EXISTENCE AND LOVE

A NEW APPROACH IN

New York

EXISTENCE
& LOVE

EXISTENTIAL PHENOMENOLOGY

William A. Sadler, Jr.

CHARLES SCRIBNER'S SONS

142.7
S126

Acknowledgments

Grateful acknowledgment is made to the following
who have granted permission for the use of excerpts from their publications:

Alfred A. Knopf, Inc. for quotations from *The Plague* by Albert Camus.
Copyright 1948, and from *Poems* by Wallace Stevens. Copyright 1959.

New Directions Publishing Corporation, J. M. Dent & Sons and Trustees for
the Copyrights of the late Dylan Thomas for quotation from "Should lanterns shine,"
Collected Poems by Dylan Thomas. Copyright 1939.

Random House, Inc. for quotations from "Alone," *Collected Shorter Poems* 1927–1957
by W. H. Auden. Copyright 1941 and renewed 1969 by W. H. Auden.

Review of Existential Psychology and Psychiatry, Pittsburgh, Pennsylvania
for a lecture delivered by William A. Sadler, Jr.,
published in the Fall 1966 issue of the *Review*, and included in
slightly different form in the second section of Chapter Nine of this book.

G. Schirmer, Inc. for quotations from the lyrics by Stephen Sondheim in
"West Side Story." Copyright © 1957, 1959 by
Leonard Bernstein and Stephen Sondheim.

To Sylvia
whose love has lightened existence

Many books have brilliantly portrayed human existence in terms of freedom, historicity, involvement, anxiety, loneliness, and the search for meaning. Yet little light has been shed upon love, and without love personal existence is inconceivable. Individual subjectivity is often analyzed so rigorously that interpersonal subjectivity tends to be ignored and the joys of intimacy, friendship, and community left out of account. With all of our scientific knowledge about human life we still are quite ignorant about love. If we are to reach an adequate understanding of ourselves and others, love is as indispensable as science. But how is it possible to bring together love and science without profaning the one or perverting the other? What, really, does love mean, not only in terms of interpersonal relationships but also with respect to personal development and human understanding? The focus of this study is upon love; its aim is to elucidate the fundamental meaning of love for human existence and understanding.

The gestation period of this book has been long; I have been working at it in one way or another most of my adult life. The initial stages of labor lasted seven months, during which time a seminar of expectant, demanding, encouraging seniors who had elected to take a two-semester course in the phenomenology of personal existence kept me producing material which was eventually molded into its present form. Most of these students were preparing for graduate studies in the social sciences, the humanities, and theology. I could count upon their intelligence and interest, but I could not expect them to know very much about phenomenology or existentialism. Part One of this book corresponds to my attempt to introduce them to existential phenomenology as it has emerged from important contributions of Husserl, Scheler, Heidegger, Marcel, Buber, and Binswanger. Though the chapters in this part are relatively introductory in nature, they are also critical at those points where I have felt correction, amplification, and even reconstruction to be necessary for the development of a viable perspective and method with which to interpret personal existence. I realize that to most readers this first part will seem much too academic to satisfy existential thirst. Perhaps they will want to skip to Part Two, where the focus upon existence and love becomes much more concrete. The individual chapters in both parts may be read as independent units; yet there is a progression of ideas throughout the book which reaches a climax in Chapter 13, followed by an epilogue in methodology in the final chapter. In a work of this nature the climax admittedly is not very dramatic; but what is said in it or in any particular chapter should be evaluated within the context of the whole work. Clearly the most important section of this book is Part Two, in which I examine the meaning of love in terms of basic human structures and then re-examine other phenomena from the perspective of existence in love. Many significant existential phenomena have quite different meanings when considered within the perspective of love from what they have if love is ignored.

The primary purpose of this book is to lead to an understanding of the distinctive nature of love and in turn to allow love to assist in the illumination of fundamental structures of personal existence. However, I have also been concerned to develop a method for continuing research and interpretation. In this respect as well as because of his insights into love, Binswanger is extremely relevant, even though he has at times been dismissed by colleagues as unintelligible, confusing, and misguided. Because he has made important contributions to existential knowledge and methodology, considerable reference is made to his works in Part Two. As I have worked at this phenomenology of existence and love I have become increasingly attracted to the possibility of building bridges between disciplines, particularly between phenomenology and the social sciences. In his own way Binswanger shared this concern and started to develop an unusual form of phenomenology which moves beyond the strict discipline of philosophy. In his attempt to understand existence from many angles but within a coherent humanistic perspective, he had much in common with American psychiatrists and psychologists, such as Harry Stack Sullivan and Erik Erikson. By bringing together the various approaches represented by these eminent students of man, I have attempted to develop existential phenomenology so that it establishes a framework and works as a coordinating principle for a truly interdisciplinary approach to human existence.

This book has been written with the conviction that an interdisciplinary method is not merely interesting and relevant but is also intrinsically important and necessary when it comes to understanding man. When grounded in love, existential phenomenology can establish a foundation for a plurality of approaches. These must be respected and allowed to provide their own unique insights if interdisciplinary dialogue is to endure. For this dialogue to advance significantly we need more than merely an increased accumulation of interesting information. If our insights are to grow into understanding, we must see human life as a whole. A vision of man in his wholeness becomes possible when science and philosophy are brought together within the perspective of love. Both in the attention paid to love and its meaning for the whole range of personal existence and in the attempt to integrate several disciplines for an illumination of distinctively human phenomena within a comprehensive perspective, this study proposes a new approach to human existence and a new approach in existential phenomenology.

Though I have written with college and university students in mind and with hopes that this book might serve in various capacities as a text, I believe it will also be useful to counselors, clergymen, and scholarly colleagues who are working toward the improvement of interdisciplinary study and communication. Because of my own interest in theology and religion, I must confess to several digressions in the text where I have seen the relevance between what has emerged through existential phenomenology and certain discussions going on about the place and meaning of religion in contemporary life. I believe that a religious perspective and religious phenomena need to be considered in our attempt to see man as a whole. So far as I can determine, a truly constructive dialogue between existential phenomenology and the study of religion is yet to take place. It is to be hoped that this new approach will stimulate some much-needed exploration and communication in this direction.

Though this expression of gratitude is quite belated, I am much indebted to Harvard University, which initiated me by total immersion into a radically interdisciplinary approach to existence and which granted a fellowship that enabled me to study phenomenology in its original European habitat. I hope that the seminar of the class of '66 at Bishop's University and other students are aware of my deep appreciation of their lively interrogations, patience, and support. I am also particularly grateful to Professor Dallas Laskey, whose trenchant criticism and friendly encouragement were sufficient to induce me to rewrite half the chapters of this book, and to Dr. Rollo May, who some years ago encouraged me to write such a book and whose comments upon reading the manuscript have been helpful. I have not always followed the suggestions of readers, colleagues or students, even though I have greatly appreciated receiving them; consequently those who have been so kind and helpful to me should not in the least be held responsible for the errors or inadequacies of this book.

Contents

xiii

PART ONE
Philosophical Background

1

In Search of a New Approach to Human Existence

1.

According to Sigmund Freud modern man has suffered three staggering blows to his ego. Copernicus delivered the first punch when he demonstrated that man is not the center of the universe but merely a tiny speck in an immense system. Darwin landed the second by revealing man's ineradicable animal nature. The hardest blow came from Freud himself. He laid bare the fact that the ego is so little the master of his own house that man is grossly ignorant of most of the dynamic activities which transpire within it and which largely determine how its business will be transacted.[1] Of course, blows to the ego may be good for one's humility, and these intellectual punches may be appreciated for their potentially beneficial impact upon our characters. Yet they provide more challenge and have greater importance than that. They require a man to reconsider his place in the universe and to ask again what sort of creature he is. Freud particularly has been tremendously influential in the fairly recent explorations of unchartered areas of human existence long regarded as beyond the pale of reason. In striking at man's misconceptions about himself he has led us to confront a crucial task: to explore what was formerly considered to be irrational and to integrate that within a broader conception of reason and meaning.[2] He was by no means the only or even the most important

[1] S. Freud, A *General Introduction to Psychoanalysis*, p. 252.
[2] See the profound and detailed study by P. Rieff, *Freud: The Mind of the Moralist*.

3

thinker who has brought new insight into the peculiar nature of human existence. Nevertheless he forced us to re-examine strongly held assumptions and to enlarge the scope of our insight when we approach man; and it is nearly inconceivable that any attempt to reach a genuine understanding of human existence could ignore the kind of challenge which Freud has presented.

To ask again the question: What is man? and to seek a wider and more illuminating perspective in which to provide an answer is not to confront an idle or largely academic task. Since Freud began his investigations into little understood and largely ignored areas of human existence, our world has witnessed unsuspected eruptions of the irrational which have been fearfully violent and destructive. Accompanying these eruptions and often inducing them has been the breakdown of previously established conceptions about the nature and significance of human life. A quarter of a century ago Susanne Langer suggested that the tremendous historical changes of our era have plowed up our entire field of unconscious as well as conscious symbolic orientation. The result has been that as we lose our hold upon convictions about human reality and its purposes, we stand in danger of losing our freedom by falling into the perspectives of a narrow rationalism or a destructive irrationalism.[3] Much more recently Erich Fromm has expressed alarm over man's inner turmoil and his lack of self-awareness. He argues that man in our age is so prone to an irrational lust for the destruction of life that the entire future of all life now stands imperiled to an extent never before thought possible.[4] A pair of psychoanalysts less given to apocalyptic utterance than Fromm has nevertheless struck this sobering note:

> We live in a dangerous world. The technical inventions of the twentieth century have hurled us into the necessity, in order to survive, of inventing hitherto unconceived social forms. Both the invention and the implementation of such forms depend on a capacity for flexibility, cooperation, and rate of change in human personality never before crucial in the history of civilization. The more we can understand about our potential for individual growth and human interaction, and about the personal illusions and

Rieff emphasizes Freud's significance as a social scientist. Cf. also the careful, yet favorable judgments about Freud's significance by European Catholics such as R. Dalbiez, *Psychoanalytic Method and the Doctrine of Freud* and A. Dondeyne, *Contemporary European Thought and Christian Faith*, p. 67, et passim.

[3] S. Langer, *Philosophy in a New Key*, p. 237, et passim.

[4] E. Fromm, *The Heart of Man*. See also my review of Fromm's book in *The Christian Century*, Vol. LXXXII, No. 39 (Sept. 29, 1965), pp. 1198-1200.

resignation that impede it, the greater the chance that people can meet the challenge for their own survival.[5]

The revolutionary changes in our historical epoch demand a certain kind of human response which is dependent upon insight into and understanding of that which is positively and distinctively human as well as that which impedes its realization. Human personality must change, not as though to adapt to a new climate but to reach its highest potentialities; otherwise it may not survive. The urgency of this task pertains not merely to the possible outcome of revolutionary changes; more deeply involved here is the very destiny of man. As Gordon Allport put it, "Most of the potentialities of man are never realized, and until we understand them better than we do they will not be called forth." [6] For man to become truly human he must understand who he is in truth. "We stand on the brink of a new age: the age of an open world and of a self capable of playing its part in that larger sphere," wrote Lewis Mumford recently. Yet that insight, full of promise, is severely tempered by his observation that man's greatest need, his need to become human, remains dangerously frustrated to a large extent because man has fallen into the grip of a narrow, mechanistic rationalism. As he also observed:

> Through over-reliance upon mechanism and automatism our generation has begun to lose the secret of nurturing man's humanness, since he gives too little care to the conditions that make each member of the community sensitive, tender, imaginative, morally responsible, self-governing, disposed to imitate human ideals and to emulate ideal examples of humanity.[7]

Torn between opposing illusions about himself, on the threshold of discovering a new world in which the highest potentialities for humanness may be actualized, man cannot responsibly put off raising the questions: Who am I? What is man? What does it mean to be human?

Most of us tend to shy away from such questions as captious, having unpleasant religious, metaphysical, or adolescent undertones. One way or another, however, the question is raised by numerous disciplines as they go about their practical work. Medicine, for example, and particularly psychiatry, has asked the question of the nature of man as soon as it questions the sufficiency of some medical goal. If the general aim of medicine is not

---

[5] J. Pearce and S. Newton, *The Conditions of Human Growth*, p. 7.
[6] G. Allport, *Pattern and Growth in Personality*, p. xii.
[7] L. Mumford, *The Transformations of Man*, pp. 183, 14.

merely the removal of disease, then the discussion often moves in the direction of healing and helping persons lead a normal life. But what is normal? Do you define normal humanity in terms of regular biological functioning or in terms of some kind of human ideal? Certainly doctors working with mental illness often tend to move in the direction of the latter.[8] The social sciences are also forced to raise the question of philosophical anthropology, of man and his essential meaning. Historians continue to debate what the subject matter of their discipline is. What are the proper data of historical research and how is one to interpret them? In writing and reading history, do we focus upon human freedom or upon the concretization of deterministic principles? If history is something which is distinctively human, what is the meaning of the term "human"? What do we look for to find it? [9] As we shall see in much more detail, sociology and psychology are faced with similar problems and the same task. Educators are also concerned with goals in education so as to develop the most appropriate educational methods. Understanding and fostering the process of education involve a working knowledge of the basic nature of man. If we are educating people to become free, responsible, and informed citizens, what is the meaning of human freedom, of responsibility, of being educated? Artists, theologians, and even politicians are in one fashion or another raising the question and working with implied answers. Needless to say, parents concerned with rearing their children ask the question regularly. As times rapidly change and various opposing views of man conflict with each other it becomes imperative *for us* to raise again basic questions pertaining to the foundations of human existence.

How do we go about such an investigation? In our empirically minded era we naturally tend to ask the question: What are the facts? It is precisely at this point that we run into serious difficulty. We tend to assume that there is really only one kind of fact. "Facts are facts," it is said; "you can't argue with them." Of course we can and must if we are to raise the question of man in such a way as to discover distinctively human potentialities. To respond directly to the challenge of new explorations into human existence it will be necessary to dispel the strong doses of positivism which have influenced many of our common-sense notions as to what are facts

---

[8] See, e.g., G. Bally, *Der Normale Mensch*; M. Boss, *Einführung in die Psychosomatische Medizin*; V. E. von Gebsattel, *Christentum und Humanismus*; M. Jahoda, *Current Concepts of Positive Mental Health*; and the existential psychiatrists in R. May, *Existence*, especially L. Binswanger.

[9] See, e.g., the discussions in *Philosophy and History*, S. Hook, ed.

and what are not. With a better understanding of the context in which facts emerge it will be possible to develop a new approach that is particularly attuned to the basic foundations and rich possibilities of human existence.

2.

A reductionistic mentality assumes that there is basically one kind of fact. Usually in our culture this mentality believes that scientific facts are really the only true ones. It is further assumed that facts of one science apply directly to those of another science, on the supposition that all sciences basically are alike and can be thought of as one. On the surface it appears that the greatest difference between them lies in the language; attempts have been made to bridge the gaps between sciences by making the same language or concepts apply in diverse areas. It is pathetic to see human studies following a course that is specifically designed to account for relatively simple forms of organic life. It may be amusing but not very enlightening to find human interaction analyzed in much the same way a physicist might discuss thermodynamics. Though the rest of us are slow to catch up, natural scientists, particularly since the development of quantum theory, have become suspicious if not incredulous of the possibility of finding a common scientific language. As the eminent physicist Robert Oppenheimer has emphasized, the language and tools of one science simply are not applicable in another. One would not suggest that the language of atomic physics is helpful when dealing with complex biological forms. Such language would obscure rather than illuminate the biological phenomena. The point is even more applicable when it comes to studying human beings and consciousness in particular:

> It seems rather unlikely that we shall be able to describe in physicochemical terms the physiological phenomena which accompany a conscious thought, or sentiment, or will. . . . Whatever the outcome, we know that should an understanding of the physical correlate of elements of consciousness indeed be available, it will not itself be the appropriate description for thinking man himself, for the clarification of his thoughts, the resolution of his will, or the delight of his eye and mind at works of beauty.[10]

[10] R. Oppenheimer, *Science and the Common Understanding*, p. 89. Werner Heisenberg has also stated that the concepts of "soul" and "life" do not occur in atomic physics and could not be derived from some consequences of natural law. "If we want

The differences between scientific languages indicate that there may be several if not many kinds of facts. The fact of consciousness is not the same kind of fact as the trajectories of molecules or the entropy of gas. The mistake in the reductionistic mentality is that it leaves the observer out of account, assuming that man can describe reality without reference to himself, his particular situation, and his special interests. Natural facts are not reality pure and simple, but portions of reality as observed within a restricted human viewpoint.

Physicists' theories pertaining to relativity have helped to illustrate the subjective nature of supposedly objective facts. Things appear to be the way they are because of the way in which man chooses or happens to see them. As it will be brought out later, one needs to have a variety of models or concepts which complement each other in such a way as to enlarge one's understanding of a given phenomenon. There is, however, an important insight to be gained from further reflection upon man's peculiar situation with regard to facts. The biologist and chemist, Michael Polanyi, has been specially helpful in clarifying the existential reasons for the limitations of any given scientific method or language. He points out that it is a mistake

to describe living or mental processes, we shall have to broaden" the models and approaches offered by physics and "introduce yet other concepts." (*Philosophic Problems of Nuclear Science*, p. 107.) The point is drawn even more strongly in his later book *Physics and Philosophy*. He shows clearly and definitively how modern physics has demolished the illusion of materialism which underlay many assumptions of classical physics and which still permeates the milieu of popular assumptions about the nature of reality. He explicitly repudiates the reductionistic assumption that methods and data can be transferred from one area of research to another with only slight modification. Relevant to our philosophical task, he maintains that we cannot expect physics or chemistry to reach an understanding of life: "If we go beyond biology and include psychology in the discussion, then there can scarcely be any doubt but that the concepts of physics, chemistry, and evolution together will not be sufficient to describe the facts. On this point the existence of quantum theory has changed our attitude from what was believed in the nineteenth century. During that period some scientists were inclined to think that the psychological phenomena could ultimately be explained on the basis of physics and chemistry of the brain. From the quantum-theoretical point of view there is no reason for this assumption. We would, in spite of the fact that the physical events in the brain belong to the psychic phenomena, not expect that these could be sufficient to explain them. We would never doubt that the brain acts as a physico-chemical mechanism if treated as such; but for an understanding of psychic phenomena we would start from the fact that the human mind enters as object and subject into the scientific process of psychology" (p. 106). Heisenberg strongly emphasizes that in physics no less than in psychology or philosophy the subjective fact of the investigator must be taken into consideration. Heisenberg also recommends Bohr's model of complementarity, which has become increasingly accepted within interdisciplinary approaches to reality. See also the position of the Oxford mathematician, C. A. Coulson, as presented in his *Science and Christian Belief*, pp. 36 ff., 70 ff. This pluralistic approach to the cosmos and life is to be distinguished from attempts to draw all of reality into a grand synthesis, as in the "hyper-physics" of Teilhard de Chardin.

to consider scientific knowledge as primary and basic. Rather, all explicit scientific knowledge rests upon a foundation of implicit personal knowledge. That is, the kind of facts which a scientist discovers depends upon how he as a person has chosen to look at reality. That is to accuse the scientist of being an incorrigible metaphysician, which is one fact that few of them care to face. It is also to bring to light that his access to facts is no more direct than the philosopher's. The scientist is first of all a man who through freedom and cultural conditioning happens to see reality in a particular way. This decision in turn forms the perspective within which his explicit, scientific knowledge arises and makes sense. The scientist's personally formed pattern of perception provides the framework within which his facts appear and are rendered meaningful. Once we change the perspective, moving from one to another, not only are the same things seen in a different light, but new things are seen. Great scientific discoveries, for example, have occurred not just because some new fact emerged in the traditional mode of encounter, but because a scientist by accident or decision approached the field with a new perspective. Suddenly things appeared in a new light, had different significance, and revealed facts which were hitherto unnoticed. Polanyi observes that it is not conducive to discovery to remain set in any one perspective or to suppose that any one approach will be successful with a variety of phenomena. It would be foolish to study a machine with the perspective and tools of chemistry or biology; so is it, he argues, if we attempt to study man with the wrong approach and methods. To him an approach which says facts are facts, such as behaviorism, is impractical and meaningless. If we are to study man as he is, then we must formulate a new kind of knowledge, one which is primarily personal rather than technical.[11]

What is at stake in these challenges to our ordinary assumptions from scientists themselves is our understanding of the nature of experience in general and the nature of perception in particular. As we presume that facts are facts we also assume that to the question: What do you see? there is only one *right* answer. The late Professor J. L. Austin of Oxford helped to clarify matters in this respect. He pointed out that the prevalent way of raising the epistemological problem in our era is to ask whether we perceive

---

[11] M. Polanyi, *The Study of Man*, pp. 29-73; see also his larger work, *Personal Knowledge*. The Dutch psychologist F. J. J. Buytendijk in *Das Menschliche: Wege zu Seinem Verständnis* has also argued that man must be understood within a personal perspective, which means to interpret his existence in terms of personal encounter. Heisenberg's position would seem to be in accord with these approaches, in particular with that of Polanyi.

material things or sense data. What do we know? Things? Or sensation of things? The hidden assumption is that the correct answer must be one or the other. As he demonstrates, this is really a bogus dichotomy which covertly imposes a tight metaphysical system that transforms the question into an argument within very limited boundaries. In fact there are many different kinds of things which we may perceive and know; consequently, many different answers are possible. When we consider what our statements mean, it is extremely important to be aware of the context in which they arise. Suppose you ask the question to several people watching a complex drill on a parade ground. A soldier will give quite a different answer from that of a citizen who knows nothing about drill.[12] There is simply no one right answer to: What did you see? unless you arbitrarily demand one. Scientists as well as philosophers have recently stressed that in considering the truth of perceptions and statements it is essential to remember the kind of situation we are dealing with. Human judgments arise from within a situation partially constructed by man's prejudices, presuppositions, and limitations. In evaluating facts we must consider the subjective factors or frame of reference; for these are irreducible factors that are part of the whole situation.

A verse taken from some poetry by Wallace Stevens presents a situation which is embarrassing to the viewpoint that demands just simple facts:

Twenty men crossing a bridge
Into a village,
Are twenty men crossing twenty bridges,
Into twenty villages.[13]

"That is to use words with poetic license, which implies pure subjectivism. What does that have to do with the facts?" you may say. Yet what do you

12 J. L. Austin, *Sense and Sensibilia*, pp. 4-42, 101 ff. Again the point has been made even more strongly by physicists. A. Eddington some time ago demonstrated that modern physics has discovered a multiplicity of frames of reference for such basic realities as space and time. Consequently the physicist has acknowledged that with numerous facts "our simple solution has been to give up the idea that one of these [statements] is right and that the others are spurious imaginations" (*The Nature of the Physical World*, p. 35). Frames of reference are now acknowledged to be relative; in assessing the truth content of any statement one must first determine the context in which it arose. Coulson puts the matter most succinctly and powerfully: "Scientific truth means coherence in a pattern which is recognized as meaningful and sensible; . . . [however] facts are never known fully and can never be completely correlated. As a result our models . . . can never be wholly satisfactory. . . . Our claim to any sort of final truth is a preposterous conceit that we must ridicule" (*op. cit.*, pp. 36-40).

13 W. Stevens, *Poems*, p. 14.

mean by facts? The facts include a bridge, a village, and twenty men who encounter this situation within a distinctively fashioned human frame of reference. To one of these twenty men the bridge may signify not primarily a means to cross a river but the spot where he kissed his first love. To another it signifies, perhaps, where he saw his father leap into the water and drown. To another the bridge leads into a village where his worst enemy lurks to fulfill his pledge of revenge. Another sees the bridge as a quaint example of rustic architecture. His companion may see it as a project which needs work done on it quickly. The village is just a spot where he can find a place to sleep, something to eat, and a bit of companionship while he works until the project is completed. To a fast-moving young man from the big city the village is a dumpy little town where he will have to spend several weeks, as though in exile. To the youth from a deserted farm it offers a world full of adventure and perhaps luring enticements. It looks like a place with a great many people whom he does not know and perhaps cannot trust. To his urban companion the village has in it nobody worth noticing. To expect that there is only one right answer to the question: What do you see? is to ignore the full situation in general and the facts of meaning in particular. To insist on one set of material facts is to ignore the people and their meaning-laden experience which constitutes that situation. Austin suggested that the motive behind much philosophy which seeks to find the only right answer embodies an unrealistic desire to arrive at statements that will be absolutely incorrigible. Completely incorrigible statements may apply to abstract constructions but not to living situations. To get at the facts of the situation demands of us that we take into account the human element which makes the situation what it is. However, the hangover of positivism from which many of us still suffer causes us to seek abstract answers to highly complex situations with the result that actual meaning-filled encounters are distilled to a condition of artificial purity. We shall do well to consider why poetry, for example, can bring to light facts close to home which our ordinary fact-conscious, scientific mentality so easily overlooks.

3.

During the nineteenth and twentieth centuries particularly, our cultural milieu was saturated with a kind of thinking that was heavily influenced by machines. The human organism was frequently conceived as a receptor of stimuli which produced in it physical sensations. These were supposedly then received by a mind that was conceived as a recorder and transmitter of messages, somewhat in the fashion of a telephone exchange. This image, however, did not describe facts; it was obviously an abstraction which implicitly presupposed what were to be considered as facts. Experiments with animals seemed to corroborate this mechanistic conceptualization, which in turn was imposed upon human phenomena. With the presupposition that nothing is in man which was not first in an animal accepted as an operating principle, the cat and the rat, which were more easily conceived in mechanistic terms, became in turn the measure of man, particularly where perception was an issue.[14] Not surprisingly, the conceptual data of this mechanistic approach became more and more remote from actual experience. The irony of a mechanistic or physicalist approach was that it set out to unravel all secrets of reality, especially those of experience; but, particularly with respect to the latter, it ended not by revealing its secrets but in denying experience.

Reflection upon the nature of scientific discourse and the implications of many principles, particularly those which assumed that there were such things as pure facts, has led many philosophers and scientists to reconsider the structure of experience in which facts emerge. As we noted already in Polanyi's work, one of the notions which has been most severely challenged is that which assumes that the mind is essentially a passive organ, reacting to stimuli fed into it through the senses and nervous system. American philosophers such as Whitehead, Dewey, and James, while thoroughly in sympathy with scientific methods, rediscovered the active, creative factor in human intelligence. In art and in life, wrote Dewey, a man "must *create* his own experience." [15] Experience is not simply something which happens to man; it is not a receptacle into which pure facts are poured that are then to be sorted out from subjective impressions. A human being is actively engaged in experience as an artist in the moment of artistic experience; every man structures the situation in which his perception will come to fruition. Man is perhaps the only creature who senses that there is more in nature than meets the eye. Nature is filled with significance; but it is significance which is dependent upon man who encounters nature within the field of his perception. Man becomes human by being creative in

14 Cf. S. Langer's discussion, *op. cit.*, pp. 18-30.
15 J. Dewey, *Art as Experience*, p. 54. This important book is still too much neglected. If American philosophers were to build on the foundations of Dewey's ideas laid down here, a distinctive American phenomenology would no doubt begin to flourish.

experience. His primary creation is, as Lewis Mumford has put it, "a new world, a meaningful world of symbolic and cultural forms which had no existence for the animal." [16] Susanne Langer has expressed this insight by emphasizing that experience is constituted by a process of symbolic formulation:

> Our merest sense-experience is a process of formulation. The world that actually meets our senses is not a world of "things" about which we are invited to discover facts as soon as we have codified the necessary logical language to do so; the world of pure sensation is so complex, so fluid and full, that sheer sensitivity to stimuli would only encounter what William James has called . . . "a blooming, buzzing confusion." Out of the bedlam our sense organs must select certain predominant forms, if they are to make report of *things* and not of mere dissolving sensa. . . . An object is not a datum, but a form construed by the sensitive and intelligent organ, a form which is at once an experienced individual thing and a symbol for the concept of it, for *this sort of thing*.[17]

Of course people have been aware of the creative function of intelligence for ages; but for some time that has been regarded as a secondary matter, particularly when it came to discussing facts. Now, however, we are beginning to realize that what we commonly assumed were pure facts are included within a situation which itself is, to a significant extent, structured by the work of intelligence. To say that facts are facts is to ignore the creative principle of experience in which facts arise; it is to ignore the primordial fact of the human world in which other facts live. Unless we choose to opt for a fantastically abstract and narrow notion of reality, we cannot talk of facts pure and simple. We never perceive mere facts but always significant facts. The late phenomenologist and social scientist, Alfred Schutz, made this point clear:

[16] L. Mumford, *The Transformations of Man*, p. 23. The emphasis upon the distinctive factor of culture which differentiates man from other animate beings is a common viewpoint among social scientists. Consider, e.g., the statement by Talcott Parsons: "Man is distinguished from the other animals, from the point of view of the social scientist, above all by the fact that he is a creator and bearer of culture. He creates and lives by systems of symbols and of artifacts; he not only modifies his environment but his orientation to it is generalized in terms of systems of symbolic meanings," etc. ("Religious Perspectives in Sociology and Social Psychology, *Reader in Comparative Religion*, W. Lessa and E. Vogt, eds., p. 120.)

[17] S. Langer, *op. cit.*, p. 72. An interesting book dealing with man's power of symbolization by an historian, P. Munz, is *Relationship and Solitude*; he develops in a way Dilthey's argument, that to understand any philosopher we must enter his experience and grasp his symbolic picture of reality within which his reflections on the meaning of data took place. See also *Dilthey's Philosophy of Existence*, trans. W. Kluback and M. Weinbaum.

All our knowledge of the world, in common-sense as well as in scientific thinking, involves constructs, that is a set of abstractions, generalizations, formalizations, idealizations specific to the respective level of thought organization. Strictly speaking, there are no such things as facts, pure and simple. All facts are from the outset facts selected from a universal context by the activities of our mind.[18]

This discussion is commonplace to those familiar with Gestalt psychology. Though it is apparent that later developments of Gestalt psychology are highly questionable, at least the basic insights are trustworthy. Human beings organize sensory perceptions into patterns. In this alone they are not unique, when higher vertebrates are also considered. Yet the insight that perceptions are not of things but of patterns (*Gestaltungen*) throws much new light upon the creativity of man, which in turn constitutes experience and enables certain facts to appear in certain ways. Things which appear are not mere things but stand in relation to other things within a perceptual field. They have significance in relation to other things within the over-all arrangement of the Gestalt. Yet the significance emerges not merely from man's seeing-things-in-relation but from his seeing that certain relations do exist. Man not only arranges his world; he can also organize perception so that it sees various arrangements in the world. Until man begins to formulate a symbolic world, "facts" will pass him by. Though quite independent of Gestalt psychology, psychoanalysis has also opened our eyes to the significance that is often hidden in the creative act of intelligence. Psychoanalysis has helped us to realize that there is much in experience of which we are consciously unaware. Our feelings and emotions, our past history and our desires all play significant roles in shaping experience so that certain facts appear downstage while others hide in the background.[19] Though psychoanalysis has emphasized the pejorative aspects of the constructive power of man to shape experience and though Gestalt psychology has tended to remain within a broad physicalist framework in which it originated, yet their underlying insights have great philosophical import. The classic distinction between subject and object, between consciousness and thing, between interpretation of

[18] A. Schutz, "Concept and Theory Formation in the Social Sciences," pp. 230-249; *Philosophy of the Social Sciences*, M. Natanson, ed.

[19] F. J. J. Buytendijk has written a most illuminating essay in which he illustrates how important are feelings as well as intelligence in the creative action of man as he shapes his situation. See "The Phenomenological Approach to the Problem of Feelings and Emotions," pp. 155-178, *Psychoanalysis and Existential Philosophy*, H. Ruitenbeek, ed.

the mind and objective facts has been broken down. Philosophical reflection and scientific insight into the creative process of the ways of knowing are here fully in accord.[20]

4.

Our attention has been brought back to living experience in which facts are known. We are beginning to see that man's basic mode of knowing is not sensation or reasoning but experience-as-a-whole. Experience is not merely a subjective event. Experience is completely a mixture of subjective and objective, of fact and interpretation, of consciousness and thing. In his massive study of perception the late French philosopher Maurice Merleau-Ponty reached the conclusion after studying numerous theories of physicalist empiricists as well as Idealists that they had all forgotten experience itself. They ignored the act of perception itself and the person who perceives. He wrote:

> Objective thought is unaware of the subject of perception. This is because it presents itself with the world ready made, as the setting of every possible event, and treats perception as one of these events. . . . Seen from the inside, perception does nothing to what we know in other ways about the world, about stimuli as physics describes them and about the sense organs as described by biology. It does not present itself in the first place as an event in the world to which the category of causality, for example, can be applied, but as a re-creation or re-constitution of the world at every moment. In so far as we believe in the world's past, in the physical world, in "stimuli," in the organism as our books depict it, it is first of all because we have present at this moment to us a perceptual field, a surface in contact with the world, a permanent rootedness in it, and because the world ceaselessly assails and beleaguers subjectivity as waves wash round a wreck on the shore. All knowledge takes its place within the horizons opened up by perception. There can be no question of describing perception itself as one of the facts thrown up in the world, since we can never fill up, in the picture of the world, that gap which we ourselves are, and by which it comes into existence for someone.[21]

All our knowledge arises from within us, from within our ceaseless encounter with our world. Our knowledge takes its place within a horizon of

---

[20] Cf. the profound insight into the significance of Gestalt psychology of Merleau-Ponty, *Sense and Non-Sense*, pp. 86-87. A similar view of experience is to be found in Dewey, *Art as Experience*.

[21] M. Merleau-Ponty, *Phenomenology of Perception*, p. 207.

meaning. This horizon is not determined by external forces. It is infinitely flexible, and its boundaries are set by the creative spirit of man within a limiting situation but not within a fixed, predetermined world.

What so many reflective studies are pointing out is that our ordinary, common-sense notion of facts is in reality part of a symbolic picture that we have formulated about reality under the influence of our culture. One has tended to assume that if he purges himself of superstition, prejudice, and presuppositions, he will be able to discover the real facts of life. What has been forgotten is that before one begins such a pursuit, he has already set the stage to determine which so-called facts shall play major roles, which shall have speaking parts, and which shall form an indiscriminate part of the background.

We have stressed the formative role of man's experience which opens us to certain kinds of significance. We should not, however, make the mistake of supposing that creativity means merely individual originality. Man is a social being; and society's creations not merely free man from nature, they also define his freedom to a large extent. The creativity of man which is so instrumental in perception should not mistakenly be considered merely an individual endowment. As man has encountered nature and produced forms, he has created what colloquially is called his second nature or culture. Experience is limited not merely by what nature offers but also but what man's second nature provides. Man's creativity applies not only to his individual experience but to the culture in which he experiences. Much of the creative formulation of his world has been given to him as he learns to identify aspects of his world and to give them names. Not merely does man participate in his culture; first of all it participates in and shapes him. In our increasingly internationally minded world we are more aware than ever that people of different cultures have quite different experiences from our own. We say that their worlds are different. Their perceptual fields are differently organized and consequently have different significance for them than roughly the same field would have for us. The thought patterns of Africans, for example, very much reflect their culture. These thought patterns may appear illogical to us; but they are logical and reasonable within their symbolic world. For example, the African mentality might well discern a personal element in natural phenomena. To us this is superstitious. Yet we miss the meaning of their perception and tend therefore to classify it as an unreal perception. However, that is not necessarily the case. The African will not project but discover a personal element in, say, a mound of rocks because the history of the tribe is closely associated with that mound.[22] His second nature helps him to perceive a fact very significant in his world, a fact which would have a hard time finding a place to live in our world.

We in the Western tradition have tended to absolutize our particular world, our set way of looking at things, our peculiar second nature. In particular we assume that facts are facts, and that anybody in his right mind using intelligence and perseverance will see the same thing we see. That is, we assume *our* facts to be *the* facts. Consequently, meanings have been treated as superficial layers covering supposedly bare facts. Much of our common-sense philosophy, particularly as it has found expression in certain sectors of linguistic analysis, has maintained that the way to get at the facts behind words is to analyze words and see how they are used. If one wants to discover, for example, what men have known about themselves he must see especially how they used words which were very familiar to them; then he may be able to transpose them into his familiar terms and discover a common meaning, as well as, perhaps, some of their nonsense. But as Professor A. J. Ayer has recently pointed out, this manner of procedure covertly brings with it a world of presuppositions including the insistence that all language to be meaningful must fit into an implicit definition of what is capable of being perceived. He singles out Wittgenstein and Ryle as examples of philosophers who sought to discover existence as it really is by becoming free of secondary interpretations. Yet they apparently failed to recognize that this very procedure was set within a primary interpretation, a symbolic world which predetermined what meaning the language to be investigated could have. As Ayer put it, how one construes a given type of statement depends upon what one thinks is possible, that is, upon one's implicit view of meaning. These two philosophers and many of the rest of us set limits to the use any given language can achieve. As he wrote, they "lay down what we are capable of meaning. . . . They do not so much elucidate our actual uses of words as determine what uses are possible." [23] Professor Ayer emphasizes that ordinary language carries with it a load of theory.

[22] Cf. the penetrating interpretation of the African mentality by John Taylor, *The Primal Vision*, p. 30 et passim.

[23] A. J. Ayer, *The Concept of a Person*, pp. 26-28. In his brief but perceptive study of epistemology Roderick Chisholm has quite recently demonstrated that our view of evidence is often very narrow. When we say we "know something" we assume that our knowledge adequately portrays whatever that something is. However, we forget

What is particularly important to us here is the insight that our ordinary language and indeed the common sense underlying it is not necessarily the most reliable guide for seeking to understand the distinctively human characteristics of man. To be in favor of scientific language or ordinary language is to adopt the conceptual system in which it arises. Professor Ayer is here in accord with our opening proposal that to get at what man is talking about when he talks of himself we must look at the perceptual system from which his statements, his expressed knowledge, arise and have meaning.[24] To get at the truth of man demands of us first of all that we consider the primary context within which whatever we already know of him has emerged. Unfortunately, our common-sense view with its many physicalist assumptions leads us to raise questions and formulate answers in a predetermined way. Our common-sense terms are not always reliable. Indeed, when it comes to uncovering the rich mystery of experience we miss much of what is going on. The trouble with relying so heavily as we quite naturally do upon the predominate cultural mode of knowing is that, as one semanticist has aptly put it, "our words get in our eyes." [25]

5.

Challenges confront us not merely from our changing historical era but also from many important endeavors within it to understand man as insightfully and comprehensively as possible. However, there is an embarrassing problem in methodology which inheres in the very nature of experience. Limitations, shortsightedness, and distortions are to be found in numerous existing approaches to man; any advance on our part must consist not simply of criticizing or adapting existing knowledge of man. Rather, it must be realized that every piece of knowledge, every statement

that whatever we know and deem adequate depends upon the particular perspective we have chosen. Thus when we consider evidence, we should not mistakenly assume that merely seeing is adequate. We must also ask the question of reasonableness. Not only should we ask: What do I know? but also: Is what I know reasonable? This in turn will lead us back to a reconsideration of the perspective within which our original questions emerged. See his *Theory of Knowledge*.

24 Ayer, *The Concept of a Person*, pp. 17-22.

25 Harry Weinberg, *Levels of Knowing and Existence*, p. 58. This book is quite illuminating of the very point we are making, because the author sets out to demonstrate that we have two ways of knowing, direct and inferred knowledge. This is the kind of bogus dichotomy, as pointed out earlier, which we should try to avoid as we approach the understanding of human existence.

about the nature of man itself, is an inhabitant of a world that has been creatively shaped by man. Man's involvement with reality is not secondarily but fundamentally creative. Experience involves the human formation of horizons of meaning within which facts emerge. There is not simply one *real* world which must be singled out from other supposedly less real or illusory worlds. The world of physics, for example, refers to a particular pattern in which things have a special kind of meaning. It is a world construed by mathematical abstractions in conjunction with a world of observed dynamics. To suppose, however, that the physical world is the really real is to absolutize merely one perceptual pattern and one framework of meaning over against others.[26]

What does our awareness of the formative nature of experience add up to as we look for a comprehensive and penetrating approach to man? In searching for a new way in which to behold and understand the most essential and distinctive characteristics of human being, it is necessary to clear away some of the obstructions from the field, particularly those basic notions in our so-called secular culture which otherwise might successfully camouflage the mysterious depths of experience. In clearing the field, I have not suggested that one particular framework of reference is to be preferred over another. Rather, I have focused attention upon the perceptual field itself and have emphasized the basic and consistent formative element in the process of human knowing. The procedure of arriving at facts is not quite what we might have assumed. The common supposition that there is a direct way at getting to reality, bypassing the human factor, is fallacious. All our knowledge is born in experience. This does not mean that we are hopelessly bound up with subjectivism. On the contrary, the traditional dichotomy between subject and object has been called into question. It is a dichotomy which emerges when one particular world has been taken for granted, one in which the very act of perceptual experience has been forgotten.

Having exposed certain obstacles, the appropriate site upon which our explorations are to commence becomes evident. This site is nothing less than the primary datum of experience itself, a site which is immensely comprehensive. Experience is no longer to be conceived primarily or exclusively as a subjective datum. On the contrary, we have at least glimpsed something of its nature as a process of interaction between man and his

---

[26] Cf. S. Langer, *op. cit.*, p. 74 and Heisenberg's argument against the absolutization of a closed world view implicit in classical physics, *op. cit.*

environing world. Merleau-Ponty perhaps expressed it best when he said that experience is really a form of communication within a given field whereby we enter into "sympathetic relation" with objects and "make sense" of them.[27] In the primary act of perception, in experience itself, we do not simply endow objects with sense or meaning. In the process by which we encounter an object, some sense is discovered as we form the field in which it presents itself to us. Sense organs themselves contribute to the kind of sense we find in things, indicating that here we find something audible, there something visible, here something edible, there something sexual, etc. Sensation, things, significance, symbolization, are all a part of experience. Our experience is no less than an existential encounter with a world which has a potentially infinite horizon. This human world is not predetermined, as common sense or physicalist language would indicate; it is a world that is open for the discovery and creation of ever-new directions for encounter, and hence open to the emergence of as yet undiscovered significance. Because our experience is a creative and thoroughly historical encounter in a *lived world*, one that is alive with our encounter of it, it is potentially open to new possibilities of significant existence. What this study shall consistently ask is: *What are the basic possibilities for meaningful human existence?* The answer can emerge only from a radical return to experience itself.

At this point in our attempt to get at the foundations of human existence, we can appreciate the distinctive approach of phenomenology. Phenomenology is best understood as a radical departure in man's attempt to know himself because it advocates complete concentration upon the givenness of experience. Phenomenology begins by insisting that we hold our common-sense notions in suspension and take a fresh look at experience. As Husserl conceived it, phenomenology does not begin by supposing that one experience is more informative about our human condition than others. Rather, he sought by phenomenology to get at the foundation of experience, or more specifically in his case, at the a priori of consciousness. He did not ask: Which act of consciousness is most illuminative or trustworthy? but rather: What is the foundation upon which consciousness is grounded so as to exist at all? This is a most unusual form of radical empiricism, which nevertheless seems to imply metaphysics from the start. His phenomenology might be considered to be metaphysical if by that one means not a formal system of principles but, rather, as Merleau-Ponty has

27 M. Merleau-Ponty, *Phenomenology of Perception*, pp. 213-219.

suggested, an attempt to rediscover the mystery of experience and to explore the paradox of experience that something which is strange and other than I is nevertheless able to enter my experience and become part of it.[28] This is certainly not, however, how metaphysics is ordinarily understood, and at this point the suggestion that phenomenology is a metaphysical pursuit should not be taken too seriously. That Husserl, Scheler, Heidegger, and others have implicit metaphysical notions about the ultimate nature of reality is another matter, and one to which attention will be given in the course of this book.

Before moving directly into a consideration of the birth of phenomenology with Husserl, and its diverse developments in Scheler, Heidegger, Buber, Marcel, and eventually Binswanger, I want to stress that I am not advocating any return to an absolute body of knowledge or a predetermined set of transcendentals. I am suggesting no more and no less than that in our search to discover the basic structures of truly human being we must return to the living, historical, contingent situations which, including man's individual and corporate creativity, constitute experience. I have emphasized that as human beings we have ideas, knowledge, prejudices, presuppositions, as well as dreams and fantasies. Rather than rush in to debate which ideas are supposedly more valid than others, I am recommending, as did Husserl, that we first recognize that we are such creatures who have ideas and presuppositions. What is necessary, as he indicated, is that we take a pause in everyday acts of judging and become aware of the living, primary fact of the full givenness of consciousness. In this way we shall become better aware of the fact of human transcendence and be on the way toward understanding its meaning.

[28] M. Merleau-Ponty, *Sense and Non-Sense*, pp. 92-97.

2

Edmund Husserl and the New Field of
Transcendental Phenomenology

Edmund Husserl (1859–1938) is rightly regarded as the father of modern phenomenology, even though the movement inspired by him has developed in diverse and disparate ways. More than merely a father who has begotten famous offspring, Husserl was a pioneer. As a pioneer he opened up new territories of reality, which prompted many thinkers to follow him and continue his explorations. Like a true pioneer he experienced numerous personal disappointments, and he suffered intense loneliness as a result of his bold enterprise in thought. Also, as happens often to discoverers, he was quickly left behind and often ignored as someone in the past by many of those who were following in his tracks. However, the vastness of his scope and the complexity of his thought even today have scarcely been fathomed. It would be both ludicrous and presumptuous to suggest that this short chapter provides a complete summary of his work. Rather, the purpose of our study here, as throughout the first part of this book, is to become acquainted with those insights and concepts which are believed to be either fundamental preludes to or indispensable parts of the ongoing development of existential phenomenology. We shall focus upon those problems Husserl confronted which are particularly relevant to the latter. Certainly my interpretation will not satisfy all followers of Husserl. It is not meant to be final; especially with the continuing publication of Husserliana, all the writings of this great thinker deserve renewed study and fresh interpretation. While every effort has been made to consider fairly what

Husserl actually wrote, in terms of considering the historical development of thought it is at least equally important to bear in mind how he was understood and interpreted by those who recognized themselves to be in his debt and whose work extended, or was thought to extend, some of the routes which he had marked out.

Though he has become famous as the promoter of an extremely pure type of philosophy which he called transcendental phenomenology, Husserl did not actually begin to work out his phenomenology until after he was forty years old. He started as a mathematician; particularly, he was interested in the theoretical foundations of mathematics just prior to the time when Whitehead and Russell were considering the possible implications mathematics might have for understanding and expanding conceptual thought. While still in his twenties he listened to the former Roman Catholic priest, Franz Brentano, lecture in Vienna. Brentano, who had acquired notoriety for his highly independent and critical thinking, was endorsing a probing investigation of experience so as to develop a scientific psychology and philosophy. In opposition to tendencies as well as doctrines in both naturalism and idealism which regarded the mind as a self-contained unit, Brentano insisted, as had the Scholastics, that the mind, consciousness, is intentional by nature. His meaning of the term "intention" was meant to suggest just the opposite of what is implied in common usage. We say, for example, "My intention is to retire early." Here intention is an interior state in the sense of a wish, an act of the will, or a fantasy. Brentano's usage was meant to suggest that in the primary reality of consciousness, "subjective" is inseparable from "objective." In other words consciousness is not exclusively subjective or interior; rather, consciousness is *of* something. Intentionality refers to the dynamic character of consciousness as being directed toward an object, without meaning to suggest that the dynamics are separate from the object. The concept of intentionality stresses the underlying connection of subject and object. It is through the intentional unity that the subject is attracted, impelled, and informed by the object. Thus Brentano used "intentionality" in a more restricted sense than had been the case in Scholastic philosophy, where it was a common term. Brentano meant by intentionality that consciousness is neither purely formal in a Kantian sense nor empty and passive in a Lockean sense. On the contrary, to conceive of consciousness as empty or detached is to misconceive it. Experience shows us that consciousness is *always* consciousness of something. The subjective element of consciousness cannot be separated from its objective content. Intentionality denotes the dynamic structure of consciousness which is inseparable from the objects that inform it.

Brentano inspired the young Husserl to turn his aspiration from a search for the foundations of mathematics toward an attempt to develop the foundations for a truly scientific psychology and philosophy. The goal was to grasp clearly and firmly the underlying structure of consciousness seen in the fullness of its intentionality. By exploring consciousness *in terms of intentionality,* one would reach the foundations for knowledge of all reality before a split between subject and object could occur. The proposed endeavor to find secure foundations for scientific and philosophical thought was not conceived as an idle academic enterprise. European thinkers were becoming aware of the limited and shaky foundations upon which their scientific and philsophical concepts were based. With the turn of the century, a crisis was dawning in which the determined, predictable, familiar universe of both scientists and philosophers was being gradually dissolved by the development of revolutionary theoretical formulations such as in the new physics. In the shifting sands of the classical theories underlying science of that time, a deep need was felt for laying a groundwork for all intellectual enterprises, a project which called for a strictly scientific philosophy. It was to meet this crisis and to establish secure epistemological foundations that Husserl's life work was dedicated.

In 1900 the first volume of his *Logical Investigations (Logische Untersuchungen)* appeared, marking Husserl as a promising and significant thinker. This work was a prolegomenon to a pure logic, that is, a logic which is based on what Husserl believed to be the irreducible logical realities of meaning and relationships unsullied by the approximations of existence. Under the impetus of thinkers such as John Stuart Mill, logic had come to be seen as an extension of psychological acts originating in experience. Though at first himself impressed with the attempt to discover logic as an outgrowth of experiential acts, here Husserl argued strongly against such an approach. He insisted that the essential categories and relationships of logic are not derived from experience but have objective validity and genuine independence from psychological acts. As a mathematician, Husserl was keenly aware of the constitutive function of the mind as it perceives mathematical essences such as the concepts of angle, number, surface, body, etc., as in geometry. These are not arbitrary concepts, nor do they depend upon the existence of some external object for either their perception or their validity. The mind can conceive of an equilateral triangle without ever seeing one. Such an object is a pure abstraction. It is realized by the mind, but not invented by it. Its objectivity is not factual or existential, but *ideal*. Such *objects* are perceived neither by induction nor by deduction; rather, Husserl insisted, they appear before the mind as self-evident and universally meaningful. They do so because the mind, consciousness, is intentionally related to these ideal realities. Thus, as we shall see, the concept of the intentionality of consciousness is absolutely essential for Husserl to construct sure foundations not only for logic but for all thinking. In this attempt to develop the foundations for a pure logic, Husserl found it necessary to attack in detail alternate theories of the mind and cognition, which he branded as psychologism and naturalism. Essentially he saw both of these as reductionistic, in the sense that they maintained that principles of thought, mental categories and their relationships, were derived from elementary psychological experiences; thus they reduced consciousness to something less than consciousness, failing to perceive the irreducible reality of the constitutive thinking of essences, which alone makes specific judgments possible and meaningful. In short, the theories were blind to the intentional nature of consciousness which was in direct relationship with essential or ideal reality.

In the following year, the second volume of this work appeared which contained numerous essays related to the program of developing a pure logic, and also two other essays that were significant as pointing ahead toward Husserl's later development. One was a discussion of the intentional nature of experience and the other suggested the formulation of a phenomenology of knowledge. What puzzled many readers who had followed him through the first volume, was that the second seemed to be a reversal of his attack upon psychologism. Here Husserl proposed a phenomenological psychology as a purely descriptive method of exploring the psyche or experience. Yet in such a proposal Husserl made a distinction which is crucial toward understanding his method and his aims. Husserl did not have in mind a new development within an already conceived field of psychology. Quite the contrary, he was extremely critical of psychology, because although it tested and measured experience in terms of cause and effect, it nevertheless did not get at what experience actually is in terms of its essential structures. As an empirical discipline, psychology is tied down to contingencies; this makes for an impure science, one whose vision is clouded by the changes and chances of concrete life. Phenomenological psychology, especially as he was later to conceive of it, was to be a pure discipline dedicated not to existential facts but to essences, to the a priori of experience. Like a pure mathematician, Husserl is primarily concerned to grasp what is essential, not what is factual, to discover the pure essence which makes the crude fact of any given experience possible. He is thus looking for the a priori of psychic life which could be a foundation for all general psychological investigations and theories. It was to be a science of the pure essence of the psychic life.

We shall return to his proposal later, but here it can be pointed out how different Husserl is from Kant and the Kantian tradition in German philosophy, an insight which will help us to appreciate the truly new direction he set in philosophy. In two obvious ways he differs from the Kantian approach. First, he does not share its skepticism of reason, but rather audaciously strikes at the very roots of the mystery of knowledge. Second, he does not conceive of the mind in Kant's formal sense; in seeking to grasp the a priori of experience he does not presuppose that the basic categories lie within the mind and are imposed upon objective material. He does not at all accept the Kantian separation of noumenon and phenomenon. Consciousness is not formal but intentional, which is to say that consciousness is immediately, directly aware of objects as they are. These objects are the phenomena as they are given to consciousness as it is aware of itself and its essential structures. The phenomena are essences which make experience possible. They are neither mental constructs nor external, factual objects, but the fundamental givenness at the core of experience. As we shall see, his notion of consciousness, and hence of intentionality, is also quite different from that of Brentano's, whom he later claimed was still caught in the cramped framework of psychologism. What is radically new here is not that Husserl emphasized that consciousness is *of* something, but that intentionality is of the very nature of reality. To this extent he was opposed to Descartes's view that consciousness is closed in upon itself as well as to Kant's view that consciousness is basically formal, cut off from direct knowledge.[1] For Husserl, the phenomenal object is not constructed by consciousness but, rather, is that which gives itself to consciousness as part of its constitution. The exploration of consciousness might thus provide a direct insight into the essential structures which make it possible for experience to occur at all. This exploration could reveal to us the fundamental meanings of experience.

[1] Cf. the extremely helpful discussion by Pierre Thévenaz, *What Is Phenomenology?* especially pp. 48-50.

In the relatively early period of his development, Husserl was looking for a pure psychology which would disclose the a priori of the psychic so as to provide a foundation not merely for psychology but for all knowledge.[2] In attempting to grasp the essence of a particular experience, he was intending to set forth the meaning of experience. For example, in the perception of a gloriously fragrant apple tree in full blossom, we are conscious of color, aroma, the image of the tree in our mind, etc. This experience, we say, is particularly meaningful. But what is the basic, underlying meaning? With numerous similar perceptions we are aware of a unity which binds together these perceptions; there is a thread of identity running through them, an essential character, a fundamental meaning. Yet what is this essential character of which we are conscious? Wherein does it lie? In the tree? The situation? The mind? The experience? What constitutes the meaning, the essence of this or any experience? Where mathematicians are clear about their essential forms, we are in an impossibly vague state as to the precise nature of the essential aspects of an experience of which we are conscious. According to Husserl we need not continue in this vague state. The essences are directly given to consciousness in much the same way that the mathematician's mind grasps immediately the essential, ideal reality of a right angle. Husserl's phenomenological psychology was to be a scientific investigation to grasp the essences which constitute all meaningful experience. It would begin, similar to pure mathematics, with an intuition which is immediately aware of an ideal reality. The objects or essences in this case refer to the different possible forms consciousness (intentionality) may take, that is, the various a priori possibilities of consciousness. Consciousness understood intentionally becomes the essential object of philosophical research. The latter will give direct access to and unquestionable evidence of every basic meaning or essence (*Wesen*). The clarity and evidence are to be provided by the pure intuition of essence (*Wesenschau*). This notion of intuition, as Husserl used it, is not what we usually mean, as though it is something sensuous or emotional; rather, it is the act of pure consciousness which immediately recognizes the unquestionable validity of a particular form of evidence when it "sees" it. Such a vision is to be attained by a phenomenological reduction.

In this brief glance at a difficult and important program, we at least

[2] For a very precise and lucid summary of Husserl's development, see the straightforward account by Walter Biemel, *Husserl's Encyclopaedia-Britannica Artikel und Heideggers Anmerkung Dazu*, pp. 246-280. The examples I use, however, are borrowed from numerous passages in Husserl's *Ideas*.

have caught a glimpse of Husserl's background, some principal themes, and
his major concern to develop a clear and certain foundation for philosophy
and psychology. In 1906 Husserl suffered a strong personal blow when his
expected appointment to the rank of professor at the University of Göttin-
gen, where he had taught five years, was rejected, largely due to the influence of colleagues who were disturbed and annoyed by his radically new
program of philosophy. This deep disappointment led him to cast doubts
upon his philosophical foundations and to re-examine in ruthless fashion
and in minute detail the entire procedure of philosophy. In a manner
similar to Descartes, who was to become increasingly a kind of inspirational
model for him, Husserl questioned each stage and basic concept of thought
so as to arrive at a thoroughly trustworthy foundation of philosophy. Some
of his anguish is revealed in this diary note written during that same year:
"I have been through enough torments from lack of clarity and from doubt
that wavers back and forth. . . . Only one need absorbs me: I must win
clarity, else I cannot live; I cannot bear life unless I believe that I shall
achieve it." [3]

This burning drive toward absolutely secure and clear philosophical
foundations led him into a third and final stage of his development. From
mathematics through phenomenological psychology, he inaugurated what
he himself called a radical revolution in philosophy with the development
of transcendental phenomenology. The ideas for it he sketched out in five
lectures delivered in the following year, and in this short time he had
already arrived at a concept of a program which was to sustain him for the
remainder of his life.

When in 1907 he developed his transcendental phenomenology, he
marked out pure consciousness as the terrain for his explorations. By "pure
consciousness" he meant the ego, or the center of the self which harbors all
of the individual's interests and recollections, and from which emerge his
thinking, acting, reacting, judging, etc. This center or core of the self is
that aspect of the personality, the pure ego, which stands in direct relation
to the world of essences, or universals, or ideas, which comprise all meaning and make experience, as we understand it, possible. The purpose of his
phenomenology is to demonstrate the direct experience of these objective,
self-revealing essences by the pure ego, which had been ignored by the
traditional science of consciousness, psychology. As he developed the series

[3] Husserl, *Persönliche Aufzeichnungen*, quoted by Herbert Speigelberg, *The
Phenomenological Movement*, Vol. I, p. 82.

of five lectures on phenomenology, Husserl realized that much more was at stake than securing a foundation for psychology. The problem was in fact the very possibility of any knowledge at all. Right along, science and philosophies had been taking for granted what must be rigorously questioned. Knowledge itself, he realized, had become a mystery.[4] What needed to be established was the constitutional basis for consciousness' own belief and claim to possess knowledge of something other than itself. Phenomenology was conceived as that philosophy which would be able to demonstrate the actual givenness of objectivity to the subjectivity of consciousness and to clarify the nature both of conscious activity and of the objective givenness.[5] Phenomenology should find the absolute evidence which would be the sure foundation for itself and which could then give science and reason their meaning.[6]

To achieve this goal, however, it was first necessary to demonstrate the fallacy in naturalistic theories of cognition which maintain that the spiritual phenomena of knowledge are caused by physical agencies. Husserl pointed out the radical difference between the two spheres of reality, factual and ideal; and he maintained that knowledge is rooted in the latter, not the former, as is commonly supposed. To understand how knowledge is at all possible, we must move beyond that natural scheme of cause and effect. The common supposition of how knowledge arises, when ruthlessly investigated, contains such anomalies, gaps, and contradictions as to make nonsense of the reality of knowledge. Clearly, knowledge requires, first of all, essences; and phenomenology emerges as the science which, unlike natural science, will study the essential sphere of reality in contradistinction to the natural or factual sphere. That distinction between empirical fact and ideal essence (*eidos*) is imperative. Though he had earlier suggested that what was needed was a systematic investigation of the a priori types of consciousness, he now turned his attention almost exclusively toward what he felt was even more basic, the *constitutive functioning of consciousness itself*. This means he would focus upon intentionality understood as consciousness in its *act* of intuiting essences. He was determined to push further into consciousness than descriptive psychology could go.

Because of the transcendent nature of the object of his pursuit, consti-

---

[4] Edmund Husserl, *Die Idee der Phänomenologie, Fünf Vorlesungen,* Walter Biemel, ed., p. 19. (*The Idea of Phenomenology,* p. 20.)
[5] *Ibid.,* pp. 10-14; English edition, pp. 8-11.
[6] Cf. Thévenaz, *op. cit.,* p. 45.

tuting consciousness or transcendental subjectivity, his method was named transcendental phenomenology; it alone was seen to be appropriate to uncover the foundations of genuine consciousness. As he consistently maintained, "transcendental subjectivity . . . cannot be found under the attitude of psychology or natural science, being no part at all of the objective world, but that subjective conscious life itself, wherein the world and all its content is made for 'us,' for 'me.' " [7] The phenomenon of transcendental subjectivity, of pure consciousness, is different from natural phenomena and cannot be discovered in the same way the latter are. From a naturalistic perspective consciousness is easily misconceived as a volatile soul substance or a thinking mechanism concealed within a physical organism; within a naturalistic framework it is small wonder that we lose so easily our understanding of human transcendence. In reality, consciousness is intentionally related to the essential structures which provide a basis for our perception and knowledge of natural phenomena. Instead of focusing upon things "out there" in the world, Husserl proposed that we reflect upon the very experience of consciousness itself as the object of philosophical research. This led him to develop quite a distinct method for the prosecution of phenomenology.

According ot Walter Biemel, the basic act in the phenomenological process is a special kind of *reflection,* wherein consciousness is turned back upon itself. This turning back upon itself, Husserl referred to as a *reduction,* which he here employed in quite a different sense from when he used the term to attack other approaches for their "reductionism." In the latter, he had in mind something like an aggressive manipulation of reality which attempts to squeeze a mystery into a concept much too small to contain it; the result is that the essential nature of the mystery is left out of account. In the phenomenological reduction Husserl is referring to an act of going back to the original source of consciousness, or as Biemel puts it, a reflection which enables man's subjective life to reach beyond individual subjectivity to the objective structure which makes consciousness possible; it is in the intuitive reflection of Husserl's phenomenology that the full reality of consciousness opens up and appears as it really is.[8] Husserl spoke of the first stage of his method as an *epochē,* a Greek term which he used in the sense of a suspension of natural beliefs and judgments. To get back to

[7] Edmund Husserl, "Phenomenology," article in the *Encyclopaedia Britannica,* Vol. 17 (1947), p. 701.
[8] W. Biemel, *op. cit.,* pp. 257 ff.

consciousness as it really is, a radical elimination of our ordinary conceptual approach to reality is necessary. We need to put our common sense in suspension. Whenever we concentrate upon something it is necessary to close our mind to distracting aspects of reality which would prevent us from achieving a clear focus upon the object to be studied. In phenomenology it is necessary, according to Husserl, to shut out of our consciousness all awareness of factual reality, the world out there. This is not to entertain a Cartesian doubt of its actuality, but merely to put all our common judgments, values, and knowledge into parenthesis as a part of methodological procedure. We are to bracket out of consciousness our relation to factual existence so that we can then focus upon pure consciousness. Once the *epochē* is put into operation, the phenomenologist must be careful not to retract it; this does not mean that he doubts factual reality but merely puts it aside, suspends his judgments about it, even as to whether it is real or fantasy, good or bad, important or insignificant. The *epochē* serves as the condition for the knowledge of essences with which consciousness is in direct touch.[9]

The *epochē* is actually the negative side of the important reductions which bring us into the domain of pure subjectivity. The first reduction has already been mentioned; it is the psychological reduction which purifies the *cogito* from ordinary assumptions and beliefs and thus provides the possibility of grasping experience in a way not confined or defined by physical characteristics. This is the bracketing of the natural attitude and factual reality. The second act is an eidetic reduction which consists in bringing out the essential forms or principles of experience through concentration upon the pure psyche; at this stage the purified ego beholds what Husserl called the *noetic* aspect of consciousness. The phenomenological method as conceived by Husserl is really an ascetic discipline in which the thinker overcomes his natural and habitual tendencies so as to reach and then reveal true spirit. In the first reduction he purifies his consciousness; in the second he purifies the content of consciousness, the *cogitatum*. This eidetic reduction brings into view both the noematic essences of experience, the ideal contents (*eidos*), and the noetic essential principles (*Wesensgesetzlichkeit*) which constitute what we recognize as the basic identities and essential structures in experiences.[10]

[9] A more complete, lucid description of Husserl's method can now be found in English. See Quentin Lauer, *Phenomenology: Its Genesis and Prospect*, pp. 49 ff.

[10] Cf. discussions by Biemel, *op. cit.*, pp. 259 ff.; Lauer, *op. cit.*, p. 52; and Thévanaz, *op. cit.*, pp. 46-51.

With his shift in 1907 toward the pure ego, toward transcendental subjectivity, Husserl conceived of yet more reductions. The phenomenological reduction which is proper and necessary to transcendental phenomenology has been set forth. In this stage, the pure subject becomes manifest. Yet as Husserl pushed more deeply into consciousness, he sensed more keenly that as intentionally structured to eidetic or essential being, consciousness would eventually lead to the foundation of the whole world. The ego is not a pale receptacle of knowledge but a real pole in the relation between consciousness and its ideal object. From about 1910 onward the constitution of all being plays the chief role in Husserl's thought.[11] First he asked: How is experience itself constituted? Then he proceeded to question: How in fact is the world and all reality constituted? If we have claim to any knowledge at all then our consciousness must be informed by the essential structures of reality which enable us to identify and thus perceive something. Phenomenological reflection reveals that these essential structures are somehow embedded in consciousness and contain an ideal content, the *cogitatum*, of our thought. The phenomenological reduction completes the *epochē* so that all external reality is thoroughly bracketed out and pure subjectivity is disclosed; as it appears, we discover the phenomenon of the constitution of the world. That is, what appears in the phenomenon of pure subjectivity is not myself belonging to a world but the *transcendental phenomenon of my self constituting the world* so that it can appear in a certain way. The more deeply Husserl attempted to probe into the phenomenon of constitution in transcendental subjectivity the more essential it became to carry out other phenomenological reductions. Quentin Lauer has indicated that there are at least six levels of reduction which presumably attain greater levels of purity approaching supposedly an absolutely pure subjectivity; yet he admits, as do others who try to follow Husserl into these pure regions, that it is next to impossible to distinguish and to classify the advanced steps.[12] This endeavor to attain absolute evidence in the pure, transcendental ego distinguishes Husserl's from other kinds of phenomenology. In his double preoccupation to search

[11] Biemel, *op. cit.*, p. 265; see also the definitive study by Eugen Fink, "Die Phänomenologische Philosophie Edmund Husserl in der Gegenwärtigen Kritik," *Kant Studien*, Vol. 38 (Berlin, 1933), pp. 370 ff. Fink emphasizes the difference made by the introduction of transcendental into Husserl's thought project; thus phenomenology came to be the way of clarifying the relation between the transcendental ego and the world in terms of the interacting process of constitution.

[12] Q. Lauer, *op. cit.*, pp. 51 ff.

for a sure foundation for knowledge by conducting an exacting analysis of subjectivity, Husserl did open up a new field for investigation, the field of transcendental subjectivity. By illuminating the constituting process in experience whereby the world receives its meaning, Husserl has led many important thinkers to rediscover and see anew the reality of human transcendence, especially as a foundation for all knowledge. But by emphasizing the apodictic, self-evident, absolute nature of his evidence which is given and becomes increasingly manifest in the purest regions of consciousness, Husserl left many of these same thinkers behind. In spite of the fact that Thévanaz, for example, has argued that Husserl's new domain was not an esoteric field but the realm of meaning,[13] yet many sympathetic minds have found it impossible to enter the deepest regions of that realm because of the inability to execute the later stages of the phenomenological reduction.

Whether or not it is possible to focus upon the relation of consciousness and universal essences when there is such a complete bifurcation of factual and ideal is a question which Husserl's methodology poses and never satisfactorily answers. Indeed it becomes apparent that his quest for an absolutely clear picture of the principles of all knowledge rests upon his underlying assumptions about the character of knowledge and its totally ideal provenance. The above bifurcation raises numerous captious problems. How is the factual ego related to the absolute transcendental ego? Though Husserl answered that each of these egos is an aspect of the same basic phenomenon, yet he did not show how this was so. The problem remains as to how transcendental phenomenology as a universal science grasping the absolute basis for all knowledge is to be related to phenomenological psychology and concrete life. As Maurice Merleau-Ponty put it:

> Husserl in his last period concedes that all reflection should in the first place return to the description of the world of living experience (*Lebenswelt*). But he adds that, by means of a second "reduction," the structures of the world of experience must be reinstated in the transcendental flow of a universal constitution in which all the world's obscurities are elucidated. It is clear, however, that we are faced with a dilemma: either the constitution makes the world transparent, in which case it is not obvious why reflection needs to pass through the world of experience, or else it retains something of that world, and never rids it of its opacity.[14]

[13] Thévanaz, *op. cit.*, p. 51.
[14] M. Merleau-Ponty, *Phenomenology of Perception*, p. 365, fn.

Merleau-Ponty went on to say that Husserl was moving increasingly in the latter direction, toward an emphasis upon an analysis of the world of living experience. Yet he has left us faced with the unsolved problem: How are the essences in my mind related to the objects of the external world? Husserl would not apparently worry deeply about this because he was concerned to uncover and illuminate eidetic, essential reality, and he argued against any attempt to consider at this level empirical methods or empirical evidence, as an intrusion of a lower power into the domain of a higher power.[15] To acknowledge the universal concept grasped by the mind does not, however, clarify how it is related to the thing before me. Husserl claimed to overcome the epistemological division of subject and object by maintaining that the object was contained and immediately given in the phenomenon of the subject because of the intentional nature of consciousness. Yet he leaves us still with a paralyzing split between factual object and constituting, ideating subject, which is one reason why so many followers of his broke away and allowed their phenomenologies to take quite different directions.

Perhaps more important to the development of philosophy than the foregoing characteristics of Husserl's novel approach to knowledge was the impetus he gave to philosophical research and the high aims for philosophical endeavor which he proposed. Husserl was a person marked with an acutely critical and deeply independent mind, and he had extremely high aspirations, if not for himself personally, definitely for the status of philosophy.[16] He expressed his understanding of the aim of any philosophy worthy of its name in a forceful essay, written in 1911, entitled "Philosophy as Rigorous Science." He had been deeply impressed with the rigor of sciences, particularly those of a deductive, calculating nature, and confessed that philosophy is sadly lacking in that quality. Tradition stands in the way of philosophy achieving a similar ideal; most obstructive of all is the traditional tendency of naturalism. He called for a radical revolution in philosophy, one which returns to the very roots of experience and knowledge. "Philosophy," he wrote, "is essentially a science of true beginnings." It must inaugurate a radical procedure which may not rest until it

---

[15] See for example his repudiation of an existential approach to anthropology in which he endorsed an absolute subjectivism which isolates consciousness from the world. Through the transcendental reduction the transcendental ego stands absolutely above the world. Husserl, "Phenomenology and Anthropology," *Realism and the Background of Phenomenology*, pp. 129-142.

[16] Cf. Herbert Spiegelberg, *op. cit.*, pp. 89-91.

has attained "its own absolutely clear beginnings, i.e. its absolutely clear problems, the methods preindicated in the proper sense of these problems, and the most basic field of work wherein things are given with absolute clarity." [17] Two things are imperative; the first is that we learn to see things as they are, and the second is to refrain from explaining them away under the prejudice which stems from our traditional way of conceiving reality.[18] His is not a naïve plea to become freed from presuppositions but, rather, a demand that we become aware of what our presuppositions are and that we do not proceed without having our presuppositions clarified. Then it becomes possible to return to things themselves and the problems connected with them. He issued the plea which has become a kind of rallying slogan for phenomenology ever since: *Zu den Sachen selbst* ("To the things themselves"). By this he advocates a return to that which is immediately given in experience, not to external objects which exist independent of our experience of them. Science ignores the immediately given by directing its attention to external things, asking not what known things are but what they do. Philosophy, on the other hand, is to focus upon the givenness of consciousness and to penetrate the essence of the object being investigated to discover what it really is.[19] The question of the philosopher is not one which leads him to look outward by asking, "What do I experience?" Rather, he is to ask, "What *is* my experience?" Asked in the proper way, using philosophical intuition, one would have a phenomenological grasp of essences, which alone would provide the philosopher with a cognition which possesses absolute certainty; for with the grasp of essences he is aware of the a priori contents of consciousness and in touch with Absolute Being. Augustine's remark, "Don't go abroad. Truth dwells inside men," [20] was here fashioned into an uninhibited, full-fledged philosophical program for investigating subjectivity without reference to external factuality. Only as philosophy succeeded in achieving this program would it attain to the status of a rigorous discipline.

With the increasing domination of the naïve naturalistic attitude through the rising success of technology, an attitude, or rather a prejudice, which Husserl consistently tried to expose and combat, combined with the turbulent state of affairs in Western society leading into and following

[17] Edmund Husserl, "Philosophy as Rigorous Science," in *Phenomenology and the Crisis of Philosophy*, trans. Quentin Lauer, p. 146.
[18] *Ibid.*, p. 147.
[19] Quentin Lauer, Introduction, *ibid.*, p. 45.
[20] Quoted in Herbert Spiegelberg, *op. cit.*, p. 88.

upon the First World War, Husserl became more convinced than ever of the relevance of his philosophical program. At the end of his life he composed an essay which declared that European man is facing a crisis such as he has never before confronted.

The cause of the crisis facing European man, Husserl claimed, is the "collapse of rationalism," for it was obvious to him that Europe was witnessing the downfall of rational culture.[21] What had led to the breakdown of reason and the outpouring of irrationalism was actually a mistaken form of rationalism emerging from the seventeenth and eighteenth centuries, a rationalism lacking the profound understanding of reason notably present in the era of classical Greece.[22] This distorted rationalism suffers from a naïve objectivism which considers the external, natural world as the truly objective. In then affirming the objective character of reason or spirit, it places spirit within nature; in effect that is to exteriorize it, and thus allow it to be absorbed in nature. Especially has this been true in psychology, which has lost sight of the spirit and focused upon the natural body, assuming that if the spirit exists it occupies the spatio-temporal realm of the natural world. The spirit or reason has been thus made into an object which is thought about; no longer is it understood as the act which constitutes all thinking. The massive methodological unclarity of both natural sciences and human studies indicates too clearly that we have an essential need for a genuine understanding of reason or spirit.[23] As long as men retain the prejudice of this naïve, objectivistic naturalism, however, there will be no improvement; for the spirit of man can never be conceived as long as it is thought to be one objective reality among others. What this attitude failed to perceive and what Husserl saw so clearly was that in the experience of man spirit does not reside in nature; on the contrary, nature as we know it is grounded in spirit. Because man has blinded himself to the foundational fact of his own creative subjectivity, he is unclear about reality and especially about his own existence.

Because of this crisis in the breakdown of true reason, Husserl saw that the task of our age consists in a methodological concentration of subjectivity upon itself: "Only if the spirit returns to itself from its naïve exteriorization, clinging to itself and purely to itself, can it be adequate to itself." [24] As he looked back on his own philosophical endeavor he realized

---

21 Edmund Husserl, "Philosophy and the Crisis of European Man," in *Phenomenology and the Crisis of Philosophy, op. cit.,* p. 191.
22 *Ibid.,* p. 179.
23 *Ibid.,* pp. 181-188.
24 *Ibid.,* p. 189.

that he had sought to commit himself fully to that task. In forging the tool of transcendental phenomenology he had sought to develop "a real method of grasping the fundamental essence of spirit in its intentionalities and consequently of instituting an analysis of spirit with a consistency reaching to the infinite." [25] Only this method could truly claim to be independent of the prejudices and interferences of other approaches and spheres of reality. It alone allowed reason to stand forth in its purity and authenticity. Hence it provided for a renewed rationalism that could save confused men from the modern crisis and impending disaster. It marked a recovery of the true meaning of reason, which is none other than spirit understanding itself in a really universal, really radical manner. The recovery of reason emerges in the form of a science whose scope is universal, wherein an entirely new scientific thinking is established, in which every conceivable question, whether of being, of norm, or of so-called "existence," finds its place.[26] Here, then, transcendental phenomenology appears in its fullness as a recovery and reinstitution of reason, as a way of exercising reason turned wholly toward subjectivity so as to establish the science upon which every other cognitive method is based; thus it is the path to absolute truth.

Unfortunately Husserl's achievements in applying his phenomenological method were extremely limited and of questionable success. His concern was not to apply but, rather, to establish the framework and provide the tools which others could subsequently use and develop. In other words, his major contribution was in the field of epistemology, a limited but important endeavor to which he was fully, indeed compulsively, committed. As he wrote in his early lectures, "We are searching for the very clear intuiting of the essence of knowledge," which leads to a concentration upon "the problem of givenness, that is the problem of the constitution of every possible kind of givenness in knowledge." [27] As we have previously noted, he sought to move beyond both epistemological skepticism and naïve arrogance, so as to establish a firm, indeed an absolutely clear basis for all cognitive endeavors.

According to his loyal disciple and interpreter, Professor Eugen Fink, Husserl's method begins in wonder and awe at the givenness of being. He then proceeds to question the existence of the world. The difference between his way of raising this question and that of traditional philosophy is

---

[25] *Ibid.*, p. 190.
[26] *Ibid.*
[27] Edmund Husserl, *Die Idee der Phänomenologie, op. cit.*, pp. 8, 14, passim, my translation. (*The Idea of Phenomenology*, pp. 6, 11.)

that Husserl questions the world as it is directly perceived by the subject.[28]
Our capacity to perceive the world at all, points to the universals or essences which underlie our perception of a particular thing. Thus his
epistemological contribution is to open our eyes to the constitutive factor
of consciousness or reason, which in turn points toward the essences that
emerge from the streaming life of consciousness, not as arbitrary constructions, but as direct reflections upon the objective realm of the ideal.
Though this method sharply divides the ideal from the factual, it does not
leave the factual world behind and out of account; but, rather, it points to
the constituting grasp of reality which contains it.[29] Thus one is directed
away from knowledge which is superficial and contingent to the *Urgrund*
of all being and knowledge.[30] Though the grasp of absolute being was seen
as a possibility, Husserl's actual claim was that his transcendental
phenomenology would provide a pure science of the spiritual subject,
an *Egologie*; this alone would provide a basis for a true, universal ontology,
but it was not his concern to develop that.[31]

It is important to note that Husserl, in his aim to achieve a clear
perception of essential objectivity, which he maintained is given in subjectivity, makes constant reference to directness, immediacy, purity, and absolute clarity. His claim, and one that is basic to his phenomenology, is that
the "things" become clarified by means of themselves, not by any outside
interference or mediation. Subjectivity is self-revelatory of its own true
objectivity. This claim stems in large part from Husserl's belief in the
capacity and veracity of the phenomenological reduction, which in turn
involves his understanding of intentionality and intuition. Husserl insisted
that it is necessary to withdraw from the prejudice of attitudes which come
quite naturally, but especially under the influence of the naïve natural
attitude described above. When the natural world is, so to speak, put in
brackets, then our judgment of things and values is suspended, so that the
true, inner reality of subjectivity may reveal itself. Husserl realized that this
suspension was itself a very difficult achievement; but it is absolutely im-

28 Eugen Fink, "Die Phänomenologische Philosophie Edmund Husserl in der
Gegenwärtigen Kritik," *Kant Studien*, Vol. 38 (1933), pp. 338-339.
29 *Ibid.*, pp. 341-342.
30 *Ibid.*, pp. 346 ff.
31 Cf. Edmund Husserl, *Cartesianische Meditationen und Pariser Vorträge*, pp. 12,
33 ff. (*The Paris Lectures*, pp. 11, 32 ff.). Heidegger was extremely critical of Husserl
on this score; he maintained that on these grounds Husserl could never get beyond his
egology to a true ontology. Hence their unhappy separation—unhappy and extremely
disappointing, especially to Husserl.

perative if we are to rid ourselves of the blinding prejudice of the natural attitude, which would deceive us into judging reality to be essentially external. If we pause and reflect, we are aware that we are conscious of the world, and that its presence to us is constituted by our act upon the world, not that of it upon us. With this insight we recognize that the world poses for us a problem of its unity and its value. This problem, as all basic epistemological and axiological problems, can be solved only by focusing exclusively upon subjectivity. As Professor Fink is careful to point out, Husserl's reduction does not disregard or deny the world; but it does bracket the natural attitude which tends to overlook and leave hidden transcendental subjectivity.[32] Nevertheless, in spite of Husserl's encouraging words and the qualifying remarks of Professor Fink, other phenomenologists have found a full reduction to be an impossibility; thus the absolute foundations for all knowledge remain tantalizing but only suggested revelations.

Bound up with his belief in his reduction was Husserl's conception of the nature of subjective or spiritual intentionality, which has been a basic term in phenomenology. In reflecting upon his own experience, Husserl was aware that his consciousness was of something, of the world, to which he was thereby united. But precisely of what is he conscious? The things of the world are not immediately presented to his consciousness; yet he was aware of an immediate presence of form and meaning. This awareness then revealed that consciousness, far from being a passive mold into which content is poured, is active in constituting the experience of the world and in designating meaning to its particulars. This suggests, indeed it was to Husserl an absolute revelation, that consciousness is directly conscious of active forms which enable it to perceive, interpret, indeed originate, the world. Thus to Husserl intentionality specifically refers to noetic consciousness in relation to noematic, eidetic reality, that is, essences. In his insistence upon the intentionality of consciousness he differed, as we have seen, both from Kant's formal view of consciousness and from Descartes's view of the enclosed, isolated consciousness, the *cogito*. To Husserl, Descartes had begun the true exploration of transcendental subjectivity; but having reached the door of the *cogito*, he merely opened it, then closed it, unaware of the ideal content that lay behind. Husserl's argument was that in the act of the *cogito* there is present a *cogitatum*, which is the intended object (noema) of which the mind is conscious. This object is part of the

[32] Fink, *op. cit.*, pp. 342-352.

subjective phenomenon, and is of an ideal rather than of a factual or existential nature. The objectivity possessed by consciousness is discovered only through subjectivity. Conceptual objectivity is immanent. It is the immanence of ideal reality in the subject which constitutes man's transcendence of the factual. This immanent objectivity enables subjectivity to transcend the world, and to contain it rather than be contained by it.

This discovery of the intentionally structured, constituting consciousness opens up to me, an individual, the world, the specifically human world as I experience it, value it, shape it, interpret it.[33] Yet what is the evidence which Husserl finds for maintaining this ideal intentionality of consciousness? That is a crucial question, because without ample indications that consciousness is so constituted the programatic claims of transcendental phenomenology are highly questionable if not extremely dubious. Husserl, who was extremely concerned about evidence, affirmed that the intentional reality of consciousness with the presence or givenness of a *cogitatum* in the *cogito* is quite simply self-evident. The ideal objectivity given to subjectivity is recognized immediately through the intuition mentioned earlier. The givenness of an essence has the same immediacy of the *cogito*; that is to say, it is indubitable. The act of consciousness which possesses an immanent objectivity contains its own evidence, an evidence which is not derived but direct; that makes it in fact infallible.[34] Thus the argument is made to rest upon what for Husserl is a direct vision of eternal essences in the phenomenon of subjectivity; we are to accept them as self-evident and hence apodictic. This is a form of validation about as appealing as a dogmatic papal pronouncement. If we can accept for the moment Paul Tillich's suggestion that angels are merely mythological versions of essences, we might then say that Husserl has attempted a grand but thoroughly secularized angelology. But his impressive demythologizing does not convince us any more easily that these transcendental essences actually exist in a reality larger than one's own private subjectivity. His intuition represents a particular version of consciousness which sees it as inherently related to a highly questionable sphere of essences which is claimed to have more objectivity than the objects before your eyes; and the validation for its presence is its intuitively perceived apodictic self-evidence. It is not so much that Husserl is mistaken in suggesting the use and

    33 Cf. Husserl, *Pariser Vorträge, op. cit.*, pp. 19, 20 ff. (*The Paris Lectures*, pp. 15 ff.)
    34 Cf. Q. Lauer, Introduction, *op. cit.*, pp. 21 ff.

validity of intuition but, rather, that he interprets it in a very narrow, absolutistic way, as a logician recognizing the universal applicability of basic principles within a given logical system. He seems rather consistently to have supposed that Being itself is ultimately logical, and that cognition, to be valid, must follow the pattern of logic as he understood it.

At the end of his famous article, Eugen Fink wrote that Husserl's position is at bottom the expression of a deep faith in the rationality of human experience. Husserl believed that the transcendental ego must be accepted as self-evident if man is to recover the true essence of spirit.[35] In his phenomenological endeavor, certainly Husserl has struck an extremely significant chord. My problem here lies perhaps in the fact that I do not share his *Weltanschauung;* to me the rich melody of life is not composed in the logically rational way he often, though not always, suggested.[36] To hear the fullness of the music, another way of listening is required. If the essence of spirit is primarily personal rather than logically rational, then the recovery of spirit and the method for understanding it will follow a different phenomenological program.

A serious snag in the program of transcendental phenomenology as a means to grasp the essential principles of transcendence is encountered when one thinks of another subject and wonders if one has access also to his subjectivity. If phenomenology reveals the essence of subjectivity, it should provide a rare and privileged insight into the essential givenness of another's subjectivity as well as into my own; for, essence is universal. Furthermore there should be between two intuiting phenomenologists absolutely remarkable communication. Husserl personally did not, apparently, experience the latter, and he was occasionally vexed about the former. Do we have direct access to another's subjectivity, so that we have transcendental knowledge of it? Husserl was at once aware that to encounter another subject means that we recognize another constituting consciousness, which by definition is an independent nature not causally affected by an external subject or object. His program would thus seem to preclude a phenomenological grasp of another's subjectivity, which in effect seems to nullify the claim that phenomenology is the door to all true subjectivity. As he worked on this problem in his first volume of *Ideas*

[35] Fink, *op. cit.,* p. 383.

[36] This criticism must be made tentatively, because though Husserl often seems to assume an underlying logical conception of reality, yet at the end of his *Cartesian Meditations* he suggests that phenomenology will lead to an ontology quite different from those of the past which have been restricted by logic. See, e.g., p. 138.

toward a Pure Phenomenology, he insisted that consciousness is indis-
solubly linked to one's body. We encounter another's body empirically, but
we do not in this way have direct access to his subjectivity, which is closed
off from us by that body. Rightly affirming the indissoluble relation between mind and body, he can find no bridge between independent subjectivities.[37] Yet in that same volume, he later maintained that there is a
transcendental community of knowledge and institutions;[38] and in subsequent writings he continued to maintain it. This statement, however, is
without justification or apparent meaning, since Husserl has been forced to
leave the ego imprisoned in its own consciousness with no direct transcendental access to the subjectivity of another. Though he affirms the subjectivity of another person, he seems in fact to be making another's subjectivity from one's own viewpoint into an inaccessible object, which is the very
sin of naturalism that he has so vigorously attacked.

In later writings such as *Ideen II, The Paris Lectures,* and *Cartesian
Meditations,* he sought to work out of this dilemma. The problem, as he
saw it, is essentially how to avoid a transcendental solipsism, whereby we
account for the genuine constituting consciousness of another person. If
phenomenology gives direct access to subjectivity, how is it possible for my
subjectivity to have access to that of another? He affirmed that the a priori
of consciousness is the same for all other subjects as it is for me. Furthermore, my experience of another person is different from my experience of
natural objects; for, I recognize over *there* in him a constituting process
like my own. We both experience the same world, and my experience of
another includes his experience of me. But how does that subjectivity over
there get over here to mine?[39] His answer is basically that the other's
subjectivity does not move to the center of my consciousness but rather
remains implicitly in my world, though on the edge of the horizon.[40] He
suggested that there is a special form of union with the other which he
denoted as sympathy (*Einfühlung*); but this term is far from being clearly
defined by him, nor does it really seem to have a place in his scheme.
What Husserl is forced to admit is that we understand another's experience by analogy but not by direct contact. The other person is in relation
to essences as I am and thus constitutes the world in essentially the same
way.[41] Yet as this manner of understanding is inferential and indirect, it

37 See E. Husserl, *Ideas,* trans. Boyce Gibson, pp. 164-168.
38 *Ibid.,* p. 213.
39 See especially E. Husserl, *Cartesian Meditations,* pp. 100 ff.
40 Cf. *ibid.,* pp. 131 ff.
41 Cf. also E. Husserl, *The Paris Lectures,* pp. 33-36.

then has no rightful place in phenomenology. Also, to assert that another's experience is constituted by transcendental subjectivity inaccessible to my own, means that his phenomenology does not open the door directly, clearly, and absolutely to all transcendental subjectivity. It is not surprising that Scheler attacked a theory of knowledge of others by analogy in his attempt to develop a phenomenology of our experience of other minds.

It is regrettable that Husserl apparently did not take Scheler's work seriously. Husserl did say in later writings that our notion of subjectivity must be expanded to a genuine understanding of intersubjectivity, which he claimed to be the true nature of subjectivity. Yet the meaning of this intersubjectivity is, it seems, restricted to the realm of essences and not to concrete social or personal life, certainly not to the subjectivity of another person who becomes a presence. In the end, he is led to assert that transcendental phenomenology evolves as a new form of Monadology. I can only posit apodictically my ego as existing. Yet phenomenology only starts with the self as a *solus ipse*; for, in the encounter with other subjectivities, we realize a plurality of monads, of consciousnesses constituting the world.[42] Thus through his pluralistic monadology he tried to solve the problem of solipsism; but he has not thereby accounted for truly personal communication. His phenomenology is essentially an egology, which inevitably places a severe restriction upon the scope of and resources available to his method. What is obviously needed is an enlarging of his framework which can account for and make sense of our actual concrete experience of others. That is, a phenomenology which focuses upon interpersonal and social transcendence is needed. Surprisingly enough, Husserl maintained the same thing only pages before he made the foregoing assertions. We need, he said, to study social acts so as to make sociality understandable as a form of transcendence and thus come to see the truly cultural world.[43] As we shall see in our next chapter, Max Scheler, who had a deep sense of the social foundation of the individual self, attempted to do just that. With the radical bifurcation between essence and fact maintained by Husserl, it is nearly impossible to see how such could be done on his terms.

An alternative to eidetic phenomenology is a phenomenology which turns toward, not away from, concrete existence in the world with others. Husserl himself considered the possibility and made a few concessions in this direction by introducing some new terms; however, these are far from

[42] E. Husserl, *Cartesian Meditations*, p. 139; also *ibid.*, p. 29.
[43] *Cartesian Meditations*, pp. 132-133.

providing what is required. Though in his later years he suggested that much investigation needs to be done on man's preconscious encounter with the world of everyday experience (*Lebenswelt*), he nevertheless made clear his opposition to an existential approach to anthropology. He insisted that phenomenology is an absolute subjectivism which is isolated from the empirically given world, focusing instead upon the subjectivity which grounds our experience of the world; for him phenomenology leads to a transcendental investigation of the ideas which emerge in the intentionality of pure consciousness. It is, then, neither an existentential nor a social science but an absolute egological science which to him is the truest philosophy of all.[44]

One of the great drawbacks, then, of eidetic transcendental phenomenology is the cleavage between subjectivity and the factuality of human existence in the world. For this reason, I find it impossible to follow exactly the path to truth as Husserl has marked it out. As Quentin Lauer has put it, "By eliminating the factual, it is true, one may arrive at the essential, but philosophically speaking, the price may be more than we can afford, if the essential must be identified with the hypothetical."[45] There is obviously much in Husserl's endeavor that smacks of a compulsiveness aggravated by a problem made insoluble because of a tight restriction upon valid evidence. Though he is not guilty of promulgating a metaphysical idealism, yet he does seem to be hampered by a view of Being which is extremely narrow; his basic ontological notion seems to be of logical subjectivity to the exclusion of personal and social being. His Logical Being is made the foundation of truth. Yet even if his program leads to a dead end, it is undeniable that he has given a new impetus to modern philosophy which is extremely valuable. He has called attention to the reality of subjectivity in an era which stands in grave danger of ignoring and denying it. He was a man of heroic dedication to truth who has prompted us to reconsider our own prejudices and predispositions, and has led us to realize the subjective nature of all our perceptions and all rational knowledge. In his call for a return to beginnings and a search for secure foundations, he has provided us with a germinating power and indicated a new direction for philosophy, which is to lead us back to experience and seek an illumination of it in its own terms. He has not presented us with a system, but has turned our gaze

---

[44] E. Husserl, "Phenomenology and Anthropology," *Realism and the Background of Phenomenology*, R. M. Chisholm, ed., pp. 129-142.

[45] Q. Lauer, Introduction to Edmund Husserl, *Phenomenology and the Crisis of Philosophy*, *op. cit.*, p. 65.

toward the spirit; by so doing he has not tied us to his peculiar vision but, rather, encouraged each of us to follow his example and learn to be a true beginner. Such is of the essence of philosophy.

This interpretative essay has tended to see Husserl tenting on the border of, if not within, the Idealistic camp. It may appear questionable that he really has a contribution to make to existential phenomenology. Yet there are tendencies in Husserl's writings which allow for the possibility of a somewhat different interpretation.[46] Merleau-Ponty saw the study of essences, not as an end in itself, but as a means by which to understand our effective involvement in the world.[47] Indeed, phenomenology is a study of essences; but different from Idealism, it puts the essences back into existence where they belong.[48] The focus of phenomenology is upon intentionality, as Husserl maintained; but we must understand that Husserl was not the first to speak of intentionality. The notion is even to be found in Descartes and Kant. What one finds in Husserl is a deeper notion of intentionality, which others, like Merleau-Ponty, have called existence.[49] Intentional subjectivity, as Merleau-Ponty reveals it, is not consciousness' identity with itself, but a movement of the self to an Other; it means to go forth and be engaged in the world with others.[50] Seen from this perspective, phenomenology is the means of revealing my (the individual's) *subjectivity in its encounter with the empirical world.* What is more, this method seeks to reveal our concrete intersubjectivity. What Merleau-Ponty has done is to establish the dialectical character of existence and the world; like Husserl he avoided talking about the causality of knowledge as from an external, foreign force, but instead he spoke frequently about the interplay of self, world, and others, and the communion and interdependence we have with them. Merleau-Ponty's *existential* phenomenology is a rich and provocative example of the stimulus Husserl's *eidetic* phenomenology may have when interpreted within the broader and more concrete perspective of human existence as it encounters the world of living, personal experience.

[46] See M. Merleau-Ponty, *Phenomenology of Perception, op. cit.,* p. 365, and passim.
[47] *Ibid.,* p. xv.
[48] *Ibid.,* p. vii.
[49] *Ibid.,* p. 121, fn.
[50] *Ibid.,* p. 426.

3

Max Scheler's Phenomenological Anthropology

Not long before his premature death from a heart attack, Max Scheler (1874–1928) wrote: "If there is a philosophical task for which our era demands a solution with unique urgency, it is that of philosophical anthropology." [1] To develop philosophical anthropology was his most enduring and major concern; as he himself said: "The questions 'What is man? What is his place in Being?' have been to me more central and essential than any other philosophical questions raised since the first awakening of my philosophical consciousness." [2] Although during his lifetime Scheler was regarded by some as an equal with Husserl in the phenomenological movement, we can see from the latter quotation that their basic interests were quite different. Husserl was primarily interested in developing a science of the sciences, an absolute and systematic insight into the essences which constitute the basis of all knowledge. Scheler's attention, on the other hand, was directed toward concrete human life and values. When as a young man Scheler met Husserl in 1900, he recognized that they were both interested in developing a methodology which would reveal the essential aspects of human transcendence; but he never apparently shared Husserl's concern to establish a truly scientific philosophy. Though they met and discussed their similar interests, their meetings were infrequent and became increasingly so as the directions of their thinking became more and

1 Max Scheler, *Philosophical Perspectives*, p. 65.
2 Scheler, *Die Stellung des Menschen im kosmos*, p. 9; my translation. Or see the English translation, *Man's Place in Nature*, p. 3.

46

more divergent. Much of what kept them apart was temperament, manner of life, and two quite distinct outlooks on life (*Weltanschauungen*). Whereas Husserl, as we have seen, thought of Being within a logical frame of reference, Scheler conceived of Being in much broader terms; he thought of Being in distinctively personal terms. To him, at least in his middle period though not at the end of his life, the essence of spirit was considered to be personal. This notion led Scheler to prize the fullness of concrete personal experience, whereas Husserl had turned away from it to focus upon what he considered to be the underlying ideal reality of any given experience. Consequently, Scheler became immersed in philosophical anthropology, psychology, and sociology, whereas Husserl consistently held himself aloof from these pursuits. Husserl worked painstakingly and in isolation, developing his philosophy in the fashion of a monologue. Scheler's philosophical habitat was a German coffee house, where he discussed his subject matter with intensity, great flashes of brilliance, and strong reliance upon his own feelings about the subject.[3]

In spite of these differences, Scheler insisted upon his indebtedness to Husserl's phenomenology; certainly his basic categories are very close to Husserl's and perhaps borrowed from him, even though his interpretations of them are markedly different from those given by Husserl himself. Furthermore, they shared an important concern for the spiritual welfare of Europe. Scheler expressed his belief that European civilization had experienced a breakdown in values; he differed with Husserl's interpretation, however, in that he did not acknowledge the cause of the breakdown to be the decline of rationalism. He attributed the collapse of spirit to the rise of a kind of rationalism associated with bourgeois capitalism which elevates technical, calculating reason so as to achieve specific, utilitarian goals. The main fault of this narrow rationalism is that it blinds men to the true values of life. For some time, Scheler identified true values with those of Christianity; and he was concerned to re-establish a Christian ethic which would emphasize the value of the human spirit as *person* above the modern values of utility and technical progress. The problem was how to direct Europe toward a recovery of unity and of spirit. Similar to Husserl, Scheler believed phenomenology to be vitally relevant to this problem, because to him it represented a means of recovering insight into the essential values of life. Like that of many others of his generation, Scheler's philosophical upbringing had been in the tradition of Kant. Scheler was particularly

[3] See Herbert Spiegelberg, *The Phenomenological Movement*, Vol. I, pp. 228-231.

perturbed by the formalism of Kantian ethics whereby ethical judgment
was made on the basis of a set of principles rather than upon the actual
perception of values. Scheler could not agree either with Kant's epistemological dichotomy between noumena and phenomena or with the
sensationalism advocated or implied in the empirical sciences of that day.
He was convinced that persons have direct perception not merely of other
beings, but also of values. In Scheler's view, values are directly given in a
particular situation to the subject who is open so as to become aware of
them. Thus Scheler saw the phenomenological method first of all as a way
of changing one's basic attitude so as to become open to values and then as
a means of beholding the given value content of an experience. His solution
to the basic problem, however, was not primarily a methodological but an
ethical one.

In one of his greatest and largest works, *Formalism in Ethics and the
Ethic of Non-Formalistic Value* (*Der Formalismus in der Ethik und die
Materiale Wertethik*), Scheler attempted to establish a foundation for a
personalistic ethic.[4] Like Husserl, Scheler stressed that he was not building
a system but was trying to discover foundations; but unlike Husserl, these
were foundations or essences, not of knowledge in general but specifically
of concrete personal values. This work is not vitally important methodologically. As Scheler himself admitted, although he maintained a phenomenological attitude, yet his phenomenology was not here spelled out. More
important is his elaboration of a concept of the person.

In Scheler's perspective, ethics is based on and part of the broader
attempt to understand man as a distinctly human being, as a person. His
argument against the Kantian tradition was that though it claims to elevate
the person above all particulars by considering the person as an end, not a
means, yet it really devalued him by making the person into a principle, an
impersonal end. In fact, it disregarded the very heart of personality.[5]
Scheler insisted that we consider the person in his act of being in the world
and thus strike at the real foundation of his being a person. By moving
away from formalism back to the givenness of experience, he had then to
distinguish himself from and to criticize the empirical sciences which considered man primarily or exclusively as an objective organism which could

---

[4] This work appeared in two volumes in the German Yearbook Series for Philosophy and Phenomenological Research in 1913 and 1916.
[5] M. Scheler, *Der Formalismus in der Ethik und die Materiale Wertethik*, pp.
381-596.

be studied with detachment. He maintained that the person can never be considered as an object. We may consider objectively his body, his inner vitality or psyche, and their unity; that is, we may consider man merely as a psychosomatic organism. But the person is an underlying unity who is engaged in an act which transcends that narrow objectivity. A personal act is not merely physical or psychological motion in reaction to external or internal stimuli. A personal act is a spiritual event which is a unity including subject and world in the meaningful order of intentionality.[6] The essence of the person consists in the execution of intentional acts which thus constitute his personal existence. Biology and psychology can have nothing to do with the latter, since they focus upon objects.[7] Only phenomenology reveals the underlying unity of act and meaning, which is the transcendental unity of intentionality. The person is a being who initiates action which is directly related to what Scheler spoke of as value facts. As a creature who acts, he is a centered being, moving out from his subjective center toward essential values and meanings. He is capable of understanding, making decisions and knowing that he has made them, and thus of assuming responsibility. As such, the person is a bearer of ethical values and one who realizes them through his personal acts.[8] The very highest value of all is the person, a value which can only truly be understood and appreciated by genuine love of another person.[9]

Though Scheler was attempting to recover a true grasp of the person as spirit, he was far from overlooking the vital or libidinal dimension of human existence. He is famous in later writings especially for his strong emphasis upon the role of feelings in man's pursuit of truth. Feeling plays an essential role in his phenomenology. To Scheler, phenomenology is not a new form of rationalism purged from emotions and feelings but a way of perceiving essences following the paths of feelings. Very important to him was the statement of Pascal that the heart has its reasons which the mind knows not of. In making value judgments, the heart plays an essential role, one which enables value perception to occur and which helps to bring clarity to the perception. Like logical reason, the heart judges with evidence; but it has evidence of its own kind. It follows a logical operation; but it is the logic of the heart, not of the mind. It has *its* own reasons, not

[6] *Ibid.*, pp. 399-400.
[7] *Ibid.*, pp. 401 ff.
[8] *Ibid.*, pp. 482-487.
[9] *Ibid.*, pp. 493-513.

the mind's or the senses'; and it has its own "reasons" or evidence for its
distinct judgments.[10] As though writing to Husserl, Scheler maintained
that if we restrict logic and perception to the mind alone, we shall have
greatly distorted the whole of reality. Without feeling, without the vision
of the heart, we are blind to the essences of value; direct perception of true
values is with the heart, not with the head. To prevent misinterpretation,
it should be remembered that Scheler's notion of true value is personal;
consequently, the heart is primarily understood to be the way we arrive at
an insight into and an understanding of the real worth of another human
being.

The emphasis upon feeling had tremendous significance for Scheler's
conception of phenomenology and also of his view of intuition. In an essay
written about 1914 while he was working on his ethics, Scheler wrote that
phenomenology differs from both science and philosophy, not primarily
because it uses a different method but because it has a different attitude.[11]
All the sciences and philosophy as well are similar to the extent that their
methods employ a basic attitude which is one of detached observation;
consequently, knowledge from this attitude is indirect. The difference in
phenomenology's method should first be described as a kind of spiritual
vision (Schauen), which opens up for it a revelation of new facts that
otherwise would be hidden. A unique phenomenological attitude is created
by a certain experience, which enables the essences upon which the phenomenological gaze is centered to be given directly. Scheler is here following what he assumed to be Husserl's teaching about the intentional structure of consciousness, although he seems to be closer to Brentano than to
Husserl. Brentano and Husserl had emphasized that the point of focus for
phenomenology was not upon either the subject or the object, but upon
their point of contact, that is, upon the inherently unified, inseparable
relation of subject and object. Scheler likewise emphasized that phenomenology is directed at the point of contact between experience and the
world of objects. Like Husserl, he maintained that phenomenology was to
be an a priori discipline, perceiving the universal rather than the accidental
contents of the experience of the world. He went further, however, to say
that though phenomenology was neither an empiricism nor an idealism,

10 M. Scheler, "Ordo Amoris," Schriften aus dem Nachlass, Vol. I, pp. 361-362;
cf. The Nature of Sympathy, "Preface to the Second Edition," p. xlv.
11 Max Scheler, Schriften aus dem Nachlass, Vol. I, "Phänomenologische Ein-
stellung," pp. 380 ff.

yet it was the most radical form of empiricism. He was the first to argue for a phenomenological realism, as opposed to the neutral or idealistic phenomenology of Husserl.[12] Scheler was not interested in essences divorced from life; similar to Merleau-Ponty, what he wished to do was to get behind them into life. His radical empiricism opposed a rationalism which presupposes a realm of absolute ideas and then devotes itself to them. He aimed at having a direct, intuitive relationship with things as they are encountered.[13] In describing his phenomenological reduction, Husserl explicitly sought to turn his mind away from values so as to perceive ideas; Scheler instead sought to set into operation an intuition which would perceive the value of things which constitute their essence, or what he called the value essence (*Wertwesen*). He maintained that these essences are objects of experience which are directly given to the subject in experience itself. Self-givenness (*Selbstgegebenheit*) is the hallmark of phenomenology.[14] Like Husserl, Scheler affirmed the immanence of the "object" of knowledge through the operation of intuition; and he, too, stressed that by directly grasping an essence, phenomenology overcomes the gap between the world and the subject's experience of it.[15] In spite of similarities of terminology and to some extent in methodology, we sense marked differences between Husserl and Scheler which, as suggested above, seem to be indicative not merely of dissimilar temperaments but of different *Weltanschauungen*. Clearly, Scheler's notion of essence in terms of a concrete personal act is radically removed from a notion of a fixed, absolute ideal.

Scheler himself was quite conscious that differing epistemological methods and their particular goals implied different intuitive perspectives of reality. He pointed to three different kinds of facts for which there are three diverse cognitive approaches. The first is the naturalistic perspective or the "natural" outlook on life (*Natürliche Weltanschauung*); second there is the scientific conception of the world which is built upon it (*Wissenschaftliche Weltauffassung*); finally there is the philosophical perspective (*Philosophische Weltanschauung*).[16] The naturalistic perspective

[12] Spiegelberg, *op. cit.*, p. 245.

[13] Cf. Spiegelberg, *ibid.*, pp. 241-242.

[14] Scheler, *Nachlass, op. cit.*, pp. 383-384; and cf. also his *Vom Ewigen im Menschen*, p. 17 and the English edition, *On the Eternal in Man*, p. 23.

[15] Scheler, *Nachlass*, pp. 384-386.

[16] M. Scheler, *Vom Ewigen im Menschen*, p. 87; *On the Eternal in Man*, pp. 93 ff. Later in life he maintained this threefold distinction, but revised it in light of his developing monism and a gnostic view of salvation. In the second category he

and the scientific conceptualizations based upon it are directed at the
environing world (*Umwelt*). The philosophical perspective arises on a
different ontological sphere and has a different object. This latter perspective grounds a spiritual act which enables the subject to participate in the
sphere of Being. As in other forms of gnosticism, Scheler maintained that
the hindrance to man's participation in Being is his exaggerated attachment to the natural world and his natural egocentricity.[17] However, man
can rise above these obstacles through an act of love. This love for Being
and value controls man's bodily impulses toward sensation and humbles his
proud ego. Thus the truly philosophical attitude is identical with phenomenology; and the essence of this approach is not a reduction but a self-
surrender to Being. The true philosopher faces reality with an outstretched
hand and an open eye which is filled with wondering love at the givenness
of Being. The essence of philosophic insight into the essential values of
reality is love; this love opens man's eyes to behold the essences and their
relationships as they exist and are given in the Absolute.[18] To obtain the
knowledge peculiar to his approach, the scientist, according to Scheler,
does not need love or true humility. Yet without love, the philosopher can
have no true knowledge at all; without it he would remain on the lower
level of the naturalistic perspective. For Scheler, then, phenomenology is
not primarily a set of mental operations; but, rather, it rests upon an
intuitive act which he has defined as love. That is to maintain that philosophical truth depends upon a specific moral act on the part of the philosopher. Heidegger also asserted that authentic knowledge of Being depends
upon a distinct moral act, which, however, he defined as a resolute facing
of one's own death. Though the emphasis upon the prerequisite moral act
for philosophical truth about man is extremely important for the emergence of existential phenomenology, it will be seen that Scheler's stress
upon the centrality of love for the full vision of man is the more important
of the two. It should now be clear that Scheler has rejected Husserl's
notion of a phenomenological reduction, but in its place he has put another act, that of love. Yet we should notice that love is similar to Husserl's
reduction in that it is an act of transcendence which goes beyond a mere
objective approach so as to reach the essences directly.

introduces a form of knowledge which builds culture. The third new category is on a
higher plane whereby the spirit achieves knowledge of essences which give man salvation through participation in the eternal. See "The Forms of Knowledge and Culture,"
pp. 13-49 in *Philosophical Perspectives*.
    [17] *Vom Ewigen im Menschen*, pp. 89-90.
    [18] *Ibid.*, p. 98.

In his study of religion, Scheler made another provocative suggestion which, although he apparently did not make much use of it, is important for existential phenomenology. In this study, he attempted to sketch a picture of the whole man, which he maintained can only be grasped from the standpoint of living under the eternal. For, to him at that time, the eternal was that element in man which makes him fully human.[19] He suggested that insight into a peak human experience will provide the fullest picture of man. The highest peak experience is an act by which man is elevated into eternity, whereby he is in immediate contact with all essentials and thus with the full potentialities of his being. Because of the intentional nature of man's spirit, a glimpse of his centered act participating in eternal reality will give the philosopher a view of man similar to God's view of him.[20] That mystical vision is perhaps higher than other phenomenologists care to go; undoubtedly it is higher than at least most of us mortals are capable of attaining, so that the full meaning of this passage is not evident. Nevertheless he has made a suggestion deserving of much consideration; that is, he has indicated that an intuitive investigation of an elevated or ecstatic experience (*Aufschwung*) will provide the best clue to discover the fullest possible picture of man. It is a suggestion which runs counter to contemporary reductionistic thinking; it indicates that by looking at man in his peak experiences rather than observing him primarily when he is at his lowest and worst we shall have a much more complete view of him.[21] In the second part of this book I follow this suggestion and concentrate upon the ecstatic experience of love.

In his mid-forties, the same time in life that Husserl underwent a radical revolution in his own thinking, Scheler also underwent a definite change of outlook and aim, leaving behind him not merely his Catholic faith but also his phenomenological enterprise. His daughter has subsequently explained that this "conversion in reverse" came about as a result of his failure to produce a theodicy for the personal religion of Christianity; he thus moved toward a tragic view of life.[22] Though he had previously dissociated himself from Husserl's systematic enterprise to arrive at ideal

[19] *Ibid.*, p. 7.
[20] *Ibid.*, p. 87.
[21] Cf. the approach of the American psychologist, A. H. Maslow, in *Religion, Science, and Mental Health*, where he reports on his studies of highest moments in human life which are so revelatory. Especially he argues for the study of love as a peak experience, whereby one's *Weltanschauung* is changed and the whole dimension and character of one's life is transformed. Freud, he argues, had only nonsense to say about love and so missed seeing the fullness of human beings (pp. 17-19).
[22] Maria Scheler, "Nachwort," editor of *Vom Ewigen im Menschen*, p. 456.

essences, he now became determined to construct a complete metaphysic which approached the monistic visions of Spinoza, Hegel, and Oriental mysticism, just those views which he had previously criticized severely.

In his final book he attempted to work out a comprehensive anthropology, but it was in reality a work in ontology, an attempt to see the place of man in the scheme of Being itself. Here he had a closer affinity to Husserl than we have previously noticed. Formerly Husserl's transcendental phenomenology with its presupposition of eternal essences divorced from historical factuality had little meaning for him. Indeed he had challenged all claims for apodictic, infallible insight into essences which supposedly ground cognition. In a brilliant psychological study, "The Idols of Self-Knowledge," he pointed up the tendency of the mind as it turns inward upon itself to construct idols. Freud had helped to reveal the self-deceptive quality of man's self-perception through the operation of repression, projection, and the misuse of terminology.[23] Now, surprisingly, Scheler himself turned inward into man's spirit so as to reach the essential concept of man.[24] He was not interested merely in the essences of the phenomenological reduction; he was interested in essences of any kind. Still, his approach to man's subjectivity was much earthier than Husserl's. Scheler emphasized the unconscious element in man, what he referred to as the vital element or libido. The libido is to be distinguished from the spirit. He saw this common vital element of life as containing a primordial layer of psyche which is to be found wherever the vital realm exists, in a manner which reminds us today of Teilhard de Chardin. Scheler affirmed the continuity of all life; yet at the same time he distinguished between the various forms of it, as higher from lower, in terms of the development of the psychic.[25] The first task in anthropology, then, is to become aware through feeling and prescience of this basic phenomenon of organic life which is immediately given and directly discernible as the basis for all genuine expression and communication.

Having established this elementary dynamic layer, Scheler affirmed that in man there is a new principle which is united to the vital level but does not emerge from it and so is not reducible to it. This reality is spirit

[23] See a doctoral dissertation which explores the psychological insights of the essay on the "Idols of Self-Knowledge" in detail; Bernard Lorscheid, Max Scheler's Phänomenologie des Psychischen; cf. also Spiegelberg, op. cit., pp. 243-244.
[24] Max Scheler, Die Stellung des Menschen im Kosmos, p. 13, or the English translation, Man's Place in Nature.
[25] Ibid., pp. 14 ff.

(*Geist*), and it is the principle of a man's acts (*Aktzentrum*) and the basis upon which he becomes a person.[26] Here he maintained that the function of the spirit is to objectify experience and thus discern the essences; that discernment occurs through a self-conscious act of concentration. What he previously might have described as an act bordering on idolatrous self-knowledge, he here declared that for man to make himself the object of his knowledge is the way for him to transcend the vital sphere and even the spatio-temporal world.[27] In Husserlian fashion he asserted the near omnipotence of human transcendence. At this point he seems to have left behind both the concrete world and his previous phenomenological method. He proceeded to devise a scheme for viewing man which goes beyond both anthropology and religion; for man, in properly using his intellectualized spiritual powers, himself becomes deified. In this last portrait, man is seen as a collaborator with an imperfect deity who becomes fulfilled in his divine being in and as man. What he was offering in this view, he wrote, is a religion of anthropotheism; it is a path of salvation for the man of intellect and courage, for the individual and the man of the spirit, who is bold enough to leave behind the old forms of atheism and institutional religion for those who are weak and unenlightened.[28]

In spite of the highly ambitious, gnostic, and mystical elements in his writings, particularly in the latter period, Scheler was able to perform phenomenology superbly, as his book focusing upon the essences of love and sympathy demonstrates so clearly. *The Nature of Sympathy* not only reveals his keen phenomenology, but also provides us with some important material necessary for the further development of existential phenomenology, particularly as we attempt to move beyond individualism. Scheler actually meant this book to be a demonstration of a principle which for him was axiomatic, what he called "the principle of the solidarity of all moral beings." [29] This principle, he affirmed, is in reality presupposed by any psychology and psychiatry which claims to have real knowledge of the mental processes of other people.[30]

The first of the three sections of this book is an attempt to work out an ethic of genuine sympathy or fellow feeling (*Mitgefühl*) by virtue of a phenomenology of the various kinds of feeling which bring us close to

[26] *Ibid.*, pp. 38 ff.
[27] *Ibid.*, p. 48.
[28] *Ibid.*, p. 91.
[29] M. Scheler, *The Nature of Sympathy*, p. 164.
[30] *Ibid.*, p. 214.

others. He first demonstrated the need for clarity here, so as to distinguish
the different kinds of feelings by which we are brought together with
others. Here Scheler showed extraordinary sensitivity and perception.
Other theories, as he examined them, had unfortunately lumped together
under a common heading feelings of togetherness which are similar yet in
reality different. By means of his acute observation, which resembles more
that of an artist than of a philosopher, he distinguished four essential types
of the feeling of togetherness. First there is what we might call a shared
personal feeling (*Miteinanderfühlen*), such as two parents might experience as they simultaneously grieve over the death of their child. Then
there is another type which we might call fellow feeling (*Mitgefühl*)
which is the state of true sympathy, as distinguished from condescending
pity. This is the feeling which structures the experience we have when we
reach deep understanding of another's situation and his feelings about it by
sharing it with him. Superficially similar but actually essentially distinct is a
third feeling denoted as emotional infection, whereby as part of a crowd
we are carried away with others by an identical feeling. Making use of
psychoanalytic studies of mob psychology he showed how radically different the feeling of identification with a group is from that of freely identifying oneself with another in his existential situation through sympathy.
Finally, there is another form of emotional identification whereby one loses
one's sense of self-identity as one is absorbed into the character of another,
such as happens sometimes during a theatrical performance; one may so
identify with the actor on the stage that he has become not merely an alter
ego but a replacement of one's ego.[31]

Operative in all forms of such feelings is the vital sphere of life, which
is not merely the basis upon which feelings arise but is also an essential
part of our solidarity with others. He pointed out that rationalism repeatedly tends to ignore this vital level, which leads it inevitably toward an individualistic view of man, seeing him in isolation from the rest of life. Yet
the naturalistic view errs on the other side by failing to distinguish the various kinds of feelings which are part of but not reducible to organic life.
There is the danger within this latter view that one will not get beyond the
feeling of identity, and thus one's personal life will suffocate in a superficial, collective existence.[32] Scheler made the point that there can be no
full knowledge of another person unless it is based upon the rudimentary

[31] *Ibid.*, pp. 12-18.
[32] *Ibid.*, pp. 32-36.

feeling of being with him in a common life (libido). Yet he rightly distinguished between mere organic feeling and personal feeling; the latter feeling is more on the spiritual level, is characterized by freedom and love, and opens our eyes to behold the truly transcendental, personal reality of another human being. Sympathy in its true sense is the way in which we transcend mere external stimuli and passing emotions so as to see the other not as an example of organic life classified as *Homo sapiens*, but as a unique, spiritual-historical being.[33]

With the distinction made between personal sympathy and emotional and vital identification, Scheler was able to make the distinctions between the kinds of knowledge that these two feelings impart. Sympathy primarily reveals the otherness of another person, which is to say, it affirms his uniqueness, whereas libido reveals our solidarity with other animate beings. Sympathy reveals that the other has an absolute privacy which cannot be rightfully invaded or denied, while emotional identity reveals that we are all one. Both feelings reveal the essential polarity in human life in terms of one direction toward independence and another direction toward mutuality and community. Scheler then affirmed that love alone can break down the barriers of individual isolation, because love affirms the absolute barrier of privacy and the uniqueness of another while at the same time affirming a life together.[34] Thus love comprehends both organic and personal feelings in its vision of the other.

Sympathy has its own peculiar content of knowledge about another person. It also has a very distinct structure. Unlike organic beings which can be observed at will, personal beings cannot be understood intuitively unless they disclose themselves.[35] Persons can never be understood as objects. No genuine sympathy can occur unless the subject first has a vital, organic feeling of identity with another; on the other hand, true sympathy cannot occur unless there is a willingness on the part of the other to reveal himself. Because of the inherent capacity for man to deceive himself, feelings are extremely ambiguous and can be highly deceptive, even when they are genuinely attuned toward another being. What makes the feeling more trustworthy is a recognition of mutuality and shared personal concern, such as is characteristic of love. To gain true insight into another, we must sympathetically share in his performance of a meaningful act.[36]

[33] Cf. *ibid.*, pp. 48-58.
[34] *Ibid.*, pp. 66-71.
[35] *Ibid.*, p. 101.
[36] *Ibid.*, p. 167.

One of the most crucial problems in contemporary philosophy re-
volves around the possibility of knowing others directly rather than by
inference or analogy. In this respect Scheler was far ahead of his time and
worked out a philosophical framework for communication and understanding which is implied in much contemporary psychoanalysis, as we shall
discover later in the book. Though the person cannot be approached as an
object, yet Scheler pointed out that he can become accessible to knowledge
through participation. Only as one participates in another's personal act,
and only as this participation serves to replace our knowledge of his external characteristics may we have a direct knowing of another.[37] This knowledge by participation Scheler labeled *understanding* (*verstehen*). Personal
understanding of others is an ultimate source of facts; it arises from intuitive data on a level Heidegger was later to call a primordial awareness of
being in the world. This awareness is not an isolated act of perception but
is a basis upon which distinct acts of perception arise; it is part of the
givenness of a man's experience. Since this awareness is primarily personal
understanding, man's primary understanding pertains to his direct participation in the personal acts of others. In other words, knowledge of persons
precedes perception of objective facts, though this knowledge is at first
nonconceptual, a rudimentary awareness of mutual participation. Thus
Scheler was led to propose an intuitive psychology which would go beyond
objective psychology by returning to primary understanding and our rudimentary life with others.[38] As we shall see, this idea was developed by
Binswanger with extremely important results issuing from it.

It is within this perspective that we can best appreciate Scheler's
notion of the unique and irreplaceable function of love in fashioning a
phenomenology of personal experience. He insisted that love is irreducible;
that is, love cannot be explained in terms of something else. It is not
derived from the libido, though certainly it is largely inseparable from it.
Nor is it merely a special kind of feeling. Love is a personal reality which
includes libido, feeling, relation, and act. As an act it is fully intentional; its
intentional object is personal value. Objective seeing perceives external
facts, personality traits, and the like; but only love can see the person in his
true worth. He wrote: ". . . love as such . . . never errs and is never

---

[37] *Ibid.*, p. 224.
[38] *Ibid.*, p. 225. Here again we see how far ahead of his time Scheler was in
several respects; his argument resembles that of M. Polanyi discussed in Chapter 1. In
some ways Scheler is more a contemporary of our time than he was of his own.

deceived, so long as man does not deceive himself as to its presence." [39] It must be understood that love is not expected to reveal facts on a biopsychic level. Specifically, love "opens our spiritual eyes to ever-higher values in the love object," values which otherwise would not be perceived.[40] Scheler emphasized that love is aimed at the enhancement of value. Love says to the one who is loved: "Become what thou art." This does not necessarily direct the beloved to develop a particular talent or character trait, nor does it present him or her with an imperative. It sees the true worth, the essence of the other as a person, and affirms that highest value. In this respect, blindness is all on the side of the detached observer.[41] To say that love is directed toward the highest moral values is to recognize that it is uniquely equipped to perceive the essences of fulfilled personal spirit.

In a subsequent writing Scheler clarified and expanded his views on love. He declared that whoever meets a person in the intentional order of love, the *ordo amoris*, truly grasps the person. That is, he sees his true spirit behind all the manifold empirical data. By participating in this order with another person one reaches the very source of the person, that is, the moral person.[42] One of Scheler's consistent affirmations is that love is a creative movement toward the highest values appropriate to the beloved. As in Dante's vision of Beatrice, the lover sees the beloved in terms of her perfection, as in heaven. Love is the active tendency to seek of each thing its essential value, its perfected value. The act of love leads us beyond the world of empirical data into the realm of the eternal. In this respect Scheler was suggesting that love, rather than religious elevation, is that act or phenomenon whereby the fullness of human existence is to be seen. As he put it, love always moves beyond what is present to what is meant to be, to the perfection of being.[43] As an intentional act, love is movement; yet it is, as he has said, a creative movement. Love not only sees to the end (*telos*) of a man, but the act of loving brings into the present that which it sees, as it were, in the future. Love is that unique form of perception which not only sees the highest value of another but creates the very reality of which it becomes cognizant. Love also sees itself as it begets itself; you cannot see love apart from love. Love's vision of itself and of the beloved

[39] *Ibid.*, p. 113.
[40] *Ibid.*, p. 156.
[41] *Ibid.*, pp. 158-160. A view of love close to that of Scheler's in this respect was worked out by Charles Williams; cf. *The Figure of Beatrice.*
[42] M. Scheler, "Ordo Amoris," *Schriften aus dem Nachlass*, Vol. 1, pp. 348 ff.
[43] *Ibid.*, pp. 355-358.

in terms of perfection is not fantasy or wishful thinking. To Scheler it was
a revelation of a new world, the world of essential values (*Wertewesen-
swelt*).[44] Though love is an exalted mode of the human spirit and the
true end of man, yet it is not by any means a reality which man attains at
the conclusion of his spiritual development. According to Scheler, love is
rudimentary; before man becomes a thinking or willing being, he is a
loving being (*ens amans*).[45]

Scheler's insight into the cognitive power of love is of crucial importance to existential phenomenology, for it proposes not merely the means
but also the basis upon which to obtain a full view of man as well as true
knowledge of other persons. Scheler demonstrated that it is extremely
erroneous to consider man primarily in his isolation; that is especially a
mistake of rationalism, which ignores the vital level and hence the intentional feeling of solidarity. By focusing upon the vital level of existence it
becomes immediately clear that there is some rudimentary involvement
with others. Love is able to see even further and to reveal a new form of
being with others. In both instances we have some direct communication
with the being of another. This shows up the inadequacy of any view which
suggests that our knowledge of others is based on analogies with our own
experience, as expressed in Husserl's writings. Actually this latter view has
wide acceptance, even among people who would be totally out of sympathy
with Husserl's perspective and aims. For example, a recent symposium of
doctors and psychiatrists concluded in their study of man: "It is generally
agreed that we can know what people are only by inference from what they
do. . . . Scientific observation of human beings uses several ways of arriving at generalizations from specific actions." [46] Scheler's study of the essence of sympathy is a carefully worked out refutation of this extremely
restricted, behavioristic view of our knowledge of others. Many views, not
just behaviorism, are blind to the reality of personal communication; they
cannot account for one's self in actual communication with another except
by a miracle.

A substantial part of Scheler's important book argues against the common view that we are basically and/or exclusively aware of our own private
experiences. This view rests on the assumption that individuals are essentially isolated from all other individuals. Scheler insisted that society is an

44 *Ibid.*, p. 357.
45 *Ibid.*, p. 356.
46 Marie Jahoda, *Current Concepts of Positive Mental Health*, p. 85.

integral part of the individual; not only do I belong to the We of society by an act of individual decision or by a process of assimilation, but the We of society is an irreducible part of me.[47] Even in his ethical writing he maintained that there are two spheres of the person, the intimate and the social. By phenomenological analysis he demonstrated that what we ordinarily consider our self-contained reflections of the self, actually, when more closely examined, reveal our involvement with others, particularly in terms of our social bond with them. In our manner of perceiving and ordering reality as well as our evaluations of it we are unavoidably conditioned by the social and cultural milieu in which we operate. For example, I might think that my perception and appreciation of the structural beauty of a Bach cantata or of a Beethoven symphony are my own particular accomplishments. However, there are other structured sounds of potential beauty which to me sound not like true tones but sheer noise. The reason that I am able to perceive and appreciate the former and not the latter is because there is a common element in my experience and in that of the composer. The examples are infinite which indicate the deep, indeed immanent nature of social reality in my personal experiences. In short, there is a givenness of content in experience; but without analysis we are not by any means certain whether the content is essentially *mine* or essentially *ours*. There is, in other words, an undifferentiated region of intentionality given in experience which needs to be recognized, marked off, and analyzed.

Scheler argued that one element of the undifferentiated given in personal experience is a general sense of I and Thou, and not primarily a sense of I as alone and apart from others.[48] This is similar to what Buber has referred to as an inborn sense of Thou, and points to the tendency in human beings, before they may have been injured or perverted by unhappy experiences of intense anxiety, rejection or hostility, to live more in community with others than in isolation. This tendency may be inborn but, if not, it is definitely an outgrowth of our early development as human beings; it is a fact of human existence that "the individual begins by living in the community to a much greater extent than he does in himself." [49] Because of this original involvement with others, something may be presented to my internal awareness regardless of whether or not I am conscious of it

[47] Scheler, *The Nature of Sympathy*, p. 230; Scheler, *Der Formalismus*, pp. 563 ff.
[48] *Ibid.*, p. 246.
[49] *Ibid.*, p. 248.

as part of my immediate experience. Certainly an initial element of perception is the infant's awareness of the other person who is significant to him, and whose presence is indistinguishable from his own sense of presence. In our early, vague general experiences it is not possible to tell what belongs to me from what belongs to us. There is in fact no crucial difference, at least at this stage, between self-awareness and the awareness of another's feelings toward me.[50] We are intuitively, though vaguely, aware of the other person's mind, when, for example, it is directed toward us sympathetically or angrily. To suppose, then, that our initial perception is exclusively of the differentiated self is fallacious; such a view suggests a self-contained soul substance locked up in a physical body. That view of man, reflected particularly in Idealistic philosophy but even transferred in slightly altered version in Freudian and Positivistic psychology, is grossly unaware of the facts of the phenomenon of man in his distinctly social dimension.

This important insight led Scheler to point out that when a phenomenologist speaks of internal perception, he does not at all imply introspection or some other form of private self-scrutiny. Internal perception conceived as phenomenological intuition will rightly refer to experience which is rooted in our participation in the many dimensions of human existence—vital, individual, personal, social and, perchance, eternal. To put it another way, phenomenological perception, as Scheler leads us to understand it, is rooted in and focused upon the intentional structure, not merely of consciousness, but of total experience. The phenomenology of love particularly has pointed toward a new understanding of intentionality in terms of our common participation in the being of others; and this participation not only is the basis of our common experience but also is the foundation upon which our insight into the other is built. Because of this common content of experience we can understand what another means even when he is unable to articulate his feelings or thoughts; similarly it is the ground upon which we base our suspicion that another is being deceitful toward us, even when there are no other grounds for suspicion. Scheler has illuminated a basic fact of human existence, the shared reality of human life, which is at the basis of all our knowledge about other people and about man in general. And he has suggested the possibility of developing a phenomenology which goes beyond individual experience and includes both interpersonal and social reality.

In spite of the tentativeness, inconsistencies, and speculative aspects in

[50] *Ibid.*, p. 251.

much of his philosophy, Max Scheler made an enormous contribution toward the advancement of existential phenomenology. He has taken many of the categories from Husserl and broadened them, giving their bare eidetic bones the substance of concrete physical, social, and personal life. Like Husserl, he was a witness to man's creative spirit in a time which was and is still threatened by the extinction of an intelligent view of spirit. Though Scheler repeatedly attacked the blindness of naturalism and scientific approaches, he nevertheless used science as an aid in revealing certain distinctive human characteristics. He maintained the irreducible, transcendent nature of man; because of Scheler's efforts, man reappears as a personal reality. He has helped to throw light upon the common as well as the private aspects of experience, pointing toward the basic existential structure of coinherence and, as well, the reality of human freedom. With his illumination it is possible to focus upon man as a person in a community of persons. Finally, he paved the way to consider love in a nonsentimental way, so as to recognize both its essential reality in human life and its cognitive power. It is not unwarranted to suggest that for the development of existential phenomenology the contributions of Max Scheler are no less important than those either of Edmund Husserl or of Martin Heidegger.

4

Martin Heidegger's Existential Analysis

In 1927 Martin Heidegger (b. 1889–   ) published philosophical fragments which he entitled *Sein und Zeit* (*Being and Time*). This relatively
large book has subsequently become a classic in philosophical literature;
and it is indispensable for the development of existential phenomenology.
That is not an easy statement to make, for the book is extremely difficult
and often enigmatic. To complicate matters, it is somewhat questionable if
that work should properly be considered as either existential or phenomenological. Heidegger has outspokenly repudiated Existentialism; to him it
is a restricted philosophy that is on another track and headed in a direction
different from that of his own thinking. Yet this work has fathered a
tremendously large share of existential thinking, and we shall find ourselves
rightly indebted to Heidegger even though we diverge from him. Not
unjustly some philosophers have considered Heidegger's approach to be
one of the most probing, comprehensive, and fruitful attempts to understand man to be found anywhere. Another complicating factor is that
some careful students of his writings have questioned if his book can
justifiably be considered an example of phenomenology, even though it was
published in Husserl's phenomenological yearbook and explicitly advocates
the use of phenomenology. Perhaps no philosopher in this century has
generated so much controversy; there are few philosophers of any era
which have had so many irreconcilable interpretations and criticisms made
of their writings as he has had of his. To sow another interpretation here
will run the risk of reaping the general whirlwind of confusion, yet the risk

must be taken. My task will be somewhat simplified, however, for my focus is almost exclusively upon *Sein und Zeit*. Though Heidegger's later writings are provocative and intriguing, they do not seem to be of immediate relevance to the task here. Before getting under way, though, a few prefatory remarks are in order.

Heidegger's entire aim and approach are daring and unusual. His basic concern has been with ontology, which is a subject matter still foreign to Americans; in that, perhaps we are fortunate. The very word rings bells of mystery in our ears. These bells make us perk up and listen; but they also jangle on our nerves. Though to my knowledge Heidegger does not use the term which we associate with Marcel's thought, the "mystery of Being," yet he is constantly alluding to it and seeking to illuminate or be illuminated by it. In this respect he seems to be a religious or quasi-religious philosopher somewhat along the lines of Oriental mysticism; Heidegger himself has somewhere remarked that he feels close kinship with Zen Buddhism. Yet Heidegger, who began his education studying for the priesthood, has repudiated the notion that Being and God are identical, as the Catholic tradition has maintained; and many have suspected that he ceased long ago to believe in God, though today that suspicion may be questioned. Heidegger is searching for Being and the meaning of Being, but not in the usual ways of conceptual thought or prayer. He has been notoriously impatient with all words in the Western tradition. They tend to "get in our eyes" so that we cannot see the truth any longer. Once men may have been open to Being; now they have become closed, cut off from their basic roots. Heidegger's search is for these roots, for the Ground of existence, for Being without which there is Nothing. Because of his interpretation of our historical stance in Being, as blinded by traditional patterns of perception and concepts, he continually plays with words and coins new ones, following them to see what new discovery of Being they will bring. What is obvious to us, but perhaps not to him, is that his word-plays are almost entirely with German terms, which he assumes are somehow particularly revelatory of Being.[1] We become suspicious of the universality of his revelations

---

[1] In later writings he has worked with other languages, especially with Greek words. However, philologists, etymologists, and classical scholars have suggested that his interpretations are extremely arbitrary if not downright preposterous. In some ways Heidegger represents a twentieth-century version of the German student of religion, F. Max Müller, who used an etymological approach to discover a basic religious experience. Fascinating as they are to read, such interpretations are frequently at variance with much if not most other evidence.

when numerous concepts and distinctions just do not come through into English or into most other languages for that matter.

Yet as enigmatic and sometimes frustrating as his language can be, I think that most of his basic *existential* categories do come through and that he has something extremely important to say to us. I shall, therefore, give attention to this major work of his, following the original text rather than the English translation, because his meanings are so much clearer in German. First I shall briefly examine the relationship between Husserl and Heidegger, which will help locate *Sein und Zeit* in the emerging picture of existential phenomenology. I shall then proceed to examine this book looking for the basic insights into existential structures or what Heidegger calls "existentials," such as transcendence, world, existence, concern, temporality, spatiality, conscience, ecstasy, and so on. These basic terms belong to each other; they all pertain to the basic phenomenon of transcendence, which Heidegger designated in his own inimitable way as being-in-the-world. As we follow his analysis we shall notice that there is considerable repetition. This is unavoidable, because these terms grow out of each other. Heidegger studies Being like a painter attending to a landscape. He concentrates upon the same phenomenon over and over again, continually seeing relations, directions, and meanings which were not at first apparent. At the end of our study we shall have achieved at least a glimpse of the penetrating vision of human being which Heidegger expressed in *Sein und Zeit*. We shall also, however, see that his picture of man has some drastic omissions, which I shall then point out.

Just how Heidegger stands in relation to Husserl and the phenomenological movement is a much debated point. According to Merleau-Ponty, Heidegger's *Sein und Zeit* springs directly from Husserl's philosophical endeavor, understood as an examination of the lived world of experience. Heidegger's existential analysis is to be seen as taking place against the background of the phenomenological reduction.[2] The authority of Merleau-Ponty is such that this interpretation carries much weight; there is truth in it, yet it is a misleading interpretation. The relationship between the two thinkers is extremely complex. Heidegger and Husserl had been friends, or at least friendly colleagues, for about ten years before *Sein und Zeit* was published. Furthermore, Heidegger dedicated it to Husserl "in friendship and admiration." When he retired from the University at Freiburg, Germany, Husserl named Heidegger to be the successor to his chair

2 M. Merleau-Ponty, *Phenomenology of Perception*, pp. vii, xiv.

in philosophy. The latter promptly left Marburg to return to his "home" university to lecture and edit the phenomenological yearbook which also had been under Husserl. This move apparently gave Husserl great satisfaction; it seemed to herald the continuation of his pioneering work in phenomenological studies. Yet things were not to work out as he had hoped. It was not a question of a student being disloyal to a former teacher. When Heidegger met Husserl for the first time, he had already completed his doctoral thesis. They had worked together as colleagues at Freiburg from 1916 to 1923. It was not until four years later that Husserl was to discover how little this potential spiritual heir had been influenced by him. When he read *Sein und Zeit* he realized that Heidegger and he were not on the same track, perhaps not even on the same wave length. Though explicitly acknowledging his admiration of and indebtedness to Husserl's phenomenology in a few places, Heidegger's project subtly ignored the architectonic structure of his former colleague's thought. Not surprisingly, their friendship came to an end shortly thereafter; and within a few years Heidegger had ceased to offer courses in phenomenology. The break between them was complete.[3] Husserl claimed that Heidegger never really got beyond the naïve natural attitude which he had so severely criticized. Heidegger's study of Kant's philosophy appeared a short while later, in which he claimed that Kant had not been able to reach the true horizon of transcendence because he had lacked a deep sense of existential time; thus Kant's notion of experience was limited to the extent that he could not escape from the dead-end street of subjectivism.[4] By implication, Husserl was also indicted; and nearly twenty years later Heidegger openly admitted that as far as he could see, Husserl had never really seen the historical factor in Being.[5]

It has become clear, especially in later writings, that Heidegger's major philosophical aim was differently conceived from Husserl's. Husserl was primarily interested in epistemology; he turned inward to consciousness in order to seek the foundations of all possible knowledge. Heidegger was also deeply involved with epistemological questions, but his concern was even

---

[3] See the detailed description of this aspect of their relationship in Herbert Spiegelberg, *The Phenomenological Movement*, Vol. I, pp. 275 ff.

[4] Cf. Thomas Langan's discussion in his *The Meaning of Heidegger*, chap. 2.

[5] Heidegger, *Platons Lehre von der Wahrheit mit einem Brief über den "Humanismus,"* p. 87. Perhaps this criticism of Husserl is the most devastating of all, since a radically historical structure of being would restrict if not prohibit any claim to apodictic truth.

vaster than Husserl's. He has sought not merely knowledge of Being but Being itself. He did not begin with a methodological doubt which throws all knowledge into question, but with an awareness of Being. Being is here, yet not here; disclosing itself, yet hidden. In a compulsive fashion, Heidegger proceeded to ask the question about the meaning of being: What does it mean *to be?* Heidegger's primordial awareness of Being points to a reality that seems to be more comprehensive and more basic than Husserl's eidetic intuition might suggest. Yet Husserl judged that Heidegger's thought was far from an advance in knowledge; he saw it as another expression of Realism, which is to locate it before the "enlightenment" of phenomenological insight.[6]

One senses at first that Heidegger's philosophical concern falls neatly into the area of metaphysics and/or ontology. Yet Heidegger has repudiated metaphysics,[7] and in *Sein und Zeit* he called for a demolition of traditional ontology. During the past thirty years, he has reflected upon mystical and romantic poetry, because he believes that poetic utterence provides more clues to the meaning of Being than do other forms of language. In *Sein und Zeit,* however, he maintained that the most reliable path to follow so as to rediscover Being was along the lines of a radical analysis of human being. Since then he has turned away from existential analysis to formulate what he refers to as a new thinking about Being, a thinking which enables Being to think itself through us.[8] Thus, whereas Husserl strove rigorously to attain ever greater precision, even at the cost of turning aside from immediate encounter with concrete reality, Heidegger has sought to follow his awareness of Being, even at the expense of becoming poetically unintelligible. To anyone reading *Sein und Zeit* in the original, it is apparent that even there Heidegger's language had a markedly poetic cast. The implications there, reinforced by Heidegger's later writings, indicate that formal conceptualizations, at least as we know them, fall far short of a grasp of Being; since Being is not a genus, it is beyond categorization. This is apparently one reason why Heidegger felt that Husserl's phenomenological reduction was irrelevant to radical ontology and why he dispensed with it.[9] Both men were deeply committed to the

---

6 Cf. Spiegelberg, *op. cit.,* p. 303.

7 See, e.g., his *An Introduction to Metaphysics.*

8 A brief, lucid, and reliable introduction to the later Heidegger may be found in James M. Robinson's "The German Discussion of the Later Heidegger," which introduces *The Later Heidegger and Theology.*

9 Cf. Spiegelberg, *op. cit.,* pp. 290 ff.

task of discovering the meaning of human transcendence; but they conceived of it differently. Husserl had emphasized the constituting nature of consciousness which is seen to be the foundation for distinctly human existence; consciousness constitutes man. Heidegger would seem to reverse this proposition, affirming that human existence engaged in the world constitutes consciousness. The whole of human existence and not merely consciousness is to be examined as intentional being-unto-the-Truth of Being. For Heidegger the term "transcendence" is much more inclusive than the term "consciousness" would suggest; human transcendence is to be understood in terms of the wholeness of its historical being in the world. In many of his writings, Husserl suggested that we bracket out concrete existence so that we may concentrate upon the essences which underlie it. Heidegger avoids becoming involved in a discussion about the distinction between essence and existence and proposes an even more radical one between Being and beings.

Though I have emphasized the original nature of Heidegger's thought, it would be misleading to exaggerate it. Certainly he bears resemblance to both Husserl and Scheler to whom he pays his brief but explicit respects. He himself also acknowledged kinship between his thinking and that of another original German thinker, Wilhelm Dilthey. Heidegger appreciated the fact that Dilthey, and Scheler, toward the end of his life, sought to grasp Being at its deepest level; and they, like Heidegger at this stage of his development, sought to grasp Being by executing historical, existential analyses of human existence. Though Heidegger felt then that Dilthey had progressed far in the direction of Being, nevertheless he fell short because he was hampered by his too broad and vague category of "life." [10] What such thinkers needed, particularly those within a "life" philosophy orientation, was a fundamental ontology. To reach this goal, *Sein und Zeit* was presented as a concrete elaboration of the question of the meaning of Being.[11] Thus Heidegger saw himself somewhat in the service of Dilthey as he proceeded to question the Being of human being so as to develop a *fundamental* ontology.

The project on which Heidegger set out was to have two parts. A significant portion of formulating a truly fundamental ontology must be a destruction of previous ontologies which, in effect, have put obstacles in

[10] See *Sein und Zeit*, pp. 397-404. See also H. A. Hodges, *The Philosophy of Wilhelm Dilthey*.
[11] *Ibid.*, p. 1.

our ontological path. Specifically, Heidegger felt the need to destroy those of Kant, Descartes, and Aristotle; these represent the gross distortions of traditional ontology, because they essentially failed to distinguish adequately Being from beings. Their orientation is what he called *ontic*, one which is riveted to beings *as beings*, or as entities.[12] To become truly ontological, we must be liberated from the prejudice of the past. Traditional approaches and categories put a screen between our vision and the presence of Being. Thus Heidegger saw his task partially as one which would unveil Being, so that we could "see it" again. The demolition of the past was to be presented in a second part of this work; it was never published.

More positively, Heidegger's intention here was to provide an original ontological investigation, one which is acutely and consistently aware of the distinction between Being and beings or entities (*Seiendes*). Even this, however, remains an incomplete endeavor, because the published portions of *Sein und Zeit* are but two of three intended sections. Nevertheless, one senses both a new departure in ontology and an original contribution simply in the title. Being is to be considered as temporal, not eternal; as historical, not beyond history. Heidegger emphatically declared that the horizon for understanding Being is existential temporality.[13] What that might mean will become clearer as this chapter progresses. However, the point which should be clear now is that Heidegger obviously judged that time had not been taken seriously enough in previous attempts to understand Being or even human being. Entities have been considered as in time; some philosophers have even stressed that man's experience of time must be regarded as fundamental to his nature. Yet Heidegger insisted that previous attempts to see the temporal and historical nature of human being have been myopic. It is in fact misleading to say that man is in time or experiences time, which suggests that time is external to the being of man. Rather, it must be seen that experience itself is temporal, that in fact temporality is the formal and concrete structure of human being and of Being itself. The being of man is radically temporal, as Heidegger attempted to demonstrate.

To avoid confusion and to assist us in criticism later, it should be borne in mind that in spite of his emphasis upon existential temporality and his proposal to execute a radically existential analysis, Heidegger's

[12] *Ibid.*, pp. 19 ff.
[13] *Ibid.*, p. 17. In some ways Heidegger did to ontology what Einstein did to physics.

primary aim was to seek Being. His underlying intention was ontological rather than existential or anthropological; that is, his task as he saw it was to illuminate Being, and the illumination of human being was merely a means to that end. This point often seems to have been ignored by numerous of his early and subsequently disillusioned followers. An outstanding example of disappointment, indeed it is nearly an accusation of betrayal, is an essay by a former disciple, Karl Löwith. He accused Heidegger of making almost an about face (*eine grosse Kehre*) from existential anthropology to ontology subsequent to *Sein und Zeit*.[14] Heidegger has admitted that he has shifted his emphasis, but nevertheless his aim has remained the same. As he wrote somewhat later: "To lead our thinking on the way on which it may find the involvement of the truth of Being in human nature, to open up a path for our thinking on which it may recall Being itself in its truth—to do that the thinking attempted in *Being and Time* is 'on the way.' " [15] It is important to stress Heidegger's primary concern for Being *per se*, for ontology rather than existential analysis; for this goal led him to draw conclusions precipitously and to manipulate evidence in a gravely unwarranted manner.

Thus, while *Sein und Zeit* is primarily an analysis of human existence, it remains basically a quest for Being.[16] By focusing upon the being which is closest to hand, namely one's own being, the philosopher is able to reach into the depths of individual being toward Being itself. The fault of previous ontologies has been that they have not seen Being as fully relational. Heidegger was aware that his own being has a "built in" relation to Being; Being is not apart from man.[17] To ask the inevitable ontological question: Why are there beings rather than nothing? leads man to ponder the Ground of his existence and to become aware of his own being grounded.[18] Thus the kind of philosophical thinking Heidegger has in mind is one which seeks to strike at the roots of all beings, not to arrive at

[14] Karl Löwith, *Denker in Dürftiger Zeit*, ch. 1. Another philosopher who insisted upon a radical change in Heidegger's thinking is F. Heinemann; he maintained that Heidegger has moved from existentialism through ontology into ontological poetry. Cf. his *Existentialism and the Modern Predicament*, pp. 90-102. A more balanced and extensive argument for the consistency in Heidegger's thought in English is presented by Thomas Langan in his book, *The Meaning of Heidegger*. See also J. Robinson, *op. cit.*

[15] M. Heidegger, Introduction to *Was ist Metaphysik?* in Walter Kaufmann's *Existentialism from Dostoevsky to Sartre*, p. 212.

[16] *Sein und Zeit*, p. 16.

[17] M. Heidegger, *The Question of Being*, p. 75.

[18] See also M. Heidegger, *The Introduction to Metaphysics*, which greatly amplifies this point of view. It should be emphasized that by "ground" Heidegger does not mean what Paul Tillich meant when he used the term "Ground of Being."

conceptions or to achieve utilitarian results, but merely to allow the ground
of our beings, Being itself, to become unconcealed. If and when that
occurs, the result would be of supreme importance. Though he does not
refer to a crisis for European man in quite the same way as did Husserl and
Scheler, yet his existential analysis makes clear his judgment about the
gravity of man's plight. To allow Being which is beclouded by our concern
with entities to become manifest would bring us to a new and creative
stage in history; in fact even to ask the question of the meaning of Being is
highly significant in his eyes: "To ask 'How does it stand with being?'
means nothing less than to recapture . . . the beginning of our historical-
spiritual existence, in order to transform it into a new beginning." [19]
Other thinkers have focused upon the waters of life; Heidegger set out to
get at the base of the spring from which they flow. This is not to suggest
that Heidegger is a crypto-theologian, for he denies that Being is God; in
fact, he has later asserted that the Being of beings is temporal and finite.
Being is basic; without Being nothing is. Being is here, because we are here;
yet it is hidden and must be brought to light. That is Heidegger's self-
appointed task. He seeks to expose the darkness of existence in which we
fail to see the difference between Being and beings, so that we may be
enlightened by the underlying identity which Being has with all beings.

To accomplish his ontological task, Heidegger claimed that the phenomenological method is peculiarly apt. Thus he affirmed that his method
in *Sein und Zeit* was phenomenology. Yet it becomes obvious that he
understood it quite differently from Husserl. Furthermore, since he provided only a rough sketch of his understanding of phenomenology in the
early part of the book, hardly referred to it again there, and in later works
has ignored it entirely, it is questionable how seriously he considered it or
how important it was to him.[20] Though Heidegger suggested that Husserl's phenomenology was a significant breakthrough for radical thinking,
yet he refrained from taking the most significant step in this method. He
disregarded the Husserlian phenomenological reduction with its implied
givenness of eidetic contents. Heidegger insisted that phenomenology is
that method which enables the phenomenon to become apparent in itself.
However, his understanding of *phenomenon* also was at variance with
Husserl's. Heidegger defined phenomenon in terms of that which shows

19 M. Heidegger, *Introduction to Metaphysics*, p. 39.
20 Cf. Herbert Spiegelberg's extended and critical discussion of Heidegger's phenomenology in *The Phenomenological Movement*, Vol. 1, especially pp. 319-325.

itself as it is; it is not merely the appearance of an entity which cannot be known in itself but, rather, it is the manifestation of Being.[21] Thus the maxim of phenomenology is rightly "back to the things themselves" (*zu den Sachen Selbst*).[22] The "things," of course, are manifestations, phenomena of Being; these disclosures in turn constitute basic phenomenological truth. Truth is the becoming-unconcealed of Being.

To engage in phenomenology does not mean, as it has for others, that one attempts to provide impartial descriptions of what appears. For Heidegger, description remains at the ontic level, thus ignoring the Being of entities.[23] It ignores the basic condition that Being is veiled, hidden from view, and thus cannot be simply described.[24] Since the phenomenon is that which shows itself as Being, the implication clearly is that Being is mostly concealed. Particularly is this apparent with human being, whose Being is not merely a mystery to himself but whose being lies ahead of him as possibility. Because phenomenology is the method which allows Being to reveal itself, it is the appropriate method of ontology; indeed, since Being is concealed, ontology is *only* possible as phenomenology.[25] Furthermore, the veil of Being which is only partially drawn aside with a particular manifestation means that phenomenology must be essentially a process of hermeneutics or interpretation. Thus Heidegger refers to his phenomenology as a hermeneutic of Being. He does not here mean by this term the interpretation of texts, as implied when used in biblical exegesis, nor does he suggest it refers to an attempt to interpret sympathetically a thinker or an historical era, such as recommended by Dilthey. Rather, phenomenological hermeneutic is the interpretive process of existence to allow Being to uncover itself in and through man himself.

Phenomenology is oriented toward Being. Seen more deeply, phenomenology is an act of Being itself, because man is the being who asks the question of Being. It is the nature of man to interrogate Being, specifically in terms of asking his own being what it means for him to be.[26] It is easier to grasp Heidegger's point here in German than in English, though at the same time the difficulty of rendering his thinking in our language suggests the artificiality of his ontological scheme and endeavor. The German word

---

[21] *Sein und Zeit*, pp. 31-34.
[22] *Ibid.*, p. 27.
[23] *Ibid.*, p. 63.
[24] *Ibid.*, pp. 35-37.
[25] *Ibid.*
[26] Cf. *ibid.*, p. 12.

for being is *Sein*; the term Heidegger uses for human being is *Dasein*, which means literally *being there*. It is a fairly common, indeed sometimes colloquial term for existence, often suggesting the connotation of being present, in contradistinction to one's possible absence. Heidegger's word-play with this term as with numerous others is extraordinary. *Dasein* is a being (*Seiendes*) who asks the question of his *Sein*; in fact his *Sein*, what we here might refer to as the dynamic principle of his self-identity and existence, questions itself, particularly as it confronts the possibility of its not-being. Hence the question of being, ontology, is raised as phenomenology, as one becomes aware of Being. The primary manifestation of *Sein* is *Dasein*, one's own existence. Since this manifestation is primary, and is obviously the closest I can come to Being, in that *Sein* is inseparable and indivisible from my *Dasein*, though not simply identical with it, the phenomenological pursuit of being must be existential.[27] My being there, however, is not fully actual. On the contrary, the most significant characteristic of *Dasein* is its *possibility* to be as well as not to be. That means that the phenomenology of *Dasein* must therefore interpret the being which I am in terms of the being which it is possible for me to be. We might here suspect that Heidegger has a hidden norm of possible being which he will arbitrarily impose on his phenomenological analyses of human existence.

Though it was far from his intention, his notion of uncovering truth resembles a process found in psychoanalysis. A therapist is confronted with the phenomenon of a patient's statement which may be a revelation of how the patient feels about himself and his world; yet the meaning of that statement is abstruse or, in familiar terminology, it lies buried in the unconscious. The therapist attempts to get behind the veil of a seemingly meaningless statement so as to illuminate its significance. This significance is partially revealed in terms of the patient's previous life history; yet at the same time it points ahead toward existential possibilities which have been thus far frustrated. The therapist attempts to interpret the meaning of the statement, but he does not necessarily seek to impose his own meaning upon it; rather, he properly attempts to allow the patient to make his own self-discovery. Thus interpretation is not necessarily a foreign element added to the phenomenon but can be an integral part of it; interpretation may reveal inherent existential possibilities.

This is not far from Heidegger's own suggestions, except that in his

27 Cf. *ibid.*, pp. 12-13.

notion of interpretation he does not introduce a second person, nor does it seem possible in his scheme for another person to play a decisive role in authentic self-disclosure. Heidegger claimed that the hermeneutical phenomenology of *Dasein* is an inherent possibility of his existence, because *Dasein* is a being who is characterized by disclosedness (*Erschlossenheit*).[28] That is, I am a creature whose being illuminates itself. *Dasein* as being is essentially dynamic in a temporal sense; he is on the move toward his own possibilities. Hence his self-illumination is not primarily of a fact, such as the historical conditioning of the present moment of his being; rather, his being is illuminated as moving ahead into its future. Thus as *Dasein* becomes aware of his own being, he emerges from the dark forest of entities into a clearing wherein the light of Being becomes visible. Phenomenology or existential hermeneutics is to be understood as an illumination of specifically human being, essentially in terms of possibility. This is an extremely important point, clarifying somewhat Heidegger's early statement that the meaning of Being will be designated as temporality.[29] *Dasein* is to be understood differently from beings as entities, for *Dasein's* existence is defined and structured by his possibilities.[30]

Heidegger's ontological-existential analysis of *Dasein* consists of a series of hermeneutical disclosures which are intended to set forth the distinct a priori of human existence which we ordinarily refer to as transcendence.[31] The a priori is here intended to refer not to some formal structures of knowledge or to contents of experience. To use Kierkegaardian language which here might be helpful, Heidegger was not attempting to conceive of the *whatness* of existence but, rather, to bring to light *how* it is to be a human being in the world in the first place.

It has been frequently enough said that one of the most urgent problems of our day is the need to articulate cogently the meaning of transcendence; and certainly it is as an attempt at such articulation that existential philosophy, and in particular Heidegger's thought, is extremely pertinent and helpful. Husserl had pointed out that transcendence was intentional in a unique sense; yet his own distinct conceptions gave that term extreme

[28] *Ibid.*, p. 133.
[29] *Ibid.*, p. 17.
[30] *Ibid.*, p. 42. It should be noted that "possibility" as an existential term has quite different connotations from "potentiality," which is most appropriate as a biological term. Potentiality refers to something which is to emerge from the past, whereas possibility refers to the not-yet-being which might emerge; if it does, possibility will emerge out of the future.
[31] Cf. *ibid.*, pp. 45 ff.

limitations. Heidegger endeavored to expand our understanding of transcendence, as he made clear in an essay published shortly after *Sein und
Zeit*, entitled "Vom Wesen des Grundes" ("On the Nature of Ground").
To him, transcendence is what we mean when we speak of selfhood. Yet
this phenomenon is not subjective, in the sense of being pent up within
the subject; nor is it objective in the sense of being an object alongside
other objects in the world. Human transcendence is relational, emitted
from Being and reaching out beyond itself to the world. *Transcendence* is
best denoted not as spirit rising above the world nor as mental intentionality but as *being-in-the-world*.[32] This phrase is meant not in a biological,
geographical, or theological sense, but in a uniquely existential way. I am a
being who cannot, except abstractly and artificially, be detached from my
experience of myself in my total environment. Yet this total involvement is
not in contrast to transcendence; it is the form of it. Though I am in an
environment, yet I am not completely determined by the forces of it, nor
do they constitute the full reality of my world. My world is not the opposite of freedom. On the contrary, my world is constituted by freedom.[33] In
my world I am myself the possibility of my approach to the ground of my
existence; freedom, which is the hallmark of being-in-the-world, is freedom
for one's ground, as the possibility to attain one's destiny in the givenness
of one's being *there*.[34] Transcendence for Heidegger is ultimately an ontological category.[35] As he makes clear in a later writing, man is never first a
subject, be that an it, an I, or a We; he is first being-in-the-world.
"World" refers not to an object over against which existence stands, but it
is part of transcendence as the very openness of Being.[36] For our purposes
it is not necessary to descend into Heidegger's ontological dimensions; it is
enough to indicate that first of all transcendence refers to existential involvement and self-discovery in the world. The fuller meaning of transcendence *Sein und Zeit* attempted to set forth phenomenologically.[37]

[32] "Vom Wesen des Grundes," pp. 19 ff.
[33] *Ibid.*, p. 23.
[34] *Ibid.*, p. 50.
[35] *Ibid.*, p. 40.
[36] Cf. "Brief über den Humanismus," *op. cit.*, pp. 100-101.

[37] Heidegger's insistence that the term "world" be understood in an existential
sense somewhat resembles the point made by William James. The latter spoke of world
awareness as a field of consciousness. An entire wave of consciousness refers to a field of
objects, but each field has its particular center of interest around which the objects are
centered. Those objects which are less and less of interest to us in terms of the particular field fade to the margin of consciousness so that the limits of our horizon become
unassignable. This reciprocal reality of consciousness and field which is structured by
our interest, the "hot place" in man's personality, and which is encompassed by an un-

Another basic disclosure of the meaning of transcendence is an obvious but often ignored fact that I am a being who is concerned about myself. Heidegger insisted that this concern is not to be interpreted, at least basically, in a selfish way. As a self in the world, I am naturally and rightly concerned about the possibility of my self being in the world. Yet Heidegger pushed this insight to extremes and made it out to be the most basic structure of transcendence. As a human being, I am altogether determined by this rudimentary concern for my own being.[38] Expressed another way, he wrote that *Dasein* exists for his own sake. In speaking of human existence, we cannot avoid the personal pronouns *his* or *hers, yours* or *mine*. Especially in a situation when we are afraid or anxious, we become quite aware of our concern for our own possible being. This selfhood concern, as we might call it, is not inverted self-centeredness. On the contrary, we are dynamic, outreaching beings encountering things in our world. As the term for existence suggests, I am *there* in the world, and the world is there for me to encounter, react to, and understand.

Thus far several features of Heidegger's thought are unusual in philosophy. In addition to new terms and new ways of approaching old problems, he has insisted that in our ontological pursuit we begin with everyday human existence. He was obviously dissatisfied with other approaches; and his repeated emphasis would appear to be especially a slap in the face to the highly abstract, technical elements of Husserl's phenomenological reduction with its claim to get back to things in themselves. Heidegger asked: How does it go with human being in his day-to-day existence? He insisted that existence itself be allowed to answer, without being silenced in favor of conceptual abstractions. Heidegger did not question, as do both sensationalists and idealists, How can I know the world? Rather, he affirmed that I already do know it. To Heidegger the skeptical question forgets our everyday familiarity with the world, and splits artificially and completely the subject from the object of his encounter. I am already in the world, engaged with it; knowing it is but one mode of being in it.[39] Traditional philosophy, he argued, has skipped over my essential "worldliness." [40]

Dasein is a being who is concerned about himself, though not always

definable horizon within which referential processes transpire is an insight that brings James very close to the existential insight of Heidegger. Cf. his *The Varieties of Religious Experience*, p. 226 et passim.

[38] *Ibid.*, p. 43, "Dassein überhaupt durch Jemeinigkeit bestimmt ist."
[39] *Ibid.*, pp. 59-62.
[40] *Ibid.*, p. 65.

consciously so. Usually in everyday life we are first of all and most of all
concerned about things which are around us to be used, counted on,
referred to as we take our bearings in our existential course through life.
These are things which are close at hand to us, such as this paper, this
pencil, this desk, that light, this room, and so on. In other words, our
everyday concern which is expressed in our worldliness, is of a practical
nature, a concern for things at hand.[41] Our world, our field of perception
and action, is shaped by practical concern. This is the world with which we
are extremely familiar. Furthermore, it is a world which makes sense, because the things in this world have fairly specific cross references to each
other. Yet the sense or meaning of the terms in my system of references
refers back to my own concern.[42] The term "world" in its existential sense
is not a biological or social environment; it is not all reality, the cosmos; it
is not a value judgment placed upon human life in a theological sense.[43]
The world in an existential sense, as an aspect of transcendence, is the field
of references upon which I discover and construct significance as I encounter my possibilities. One specific sense of the term "world," then,
appears in everyday usage; it is our practical frame of reference in which we
respond and act. In the broadest sense *world*, within an existential, phenomenological perspective, refers to our encountering-understanding relational involvement with that reality toward which and through which we
express our concern.[44]

This interpretation of the world might seem hopelessly inadequate
and subjective to one who is accustomed to think of reality in terms of its
objectivity. What about the world out there which is measured, analyzed,
controlled—the world of nature and science? Heidegger has not ignored
this meaning of the world, but he has pointed out that the so-called
objective world emerges not as a primary but as a secondary factor in
human existence, a point which has recently been conceded even by eminent scientists, as mentioned in Chapter 1. Man is first of all in the world
as a being who is close to things in a practical, familiar way. He may
subsequently stand back from these familiar things and ask about them in
a detached manner. That is, he may consider them not as things at hand,

---

41 *Ibid.*, pp. 66-69. The German word for "at-hand" is *zuhanden.*
42 *Ibid.*, pp. 76-83.
43 Cf. Rudolf Bultmann's definition of the world as "existence in bondage," in
the darkness of sin, hidden from God's truth, *Theology of the New Testament*, Vol.
II, p. 16 et passim.
44 Cf. *Sein und Zeit*, pp. 84-86.

but as there in reserve; he may take stock of them as things on-hand (*Vorhanden*). This type of relationship to things is artificial; but in our artificial environment, such relationships are necessary. The attitude underlying this type of objectifying-analyzing relationship to things is the basis of both theory and science.

Through the phenomenology of *Dasein*, Heidegger has revealed three dimensions of being in the world, or three modes of understanding beings in the world. There is the practical mode, the scientific-theoretical mode, and the basic existential mode of being-in-the-world. For Heidegger the all-embracing structure of being-in-the-world is concern (*Sorge*). The existential structure of concern precedes any discovery of the world at all and shapes the significance of every encounter.

Consistent with his aim to investigate what is basic and primary in human being, Heidegger left behind the analysis of secondary features so as to concentrate upon the existential structure and meaning of being-in-the-world. "World" has come to have a distinctly existential meaning, similar to the phrase "one's field of significance." Not only is world to be understood existentially; so, too, is the manner of one's "being *in*" it. Certainly I am *in* the world differently from objects occupying worldly space. This suggests that space also has an existential meaning. Since the location and worldly references of objects are discovered by man, his spatiality can neither be defined in terms of things at hand (practical spatiality) nor of things as regarded by either theory or science. *Dasein* is *in* the world in the sense of his concerned, familiar involvement with the beings he encounters.[45] His location is therefore defined in terms of his concern. I can be proximate to something which is insignificant and so for "all practical purposes" distant; on the other hand, I can feel close to something about which I am vitally concerned, even though geographically it is some distance away. That is not subjectivism; on the contrary, that is how it is to be in the world. To Heidegger, existential space is primary and is the ground upon which our geographical notion of space is founded.

In one of his most brilliant but all too brief displays of phenomenological acumen, Heidegger portrayed the distinct character of existential spatiality.[46] Existential spatiality is characterized first by my capacity to become distant from my environment; by the dynamics of "distancing" myself from things I am able to "take them in" or avoid them. Second, it is

[45] *Ibid.*, p. 104.
[46] *Ibid.*, pp. 105-110.

characterized by "directedness" (*Ausrichtung*), which points to my dynamic orientation toward things. This setting of a direction is clearly determined by my concern. As I approach or withdraw from things, depending upon the quality and weight of concern I have for them, I shape the meaning they have for me in my world. Both of these existential characteristics are constituted by what can be considered the basic action of existential spatiality, which is "to give place" or "make room for" (*Einräumen*).[47] To establish distance and take a direction toward a thing means to give it a place in my world, to designate its position, to set its location whereby it obtains its significance for me. Existential space is not *in* the subject, nor is the world in space. Spatiality conceived existentially is an existential a priori, a basic structure of human existence, to be interpreted in terms of the spatializing of concern for possibilities of meaningful being. The existential analysis of spatiality investigates the human event of making space within the boundaries set by concern.

One of the most elementary existential questions pertains to one's personal identity: Who am I? Who are you? Who is man? Heidegger has already set the stage for at least a preliminary answer. The *who* of this question is a being who is predominantly absorbed and fascinated by (*benommen*) his world. Furthermore, his being *in* the world is constituted by a unique, existential mode of spatiality which must be specially considered. Thus to find out who one is will lead us to investigate the kind of world he lives in, how he spatializes it, how he is immersed in the world, especially in his everyday life. Yet since *Dasein* is a being who is essentially possibility, it will not at all be accurate to restrict oneself merely to an analysis of his present world; one is not yet the being he is to become.[48] Even more inhibiting to judgment, however, is that everyday, ordinary existence, according to Heidegger, is not authentic. Consequently any answer to the question; Who am I? which is based merely on descriptions of everyday existence will be grossly shortsighted, especially in terms of man's authentic possibility.

In one of the most quoted sections of *Sein und Zeit* Heidegger characterized human inauthenticity in its average, everyday world as anonymous existence (*das Man*). "On the average" I am just somebody, one with a public image, part of a crowd, just an ordinary fellow like others.[49] This

47 *Ibid.*, p. 111.
48 Cf. *ibid.*, pp. 113-116.
49 Cf. *ibid.*, pp. 126-130.

characterization of the anonymous average "someone," which is extremely reminiscent of Kierkegaard's description of "the Public," portrays how *Dasein's* concrete mode of existence is inauthentic. Concern is properly the foundation of the self's unity. In the everyday mode, however, concern is scattered among public interests. In the everyday of average life my concerns are elsewhere directed than toward genuine existential possibilities. Both in public life and in relations with other individuals *Dasein* is fragmented and anonymous, living on borrowed identity, and consumed by trivial cares. Heidegger went on to interpret the inevitable inauthenticity of everyday existence as a fallen state of being. Before moving on to that interpretation we must shift gears for a minute to examine in more detail his method, which will then enable us to proceed to further illumination of human being.

In his epistemology Heidegger sought to move beyond rationalists and naturalists so as to return to Being. We have seen that he began with an awareness of Being, particularly with an awareness of his own being as given, as simply *there*. Furthermore, he maintained that man is a self-disclosing, self-revealing being; he is a being who is aware of himself as being-in-the-world. That in itself says a great deal which Heidegger judged to have been ignored by traditional methods. We have seen that phenomenologists have put great stock in their term "intuition." Heidegger, however, avoided the term and suggested that it was a secondary phenomenon.[50] By dropping "intuition," Heidegger was able to discover the even more basic existential or primordial awareness of self which opens us up to the "first truth" of man. What constitutes the insight of my awareness is not a rational judgment or a concept but a mood, or feeling, or state of mind (*Befindlichkeit*).[51] Heidegger here seems to come close to Scheler's insistence that phenomenology begins with feeling; but Heidegger did not suggest that this feeling has anything to do with libido or one's sense of solidarity with others. He was much less precise in his analysis of feeling than was Scheler. To Heidegger this primordial feeling or mood is apparently global, in the sense that it is not restricted, located, or concentrated in any particular part of one's body. It is just a vague sensing *that I am*; it reveals to me the *fact* of my being in the world.

To Heidegger the most revelatory state of mind is constituted by anxiety. Anxiety opens up to *Dasein* his being as a possibility, a possibility

of being that is threatened with the possibility of not-being. Borrowing
from Kierkegaard's now well-known distinction between anxiety and fear,
Heidegger stated that anxiety arises in man's confrontation with Nothingness (das Nichts); consequently anxiety is unlimited, whereas fear is restricted to the object upon which it has become attached. Fear is unquestionably a basic state of mind, but it is of a secondary nature; anxiety is
transformed into fear by becoming attached to an object.[52] Yet though
they must be distinguished, both anxiety and fear reveal to me not only
that I am but also *how* my being-in-the-world is constituted.[53] My basic
mood reveals that I have been thrown by Being into the world.[54] *Being-
thrown* constitutes what Heidegger referred to as *facticity.*[55] That is, the
actuality of the fact of my existence is now seen in terms of its being
thrown into the world. Thus Heidegger has suggested that the first step in
existential analysis is not a bracketing out of existence so as to achieve an
intuition of essences, but a turning toward one's mood, particularly toward
anxiety, which provides one with a primordial existential awareness of the
fact of one's being as *thrown away* from Being *into* the world *toward* one's
possibilities. As provocative as this suggestion is, one wonders why Heidegger restricts basic moods to anxiety and fear. By starting with other basic
states of mind or feelings such as gratitude, trust, and sympathy, one will
come upon quite a different meaning of one's facticity.

The primordial feeling reveals to oneself one's being-in-the-world; the
most primordial feeling or state of mind is anxiety that reveals the particular nature of my facticity as thrown. Thus begins the development of
existential knowledge or what Heidegger referred to as basic existential
understanding (verstehen). This understanding of human being arises
from within my global self-feeling and begins to "take shape" as my awareness develops into a perspective of myself in the world. In Heidegger's
terms, my feeling of thrownness, of *being-projected* by Being, expresses itself in a *projection* of my being-in-the-world (*Weltentwurf*).[56] This existential projection is not at all to be mistaken or confused with a psychoanalytic
conception of the projecting of unconscious thoughts and feelings onto
one's present environment. Rather, it is our rudimentary awareness coming
to form a picture of reality as reality opens itself up to our concern. Since I

52 *Ibid.*, pp. 140 ff.
53 *Ibid.*, pp. 184 ff.
54 *Ibid.*, p. 135.
55 *Ibid.*, p. 56.
56 *Ibid.*, p. 145.

am essentially a creature of concern, according to Heidegger, it is not surprising to discover that my existential projection includes, indeed is intentionally constituted by, my understanding of myself in terms of what I am in the world *for*. As a creature of concern, I understand my being in the world in terms of my own possibilities. The project of my life thus unfolds within my existential world projection. My being in the world is essentially for the sake of (*um willen*) the authentic possibilities of my being. My failure to understand this is a sign of my inauthenticity. Since this world projection is essentially temporal, it looks ahead toward the attainment of my own most possibilities. Thus in Heidegger's scheme existential analysis follows the course of primary existential understanding, returning to the basic feeling state and the world projection which projects toward one's authentic possibilities.[57]

The process of existential understanding which is aimed at the discovery of the meaning of Being through the uncovering of the meaning of human being proceeds through a next stage, which is properly denoted as interpretation.[58] If interpretation of existence, which is intended to see basic possibilities, is to escape arbitrariness, it must be grounded upon one's primordial prescience or feeling state. That is, existential interpretation must be informed by the full weight of one's facticity; properly, interpretation is not the imposition of meaning upon understanding but the elaboration of understanding. Nevertheless, interpretation runs the risk of error because it involves foresight as well as hindsight. That is, it involves forming some notion as to where in the world I think I am going or ought to be going.[59] It is at this point in his existential analysis that Heidegger becomes particularly vulnerable to criticism because his interpretation of everyday existence is a judgment that it is *fallen*. Facticity is now a "revealed truth" of my being-in-the-world, but it is not the whole truth. The being that I am is fallen away from authentic possibilities and lives in the fallen state of inauthenticity. All basic modes partake of fallenness. Speaking, which properly is to be a mode of revelation, such as in great poetic utterances, in the everyday mode occurs as idle talk. Existential understanding, which should be directed toward authentic possibilities, has fallen into curiosity about things, even to the extent that Being and human beings are considered with curiosity as things in a thing-world. Even my

[57] *Ibid.*, pp. 143-145, 295.
[58] *Ibid.*, pp. 146-148 ff.
[59] Cf. *ibid.*, pp. 150, 151 ff.

primordial state of mind, which could reveal directly to me the basic fact
of who I am and might become, has fallen into a state of ambiguity.[60] The
intention of Heidegger's judgment is not that of a moralist or preacher.
Rather, it is in line with his entire ontological project, which is to point out
the darkness of the ordinary way of seeing reality which has thrown up a
barrier to our understanding of Being. If we are truly fallen into inauthenticity, then our everyday being in the world is not simply a disclosing being.
I am not simply an openness to Being itself or to my own human being.
I also constitute a barrier to my true self and to the truth of Being. For this
reason Heidegger urgently suggested that we find some way of looking
beyond the "fall" so as to catch a vision of the wholeness of authentic
being. Thus we must seek some modification of daily existence, one which
will be radically different from the average.[61] At this point consideration
of temporality becomes imperative.

Thus far the basic phenomenon of human transcendence has been
illuminated as being-in-the-world, which for Heidegger is essentially structured by concern (Sorge). Whether authentic or inauthentic, concern is
what grounds my being and holds it together; it underlies all my awareness,
cognition, and volition.[62] This illumination arises insofar as I am
a being who is open to my existence in the world, an openness which
discloses my being through the existential modes of awareness and understanding. My truest orientation is primarily toward my own possibilities. If
I allow anxiety to perform its function of opening up what I am and am to
become, then I realize that my truest orientation is toward my most authentic existential possibility.[63] To understand and interpret this possibility requires an elucidation of the meaning of time. It is time constituted by
human concern for one's future which Heidegger designated as *existence*.
He used the term "existence" here in a precise way, meaning to stand forth
"toward being true." Existence includes the other modes, *facticity* and
fallenness, but only as it ecstatically reaches for the future does it truly
highlight the deeply temporal nature of human being.[64] By investigating
existence now as existential temporality, a true vision of the wholeness of
human being may emerge.

Because of his emphasis upon possibility, it is not surprising that for

60 Cf. *ibid.*, pp. 166-175.
61 *Ibid.*, p. 130 et passim.
62 *Ibid.*, pp. 192-194.
63 Cf. *ibid.*, pp. 182-188.
64 *Ibid.*, pp. 231 ff.

Heidegger existential time, or temporality, is largely to be understood in terms of the future rather than in terms of the past and present. His discussion of temporality is one of the most heuristically valuable and exciting sections of this work, though aspects of it are also the most vulnerable to empirical criticism. He has already implied that temporality is to be understood in terms of one's concern for one's own possibility; concern interprets human time. Yet temporality is the meaning of concern; for, it is temporality which grounds human existence.[65] The essence of existence is temporality. As a temporal being, I am always in my future; and my future is always coming toward me into my present, enabling me to interpret the whole of my concern. Thus the being that I am "in truth" is ontologically the farthest away; that is why ontic descriptions and analysis are so short-sighted, so inauthentic [66] I am never primarily the result of my past; my past history does not necessarily establish the framework within which my existence is to be interpreted. Rather, the primary meaning of my existence is to be found in the future.[67] Also my being free can be understood fully only in terms of the future. The future grants me my freedom and provides the perspective which enables me to understand the meaning of my past. My existence is toward the future. It is also constituted by my having been in the past; yet my past, my history, is always moving ahead of itself into my future. My history should not be regarded as something finished and done with, at least not until I am dead. My *having been* constitutes my *facticity*, while the future that I am in truth, but factually am not yet, defines my existence; and the whole of my temporality moving into the future constitutes my *historicity*.

Existential temporality is self-begetting. My existence temporalizes itself, as my future becomes my present and interprets my already having been. Having been, the present, and the future constitute a unity held together by concern. Yet in my fallen condition, my existential unity is fractured through distorted understanding; I often think of my future as divorced from the present and I think of the present as cut off from a dead past or as dominated by an unconscious one. Hence I misunderstand my temporality. When the temporal unity of existence is seen, however, I become aware that existence is essentially *ecstatic*. The *ecstasy* of human time refers to my existing as standing forth from the mere here and now

[65] *Ibid.*, p. 234.
[66] *Ibid.*, pp. 311-312.
[67] *Ibid.*, pp. 327 ff.

and embracing the wholeness of my being-in-the-world.[68] Human time is basically ecstatic, as contrasted with the time of things which are embedded in and pass through successive temporal periods. Heidegger's term "ecstatic" is an apt ideogram illuminative of the transcendent quality of human time; yet it must be used carefully. The ecstasy of time appears as I run forward into my future, not disregarding my having been, but affirming its continuity with the whole of my existential progression. The ecstasy which is lost in a fallen condition may be recovered by a special resolution on my part. If I deny my having been, I deny a mode of my being-in-the-world. When I cease to be oriented toward my future in terms of authentic possibility, the ecstatic quality diminishes and I become fallen even deeper into inauthenticity. Since the primary phenomenon of original and authentic temporality is the future,[69] it is legitimate to say that as the future diminishes in importance, I become less an existential being and more like an entity in the natural spatio-temporal succession. Existence temporalizes itself properly as I am a being who anticipates the future which in turn provides the reason (Grund) for which I exist.

Heidegger has said that Dasein is a being who is open and who dwells in the openness of being. The true meaning of openness is to be conceived not in spatial terms but in temporal ones; for, I am open as existing in a mode of projecting understanding toward my own most possibility. Ecstasy dawns in openness.

Insofar as my being is authentic, I live in the future. Authentic existence is running ahead of myself (Vorlaufen), as a kind of eschatological anticipation of a future possibility which is already in a sense here.[70] Of course Dasein is fallen away from himself. He turns away from his genuine possibilities. He often concentrates upon the present as a perpetuation of the past either in terms of retaining the status quo or developing it. In fallen existence I expect something to develop; but as my existence opens up toward authenticity, I go beyond mere expectation. I am already ahead of myself as my future possibility becomes actualized as the being who I am. The authentic present is then the moment (Augenblick) of ecstatic coming to oneself through anticipatory, proleptic resolution;[71] and the moment of awareness-response constitutes the emergence of conscience. This temporal projecting quality of existence toward the future in

68 Cf. ibid., p. 350.
69 Ibid., p. 329.
70 Cf. ibid., pp. 335-337.
71 Ibid., pp. 338-339 ff.

no way eliminates or disregards my having been. On the contrary the rudimentary state of mind, by becoming truly temporal, enables *Dasein* to recover the having been of his facticity.[72] As I respond to the voice of conscience which calls to me from my future, the whole of my existence stands out from fallenness and moves toward authenticity.

Not merely is the "being" of being-in-the-world temporal, but the entire category of transcendence must be understood temporally or historically. World itself, as an existential term, is best clarified not spatially but temporally. My world is not a finished product or an established field. It is an open world because it is one which temporalizes itself (*zeitigt sich*).[73] The world is not an external network of forms outside a worldless subject. Time is not an element of the spatio-temporal sphere of a supposedly external world. On the contrary, existential temporality is the ground upon which the natural temporal-spatial realm is perceived and interpreted. The world is the horizon against which I am "located," but its boundaries are not primarily spatial; they are temporal, lying ahead of me, beckoning me forward, opening up to me the possibility of authentic selfhood. As being-in-the-world I am defined by my concern; but the meaning of concern is to be discovered in my temporality.[74] Thus the analysis of human being proceeds to open up in a brilliant and novel way existential essence as temporality. Interpretation of temporality enlightens our understanding of the meaning of Being,[75] and first of all of human being.

Authenticity requires that I face my own most authentic possibilities. But more precisely just what does that mean and how is it to come about? The answer is crucial, not merely for pressing existential reasons but also for the philosophical illumination of human being. A revelation of authentic human being is needed to provide a truthful answer to the question: Who is man? Heidegger maintained that it is by facing his own death that *Dasein* becomes directed toward his own most possibilities.[76] According to Heidegger, by facing one's death, one faces the end possibility in an isolation that is true freedom. This being unto one's own death will, then,

---

[72] Cf. also *ibid.*, p. 340.
[73] *Ibid.*, pp. 366 ff.
[74] *Ibid.*, p. 367.
[75] Cf. *ibid.*, pp. 436 ff.
[76] *Ibid.*, p. 250; "Own most" is, I think, a somewhat closer translation of *eigentlich*, at least in some places, than "authentic." *Eigentlich* in ordinary German means "authentic" or "genuine"; but its root suggests that it in some way belongs to a person, as his *own*, as being the most appropriate. Cf. the somewhat similar sense of self in Gordon Allport's discussion of self as "The Proprium," *Becoming*, pp. 41-58.

reveal the wholeness of *Dasein;* in this moment one gathers up into an ecstasy of finality the whole of one's existence. As we say in colloquial English, in a moment of anxiety, as we confront the possibility of death, our life stretches out before us. Here our most vital concern becomes apparent, because death cuts us off from other concerns which are of less than ultimate interest; facing death we are called by our very being to direct ourselves to our true selfhood. Only as one has faced his own death can one hear the authentic voice of conscience and live authentically in the world with concern for things and others; unless one has thus directed himself toward his own most final possibility, he will fall into banality and triviality of public life.[77]

Heidegger's existential solution is, with certain qualifications, voluntaristic. You must resolutely affirm your being in the face of nonbeing.[78] Only out of the resolution of an authentic selfhood may there arise authentic relations with others.[79] To see and seize the real possibility of my existence, I must confront the possibility of my nonexistence.[80] In order to appropriate the authentic future I must hurl myself away from any concerns which externally confine my transcendence; I must throw myself into the isolation that comes from facing death so as to discover my authentic future.[81] The isolating possibility of death frees me to face and choose my self in its wholeness. In this ecstatic vision of the whole of my self I also am presented with the most authentic vision of the meaning of existence. Resolute being-unto-death is the act which achieves the necessary transcendence beyond the fallenness of everyday life and in which the meaning of human being as grounded in temporality becomes manifest.

The solution to the problem of existence and existential understanding is the goal of Heidegger's interpretation. Nevertheless Heidegger's existential analysis has suffered distortion due to an ulterior motive on his part to get beyond human being so as to formulate an ontology: "All our efforts in the existential analytic serve the one aim of finding a possibility of answering the question of the *meaning of Being* in general." [82] His brilliant phenomenology of human existence, albeit much of it borrowed from Kierkegaard, Dilthey, and others, is dominated by his over-all aim. This has

---

[77] *Ibid.*, p. 263.
[78] *Ibid.*, pp. 267 ff.
[79] *Ibid.*, p. 298.
[80] *Ibid.*, p. 329.
[81] Cf. *ibid.*, p. 339.
[82] The English translation, *Being and Time*, p. 424 (SZ, p. 372).

led him to neglect some important factors and to evaluate others in a predetermined or prejudiced fashion. His characterization of existence as fallen, with the distinction between authentic and inauthentic existence, is perhaps an expression of ontological prejudice.[83] I am not here claiming that his judgment is mistaken. What I wish to point out is that his interpretation and solution are imposed upon the material, not elicited from it. If I am to ask: Who am I? it well may be that the most appropriate answer lies in my future, understood as existential possibility. Yet Heidegger's scheme portrays that possibility too abstractly and much too narrowly. Certainly Heidegger has helped us to realize that if we are to understand man we must seek to grasp the whole of existence as temporal being and not to focus upon him as a mere entity in time. Furthermore, he has pointed out that one's everyday mode of existence in the world may actually misrepresent what is essentially human. However, to judge as fallen all forms of concrete existence except that which is grounded in one's resolute facing of death is an arbitrary assertion which deserves to be questioned and thoroughly investigated.

Heidegger's description of existence as shallow, impersonal, anonymous, and conformist, as *das Man*, strikes a strong, true note. It is in line with what many other writers representing extremely diverse backgrounds have been expressing for at least the past two generations. It is especially close to the insights of psychologists, sociologists, and artists of our times. Yet for all its truthfulness this characterization is really very close to what Max Weber called an ideal type, which is to say an artificial abstraction, an approximation of a fairly general style of existence. If that is the case, then to what extent is Heidegger's *das Man* truly a phenomenological revelation, a manifestation of "things themselves as they really are"? Many people will feel that his rather gnostic condemnation of all worldly life as fallen is a distortion of "how it really goes" with man. Is there no grace in idle talk or secular amusements, in technical endeavors, in social and political activity? Heidegger apparently would give a resounding No! Actually Heidegger's authentic *Dasein* strongly resembles the portrait of the man seeking his own truth in Herman Hesse's novel, *Steppenwolf*. This lone wolf can find no roots in public life or even in ordinary fellowship; he senses that he must turn away from the everyday world to find his truth within himself in isolation. Like Hesse at this point, Heidegger emphasized

[83] The burden of my doctoral thesis had to do with the dangers of allowing ontology to encroach upon existential analysis. See Sadler, *op. cit.*

the isolation of the individual and his need to find his individual roots. But is this not arbitrary and perhaps terribly mistaken? If one emphasizes as basic states of mind anxiety and fear while ignoring trust and gratitude, one will naturally see man as solitary rather than in terms of solidarity. If one dogmatically asserts that a human being is isolated and by himself must find his own truth, then one will turn away from the common world of man in mystic fashion to seek the Being which lies "beyond." Yet philosophers such as Buber and Marcel have intuitively analyzed concrete everyday existence in the world with others. They, too, have discovered the fallenness which Heidegger illuminated; but they also detected the presence of grace in love as the manifestation of true Being. At least at this point we may wonder if Heidegger's picture of the authentic wholeness of existence is really trustworthy.

Heidegger's absolutizing of concern as the underlying and all-embracing structure of existence carries with it serious defects that show up in aspects of human life which Heidegger gives short shrift. Marjorie Grene raised this pertinent question in her otherwise unjust and bitter book, *Dreadful Freedom:*

> What one wonders is this: What happens to the individual's relationships to others when he resolves to be, not a mass of conventions, but himself? In other words, what does Heidegger do with the question of our existing-together-with-others outside the conventional and unauthentic level of existence? The answer is clearly, "Next to nothing." My freedom is mine and the awareness of it bears no intruders, for it is "freedom to death"; and from my loneliness in face of death no one can save me; nor can I if I would, save or even pity another.[84]

A more patient and admiring critic has pointed out that Heidegger's notion of man's end or Ground is bound up with his philosophical option to see freedom essentially in terms of death, of nothingness where there can be no extraneous limitation to one's self-projection.[85]

Several things can be said at this point. It could be questioned if people generally see the whole of their lives stretched before them as they resolutely face death. There is considerable evidence that some people's perspective becomes extremely restricted in such moments. Furthermore, anxiety rarely has been demonstrated to have the revealing properties Heidegger claims for it. Usually it blunts and distorts man's vision of

---

[84] M. Grene, *Dreadful Freedom*, p. 69.
[85] T. Langan, *op. cit.*, p. 214.

himself. As we shall see in Chapter 12, Heidegger has scarcely touched the real meaning of existential anxiety. Furthermore, in the moment facing death some people do not find the supposedly liberating isolation Heidegger refers to but, rather, sense a deep communion with loved ones and/or God. Heidegger remained dogmatic in his position:

> The more authentically Dasein resolves—and this means that in antici-pating death it understands itself unambiguously in terms of its ownmost distinctive possibility—the more unequivocally does it choose and find the possibility of its existence, and the less does it do so by accident. Only by the anticipation of death is every accidental and "provisional" pos-sibility driven out.[86]

This is sheer assertion and far from being self-evident. There is no justify-ing phenomenology or any other kind of evidence to substantiate it. Miss Grene's brittle pen makes the criticism clear:

> The emphasis on the single isolated person is disastrously limiting. Even the emphasis on death, in the fashion in which Heidegger presents it, involves an inescapable narrowness which warps the total conception of the authentic individual.[87]

The argument at this point is not that the individual's resolution toward death is unimportant, but merely that it cannot arbitrarily be made to stand either as the basis for authenticity or as the way to realize the full picture of man. It would seem that Heidegger has borrowed from the perennial wisdom of the Psalms: "So teach us to number our days that we may get a heart of wisdom" (Psalm 90:12); but in a religious context it is ultimately not the humble acceptance of one's mortality but faith which provides the moment of authentic insight.

It should be obvious that the entire Heideggerian scheme, as a coher-ent framework, is worked out so as to provide him with a logically satisfac-tory method for arriving at a view of the whole of existence. Facing death is the solution to the vexing problem of how to grasp the whole. But this whole is existence isolated by not-being, through a resolution that is exclu-sive of significant involvement with others. To a reader with a sense of the priority of social life and social concerns, this individualistic solution within one's private time will appear to be exasperating, trivial, and mistaken; reaction to Heidegger could be similar to that of a socially oriented Chris-

---

[86] *Being and Time*, p. 435 (SZ, p. 384). Cf. a different interpretation of facing death by the psychoanalyst, H. Hendin, *Suicide and Scandinavia*.
[87] Marjorie Grene, *Heidegger*, pp. 51-52.

tian confronting a pietist who is almost exclusively concerned about the
salvation of his supposedly immortal soul. Heidegger's secular eschatology is
too private. Though he has made a real breakthrough in existential phenomenology by opening up the dimension of the future as basic to our
understanding of human transcendence, yet his ontological bias has apparently restricted his vision to that of the isolated individual; this has certainly contributed to his ignoring of the underlying reality of community
and the implicit notion of an authentic corporate future. Hence his picture
of the whole of existence is far from complete, not just in the sense of
being an unfinished sketch but also as having omitted in the plan basic
other figures. By leaving out the being of others in any authentic sense,
even his wonderfully grand notion of freedom is indigent.

Heidegger's *Sein und Zeit* is unquestionably the work of an extraordinary man, a genius; and it has sometimes had the effects of prophetic
utterance.[88] It has stimulated people to turn from distractions and superficiality and to think originally and excitedly about the significance of
human being. He has provided contemporary man who feels his existence
being torn, dissipated, and buried in an increasingly technical, overly conformist, manipulative, anonymous urban society with a vision of ecstatic
existence—the possibility of rising above the ephemeral, inner worldly
beings and cares into meaningful existential wholeness. He has challenged
man to authenticate his transcendence, to be himself; and he has provided
an existential rather than a biological or mundane way of understanding
his vocation *to be*. To become a man is to achieve existential ecstasy—to
become your future which rushes through your present giving meaning to
your past. He has given us a vision of existence and a method which are
indispensable for building up existential phenomenology. Yet for all the
excitement and heuristic value, it is necessary to question his portrayal of
the ecstasy of authentic existence as a thoroughly reliable vision or criterion
of the whole of human being. Certainly his solution to our question about
man is a more plausible and more easily executed one than Husserl's
eidetic reduction and more basic than Scheler's phenomenology; but it has
nevertheless left out a place for significant others in the existential quest
for truth.

To anticipate countercharges, I have not overlooked Heidegger's discussion of social existence (*Mitsein*) and existence with others or inter-

---

[88] This aspect of Heidegger has had its demonic side, especially when he "spiritu-
ally ratified" the Nazi takeover in Germany.

personal relations (*Mitdasein*). As a conclusion to this chapter and a preparation for what is to follow, a brief examination of this particular section
of *Sein und Zeit* is necessary. Heidegger has brilliantly delineated human
transcendence as being-in-the-world. He has demonstrated that to discover
the meaning of this key term involves a radical process of existential understanding. Furthermore, he has shown some basic existential structures and
has indicated how they are fundamentally temporal phenomena. The
underlying structure of *Dasein* he has designated as concern; and this
concern is always for the sake of itself in terms of historical possibilities. As
historical being, the world of *Dasein* is not completely isolated from other
people; his world is always a social world, Heidegger has said. *Dasein's*
being *in* the world is for himself but it is also a being *with* others in a
world which is shared. In fact, being-in-the-world in itself is being *with*
others.[89] Heidegger stated that being-*with* is basic. It provides the ontological basis for concrete being with others; as ontological it *is* even if relationships with concrete persons are missing, as for example with Robinson
Crusoe. Yet just what this might mean in Heidegger's context is certainly
unclear, and again there is no phenomenological evidence presented.[90]
Heidegger here merely asserted the ontological priority of *with*; having
done so he proceeded to qualify it and then ignore it altogether.

Heidegger insisted that *Mitdasein* must be understood to exist within
the structure of concern. He then qualified this type of concern. The form
of concern applicable to things (*Besorgen*) is inappropriate for another
human being; hence the personal expression of concern is a concern for the
welfare of others (*Fürsorge*).[91] To become authentic this mode of concern
must set another free for his own possibilities.[92] Certainly in our relationships with others, if we treat them with the respect appropriate to a human
being, we shall properly attempt not to dominate or possess them; proper
concern is to free them to become themselves. Surely we are not in disagreement with Heidegger here. Yet it is highly questionable if this even
begins to suggest the depth and complexities which are inherent in authentic interpersonal relations. Heidegger did not say here that authentic concern for self totally isolates the other from me, for there is the ontological
priority that the other is already with me.[93] Yet, what can this mean when

---

[89] *Sein und Zeit*, p. 118.
[90] *Ibid.*, p. 120.
[91] *Ibid.*, p. 121.
[92] *Ibid.*, p. 122.
[93] *Ibid.*, p. 123.

it is said that I am and must be alone confronting my death, which cuts off all possibilities save that of my own being ahead of myself into the future? Is it not significant that Heidegger does not bring up the ontological *with* in discussing resolution toward death? Is it not also significant that whereas he discusses at length authentic existence as being-toward-death (*Sein-zum-Tode*), he speaks phenomenologically only about inauthentic, fallen forms of social and interpersonal existence? The temporality and concern of being with others are seen only as fallen into the public sphere, the dimension of *das Man*.[94] Where in his whole scheme is the possibility of my discovering the authentic truth of another being? Virtually nowhere. He must do that in and for himself, as I must. Here Scheler's illumination of the idols of self-knowledge as well as the evidence of love, friendship, and psychoanalysis suggest both the danger and the falseness of Heidegger's position. At least we must consider the possibility of a shared truth as well as the possibility of deeply shared existence as authentic. Heidegger tended to individualize genuine interpersonal terms. Even fidelity is interpreted as constituted by existential resolution toward one's own self.[95] To Heidegger, *Dasein*'s world is existential, but it is *in its authenticity a private world*; the world horizon for the manifestation of being is structured by my concern for my own existence. Though he has affirmed the presence of *Mitwelt* it would seem impossible to give it any ontologically authentic meaning; surely it has little positive existential meaning. Though Sartre's criticism of Heidegger as solipsistic is probably unjust, there seems to be an inescapably individualistic understanding of human existence which is incapable of touching the most authentic interpersonal reality of love.[96] As Binswanger was to say later, love stands freezing outside the doors of Heidegger's existential world.

[94] *Ibid.*
[95] *Ibid.*, p. 391.
[96] Jean-Paul Sartre, *Being and Nothingness*, pp. 244-252.

5

Witnesses to Love: Some Contributions of Martin Buber and Gabriel Marcel

Even brief exposure to three leaders in the phenomenological movement is enough to indicate that phenomenology can have strikingly different meanings, depending upon the philosopher who attempts to apply it. Nevertheless the thinkers already considered have shared certain basic views and aims, and some foundations for the development of a new approach to man have been established by them. It is my conviction that Heidegger has been the most significant with regard to the formation of a new approach, incorporating many important insights of Husserl and Scheler into his own vision of human transcendence. Heidegger's vision of existence is magnificently profound yet dangerously inadequate. In common with other phenomenologists he has drawn our attention to the givenness of experience; and he has illuminated its broad intentional structure in terms of existential historicity. His hermeneutical analysis of the lived world has clarified the unique characteristics of human space and time, which in turn has thrown fundamental features of existence, such as freedom, conscience, ecstasy, authenticity and inauthenticity into a new light. There can be little doubt that Heidegger's existential analysis presents an indispensable operational base for continuing research into basic human phenomena. However, from the viewpoint of Scheler, it is clear that Heidegger's vision of human existence is lacking in awareness of the personal dimension, insofar as it ignores the deeply interpersonal sphere of reality. It might be said that Heidegger's picture of being-in-the-world is a vision of just one particular mode of human existence. Heidegger has stressed the presence of Being, but he has failed to take notice of even the possible authenticity of the revelation of Being in and through the presence of another human being. It is in view of this inadequacy that the philosophical anthropology of Martin Buber becomes extremely pertinent.

1.

A short comparison between Martin Buber (1878–1965) and Martin Heidegger's respective approaches to man will enable us to expand our existential picture and sharpen our phenomenological focus. It is appropriate to compare these two thinkers because they have much in common. Buber addressed himself seriously to Heidegger's existential anthropology, but in a misleading way, because he suggested that Heidegger's analysis in *Sein und Zeit*, by closing itself off within an isolated self from the genuine reality of relation, does not reveal what man is, "but only what the edge of man is." [1] That is not the case, surely; but a comparison will indicate a severe enough criticism of Heidegger. An American interpreter of Buber, Maurice Friedman, has suggested that for all the major contributions he has made in diverse areas of thought and scholarship, Buber's underlying interest was philosophical anthropology. [2] Thus he shared with Heidegger in *Sein und Zeit* a concern to understand man, as well as a deep dissatisfaction with traditional attempts to do so. Furthermore, Buber and Heidegger agreed that what is essential is for us to catch at least a glimpse of the whole structure of human existence. As Buber wrote, the subject of philosophical anthropology is "man in his wholeness." [3] With all the phenomenologists and existentialists, Buber shared an abhorrence of the tendency in modern thought to reduce human being to biological or psychological categories: "Every attempt to interpret human action in biological terms . . . is a trivialization; it is a poor simplification because it means the abandoning of the proper anthropological content of that which constitutes the category of man." [4] Yet, like Heidegger, he did not resort to a rationalistic fallacy divorcing man's spirit or mind from his involvement in

---

[1] Martin Buber, *Between Man and Man*, p. 181.
[2] Cf. Maurice Friedman, "Martin Buber's Final Legacy: The Knowledge of Man," in *Journal for the Scientific Study of Religion*, Vol. V, No. 1 (Fall, 1956), pp. 4-9; also his *Martin Buber: The Life of Dialogue*.
[3] Martin Buber, *Between Man and Man*, p. 123.
[4] *Ibid.*, p. 72.

the world, which is to forget man's essential worldliness. Throughout his writings, and surprisingly enough especially in his theological works, he stressed man's necessary involvement in the world; in Buber's view man does not find God by turning away from the world but by opening himself to the world for genuine encounter. Similarly man does not find himself by ignoring or retreating from worldly involvement.

Yet Buber looked upon the existential world in a way different from Heidegger's. To him "the man who knows a world is man *with* man." [5] This statement might well have been written by Heidegger in the previously discussed section of *Sein und Zeit*. Yet Buber meant by the preposition *with* in this context something much more profound, dynamic, and intimate than Heidegger did. For Buber the *with* refers to the realm *between* man and man, the deepest possible relation one person can have with another, the sphere of dialogue. For Buber there are three possible ways to consider another person. First, you can assume the role of an observer, remaining detached, fixing your gaze upon him, and then describing what you see. The second way is that of an onlooker who withholds immediate description to wait for the person to describe or reveal himself, such as an artist might do who paints a portrait. Third, there is the most authentic mode, which is to become aware of the other person as a whole being with whom you are engaged in intimate, honest dialogue. In this relation the person over against you is encountered as a being who addresses you as a whole, calling you to participate in his being.[6] Thus one enters into the primary relation of what Buber calls I-Thou. In the I-Thou relation the whole of human being is revealed. Like other phenomenologists Buber has also moved beyond description in his attempt to express the truth of existence.

It is well enough known that Buber distinguished between two basic types of relation a person may have with others and with the world of things: "There is no I taken in itself, but only the I of the primary word I-Thou and the I of the primary word I-It. When a man says I he refers to one or the other of these." [7] With this statement and many others like it Buber placed himself adamantly against all views of man which fail to see him in terms of relation. In this he is also similar to Heidegger, Scheler, and Husserl who, as we saw, stressed the relational reality of the being of

[5] *Ibid.*, p. 155.
[6] *Ibid.*, pp. 8-10.
[7] Martin Buber, *I and Thou*, 2nd ed., p. 4.

human beings. Like Heidegger, Buber emphasized man's facticity, his awareness of himself thrown into the world and engaged in it. The primary words I-Thou and I-It which emerge from man's twofold attitude toward the world "do not signify things, but they intimate relations. . . . [they] do not describe something that might exist independently of them, but being spoken they bring about existence." [8] These primary words are symbols, expressive of basic existential reality, not merely something which is added to it as an attribute. But this dual possibility of relation by implication challenges a single structure of concern. For Buber, man is in the world in a twofold way. I shall elaborate on this possibility in later chapters.

The mode of I-It is what Buber referred to as the world of experience. Again we notice a similarity to Heidegger, though it should be noted that Buber's classic work appeared five years before *Sein und Zeit*. In the mode of I-It we exist not separate from things; on the contrary, our experience is structured by intentionality. As Buber put it, I am never aware of my perceptions apart from the object of my perception; always "I perceive something. I am sensible of something. I imagine something. I will something. I feel something. I think something. . . . This and the like establish the realm of it." [9] This notion of intentionality sounds more like Brentano than Husserl; but, as we see it developed, it resembles Heidegger most of all. As one experiences things, he formulates a picture of the world. This world is not exclusively a reality outside man but within him as well, as an image; yet in truth the inner and outer world are mutually included.[10] Like Heidegger's discussion of the intentional structure of concern in terms of its rudimentary practical aspect, Buber maintained that experience of things is basically for the purpose of utilization: "The primary connection of man with the world of It is comprised in *experiencing*, which continually reconstitutes the world, and *using*, which leads the world to its manifold aim, the sustaining, relieving, and equipping of human life." [11] Buber did not distinguish here between the practical and the scientific-theoretical modes as did Heidegger. Yet they both would agree that although man cannot live apart from these modes, he does not truly exist unless he *stands forth from* them.

It is in their picture of man's standing forth, as truly *ex-sisting*, that

8 *Ibid.*, p. 3.
9 *Ibid.*, p. 4.
10 *Ibid.*, p. 93.
11 *Ibid.*, p. 38.

these two thinkers, who so far seem to be amazingly similar, differ radically. For Buber the way for me, the individual, to gain wholeness is not to affirm my own being in the face of possible death, but to "face a human being as my Thou, and say the primary word I-Thou to him." [12] By saying Thou the whole of my being is evoked; I am no longer restricted by any *thing*, for the "Thou has no bounds." [13] In the world of I-It, I perceive a world with definite boundaries, of things which occur in a given space and at a particular time. Both the events and the objects are measurable, and the relationships between events and things are ordered, analyzable, and predictable. The organization of things in events can be surveyed and manipulated and depended upon. This is a familiar world, which is always there, as my object.[14]

In the world of I-Thou, on the other hand, I meet the other only as a single being who opens up to me in an unpredictable fashion. This unpredictable, surprising openness breaks the boundaries of the familiar object world of It. The space of this I-Thou world is not bounded by things; it is unbounded. Time in the I-Thou world is not measured in terms of sequence, but is felt to be an event that finds its own fulfillment in itself.[15] I-Thou time is lived as a duration which has nevertheless the characteristic of simultaneity; for this time is not linked to a series of causes but was where beginning and end are one. Personal time is characterized by a boundless Present.[16] The meetings of I-Thou are not predictable, nor can they be organized or measured. Thus this world of I-Thou seems unreliable and uncertain, if one adopts the world of I-It for his standard of measurement. I-Thou is a reality which cannot be surveyed according to Buber; it cannot be had, for if you grasp at it, it vanishes. It is not a world of experience, of subjective intentionality, or of utilization. To Buber the world of I-Thou is a reality of mutuality, of freedom, of personal coinherence, which are in marked contrast to I-It characteristics. I-Thou is temporal existence in ecstasy, beyond the domination of spatiality. I-Thou is the authentic present where you are fully present to another human being and he to you. In the relation of I-Thou, the relation is not simply constituted by what I as a subject do to you as a subject or vice versa; authentic "relation is mutual." [17] When the *meeting*, which is constituted by this

12 *Ibid.*, p. 8.
13 *Ibid.*, p. 4.
14 *Ibid.*, p. 31.
15 *Ibid.*, p. 32.
16 *Ibid.*, p. 30.
17 *Ibid.*, p. 15.

mutuality, happens, then you are beyond the world of It and in the
"heaven of Thou." [18] Buber emphasized that this mutuality is not a reality
which is inherent in man as an inner potentiality; nor can it be contrived.
When a genuine meeting occurs, it is always a gift of grace; and to receive
it we can only be open and ready.[19]

It is obvious that Buber's vision of the wholeness of man, of existence
in ecstasy, is radically different from Heidegger's. Yet though their views of
the whole differed, they both agreed that man is fallen in the world and
thus exists inauthentically. We are surrounded and enticed by the world of
It, a world in which it is comfortable to live and which offers us excite-
ments, activities, and knowledge. In this world of It the moments of I-
Thou appear to be strange, lyric, seductive, and magical, tearing us away to
dangerous extremes, loosening the well-tied contexts, and leaving us with
unanswered, perhaps unanswerable questions. The authentic moments of I-
Thou are rich but uncanny; and from the view of the world of It, we
should dispense with them. To live in this world, it is impossible to live
without I-It relations; "but he who lives with It alone is not a man." [20]
Today, wrote Buber, we are in perilous danger because of the "progressive
augmentation of the world of *It*" in technology, commercial expansion,
the scientific outlook, etc.[21] Thus we are losing the truth of the person.

Like Scheler, Buber was also seeking to get a clear, honest view of man
as a *person*; and he realized that a person is not to be seen either as an
object or as a subject. To achieve a vision of the person, he insisted that we
need to recover the reality of I-Thou, letting the spirit of meeting blaze
into presentness.[22] Buber is more helpful than Scheler at this point because he suggested a new framework within which to view I-Thou relations; Scheler did not seem to have succeeded in breaking loose from the
individual-collective antithesis. Though Heidegger and Buber differed in
their solutions, the one being voluntaristic while the other adamantly resisted any voluntaristic solution, they were significantly similar in that they
both encouraged the triumph of temporality over spatiality. For Buber we
are to recover the Present, interpreted as mutual Presence, whereas with
Heidegger we are to achieve the authentic Moment, the present as fulfilled
by the future. All three thinkers agreed that what obstructs man's existen-

---

18 *Ibid.*, p. 9.
19 "Postscript," *ibid.*, p. 131.
20 *Ibid.*, p. 34.
21 *Ibid.*, p. 37.
22 *Ibid.*, p. 40.

tial fulfillment is an absolutizing of a practical and utilitarian outlook; the latter indicates the tendency of man to deceive himself about the nature of his true being. As Buber put it, man is a being who lies about himself, about the values of reality, about being, and about the truth of God.

These thinkers are concerned that man be recovered from his fallenness. They agree this can occur only as man becomes open to the truth of his being. Buber's solution, vague as it may be, is most trustworthy. He maintained that if a person turns from his deceptive fascination with the world of It and is open for another Thou, and if a meeting occurs wherein there is genuine mutuality, where the primary word I-Thou is spoken, then one enters the true world of relation, the world of love. Buber did not mean literally that one lives then in two worlds. To him, these terms referred to two poles of being in the same world. Both are necessary; and man must live in tension "swinging" between the two extremes. Fallen existence means to be trapped at the pole of It; authentic existence happens in the encounter of Thou. "All real living is meeting." Personal relationship is authentic, is real, not only in terms of a fullness of being and of value, but also as a revelation of who I really am. In the relation of love, the other, to whom I say Thou, reveals me to myself, as a Thou. It is in love that deception is cleared away, and we see ourselves as persons in relation, each evoking the being of the other and revealing to the other his true being. Buber is adamant: this is the truth—"The man who does not know this, with his very being know this, does not know love." [23] Such a man, to Buber, would be very strange indeed. For he insisted that the I-Thou relation is not a rare, mystical experience enjoyed by an elite. On the contrary, he maintained that all men some time have had such a meeting; it is reality familiar to all persons.[24]

The mistake Heidegger and most Western thinking about man has made is that it begins with man as a single, individual unit. To Buber's way of seeing reality, that is false not only to nature but to spirit. What we must not overlook is the primary fact that "we live our lives inscrutably included within the streaming mutual life of the universe." [25] So, the first word about man is not the individual; but rather, "in the beginning is relation." [26] Like Scheler, Buber insisted upon a fundamental solidarity that I, the individual, have with the rest of reality.

---

[23] *Ibid.*, p. 15.
[24] Cf. *ibid.*, pp. 53, 130, passim.
[25] *Ibid.*, p. 16.
[26] *Ibid.*, p. 18, also pp. 25-28 ff.

The primary reality of human existence is relation, the reality of the *between*. Buber saw human growth as a process of exchange, involving at first a rudimentary mutuality between an infant and his immediate environment. There is a primal effort to enlarge and strengthen this relation of mutuality into a distinctively personal relationship; this interpretation is deduced from the infant's apparent need to establish contact and to find tenderness.[27] When one finds a relationship of tenderness and trust, one's being is then brought forth in individuality. That is, the individual is born in relationship; he does not emerge out of himself and then establish relationship: "I become myself through my relation to the Thou; as I become I, I say Thou." [28] Buber's view is thus diametrically opposed to the common notions of individualism, for example, that you must develop self-confidence before others can become confident in you. Rather, it works the other way around, as we shall see in later chapters. Without trust, one is bound by anxiety and restricted to the narrow world of measurable dependability, the world of It. When you have entered the loving relation of I-Thou, you find your being in "a world that is homely and house-like." [29] True, it is not an ordered world like that of an IBM plant; but its uncertainty belongs to spontaneous moments of surprise such as arise in a love-filled home.

Yet we might wonder if with the insistence upon solidarity and relationship Buber has done justice to what individualists, such as Heidegger, mean when they speak about authentic individual existence. Buber confronted this problem, specifically and at length, in a critical discussion of Kierkegaard's concept of the solitary individual. Though Buber had been deeply influenced by Kierkegaard, nevertheless at this point it became necessary to part company with him; for to Buber, Kierkegaard's solitary individual before God is an abstraction, and the attempt to emulate "it" is a turn not toward God but away from Him. Authentic existence requires a turn toward the other; for in the other one will find God, as the Thou of all Thou's.[30] There is a place in life for being solitary, which is to withdraw for reflection about life; but solitariness is for the sake of returning to the world and entering more fully into relation.[31] Solitude does not

---

[27] Cf. Gotthard Booth, "Values in Nature and in Psychotherapy," in *Archives of General Psychiatry*, Vol. I (Jan., 1963), pp. 38-48.

[28] *I and Thou*, p. 11.

[29] *Ibid.*, p. 54.

[30] Cf. *Between Man and Man*, especially pp. 40-57.

[31] *Ibid.*, pp. 54, 55, 92.

amount to the same thing as isolation; it does not sever relationship.[32] Buber has later emphasized that solitariness is to be encouraged; yet it must also be pointed out that there is the danger that one might begin to consider it a good in itself. Solitariness, being by yourself to be with yourself, thus seems to be for Buber on the plane of utilization; it is good, but it is for the purpose of relationship. Even though some solitariness is necessary to establish distance between yourself and another, the distance is for the purpose of relation, is for the other, not yourself alone.[33] In returning from solitude you are better prepared to enter what he referred to as the process of identification with the other, that is, of participating in his being, and experiencing "the other side." [34]

As valid as all this may be, one constantly wonders when one reads Buber: What is happening to my individual self, which I cannot deny exists? If Heidegger does not do even scant justice to I-Thou, Buber does not seem to do full justice to the Kierkegaardian-Heideggerian individual. To put it another way, he does not seem to illuminate the full dimensions of freedom. Buber has rightly been called an apostle of freedom; yet he is an ambivalent apostle: "Freedom—I love its flashing face; it flashes forth from the darkness and dies away, but it has made the heart invulnerable. I am devoted to it . . . I love freedom, but I do not believe it." [35] Buber emphasized that freedom is not an action in isolation, but is purposive; ultimately, freedom is one with relation. Freedom is *for* relation, for meeting with another. Freedom creates a bond between us; and so it is inseparable from responsibility. Yet for all the truthfulness in Buber's position, what about the individual who feels crushed with responsibility and burdened with relations that curtail his freedom? Buber does not, I think, really offer much help to us on this score.

As valuable as Buber's thinking is to combat individualism and to suggest an alternative view, one is never quite sure just what to do with his anthropological statements, especially if one is a phenomenologist. It is usually impossible to find verification for his conclusions. The trouble here is twofold. By affirming that I-Thou is beyond experience, Buber logically concedes that meeting is beyond description.[36] Yet he insists that meetings reveal a pure truth, such that: "No deception penetrates here; here is

---

[32] *I and Thou*, pp. 103-104.
[33] Martin Buber, *The Knowledge of Man*, see chapter, "Distance and Relation."
[34] *Between Man and Man*, pp. 62, 96.
[35] *Ibid.*, p. 91.
[36] *I and Thou*, p. 10.

the cradle of Real Life." [37] Now how does he move from this personal revelation of the truth of human being into the conceptual, systematic framework of his writings? His affirmations often drop from "out of the blue" much like Heidegger's ontological assertions. Both of them write as though once they have made their pronouncements upon any given matter, the issues are settled. Buber has suggested on occasion that his writings are like those of an artist, designed not to describe reality but to evoke it in the reader.[38] Seen as artistic, evocative works, his writings are amazingly successful. He states his case with artistic conviction in ways which are sometimes stunningly brilliant, though at other times his statements are confusing, eccentric, and open to question. Frequently in just those areas where we would want to question him, his statements are apodictic pronouncements, like those of a prophet. Perhaps he shared with Husserl a faith that his truths were self-evident.

However great as well as puzzling and frustrating, Buber's anthropology is not in the genre of secular existential philosophy. It is basically religious writing in the prophetic tradition. Buber knows of no life in any world which might separate a man from God, even though God may be hidden as in an eclipse. What is described as separation from God is merely life alienated from its personal truth in the world of It. All genuine personal relations are symbolic, pointing to God: "He who truly goes out to meet the world goes out also to God." [39] In spite of anthropological exaggeration and methodological shortcomings, Buber has pointed in his own unique way to concrete existence in the everyday world; and what is most important is that he has seen there a reality which Heidegger overlooked. Buber would designate Heidegger's existence *individuality*; this existential mode is, as he says, marked by a sense of yours and mine as well as by a sense of detachment from other people and things. His own view opens up to the *person*, whose existential reality is beyond the modes of possession and isolation. The aim of individuality is self-differentiation, epitomized by the individualized single one of either Kierkegaard or Heidegger. The person, on the other hand, affirms his solidarity with others. Within this latter perspective a person can nevertheless become truly solitary and discover the fullness of solitude. The goal of solitude within a personalist perspective is not self-differentiation; it is relation. To be a

[37] *Ibid.*, p. 9.
[38] *Between Man and Man*, p. 35.
[39] *Ibid.*, p. 95 et passim.

person is to exist beyond the isolated self in direct contact with and sharing of the reality of Thou. It is from this viewpoint that the personal I becomes authentic; or, as Buber would say, in I-Thou the I becomes real through sharing.[40]

2.

Further progress in our attempt to expand, deepen, and correct Heidegger's existential view of human being can be made by moving on and taking a quick look at the rich fabric of Marcel's thought. Gabriel Marcel, who was born in the same year as Heidegger (1889–   ), is in some ways also much like Heidegger; and yet, too, he is very different. They have both reacted against German Idealism; yet Marcel's reaction has been within French culture and in the midst of Parisian intellectual and artistic circles, which has contributed to his creative thinking a flavor different from that produced by his counterpart in the *Schwarzwald*. Though both Marcel and Heidegger have been classified as Existentialists in many books about Existentialism, both of them repudiate the label as inapplicable to themselves. Though each has concentrated upon interpreting human existence, the scope of their philosophy is broader. Marcel, as we have seen of Heidegger, is also an ontologist, though that term has even less precise meaning with him than with Heidegger. He definitely has deep admiration for Heidegger's thinking and shares with him a certain affinity for a pre-Socratic quest for the meaning of Being. Both thinkers have warned against the arrogant presuppositions contained in much traditional and contemporary conceptual thought. Marcel also has a particularly deep appreciation of imaginative artistic expression. In fact, most of his life he has been an active dramatist; in addition, he has written some poetry and a bit of music as well. Like Heidegger and Buber, Marcel has been perturbed by the tendency of thought, especially predominant in our era, toward a form of abstraction that has the goal of making knowledge useful. This tendency reduces reality to the level of technique. The evident technocracy of our times, he feels, is causing us to lose a sense of the mystery of being; life for us is becoming flat, shallow, toyed with but not loved.[41]

Not dissimilar to both Heidegger and Buber, Marcel sees man as

[40] Cf. *ibid.*, pp. 62-63.
[41] See his book-length exposition of this subject: Gabriel Marcel, *Man against Humanity*.

living on two levels; he refers to the two modes as the level of *being* and the level of *having*. We must distinguish what we have and the inherent attitude in having from what we are; to come to an awareness of ourselves in terms of our being involves a sense of the mystery of our existence.[42] This distinction is comparable to Buber's I-Thou and I-It, but also to Heidegger's distinction between existential concern and practical scientific-theoretical concerns. Like Heidegger, Marcel affirms that man is a being who can be open to being; indeed, *openness* is a category extremely important to Marcel. Openness is basically a temporal structure and is constitutive of human freedom. Man is to become open to find his truth and live it. Marcel, too, has strongly emphasized the dynamic progression of existence; one must constantly become what one is to be. He has maintained that a human being is essentially *Homo viator*, man en route. The essence of man is active.

Although we can find numerous similarities between him and others, Marcel is much more consistently a phenomenologist than most; his philosophy, like his dramas, attempts concrete illumination of existence as we find it. His probing investigation of everyday life leads him to the opposite pole from Heidegger; where Heidegger sees the individual becoming authentic as he becomes autonomous, Marcel views autonomy as a barrier to existential fulfillment. To him, the true man is one who realizes his solidarity and actualizes his freedom in love. Though thus far Marcel might merely appear to be a French, Catholic version of Buberism, there are yet significant differences between these two. Especially important, however, is the fact that Marcel has articulated his own understanding of the phenomenological method which will enable us to explore the mystery of love and freedom more clearly. Marcel has said that the best way to consider his method and all *true philosophy is as research*; it is a probing, illuminating *search for* the fundamentals of being.[43]

Marcel's research into the mystery of human being is a concrete one. It is based on experience and is an exploration of experience as given to us, given as a massive presence.[44] This concrete approach involves a presentiment or forefeeling, a kind of intuition which leads us to say, "This is reality." [45] Like Heidegger, Marcel understands the quality of this initial reaction to experience to be a deep wonder at that which is. This wonder-

42 Gabriel Marcel, *Being and Having*, pp. 155 ff.
43 Gabriel Marcel, *The Existential Background of Human Dignity*, pp. 5 ff.
44 Gabriel Marcel, *Mystery of Being*, II, p. 53.
45 Gabriel Marcel, *Metaphysical Journal*, pp. viii-x.

ing at being includes both a sense of admiration and a restlessness, what he
has referred to as a metaphysical need or disquiet that constitutes man's
appetite for being, for further searching for that which is.[46] Marcel's
search for being, however, is not like that of a spectator who patiently
watches for some new thing to appear on the stage. The search makes man
an actor, a participant in the drama of being. Marcel has also repeatedly
emphasized the importance of music to his entire outlook; his approach is
like that of a musician who listens to the voices of beings who are in
company with him in a grand symphony of being.[47] Music as an image of
being suggests that it is a mystery beyond visual conceptualization, a mystery which is impossible to locate, within me and beyond me, encompassing us yet between us, penetrating but capable of being faded out, suscep-
tible of multiple interpretations, and so forth. As I shall elaborate in
Chapter 7, a phenomenologist is one who listens to the music of experience, not by detaching himself—for that would be to stop hearing—but by
participation. Yet Marcel has emphasized that though we come closer to it,
the mystery remains a mystery for all our investigation; it is a fundamental
quality of our existence which cannot be converted into the content of
thought. We can only allude to this mystery as do poets and musicians.[48]

Now, in this research, what does one listen to? That which is first to
call us to attention is a sense of our bodily being. Marcel has also stressed
facticity, but somewhat differently from Heidegger. Marcel approaches
facticity in terms of bodiliness. I am aware of my body, yet basically I know
that my body is not something which I have; it is not an instrument for me
to examine and manipulate, though it can become so. To consider my body
as an object which I possess is to resort to an abstraction which restricts my
awareness to the level of having. It is not basically correct to say: I *have* a
body. Rather, I *am* my body. Primordial self-awareness is to sense what
Marcel refers to as the "existential indubitable": *I am alive!* I sense this
even though I do not say it in so many words. As I wonder at my being,
there arises an "exclamatory awareness" of myself.[49] This is where
phenomenology begins: with an affirmation that I am.[50] This existential
affirmation or vibrant self-awareness provides me with the basic understanding that I am an incarnate being. What Marcel has designated as

---

[46] *Ibid.*, p. 290 et passim.
[47] Gabriel Marcel, *Existential Background of Human Dignity*, pp. 82-83.
[48] *Metaphysical Journal*, p. 299.
[49] Gabriel Marcel, *Mystery of Being*, I, pp. 91-101.
[50] Gabriel Marcel, *Being and Having*, p. 140.

"incarnation" is not a theological doctrine about Christ but a term which points to the basic fact that I am my body. As such I am engaged in a situation, not as a spectator but primarily as a participant. Thus it is as an incarnate being participating in a concrete situation that I am to carry on phenomenological research, that quest for something which is beyond us yet which is also essentially here.[51]

Marcel, like Heidegger and Scheler, thus affirmed the primacy of feeling as a total awareness of self as the beginning of phenomenology; from there he has sought to proceed toward conceptualization. These thinkers, Heidegger and Marcel especially, should not be interpreted as advocating irrationalism or sentimentalism in thought. To use the image of light, which is extremely important to both of them, the truth emerges not as an object buried in a chest but as a light, which, when we follow it, sheds more and more light upon the being that we are. Phenomenology is a method of thought which follows the light emanating from our concrete existence by reflecting upon that which we have encountered. It is a form of contemplation which arises from our awareness of participating in the being we are trying to illuminate.[52] Marcel's method, as he says, is an attempt to work from life to thought, but then back to life, to throw more light upon our lives.[53] This is a *method of recollection* or *reflection*, which he sees as springing spontaneously from our exclamatory self-awareness.

Marcel distinguishes between two kinds of reflection. What he calls primary reflection is analytical and abstract. Such work is necessary, but if that is as far as the mind goes, it will distort rather than illuminate experience. A secondary reflection is required for phenomenology, which enables us to recover the unity of experience.[54] This secondary reflection requires the work of man's imagination, which enables him to transcend the abstractions of analysis so as to recover the original givenness of being, seen in clearer light. Here Marcel is obviously close to Heidegger's notion of hermeneutics. Heidegger asserted that interpretation must be made of a phenomenon, not merely because it is veiled, but because as temporal its fullness lies in the future; that is why it was so essential for him to have a complete view of man in terms of his future possibilities. His arbitrary,

---

51 Cf. *ibid.*, pp. 11, 151 ff.; also *The Mystery of Being*, I, chaps. 6, 7; and *Creative Fidelity*, chap. 1.

52 *The Mystery of Being*, I, pp. 13-19, 117 ff.

53 *Ibid.*, p. 41.

54 *Ibid.*, pp. 81 ff. Readers familiar with the literary criticism of S. T. Coleridge will recognize here what the latter described as the work of man's imagination. It is not surprising that such is the case, for Marcel did an intensive study of Coleridge as a young man; he has obviously been influenced by him.

schematic view of the wholeness of existence, however, was imposed upon the phenomena of everyday existence. Not having the ambitious ontological goal of Heidegger, Marcel was not so impatient to impose his evaluative categories upon existential phenomena. In a relaxed manner he has allowed his insights to emerge from the phenomena themselves. In his secondary reflection there is what he calls an act of recollection, which enables *me* to recover *my* being as a unified whole. This is the opposite of being resolutely set toward transcending what is given; rather, it involves a relaxation, a release from both resolution and detachment into the depth of my self-awareness. This act arises from an abandonment of those powers which I possess and enables me to sense again the being that I am. To engage in this act I must obviously, as he points out, have a basic trust in being or reality. Such trust allows me to re-establish contact with the very source of illumination. Certainly in this act I take a stand, but it is not at all an act of defiance or breaking loose; it is an entrusting of myself to being, which I sense as presence. As an act of recovery of self-unity and further illumination of the mystery of one's being, this recollection is a realization of what one rightly calls freedom.[55]

Were we to stop here, one would conclude that Marcel sounds like a mystic, not a philosopher. His methodological remarks could be taken as leading us to transcendence which is beyond the experience of ordinary men, certainly to regions as lofty as those intimated even by Scheler and Heidegger. But Marcel's methodology is inseparable from the concrete subject matter which he attempts to illuminate. When he speaks about recovering a unity of oneself he is not speaking primarily, if at all, about either a mystical or a psychic process of individuation. Concretely what he sees is that the existentially indubitable reality of himself does not stand alone. In illuminative recollection I realize that the life that I am is not mine as a possession, but comes to me as a gift.[56] The sense of mystery arises, not out of my isolation, but from the fact that my self exists in a living tie with other men. Of course we are trapped in ambiguity, as Heidegger points out; but we shall never get beyond it unless "we pass beyond the limits of the ego." [57] The reason we are able to trust the underlying being in which we sense our rootedness is because that being is love. As a former agnostic who became a convert to Catholicism, Marcel believes deeply that the original reality is the love of God, so that his

[55] Cf. Gabriel Marcel, *Existential Background of Human Dignity*, pp. 86-88.
[56] Gabriel Marcel, *Being and Having*, p. 199.
[57] Gabriel Marcel, *Existential Background*, pp. 136 ff.

statements might well have deep theological undertones. Yet he is not at this point speaking about theological reality. In a concrete phenomenology of the mystery of family life, Marcel's reflections led him to realize that his being is intimately related to the members of his family, even those who died before he ever knew them. Since his mother died when he was a small boy, the thought of those who came before him has naturally occupied much of his reflections.

As an incarnate being, I sense I am inherently linked with others. This unity is neither merely spiritual nor physical—it is existential, involving the whole of my being. Reflecting as a member of a family, I am aware that I am in continuity with others; yet my being is unique and I must affirm it. As an individual being I cannot find my truth in isolation from my roots; finding truth involves fidelity. Yet for me to become myself it must be a fidelity which is creative, transcending the given into the new reality of myself in free relations with others. The very essence of personal existence, my life with others, is what Marcel calls creative fidelity.[58] To be faithful is not a restriction of freedom, but is creative receptivity. Consider the fidelity of an artist who is open to all that is received and is responsive to it in such a way as to inaugurate action which may be said truly to be creative. Freedom and fidelity are inseparable.

Though Marcel's awareness of the mystery of his being is rooted in his reflective awareness operating on the basis of love, he is neither a naïve sentimentalist nor ignorant of the hatred, deception, distrust, and mutual manipulation which persist in many relationships. His numerous plays reveal uncomfortably penetrating insights into loveless situations where communication and communion have collapsed. Yet his point is precisely that love in many situations has broken down. It is the task of phenomenology as part of personal existence to overcome the obstacles obstructing genuine interpersonal communication. Only as we come to know one another and share in a reciprocal underlying reality do we recover a sense of who we really are. This underlying reality is love, and Marcel illumines it to be an intersubjective nexus in which we are mutually involved. It is a mistake to see love exclusively as an action of one subject toward another, thus ignoring the underlying reality of intersubjectivity.[59] Intersubjectivity structures

---

[58] Cf. Gabriel Marcel, *Homo Viator*, pp. 68-97, and *Creative Fidelity*, ch. 8.

[59] See, for example, Erich Fromm, *The Art of Loving*, which goes so far as to define love as an act, completely ignoring the interpersonal, coinherent reality of presence—that is, the phenomenon of presence as a reality in which we mutually share, not of a foreign presence which I stand beside.

the loving situation and genuine community. For Marcel, the real impetus for phenomenological research as a search for the further unfolding of the mystery of being arises from my reflective sense of participation in this underlying reality whereby I am united with others.[60] Much of our lives is spent with a sense of detachment from others; but such a mode of existence is not one which could rightfully be designated as involvement. "Being involved" is a fundamental condition of our human situation to the extent that it coincides with love. To become truly involved in a situation as a man is not to become submerged in external forces; for Marcel, to become existentially involved is to open up to a situation, to receive it inwardly, and respond to it with creative fidelity.[61] When Marcel affirms that love is the starting point for revealing the mystery of man, he means that phenomenological research is to begin with man in community and then to recognize barriers which are significant and tragic because they frustrate or prohibit community.

Phenomenology is concrete for Marcel because it marks the return to one's neighbor as the approach to being and truth.[62] The phenomenology of existence demands personal involvement with others. Like the previous phenomenologists we have considered, Marcel posits a preliminary action for the envisioning of truth. It is not a Husserlian phenomenological reduction or a Heideggerian resolution of oneself unto death but an action which repudiates the deceptive prison of egocentricism by recognizing the reality of intersubjectivity. Marcel's beginning, then, is similar to Scheler's, but he travels along slightly different lines. For example, to begin with love means for Marcel that I, the individual, become aware that my being does not belong to me, that the best part of my personality is granted to me as a gift.[63] Thus one becomes open to one's own concrete situation and ready for a full encounter with it and creative development within it, not merely with a feeling of solidarity, but also with an act of gratitude.

Marcel's view of the individual greatly differs with views which emphasize rigorous self-delimitation or differentiation as an autonomous unit. He pictures the development of human being in an expansive way. To be a person means to be engaged in a community situation which requires consistent openness or availability to what is given and then a binding of oneself to this presence. This view suggests that truth and authenticity

[60] *The Mystery of Being*, II, pp. 10-17.
[61] *Philosophy of Existence*, p. 9, and The *Mystery of Being*, I, pp. 138-145.
[62] Cf. Gabriel Marcel, *Man against Humanity*, p. 198.
[63] Gabriel Marcel, *The Mystery of Being*, II, pp. 32-34.

require some form of commitment within encounter; yet Marcel's commitment is much less a resolution of the will than a giving of oneself for
participation.[64] His sense of ever increasing and expanding involvement in
the being of others emerges from his awareness of the *reality of presence*,
an admittedly slippery term, but one which refers to a very concrete experience such as we signify when we ask another, "Are you with me?" If the
question is genuinely asked and the answer is genuinely, "Yes, I am with
you," the two persons discover that there has been an exchange as in an act
of sharing which has involved them in a total way. Marcel describes this
presence as a phenomenon which reveals an exchange of free acts; it is a
mutual response which signifies to me that the other person is not placed
there in front of me but that *we* transcend external spatiality in a personal
reality of sharing.[65] To be incapable of presence is to be restricted to the
prison of autonomy, to be encumbered with yourself apart from community. Thus presence is far from an encroachment upon one's freedom; on
the contrary, freedom involves being able to recognize that my being is a
gift and that my being extends beyond my body in the being of others.
Freedom is the opportunity to attain one's destiny; my destiny is not to
become an isolated self, a Prometheus, but to recover and enjoy the creative possibilities in living with others.[66]

Moving from incarnation to intersubjectivity enables Marcel to see
freedom in quite a different light from what it has been thus far. To him,
freedom means essentially *to be creative within a situation*. It is misguided
to say that man is free, as though born that way. It certainly is not accurate
to say, with Sartre, that man is condemned to be free. Rather, as man
opens himself to being in a situation he opens the possibility to himself of
becoming free. Our condition as men living in broken situations encumbered with barriers to communication is a captivity; man has the task to
become free, to achieve freedom. How is that possible? What will inspire
man to become creative in his situation? It is not anxiety, but trust, gratitude, and hope. Concrete recollection reveals that trust is needed for genuine freedom. Consider the refugee who has been freed from certain hard-
ships and restrictions in his native land. Yet as he is conscious of being a
refugee, his freedom is curtailed; he is aware of being tolerated, not loved,
and he must be on guard so that his words and gestures will not arouse

[64] Cf. Gabriel Marcel, *Homo Viator*, pp. 21-23, 126.
[65] Cf. Gabriel Marcel, *Philosophy of Existence*, pp. 24-28.
[66] *The Mystery of Being*, II, p. 155.

suspicion. To find freedom he must learn to feel at home in the new situation.[67] In Marcel's eyes the freest man is the one with the most hope, whose trust in the gift of being is such that he can look beyond the disappointing aspects of the immediate present to affirm the intersubjective reality in which he can find life meaningful. The man of hope is one who is able to give his existence the richest significance, to make the most of it, not as a dilettante but as a participant in the presence and freedom of others. The free man is one who can enter into relationships with others with the full weight of his being; thus, the freest man is the most fraternal, who is linked to his neighbor, freeing himself and the neighbor from the restrictions of self-centeredness.[68]

Though similar to Heidegger in that he sees freedom in terms of temporality, Marcel's view of temporality is significantly different. He has little patience with Heidegger's scheme about being-unto-death. Knowing you may die, he comments, may become a thought which will overtake you as an obsession and might, as so often happens, make life appear as being without meaning, without color. Marcel feels that one of the great tragedies of our era is that life is not loved; we are suffering a "spiritual asphyxia" which has caused us to lose a keen taste for living.[69] To overcome this asphyxia we must face the future as men with hope. Marcel has sketched out a phenomenology of hope in which he distinguished it from mere expectation or wishing for something to happen. Wishing is on the level of having. Hope is a response to presence. That is, at the root of hope there is a gift which demands a response of openness and affirmation. To hope is not essentially to hope for something, but to hope in someone. "I hope in Thee for us." Hope is in a Thou who shares with me in a present, who makes his presence available. To hope in this presence is to say that in spite of what happens I shall be faithful, I shall affirm our reality. As such, hope is inseparable from love; it is an act of creative fidelity, an act of transcendence which fulfills a situation. To hope is to continue in communion and to win the freedom to live in community, outside the prison walls of isolated self-centeredness.[70] Quite different from either Stoic or Heideggerian resolution, this existential mode of expressing future temporality does not require a stiffening of the will but a relaxing of oneself in response

[67] Gabriel Marcel, *Existential Background, op. cit.*, p. 151.
[68] See *Existential Background, op. cit.*, pp. 145-148.
[69] *Ibid.*, p. 144.
[70] Gabriel Marcel, *Homo Viator*, pp. 29-67.

to the gift of presence.[71] Hope is an act of freedom, but it is not a creation *ex nihilo*. It is an affirmation projected into the future which enables both courage and vision for the present. Hope, fraternity, and freedom are, for Marcel, basic qualities of human existence that reveal and establish its truth. Without them we shall scarcely begin to see man in his wholeness. It must be admitted that Marcel has not provided us with so great and heuristically valuable a scheme for interpreting existence as has Heidegger; yet he has, in a phenomenological way, given us concrete reflections with which to develop a truthful vision of human transcendence and which accounts for the mystery of existence and love. Surely any philosophy which attempts to account for the full reality of existence must heed the vision of artists and lovers; as W. H. Auden put it:

> Whatever view we hold, it must be shown
> Why every lover has a wish to make
> Some other kind of otherness his own:
> Perhaps, in fact, we never are alone.[72]

The primary aim of this chapter has been to call attention to what I believe to be an essential possibility for and the foundation of genuinely personal existence, the phenomenon of love. Secondarily my intention has been to suggest that love plays a basic role not merely in human existence but also in any phenomenological research which aims to illuminate that existence. Poetry has long served men by articulating a concrete need for and an awareness of the loving presence of another. Buber's philosophy of I-Thou has formulated in universal terms a perspective within which such poetic utterance becomes most significant. Marcel's philosophy is essentially in agreement with Buber's insistence upon the distinctively personal sphere of human existence, so there was no need to reduplicate our point by delving more deeply here into Marcel's thought. Both agree that subjectivity, including freedom, only finds its full significance within the context of loving intersubjectivity. Furthermore, Marcel has provided some strikingly important suggestions for working out a method which is both truly existential and phenomenological. We shall come back to these later, especially in Chapter 14. Before executing a full-fledged phenomenology of existence and love, however, it will be helpful first to examine Binswanger's existential analysis which integrated the empirical and phenomenological approaches.

[71] Gabriel Marcel, *Philosophy of Existence*, p. 20 passim.
[72] W. H. Auden, *Collected Shorter Poems*, 1927-1957, p. 200.

6

Ludwig Binswanger's Way to Freud and beyond Him to Phenomenology

1. PREFACE

Martin Buber once wrote:

> A legitimate philosophical anthropology must know that there is not merely a human species but also peoples, not merely a human soul but also types and characters, not merely a human life but also stages in life; only from the systematic comprehension of these and of all other differences, from the recognition of the dynamic that exerts power within every particular reality and between them, and from the constantly new proof of the one and the many, can it come to see the wholeness of man.[1]

That statement, so pregnant with possibilities for the development of a new and comprehensive approach to the understanding of human existence, found incarnation in the philosophical anthropology of Ludwig Binswanger (1882–1966). Thus far the background for existential phenomenology has consisted in the work of men who have been for the most part philosophers. All of them, however, have repudiated speculative, idealistic philosophy and have called for intensive research into the immediacy of experience. At least in this respect their approaches approximate something like what Americans think of in a general way when the terms "pragmatic" and "empirical" are used to designate method. This rough similarity would imply that phenomenology and empirical approaches to the phenomenon of man can and should be brought together. Admittedly

[1] M. Buber, *Between Man and Man*, p. 123.

115

phenomenology has denounced the absolutization of an attitude underlying or consistent with natural sciences; but quite a different attitude may be found in the social sciences. As long as sciences admit that there is no one absolutely constant scale of measurement and that frames of reference are relative, the possibility for dialogue with phenomenology is open.[2] On the other hand, our own refusal to accept without question the authoritative statements of eminent phenomenologists indicates clearly that some kind of testing, some process of validation of phenomenological insights by empirical methods, is not only desirable but necessary. Because the rich complexity of man's unique being in the world requires both philosophical reflection and scientific analysis, the contribution of the Swiss psychiatrist, Ludwig Binswanger, becomes both pertinent and important.

Dr. Binswanger came from an established medical family which had an honored reputation in medicine in general and psychiatry in particular. Emerging from a tradition which emphasized scientific rigor and empirical methodology, Binswanger consistently paid close attention to the facts and methods of the natural sciences. Yet early in his career he realized, as many social scientists have realized, that the "object" of study in psychiatry cannot be reduced to biological terms. Particularly significant to him were the insights of psychoanalysis which emphasized the psychic nature of pathological phenomena. Most of his life Binswanger acted as a mediator between psychoanalysis and general psychiatry with its biological orientation. In so doing he strove to formulate a general psychology which would include and correlate both approaches; but in the process he discovered philosophical implications underlying these approaches to human existence. He then turned to philosophy for help in understanding both man and man's approach to himself. Starting from a neo-Kantian background he progressed through the *life* philosophies of Dilthey and Bergson into the phenomenology of Husserl, Scheler, and finally Heidegger. His search for a truthful picture of man was motivated primarily not by a need to achieve academic respectability but by a desire to work successfully with disturbed patients in his family's clinic. Though he could philosophize as

---

2 For a clear statement of the new outlook in science that has emerged with the discoveries of modern physics see A. Eddington, *The Nature of the Physical World*, especially pp. 8-35. He demonstrates how and why physics has given up the idea that only one answer or one frame of reference is right when it comes to explaining the behavior of particular phenomena. The flexibility of science to a multiplicity of approaches opens the door once again for genuine dialogue between philosophy and science. Cf. also the discussion by Heisenberg, *op. cit.*

systematically and abstractly as any Idealist, his writings also clearly indicate that he was amazingly open to the varied insights of philosophers, psychologists, sociologists, literary artists, as well as those gained from his personal and professional experiences. Unlike the eclectic approach which is so prevalent in America, Binswanger's aim was to achieve an integrated, consistent framework so as to become aware of and understand the full reality of human existence as a personal whole. Eclecticism to him represented an untenable outlook, an intellectual hodge-podge which has not done the work of formulating the interrelation between its insights.[3] Binswanger's approach in itself represents a dialogue between social sciences and phenomenology; and it also represents a phenomenological approach which builds upon Heidegger's existential analysis while at the same time being constantly attuned to and tested by everyday experience.

We shall in this chapter follow Binswanger's relationship to Freud's approach. For our purposes Freud may be considered a representative of a social-science approach to human existence, though one which leans hard in the direction of natural science. In the dialogue between these two men we shall see how Binswanger gradually conceived a phenomenology that would act as a framework within which to interpret existentially the data of psychotherapy. The kind of phenomenology represented by Binswanger moves through ideas back to life and not through life to ideas as a kind of a goal. In this as well as in his emphasis upon love, Binswanger closely resembled the concrete approach of Marcel.

Binswanger's expressed aim was to reach the foundations, the existential a priori, of distinctively human being.[4] This may sound like too much

[3] Cf. L. Binswanger, *Ausgewählte Vorträge und Aufsätze*, Vol. I, p. 345. For a much more extensive and detailed critical study of Binswanger's major writings the interested reader is referred to my doctoral dissertation, *Ludwig Binswanger's Existential Phenomenology*, copyright 1962, 402 pp. Bound copies as well as microfilm are available through the Harvard University Library, Cambridge, Massachusetts.

[4] Jacob Needleman presents an interesting, descriptive study of Binswanger's attempt to elucidate the existential a priori in his "Introduction" to *Being-in-the-World*, pp. 9-31, 84 ff., 139-145. Though helpful for those unfamiliar with phenomenology, he apparently has failed to grasp the distinctive point that is to be made about Binswanger's position with relation to Heidegger. For Needleman adopts the Heideggerian a priori of "concern" as *the* basic ontological structure. Binswanger himself consistently and at length in *Grundformen und Erkenntnis des Menschlichen Daseins* attempted to refute Heidegger's absolutization of concern. Actually a controversy has arisen about this issue, which I have discussed in my thesis, pp. 233-241. Heidegger has refused to accept Binswanger's criticism; in collaboration with the psychoanalyst Medard Boss he accused Binswanger of perpetuating subjectivism. Cf. M. Boss, *Psychoanalyse und Daseinsanalytiker*, pp. 88-97. Boss told me personally that Heidegger had "corrected" his manuscript. In the much enlarged English version, *Psychoanalysis and Daseins-*

high-flown philosophizing to empirically minded Americans; but that would be to misunderstand Binswanger. Erik Erikson has repeatedly affirmed that the student of man, and in particular a psychoanalyst, cannot be content merely to consider, however fully, an individual's life history; nor is it enough to add to that a study of the pattern of his relationships. Any perspective of a person will be inadequate unless it also takes into consideration the social dimension which forms a significant part of man's development.[5] Erikson has contended for a multiple approach to man that incorporates the insights of biologist, psychologist, sociologist, and historian. Binswanger was fully in agreement with this appeal for a multiple or interdisciplinary approach; but he would have insisted that it must occur within a frame of reference in which the various phenomena make existential sense. To seek for existential a priori or basic forms of human existence is to look for those dynamic structural foundations which make it both necessary and possible for us to approach man in different ways so as to discover the meaning of the human world. Thus in this chapter we shall also examine the incipient stages of a phenomenology which is truly attuned to and informed by human existence in its everyday world and which is directed toward seeing existential a priori. Along the way we shall also see more deeply into the particular being of Sigmund Freud, to whom every effort to know man in our day must stand in appreciative debt.

analysis, done apparently without Heidegger's assistance, the criticism is less clear and to the point. Binswanger, in a letter to me, acknowledged that some of Heidegger's charges were accurate, that he had in fact misunderstood the nature of Heidegger's ontology; however, he hoped that his own development of a Heideggerian type of existential analysis would be considered a fruitful misunderstanding. Heidegger, Boss, *et al.* do not seem to realize the real challenge of Binswanger's position; for the latter has uncovered basic existential structures, especially love, which simply cannot be fitted into a strictly Heideggerian scheme. My own position would be that the argument should move off the ontological playing field; for ontology seems not only to befog basic existential issues, but also to distort and conceal the radically historical and personal nature of man. The argument of my doctoral thesis was that existential phenomenology is not an auxiliary of but a different approach to the mystery of being than ontology. The thesis includes not only a study of Heidegger but a detailed criticism of Paul Tillich's ontology; it is demonstrated that ontology lends itself to a dogmatic approach which continually forces existential phenomena into an ontological Procrustean bed. See Sadler, *op. cit.,* pp. 311-364.

   [5] E. Erikson, *Childhood and Society,* p. 207 et passim; see also his *Young Man Luther,* p. 20.

2. INTEGRATING PSYCHOANALYSIS INTO PSYCHIATRY

In February of 1907, Dr. Sigmund Freud greeted in his home in Vienna two psychiatrists who had just arrived from the Burghölzli Mental Hospital in Zurich. The one who had initiated and planned this visit to Freud was Dr. Carl Gustav Jung. With him was a twenty-five-year-old physician who had just completed his medical examinations and was now Jung's assistant. His name: Ludwig Binswanger. The relationship Jung established during this first visit with Freud was unsteady, then turbulent and short-lived.[6] However, for Binswanger this meeting was the start of a placid, steady friendship which lasted until Freud died nearly thirty years later. As might be expected, the young Swiss doctor was deeply impressed with the slightly notorious medical pioneer who was more than twenty-five years his senior. His admiration led him to study the early theories and findings of Freud which commenced what Binswanger called the first of five stages in his relationship with Freud.[7] A second visit to Vienna three years later, which afforded him the opportunity to participate in psychoanalytic discussions, convinced Binswanger that Freud was a thoroughgoing natural scientist whose method adhered to the facts of experience. Then began the second stage in which Binswanger intensified his study of Freud's doctrines and tested them clinically.[8]

Not long thereafter began a third stage in which Binswanger set about to demonstrate the significant contribution Freud had made to psychiatry. Freud's approach counteracted the strong trend at that time to regard mental disorders exclusively as a result of neurological impairment. Binswanger's project was to investigate Freud's technique in detail so as to get at its basic concepts and the reasons for them. This was to lead him into a consideration of the presuppositions of Freud's science which, he discovered, were markedly different from the predominant ones in psychiatry at that time. He then had to establish criteria for estimating and evaluating Freud's influence upon psychotherapy. Freud's clinical approach and the general psychiatric practice had two basically different concepts for operation. Psychiatry then concentrated upon the brain as the center of

6 See Ernest Jones, *The Life and Work of Sigmund Freud*, Vol. II, pp. 27-152.
7 See Ludwig Binswanger's essay, "Mein Weg zu Freud," *Der Mensch in der Psychiatrie*.
8 See *ibid.*, pp. 37 ff. and also Binswanger, *Sigmund Freud: Reminiscences of a Friendship*, pp. 88 ff.

disturbances within the human organism, an orientation Freud had himself shared while he worked several years in neurological studies before practicing medicine; however, during the course of his clinical practice, Freud had come to focus upon instincts as determinative for neurotic mental disorder.[9] Although he sided with Freud's position against the limited perspective of brain pathology, Binswanger began to be disillusioned with Freudian doctrine because of its apparent reduction of the dynamics of human behavior to instincts. He was beginning to develop an ambivalence toward Freud which persisted through the years of friendship. He expressed greater respect for Freud than for his admired teacher, the psychiatrist Eugen Bleuler; and he affirmed that Freud's therapeutic method was superior to other methods. Yet he became severely critical of Freud's theories which he had set out to defend. Their exchange of letters at this time reveals that Binswanger was deeply indebted to Freud's trenchant analyses of the disorders of Binswanger's own patients; yet he regretted what he felt were unnecessary topographical and biological descriptions. He gradually realized that Freud's theories carried with them weighty philosophical implications which were one-sided; they needed investigating and balancing, as a remark made by Freud to him in 1910 itself suggested: "None of us has acquired the habit of thinking simultaneously of the ego and conscious processes on the one hand, and the process of the unconscious and sexual instincts on the other." [10] Binswanger was indirectly incited by Freud to reach an understanding of man that would eventually be more comprehensive than psychoanalytic theories, keeping in view both human consciousness and biological processes.

During this third stage, Binswanger assumed the role of a mediator between Freud and general psychiatry, a role which, as he wrote forty years later, was perennially important to him: "Throughout my life I have tried to clarify the scientific foundation of psychoanalysis and its status as a branch of psychiatry." [11] He tried to indicate the needed influence of Freud for psychiatric practice while at the same time going beyond the limitations of Freudian theory by developing a general psychology. In an essay written in 1920 he contrasted psychoanalytic method with other current psychiatric practice, indicating the former's value for therapy.[12] He

---

[9] L. Binswanger, Der Mensch in der Psychiatrie, pp. 39 ff. See also E. Jones, op. cit.
[10] L. Binswanger, Sigmund Freud, op. cit., pp. 6-7.
[11] Ibid., p. 23.
[12] L. Binswanger, "Psychoanalyse und klinische Psychiatrie," Ausgewählte Vorträge und Aufsätze, Vol. II, pp. 40-66.

outlined three major tendencies in clinical psychiatry, ranging from the strict anatomic approach of Bleuler through the descriptive psychological approaches of Kraepelin and Jaspers, to Kretschmer's characterology, which sought to get beneath symptoms and syndromes to inner experience.[13] Though all these approaches were helpful, none had revealed the sick person so well as Freud, who demonstrated as had no other psychiatrist actual psychic conflict.[14] The superiority of the psychoanalytic approach stems from its attempt to understand the personality which has been afflicted by a disorder in its development. Instead of merely classifying symptoms and attempting to trace them back to neurological disorders as was the habit of prevailing psychologies then operative in psychiatry, psychoanalysis plunged into the inner depths of the person, revealing psychic conflict and the intentionality of consciousness.[15] Though he later was to modify the following interpretation of Freud, he here affirmed that Freud's method focused upon a knowing, judging, spiritual being, that is, a man who is not merely an organism caught in the chain of stimulus-response, but a being who is intentionally and creatively oriented toward norms and values. Yet he pointed out that these therapeutic insights were distorted and misinterpreted by Freud's conception of a psychic apparatus; this theoretical apparatus threatened to lose sight of the person by explaining personality quantitatively in terms of the amount of libido which had been either released or repressed. Such quantitative explication would make nonsense of intense inner conflicts in, for example, Hamlet, Antigone, and Lady Macbeth, who manifest phenomena which psychoanalysis of all psychologies is particularly attuned to appreciate. Freud's invaluable contribution was to curb the tendency of followers of Wernicke and Kraepelin to reduce psychic phenomena to the brain structure; yet Freud's reduction of psychic phenomena to instincts was equally mistaken. As later modifiers of Freudian doctrine have also pointed out, if a psychic disturbance is primarily a result of unsatisfactory relationships to other people, then it is illogical and misleading to suggest that the root of the problem is to be discovered in some hypothetical inner mechanism.[16]

---

13 *Ibid.*, pp. 40-49.

14 A more emphatic and detailed account of Freud's contribution with respect to revealing psychic conflict may be found in Philip Rieff, *Freud: The Mind of the Moralist;* see especially ch. 2.

15 L. Binswanger, *op. cit.*, pp. 49 ff.

16 The object-relations school of psychiatry represented by Melanie Klein and W. R. D. Fairbairn has pointed out the defectiveness of the Freudian model; if we are to think of a patient's behavior as determined by relationships to people and primitive feelings about them, then we cannot at the same time think of behavior as determined

In this early essay Binswanger sought to demonstrate what has subsequently been claimed by a host of Freudian revisionists. He claimed that Freud actually had two approaches, a qualitative personal one in therapy and a quantitative, biological-teleological one in the construction of his theories. His conclusion was that the one could not be reduced to the other. Rather, psychiatry of necessity has to consider the human organism in terms of the nervous systems and biological drives, but also it has to study all possible dynamic structures; and to do so it must have the whole man in view. Thus Binswanger, encouraged by Gestalt psychology and phenomenology, was beginning his search for what he himself referred to as the wholeness of man in terms not only of his organic structural dynamics but also his historical uniqueness. To aid him in his quest he suggested that the phenomenological research stemming from Husserl would prove to be extremely helpful and significant, as indeed it was.[17]

In 1922 the first volume of Binswanger's *Introduction Into the Problems of General Psychology* (*Einführung in die Probleme der Allgemeinen Psychologie*, not translated) appeared, dedicated significantly enough to both Bleuler and Freud, the distinctive representatives of very disparate psychiatric positions. However, a second volume which was to elaborate the principles of psychoanalysis, a volume which Freud eagerly awaited, never appeared. In preparing this work, Binswanger had delved into the writings of literary artists and philosophers who also had described and elucidated psychic phenomena; and he began to realize that Freud's explanation of human dynamics was too simplistic, leaving too much unaccounted for. Furthermore, Binswanger was increasingly convinced of the intentional nature of consciousness. Even Freud had stressed intentionality when he referred to the factor in man which has meaning, is oriented to goals, has aims and intentions, and which, strictly speaking, is a mental phenomenon distinct from an organic symptom.[18] Yet Freud's libido theory in effect undercut this intentionality. Binswanger had thus turned to the investigation of intentionality as executed by Brentano and Husserl

by an inner mechanism as visualized by Freud. See Nigel Walker, *A Short History of Psycho-Therapy in Theory and Practice*, pp. 102 ff. The French psychologist Roland Dalbiez, with a perspective not unlike that of Binswanger, has affirmed that only Freud enabled us to realize the truly psychic element of neurosis in terms of inner conflict; but his interpretive model which reduces human phenomena to a biological level would abrogate his original and profound contribution to our understanding of man. See his *Psychoanalytic Method and the Doctrine of Freud*, Vol. I, pp. 201 ff., passim.

17 L. Binswanger, *op. cit.*, pp. 52-64.

18 E.g., see Sigmund Freud, *A General Introduction to Psychoanalysis*, pp. 54 ff.

and by so doing realized that even the scope of his own general psychology was too narrow. What is essential for the progress of psychiatry is nothing less than research which focuses not upon an organism but upon *man as a person*.[19]

As an essay written several years later dealing with the relationship between psychology and psychiatry makes clear, Binswanger was not by any means dispensing with psychology. However, he felt that its usefulness was as a method whereby we become acquainted with universal psychic principles but not necessarily with specific content.[20] The issue is not primarily a methodological one but has to do with the subject matter upon which research is to focus. Granted that in medicine the patient must be viewed as an organism. In this respect Bleuler and others were correct; but they did not have the final say. By this time Binswanger had become acquainted with the writings of the French psychiatrist, Eugene Minkowski, who had been influenced by Bergsonian philosophy. Minkowski had been making a thrust similar to Binswanger's and had pointed out how indigent a strictly organic approach was in terms of explaining the differences between similar but not identical psychic processes, such as the inability to distinguish cognition from recognition, or the different quality of appreciation to be found, for example, in people listening to a great work of music.[21] An organic approach scarcely touches complex phenomena such as aesthetic appreciation, reflection, and memory, whereas to Binswanger phenomenologists in just a few remarks had thrown more light upon them than his entire medical training.[22] His reading of Husserl, Cassirer, Scheler, and others led him to become increasingly disillusioned about the capacities of natural science. He was becoming aware that natural science, as Husserl had so brilliantly demonstrated, was not as matter of fact and empirical as its proponents had claimed; on the contrary, it was beginning to appear to be as much a construction as any other approach. With additional help from the writings of Wilhelm Dilthey, Binswanger realized that there are different kinds of knowing; in science, the mode of knowing is detached and analytical, whereas a more basic form of knowing is understanding

[19] See L. Binswanger, *Der Mensch, op. cit.*, pp. 40 ff. and *Vorträge, op. cit.*, pp. 22, 139. The term *person* here best translates *Mensch*, which in German often has the connotation of "real person" in English. Certainly Binswanger uses it so.

[20] L. Binswanger, *Ausgewählte Vorträge*, Vol. II, pp. 111 ff.

[21] A sample of Minkowski's approach which illustrates his concern with an understanding of existential time may be found in *Existence, op. cit.*, pp. 127-138.

[22] L. Binswanger, *op. cit.*, pp. 122 ff.

(*verstehen*) which involves feeling and imagination.[23] There is no need, Binswanger realized, for a man of medical science to be afraid to admit the important role played by feeling in his perception and understanding of patients. As Bleuler was said to remark that he became aware of schizophrenia in patients when he felt in their presence that they were more foreign to him than the birds and flowers in his garden;[24] so Binswanger confessed that he was most often aware of schizophrenia not by observable symptoms, which are always capable of various interpretations, but by a feeling of lack of rapport. Often when a schizophrenic would enter his office he sensed something like an inner freezing up, which was a kind of barrier he encountered that made community very difficult if not impossible. In a similar way the unity of the person is perceived not by detached analysis but through the eyes of feeling. If the doctor carries with him into a clinic a theoretical construct which has already splintered the person into parts and functions, it is nearly hopeless to expect him to *understand* the *person* who suffers from a split personality. The task of the psychiatrist is to understand the person, however strange he might be.

3. DEVELOPING PHENOMENOLOGICAL PSYCHOANALYSIS

Clearly Binswanger was on his way to developing a new kind of psychology which begins by criticizing the scope, content, and method of existing psychologies. In so doing we can see him beginning to formulate a phenomenological psychology such as suggested by Husserl in his earlier writings. Yet the influence of Scheler and of Binswanger's friend, the Swiss philosopher Paul Häberlin, was extremely marked. Like Scheler, Binswanger put tremendous emphasis upon feelings, and he did not consider them to be merely subjective experiences, inner movements revealing nothing but the interior state of an individual whose psyche is supposedly pent up within his body; on the contrary, Binswanger, again like Scheler, emphasized the intentional nature of feelings. Feelings can reveal directly how we stand with another "object"; thus they can present us with an immediate perception of the other person and of the relationship we may have with him.[25] Also similar to Scheler we see that even at this early stage in

23 *Ibid.*, pp. 131 ff., 146.
24 See R. D. Laing, *The Divided Self*, p. 28.
25 See the essay by F. J. J. Buytendijk, "The Phenomenological Approach to the Problems of Feelings and Emotions," pp. 155-178, in *Psychoanalysis and Existential Philosophy*, H. M. Ruitenbeck, ed., for an extensive, clear argument for seeing feelings as intentional rather than as merely subjective.

his development Binswanger was pressing hard toward a "science" of the person; and like Scheler he interpreted Husserl's phenomenology in such a way as to see it as a wonderfully appropriate method for viewing the person as a whole, in a manner simply not possible to natural sciences. He seems to have been quite unaware or at least unconcerned that the phenomenologists differed, often strongly, among themselves and that Husserl had been stumped by the possibility of a phenomenon which Binswanger took for granted, namely, the direct knowledge of other people. Where Binswanger differed from other phenomenologists was that without perfecting his method he applied it regularly to actual clinical experience; for to him phenomenology gave the doctor a tool which enabled him to analyze his clinical encounter and to distinguish those elements in his experience which came merely from his own subjectivity and those which were actually given by the patient. Particularly relevant was the phenomenon of inner psychic conflict, data which Freud had made available by his unusually perceptive approach to patients,[26] but which his theory elucidated imperfectly.

As a practicing psychoanalyst Binswanger's daily concern for his patient's "history" had an effect upon his evolving conception of phenomenology which made considerable impact upon his later conceptualization of it. By focusing upon the development of the historical person Binswanger shared in the perspective of Dilthey. He differed with the latter in that Dilthey had proposed, as an alternate to natural science's study of man, a science of the spirit (*Geisteswissenschaft*); proposed in this way, Binswanger maintained that it created a bifurcation between nature and spirit which is in fact false to the reality of human existence. Thus Binswanger advocated a science of the person which would incorporate all dimensions and aspects into a whole view. Yet he was inclined to follow Dilthey's direction in seeing the individual person historically rather than to seek the essence of him in one of his acts. In seeking to view and understand a person from the perspective of his whole history, Binswanger was exhibiting a psychoanalytic approach which he had learned from Freud. From this point of view he came to feel that Husserl's idea of consciousness was a lifeless abstraction far removed from the actual person confronting the doctor.

What was disconcerting to Binswanger was that though Freud's method had taught him to focus upon a historical person in the therapeutic encounter, yet Freud's theories reduced man to a vital, organic abstraction. In the unpublished second volume of his general psychology

26 Cf. L. Binswanger, *Ausgewählte Vorträge*, Vol. II, p. 141.

Binswanger had demonstrated to his own satisfaction that Freud was not
nearly so empirical as he claimed to be. In reality, Freud's science was not
based upon actual perception of phenomena but upon the assumption of
hidden dynamics such as strivings, aims, and tendencies. The process of
psychoanalytic theorizing was an original constructing experience, producing such questionable constructs as the "unconscious." [27] Binswanger here
was not disputing the actuality of the data but the validity or the helpful-
ness of the construct. The data had also been illuminatingly presented by
other methods, such as in the creative and philosophical writings of
Schopenhauer, Nietzsche, Dostoevsky, Leibniz, and others.

In an essay published in 1926 Binswanger examined the psychoanalytic modes of experience, understanding, and interpretation, and he
articulated his view that Freud's actual experience with patients was primarily personal and open to personal meanings; because psychoanalysis
involves a special kind of experience, its method of interpretation cannot
be restricted to the boundaries of natural science.[28] Thus it was not Freud
as scientist but Freud as an intuiting human being who had come nearer
the truth of human existence than any other psychologist. Freud covered
up his intuition by a scheme which depersonalized the patient by reducing
him to a biological, almost mechanical apparatus. Yet his vocabulary belied
the scheme; the personal reality which really held the attention of Freud is
disclosed by the numerous personifications employed in speaking about the
psychic apparatus. Freud's famous saying, "The ego is not master of his
own house," is an obvious example. These personifications do not refer to
parts of an apparatus but to a *you* and *me* who initiate or suffer a particular
action.[29] To substantiate his strongly felt awareness of the truthfulness
behind Freud's cumbersome and grossly misleading theories, Binswanger
devoted himself to understanding psychoanalysis critically, which meant to
see it within a larger framework than that adopted by Freud himself. As he
wrote later, "My entire scientific development, in positive as well as negative respects, has been determined by my efforts to formulate the philosophical as well as the scientific basis for psychoanalysis." [30]

Binswanger's basic criticism amounts to a disagreement over the actual
content of psychoanalytic experience and interpretation. The problem was

27 Cf. L. Binswanger, *Der Mensch*, p. 43.
28 See L. Binswanger, *Ausgewählte Vorträge*, Vol. II, pp. 67-80.
29 L. Binswanger, *Der Mensch*, p. 47.
30 L. Binswanger, *Sigmund Freud*, p. 23; see also p. 73.

posed and illuminated in an unforgettable way during a conversation the two had during the summer of 1927. Binswanger, in discussing his disappointment with the outcome of some of his cases, inquired of Freud why some obsessional neurotics fail to take the final step in therapy toward genuine psychoanalytic insight, especially when everything in the course of analysis had prepared them for it. To Binswanger the only answer which could account for the facts was a lack of spirit, by which he meant an inability to rise to the level of personal communication with the doctor and to make a decision for authentic existential meanings. Freud's theories, of course, would leave the spirit out entirely. To his great surprise, Freud replied, "Ja, Geist ist alles." ("Yes, spirit is everything.") [31] Binswanger thought he had misheard Freud; but then the latter went on: "Mankind has always known that it possesses spirit; I had to show it that there are also instincts. But men are always discontented, they cannot wait, they always want something whole and ready-made; however, one must begin somewhere and one progresses only slowly." Their moment of apparent unity was soon shattered when Freud presented to Binswanger a copy of his recently finished, *The Future of an Illusion*. In this, as in most of his theoretical writings, Freud's more consistent belief was patent: the physical constitution of man is everything. As Freud remarked to Binswanger, he stayed in the basement of the dwelling of man's existence. In fact, however, he believed the cellar is all that exists; the upper stories are mere illusion. He had succeeded in demonstrating that the building did have a basement; eventually he or his followers would show it to have only one level.[32] Yet personal communications from Freud, such as his letter of consolation upon the death of one of Binswanger's sons in 1929, revealed a touching expression of the man Freud that went far beyond what one would expect after reading, for example, his essay on mourning. These signs as well as the "Freudian slip" above were sufficient to show "how far Freud the man surpasses Freud the scientist in largeness and depth of humanity." [33] Thus Binswanger felt justified in going beyond Freud's theories, because in so doing he would not only serve his patients better but also be more loyal to the person, insights, and major contributions of his friend.

[31] See L. Binswanger, *ibid.*, pp. 80-81; also the translation of his essay, "Freud and the Magna Charta of Clinical Psychiatry" in Needleman, trans., *Being-in-the-World*, p. 182.
[32] *Ibid.*, p. 21, fn., and pp. 96-99.
[33] *Ibid.*, p. 85.

Binswanger was intent upon developing a phenomenological psychology which grasped the wholeness of the person; that is, he attempted to get
at the basic structure of human existence before making a distinction
between healthy and sick people.[34] This led him to focus upon different
kinds of phenomena than had Freud; whereas the latter gave special attention to pathological symptoms, Binswanger also devoted himself to the
study of a variety of phenomena we commonly regard as quite healthy.
Originally he followed Husserl's direction to seek the essential structures
and content of consciousness. Yet in an early essay he emphasized that
phenomenology differed from other methods in that it enabled us to participate in the object itself; it thus overcame the distance set by acts of
judgment, to say nothing of prejudgment or prejudice. Thus to Binswanger
the phenomenologist does not act like a scientist but much more like an
artist, who describes sympathetically the essential features of an object as
these have become manifest to his aesthetic vision.[35] He definitely was not
interested in attempting to execute the advanced stages of Husserl's phenomenological reduction. What was important to him was to recognize the
basic intuition which opened up directly the essential forms of ordinary
experience, much in the manner suggested by Scheler. The intuitive grasp
of the basic human structures would enable the doctor to view the otherwise "foreign" patient within a framework that was common to both of
them. Thus phenomenological intuition for him was nearly identical to
Scheler's theory about the feeling of genuine sympathy (Einfühlung-
theorie) and not the eidetic intuition as suggested by Husserl.[36] As he
made clear, this feeling of sympathy was not a subjective phenomenon but
an intersubjective one; it was an inner perception whereby I have direct
grasp of another's psychic life. Genuine sympathy is a reality that a subjectivistic psychology which talks about self-contained inner states and projec-
tions can never understand.

It is interesting to see how the method worked in Binswanger's hands
at that time. Phenomenology in the clinic does not proceed as merely
descriptive psychology, which records what the patient says, makes judgments, forms concepts, and then carries out investigation as it sees these
concepts applying within a predetermined framework. The phenomenologist refrains from this process by attempting to enter sympathetically the
phenomenal expression of the patient and by seeking to visualize what the

---

34 See L. Binswanger, Ausgewählte Vorträge, Vol. I, p. iii.
35 Cf. ibid., pp. 25 ff.
36 Cf. ibid., pp. 34 ff.

words mean to him; that is, the phenomenological psychoanalyst moves from what is uttered to what is meant, which is to say, the intentional object which gave rise to the phenomenal utterance. In other words, the doctor as phenomenologist seeks to enter into the intentional structure of the experience so as to get at the meanings to which the patient's words refer.[37] As indicated earlier, Binswanger was not advocating only the use of phenomenology nor was he disparaging the use of other ordinary methods. Actually he was suggesting an interdisciplinary approach to the person; yet man is best seen as person from within the perspective of phenomenology. Thus, for example, in dealing with a schizophrenic Binswanger would perform an analysis of the patient's behavior; but a diagnosis of autistic thinking would not illuminate what was behind the strange, bizarre behavior. Binswanger refused to acknowledge the impotence of psychoanalytic method with such people, as was the standard practice then. With the aid of phenomenology he saw a way to conceptualize how autism really feels,[38] as we shall see in detail later in the book. Binswanger realized that by feeling our way into the schizophrenic's experience we discover a person whose basically personal intentional structure has been disastrously altered. His relations to the external world, to people, to himself, to values of all sorts have been so altered that we see that he has undergone a radical change in his outlook on life (*Weltanschauung*). What we find here is not a "loss of reality" but a distinctive qualitative change in orientation to value and especially to the value of other people (*Mitmenschen*).[39]

To see a changed outlook in a person requires the psychiatrist to see the person in terms of his total life history, as he wrote later in another essay.[40] This emphasis had two implications for his development. First, it meant he discarded the tripartite anthropological scheme suggested by Scheler in which the person is conceived as containing three levels: the somatic, the psychic, and the spiritual.[41] His emphasis was upon the integral interaction of the various processes in existence which this view may tend to distort or ignore; [42] that is, Binswanger early adopted a view which has become commonplace through the development of psychosomatic

---

[37] *Ibid.*, pp. 36 ff.
[38] *Ibid.*, pp. 38 ff.
[39] *Ibid.*, p. 43.
[40] L. Binswanger, "Lebensfunktion und innere Lebensgeschichte," *ibid.*, pp. 52 ff.
[41] *Ibid.*, p. 54; cf. Scheler's *Die Stellung des Menschens im Kosmos*.
[42] The dangers of working with a tripartite structure can easily be observed in the writings of a Viennese psychiatrist, Viktor Frankl, who consistently stresses the radical independence of the human spirit in its attempt to achieve meaning. See bibliography for details of his writings.

medicine. At the same time, however, he insisted that the medical practice
had focused almost exclusively upon what he called "life functions," and
especially what we usually think of as functional disturbances in the organism. Yet, as he indicated to Freud, the doctor must also take into consideration the spiritual factor, or what in English we might call the "human
element" in a situation. It is only by considering the spiritual in man that
we can account for the continuity of the person of which we are intimately
aware. This inner continuity, which includes and connects the vast variety
of contents from an individual's experiences, he referred to as *inner life
history* as distinct from life function. By giving his attention to inner life
history a doctor has a way of grasping, for example, hysterical psychosis as a
genuinely human phenomenon which can be understood, not merely analyzed as a peculiar psychosomatic occurrence to be treated without understanding. By distinguishing between life functions and life history, both of
which must be given consideration by the psychiatrist, Binswanger opened
up a way for genuine psychotherapy for schizophrenic patients who
otherwise would have been deprived of it.

In focusing upon inner life history, we are immediately dealing with a
dimension of experience in which the principle of causality is simply not
applicable, at least not in the way it is within an organic perspective.
Historical response within the intentional structure of meanings is quite
different from mere motor reaction to external stimuli; this response involves the developing character of an individual including his life aims, his
fears, his immediate goals, the quality of his relationships, and his decisions. These are all aspects of his freedom. We see Binswanger here working his way toward a position which will find itself amazingly compatible
with Heidegger's existential analytic and away from any notion of an instantaneous grasp of essence; for to Binswanger, the essence of the person is
unfolded in his history.[43] As he makes clear in another essay, by investigating the inner life history of a person one focuses upon the spiritual
becoming of his individuality.[44] This is quite a different phenomenological
object from the pure essences sought by Husserl in transcendental subjectivity. What Binswanger is interested in is the insight into and the interpretation of the formative development of a historical individual, which is

---

[43] L. Binswanger, *op. cit.*, p. 64. His position here is amazingly similar to that of
Gordon Allport. It is puzzling and ironic that Allport showed little appreciation for
Binswanger's writings.

[44] See L. Binswanger, "Geschehnis und Erlebnis," *Ausgewählte Vorträge*, Vol. II,
pp. 141 ff.

also the very subject matter of good biography and of much social science. Binswanger's interpretation of historical experience indicates that an individual is not best viewed in terms of striving toward some separate universal meanings, a questionable view, suggesting that the individual is devoid of meaning to start off with. Rather, the person acts in response to meanings which represent various modes of existential possibilities. Unless meanings and essences are related to possible existential modes in terms of life histories, they are concepts which merely hang in mid-air.[45] Presumably, Binswanger would thus highly endorse such excellent psychoanalytic biography as provided by Erik Erikson in his study of the young man Luther, which sympathetically portrays a unique spiritual individual in his wholeness, including his life functions, basic strivings, and personal meanings within his unrepeatable social-historical situation.[46]

In an essay on dream interpretation appearing in 1930, we see further how his method applies to the illumination of human existence. Although this essay is tediously long and in parts is highly questionable today, nevertheless it marks a radical departure from typical psychoanalytic hermeneutics, and one which has had increasing support.[47] As is now well known, Freud introduced a new conception of meaning as it applied to dreams. Most of Freud's predecessors conceived of dreams, as well as autistic lan-

[45] Cf. L. Binswanger, *Vorwort, ibid.,* pp. 24-25.

[46] E. H. Erikson, *Young Man Luther;* see also his recent article, "The Nature of Clinical Evidence," *Insight and Responsibility,* pp. 49-80, in which he argues for a position not far removed from Binswanger's, one which includes the structural, dynamic, genetic, and adaptive viewpoints needed in psychoanalysis but also stresses the immediacy of clinical evidence which results from the personal communication between therapist and patient. Erikson rejects an absolutization of the Freudian instinct theory. The so-called instincts are not inborn, but are *drive fragments,* as he calls them, which must be assembled and given meaning throughout the process of child training and maturation. (*Childhood and Society,* p. 95.)

[47] See Binswanger, "Traum und Existenz," *Vorträge,* I, translated by Needleman, *Being-in-the-World,* pp. 222-248. A much more penetrating and reliable study in this vein is the book by Medard Boss, *Der Traum und Sein Auslegung,* translated as *The Analysis of Dreams.* Boss refuses to see the dream merely as a symptom of an inner disorder or psychic wish, but stresses that it is also and primarily an existential phenomenon which includes deep insight into one's world, one's basic attitudes, fears, hopes, and even indicates an aspect of genuine freedom. The clinical material here as well as in his study of sexual perversions is convincing. He strongly criticizes Binswanger for not seeing the truly existential character of dreams, and the latter's more recent statements suggest that he accepted the criticism. Binswanger, at the time of the essay in question, was engaged upon a study of Greek philosophy, especially that of Heraclitus, which had little practical value to his phenomenological development and led him to write extraordinary pieces that from one level seem mostly to be manifestations of intellectual exhibitionism; see for example his *"Heraklits Auffassung des Menschen,"* in *Ausgewählte Vorträge,* Vol. I.

guage, as disturbances of logic due to a disorder or relaxation of physio-
logical functions, without seeing its inherent connection with other psychic
events. Freud maintained that dream images were connected with previous
experiences, that they had primarily psychic rather than merely physical
causes, as is easily suggested by the method of word association. To Freud
dream images were symbols of unconscious processes.

Yet it is questionable if the term "symbol" as used by Freud is appropriate here. Properly, a symbol is something which communicates the
meaning of what it represents; however, the traditional psychoanalytic
method involves imposing a constructed meaning upon each manifestation.[48] Thus, in a dream where one stands at the base of a tall tree, it
would most likely be said that the tree is a phallic symbol and represents
some sort of repressed wish. Yet one should pursue the matter further and
inquire, if such is the case, what a phallus means to this particular person.
Is it a symbol of aggression or pleasure, a source of anxiety or pride, a sign
of a central or a peripheral concern, etc.? Freud's technique really converts
a symbol into a sign, which is merely a manifest substitute for a latent
reality. Whereas a symbol is a communicative representation, a sign is an
arbitrary substitute. Freud's symbol is a psychic sign in most cases, and acts
as a symbol only with reference to one mode of existence; it communicates
only on one level of meaning. In other words, his symbol is hardly more
than a symptom.

Binswanger rejected a rigid libidinal framework which involved constant imposition of sexual meanings upon dream images. He suggested a
different interpretation of dream symbols, which would see them in terms
both of inner life history and of life functions. In studying the dreams of
numerous patients, particularly manic-depressives, he was struck by the
images of rising and falling, of being carried up into the sky, falling off
cliffs, of being struck, as we say, from "out of the blue." A tree might just
as well signify an existential aspiration as a repressed sexual wish; and at
the same time it might suggest anxiety over the danger of falling and being
broken to pieces in the process. At that time, because of the newness
of his contribution and under the influence of his studies of Heraclitus,
Binswanger unwisely segregated dreaming and waking into the respective
categories of life function and inner life history; nevertheless, he did

---

[48] See the more detailed discussions of this problem in Roland Dalbiez, *Psychoanalytic Method and the Doctrine of Freud*, Vol. II, pp. 98-153 and also Needleman,
op. cit., pp. 60-77.

affirm the unity of the phenomena within the person. Unlike the tendency of Freud's theory, he refused to allow the phenomena of the spirit of man to be reduced to bio-psychic process. The concept of instinct and the concept of spirit are simply incommensurable.[49] The analyst, to be true to the human reality of himself and his patient, must see psychic manifestations truly as symbols of the spirit within the inclusive process of becoming a person.

Another graphic example of how Binswanger's phenomenological method differs from strictly Freudian analysis can be seen in his interpretation of greed as an existential possibility. Freudian thought characterizes greed largely as an extension of an unresolved conflict from the supposedly anal stage in personality development; a miserly individual is often said to have an anal personality. Binswanger did not deny genuine Freudian insights which point to psychogenetic factors that may well be prevalent in a greedy individual. Yet he revealed so much more than a strictly Freudian approach.

A greedy person is one whose dominant existential mode is that of filling, such as filling up bags and boxes with gold. This filling does not derive from simple selfishness, from not wanting to give up, but much more from a delight and passion for filling; this is a primary meaning, and not any fondness for money or feces. Binswanger sought to get at the real "motives," the dynamics which lie behind the possible psychogenetic origins of greed. That is, he wanted to see what it "means" to be greedy. He went on to illuminate greed in this way:

> In the need to fill and pile things up we see one of the basic traits of the feeling tone of a greedy person; this extends to his body as a container as well as to boxes and barrels, socks and sacks. The hollow spaces not only serve for piling things up; they also serve for hiding things from the looks and grasp of his fellow man. It is thought best to keep them remote and well hidden. Along with this goes the fact that the greedy one also sits or squats on his money as a hen on her eggs, so as to cover it with his own body and defend it from the outside. Pertaining in an essential way to his passion are the secrecy and seclusion of his possession, as well as his association with it. Instead of a desire to give and to part with, such as is possible only through contact with one's fellow men, here there is a desire for secret inspection and handling, or just intellectual handling, which is counting. It is in such activity that the secret delight and orgies of this kind of feeling lie. I don't believe that in this case we have a fetish trait.

[49] L. Binswanger, *Being-in-the-World*, p. 246.

. . . Money can scarcely represent as a fetish does the power and enjoyment of the real thing, such as a tuft of hair representing the whole
woman. The irrational trait of greed is precisely the Molochlike quality
which has, as a consequence, a definite spatial interpretation of the world,
that is, a strong emphasis upon the significance of space which is filled up,
secluded, covered, and hidden; along with this, the body is conceived as
a hollow. A definite manner of body consciousness pertains essentially to
greed. Psychoanalysis saw that rightly. But even so, there is also a definite
interpretation of time which pertains to greed. Time doesn't stand still
for the greedy one, as it does for some neurotic who is constantly forced
to revolve around himself and thus loses his sense of history. Here time
receives its meaning only from images of snatching and filling; it is not
counted by hours and years but in terms of the possibilities for filling.
One's personal, experienced sense of time is thereby given its arrangement
and tempo. One can be greedy with one's time, which shows that time
has been spatialized in a Molochlike way, insofar as little spaces of time
are busily and constantly stuffed, as though in a box, and are locked in,
piled up, and jealously guarded. Not wanting to give up time is only a
secondary aspect of greed. Temporalization, historical becoming, actually
loses its possibilities through the stultifying monotony of greed, which
becomes the monomania of the greedy one. What happens to time is that
it becomes time sums which can be added like bits and pieces.[50]

Binswanger continued to elaborate on the pervasive and determining character of greed as it affects one's sense of death, interpersonal relations, the
social world, and participation in historic events. In each case there is a
pronounced lack of possible meaning because in each case the existential
possibility is shunted off into categories of grabbing, possessing, hording,
and keeping oneself safely withdrawn from the possible possession of
others. Other people are thought of primarily as means to an end, not as
persons in whose developing lives we might share. A greedy person will
relate to others in terms of how he can take hold of them, impressing
them, catching them at a weak spot so as to seduce them, embarrass them,
sell them something they don't really need, force them into something
they don't really want, and so forth. These impersonal relations with persons are not necessarily manifestations of sadism, but are just another
expression of a tendency to expand one's possessions, to fill one's life with
stolen meanings. The greedy individual is also, however, quite alone with
himself and his demon. Psychoanalysis was correct, Binswanger pointed out,
to demonstrate the close connection between greed and the abdomen, for
such a person lives much more for the "belly" and what it takes in rather

50 L. Binswanger, *Ausgewählte Vorträge*, II, pp. 170-171; my translation.

than by or for the mind or spirit. In terms of the existential possibilities of love, art, and religion, it is a form which never gets off the ground.

This phenomenological study is not of any one individual; nor is it a portrayal of an essential structure of human existence; nor is it really an ideal type as defined by Max Weber, which would make it out to be a useful but nevertheless fictional approximation of a concrete actuality.[51] In fact it is a manifestation of an existential possibility. For us in this era of carefully calculated time, which Benjamin Franklin taught means money and is thus to be spent wisely, not wasted, Binswanger's analysis has frightening and widespread implications; it is a possibility which is becoming all too prevalent and, perhaps, comes too close to home. It presents us with a picture that sees the essentials of what we usually call a personality trait in terms of existential wholeness. It neither hangs in the air of abstract speculation nor is it a possible result of ordinary scientific methods. In fact what we are beginning to see here is the development of a new kind of empiricism which truly lets the facts speak for themselves.[52]

In this analysis of greed Binswanger had expanded his concept of interpretation so as to include life functions and even parts of the body within an existential perspective. He told of an incident that occurred in a ward of his clinic which brought home to him the truth that bodily functions themselves are often symbolic of existential meaning and thus must be understood existentially. An extremely withdrawn patient, one who had not communicated verbally for a long period, one day developed a severe coughing spell which brought about such violent choking that it was feared she would die. Binswanger broke psychoanalytic rules by forcefully intervening, shaking the patient so violently that the choking stopped. This intervention, he discovered intuitively, met with a vague personal response.

---

[51] See Weber's description of an ideal type in *The Methodology of the Social Sciences*, pp. 89-95. Weber's "type" would probably receive the same censure from Binswanger that Freud's concepts received, because in this case it is a deliberate construction imposed upon a situation; yet if seen from the viewpoint of sympathetic, imaginative visualization of basic characteristics in a given social situation this concept of Weber's might prove to be exceedingly useful in establishing a dialogue between sociology and phenomenology or what we might call existential sociology.

[52] Much more extensive analysis of this personality type can be found in Binswanger's study of manic-depressive psychosis, *Über Ideenflucht* (1933). In this book he revealed, for example, that a manic phase is really a particular mode of existence that can be characterized as a "springing" one—in which a person springs from one meaning to another without integrating the individual meanings into any coherent pattern other than to keep springing. It is thus a life characterized by exceptional superficiality, such as suggested by the person who jumps hastily from one subject to another without remaining long enough with any given subject to learn anything or receive anything from it.

Such a response on the part of the patient, he explained, occurred because the event took place within a context of trust, which enabled the patient to interpret the violent handling as a sign of sympathy on the part of the doctor.[53] Binswanger had intuited the choking, a life function, in terms of a personal communication, not merely as a call for help to relieve the choking but as a call for sympathetic understanding and a cry for genuine concern. In the same way the patient "heard" the doctor's answer through his violent gesture. Thus long before the penetrating studies by Marcel and Merleau-Ponty on the same subject, Binswanger realized that I do not merely *have* a body; also, and more basically, *I am my body*. The body, he pointed out in this same essay, has a language of its own. Hysteria, for example, to a perceptive person can reveal an inner life history, which is actually an insight underlying much of Freud's otherwise misleading theory. A twitch, for example, does not merely indicate a nervous disorder; it shows that there is something wrong with *me*. Bodiliness thus takes on a new meaning within an existential perspective. How one considers one's body, the attitudes one has toward it, are extremely important. In some neurotics and psychotics the body becomes envisaged as the hiding place for threatening powers which can torment a person and drive him to existential emptiness, boredom; this happens especially when the environing world, and especially social reality, becomes meaningless. Lack of meaningful relationships with others drives an individual back to himself where the bodily condition becomes predominant, where life functions dominate life history; such had occurred with the above catatonic patient. When one's past becomes buried and the future is cut off from significant possibilities, one is then stuck in an isolated present. And what is more present than one's body? [54] Thus, as Binswanger was to say in his notable address on the occasion of Freud's eightieth birthday, there is more than health to think about; undoubtedly it is one of man's greatest goods, deserving the full protection of society, but it must be incorporated within the total significance possible to human existence.[55]

[53] L. Binswanger, *Ausgewählte Vorträge*, I, pp. 136 ff.
[54] See R. Laing's *The Divided Self*, ch. 4, for a penetrating existential examination of two basically different attitudes toward one's body and the implications they have for the development of one's total outlook. He contrasts what he terms the embodied and the unembodied self; the latter is typical of some existentialists, psychotics, and gnostics whose negative attitude toward their own bodies lead them to formulate theories of existence which are extremely negative. Their deep suspicion of the worst in man is, he suggests, a result of the lack of love.
[55] L. Binswanger, *Being-in-the-World*, p. 166.

4. RE-EVALUATING FREUD IN THE LIGHT OF
EXISTENTIAL PHENOMENOLOGY

In the latter address Binswanger had an opportunity to re-examine his attempt for over twenty years to understand and interpret Freud's psychoanalytic theories and to integrate them within his own developing existential perspective.[56] At this time Binswanger realized that much of his difficulty in past attempts to interpret Freud resulted from trying to understand his theories within a perspective of psychology. To understand Freud's basic idea of a psychic apparatus, however, one should begin instead with a perspective of biology. For, it was Freud's intention to trace psychic phenomena back to the organism, especially in terms of instincts.[57] Thus, as he said in his address, Freud's basic working conceptualization of human existence is *Homo natura*, man as natural being, interpreting nature in the usual sense understood by natural science.[58] As he had pointed out at length previously, this idea is a scientific construct which reduces man to one dimension, the level of bodily functions. The mistake in absolutizing natural science, as Freud seems to have done, is that one then ignores the fact that there are various modes of perception which cannot be reduced to other modes or translated into other categories.[59] Natural science approaches reality with a perceptual mode fixed upon the past in attempting to trace effects (or symptoms) in terms of antecedent results (causes). Psychology, however, cannot be restricted to this orientation, because it must focus primarily upon the historical present.[60] Freud's mistake in reducing man to a strictly natural level, in which physical needs are given authority over the whole of existence, is that he puts man in a world which is devoid of existential meaning.[61] This produces a dangerous distortion, one which has drastic cultural implications, as our era has witnessed all too vividly.

[56] L. Binswanger, "Freuds Auffassung des Menschen im Lichte der Anthropologie," *Ausgewählte Vorträge*, I, pp. 159-189; translated by Needleman, *Being-in-the-World*, pp. 149-179, which from here on are the pages cited in the notes.
[57] See Binswanger's article written in the same year, "Freud and the Magna Charta of Clinical Psychiatry," *ibid.*, pp. 194-198.
[58] L. Binswanger, "Freud's Conception of Man in the Light of Anthropology," *ibid.*, pp. 154-155.
[59] *Ibid.*, p. 173.
[60] *Ibid.*, pp. 155-156.
[61] *Ibid.*, p. 175.

Freud's theories have undoubtedly been extremely useful in showing up the economy of human dynamics; the phenomenon of repression is a prime example. Nevertheless, his underlying perspective of *Homo natura* prevented Freud from penetrating as extensively as he might have into a fuller understanding of human dynamics. So long as Freud spoke about the *wish,* which for him set the psychic mechanism into full operation, he was referring to a realm of meaning which goes far beyond mere physical satisfaction.[62] Yet Freud's constructive idea is not open to the multiplicity of meanings which fuel and set the course of human life. Though Freud had called attention to man's historical development, his theory fails to appreciate genuine historical change by its exaggerated emphasis upon a constant factor, the instincts. Thus his psychic mechanism tends to eliminate human freedom, which from a therapeutic viewpoint is what the therapist is attempting to help the patient achieve. By eliminating meanings and freedom it would become impossible to conduct psychotherapy and to appreciate the genuine greatness even of Freud's own existence. For within his naturalistic perspective one cannot really tell why a man would give himself so tirelessly to a search for truth, nor why he saw it to be his mission in history to suffer so as to wrest the truth from its hiding place in man's ignorance and self-deception.[63]

We find here a consistent theme of Binswanger that a genuine appreciation of Freud the man will prevent us from identifying his theoretical constructs with the whole of his existence or with the existence of any man. In this interpretation and tribute to Freud, Binswanger would certainly agree with the eloquent statement by a French interpreter, Roland Dalbiez:

> Psychoanalytic investigation does not explain the philosophical aspect of philosophy, the artistic aspect of art, the scientific aspect of science, the moral aspect of morality, or the religious aspect of religion. The specific nature of the spiritual values eludes the instrument of investigation which Freud's genius has created. . . . [We might say, then, that] Freud's work is the most profound analysis that history has ever known of the less than human elements in human nature.[64]

Not only do Freud's theories fail to indicate the human greatness of their originator but they also inadequately point to a burning moral con-

---

[62] *Ibid.,* p. 164.
[63] *Ibid.,* p. 171.
[64] R. Dalbiez, *op. cit.,* Vol. II, pp. 325-327. See also J. Nuttin, *Psychoanalysis and Personality* for a critique of Freud's reductionistic model, pp. 42-60.

cern which underlay Freud's theory and practice. As Binswanger pointed out, Freud was deeply against man's all too prevalent tendency to live "beyond his means." [65] Freud strongly opposed man's reckless phantasy whereby one perpetuates wishful thinking so as to avoid facing the difficulties involved in assuming responsibility for the physical and unconscious aspects of his life. Thus man perpetuates what Sartre has called "bad faith"; [66] it was Freud's goal to free man from this delusion so that he could find the freedom to live his truth. Binswanger pointed to the deeply moral character of Freud which a superficial or literal acceptance of his theory of instincts and psychic apparatus would conceal. As Philip Rieff has also demonstrated at length, Freud's concentration upon the suffering individual really breaks the identification between psychology and natural science, because he revealed the moral subject in the midst of conflict struggling for decision and self-mastery. Yet at the same time Freud was prisoner of a naïve concern for the nature which drives men's history, so that he constantly looked at prehistory, at nature, in such a way as to ignore theoretically what really held his attention. Freud, acting within the role of scientist, was really a moralist who has helped us tremendously to grow unsentimental about ourselves so as to live honestly with ourselves and others.[67]

Binswanger's insight into the deeply moral and highly complex factors in Freud's own personality, an insight now shared by many others, nevertheless does not answer the question: Why should Freud, with his extraordinary intuitive penetration into the depths of man's spirit, have chosen a "natural" model in which to express his insights, a model which proved to be so inappropriate and misleading? Binswanger pondered this question and twenty years later gave his answer in an address honoring Freud's one hundredth birthday. Marking what he called his fifth stage in his relationship to Freud and his teachings, Binswanger expanded his interpretation of Freud's underlying idea of *Homo natura*. Freud at times operated as a natural scientist with a cool, detached, highly analytical deportment with respect to his subject matter. Yet there was another side to his concept of nature that had been frequently overlooked. In fact Freud had implicitly proposed a new conception of nature, as is indicated by the development

[65] L. Binswanger, "Freud's Conception of Man," *op. cit.*, p. 177.
[66] Jean-Paul Sartre, *Being and Nothingness*, pp. 47-70.
[67] See Philip Rieff, *Freud: The Mind of the Moralist*, especially pp. xiii, 18, 193, 308-328.

of his theory of the death instinct in conflict with the life instinct.[68] Actually Freud's vision of nature was extremely romantic; it was not merely scientific. It is quite significant that his decision to enter medicine came after reading the highly mythical and romantic *Fragmentes über die Natur,* once ascribed to Goethe. Another indication of his romanticism is seen in his childhood remembrance of Leonardo da Vinci; another clear indication of it is to be found in his letters written during trips to the Alps and to Italy. Freud's deepest attitude toward nature was Greeklike reverence; he was awed by it, he respected it, and he sought to penetrate its mysteries. Here his positivistic background was humbled before the unfathomable, unknowable mystery of nature.[69] Binswanger's unusual interpretation is easily documented; in addition to those instances already cited, we find Freud's articulate sense of mystery in attempting to interpret dreams. Although it is possible to get from the manifest to the latent content in a dream, the therapist ends by confronting an unknowable mystery in the deepest level of the unconscious process, which, he wrote, "is the obscure, inaccessible part of our personality; the little we know about it we have learnt from the study of dream-work and the formation of neurotic symptoms, and most of that is of a negative character, and can only be described as being all that the ego is not." [70] For all the analytic concentration given it, the unconscious remains for the most part concealed, and one remains hesitant to say what exactly is its basic nature.[71]

With the aid of his phenomenological method applied to an interpretation of Freud's writings, Binswanger discovered the essence of psychoanalysis to lie not in its supposedly scientific theory but in its reverent respect for the unfathomable being of man conceived as nature, a respect which is inseparable from Freud's perseverance and unclouded purity of heart. Freud not only created a new applied science or technique for cure, he also provided a new and different kind of possibility for experience and scientific exploration with regard to the unconscious, and especially unconscious intentionality. Thus in the image he presented of man, Freud actually brought human existence and nature closer together.[72] Before him we

[68] L. Binswanger, "Mein Weg zu Freud," *Der Mensch in der Psychiatrie,* pp. 53-54 ff.

[69] *Ibid.,* pp. 57 ff.

[70] Freud, "Revision of the Theory of Dreams," *New Introductory Lectures on Psychoanalysis,* p. 98 et passim.

[71] L. Binswanger, "Mein Weg zu Freud," *op. cit.,* p. 59.

[72] Though his emphasis is different, Binswanger would agree with the interpretation offered by Erik Erikson in his address on the same occasion, that Freud presented

thought we lived mostly in a world of mere consciousness. Freud disturbed that narrow world and showed how small, restricted, and dishonest it is; he also showed how deep-reaching into nature the psyche of man is. He gave us a conception of nature in which the subject is viewed as a natural event within the natural order.[73] It might be said that Freud's vision rediscovered nature in man, that man might become truly natural; but in so doing Freud has suggested to us a new, richer, broader concept of nature, which is our *human* nature.

Even though Binswanger's admiration for the genius and contribution of Freud was tremendously profound, it is obvious that he could not be satisfied with an image and structural framework for conceptualization which essentially depersonalizes man. Both the therapist in his confrontation with his patients, as well as each individual man in his historical development, must be open to the personal reality in which transpires the essential relationship of I-Thou. As great a help as psychoanalysis has been to overcoming the deficiencies in the narrow scientific constructs of the past, yet reductionistic concepts in both natural science and psychoanalysis, when applied to the reality of spirit or human existence, make as much sense as a man who tried to understand music by investigating the radio that transmits it. Human existence must be seen within a larger approach that is appropriately attuned to it, one which especially appreciates the struggle man lives to become truly human; as Binswanger wrote some thirty years ago:

> Man is no longer merely an animated organism, but a "living being" who has origins in the finite life process of this earth, and who dies its life and lives its death; illness is no longer an externally or internally caused disturbance of the substance or function of the organism, but the expression of a disturbance of the "normal" course of a life on the way to its death. But, we must add, here "man" is not yet man in the full sense of the word, for to be a man does not mean merely to be a creature begotten by living-dying life, cast into it and beaten about, and put in high spirits or low spirits by it; it means to be a being that looks its own and man-

us with a new focal awareness of man leading to responsible self-awareness which overcomes illusion; the object of this focus transcends the natural-science scope because of Freud's unique method for acquiring evidence, namely, the psychotherapeutic contract, which involves a qualitative relationship beyond the level of subject-object as ordinarily conceived. See his essay in *Freud and the 20th Century*, Benjamin Nelson, ed., pp. 79-101, also included in *Insight and Responsibility*, *op. cit.* In some ways closer to Binswanger is Jerome Bruner's description, that Freud sees man as an unfinished product of nature, which is really a new natural image. In the Nelson volume, pp. 277-285.

[73] L. Binswanger, "Mein Weg zu Freud," *op. cit.*, p. 61.

kind's fate in the face, a being that is "steadfast," i.e. one taking its own
stance, or one standing on its own feet. . . . The fact that our lives are
determined by the forces of life, is only one side of the truth; the other is
that we determine these forces as our fate. Only the two sides together
can take in the full problem of sanity and insanity. Those who, like Freud,
have forged their fates with the hammer—the work of art he has created
in the medium of language is sufficient evidence of this—can dispute this
fact least of all.[74]

The man who shapes his fate is a human being such as portrayed in
the framework of Heidegger's analysis. It was his analysis that Binswanger
discovered to be the most helpful in formulating a perspective that illuminates the wholeness of man. The unusual interpretation and development
Binswanger made of Heidegger has immensely furthered the progress of
existential phenomenology. With the help of Heidegger, Binswanger enlarged and refined our understanding of personal existence; yet as he himself would have been the first to admit, he might not have done so without
the insights and stimulus of that historical existence known as Sigmund
Freud.

[74] L. Binswanger, *Sigmund Freud*, p. 90; also *Being-in-the-World*, p. 204.

PART TWO

Developing a Phenomenology
of Personal Existence

7

⌒⌒⌒

Exploring the Meaning of Existential Space

1.

The phenomenologies already examined have been quite different in many significant ways. Nevertheless all of them have had some essential points in common. Each philosopher has had a deep sense of crisis in the important matter of man's self-understanding. Phenomenology as a whole represents a profound criticism of narrow attitudes toward reality. In particular it has attacked notions about human existence which lie deeply embedded in much of our so-called common sense and which in turn underlie many philosophical and scientific theories. Phenomenologists have devastatingly attacked an intellectualist approach to reality, such as associated with manifold forms of rationalism and idealism. Perhaps more relevant to the American scene, they have also exposed and criticized physicalist assumptions pervasive in much contemporary Western culture. Reared on strong doses of Positivism in which natural sciences were absolutized as the only legitimate avenue of truth, our cultural tendency has been to forget the sphere of existential meaning or to dismiss it as beneath the dignity of serious intelligent analysis. Thus we too easily lose sight of human transcendence in which all knowledge and science are grounded. In both intellectualism and physicalism experience is leveled. On the one hand, the rich mystery of the lived world is ignored; on the other, it is reduced to one fact among others. The latter reduction leads to the unwarranted assumption that all reality exists upon a homogeneous, one-dimensional plane. Phenomenology has called for a return to the immediacy and the original givenness of experience, of which science is but a second-order expression.[1] In order to understand the particular truths of science and to discover the truth about distinctively human existence, phenomenology has attempted to evoke an immediate awareness of the basic experience of our existence in the world.

One aim of *existential* phenomenology has been to investigate our primordial awareness so as to develop insight into basic existential structures in which knowledge and conceptual truth emerge. On the basis of such insight existential phenomenology attempts to delineate these basic structures or existential a priori, which constitute the essential givenness of experience. Phenomenological analysis has already elucidated many universal structures of both individual subjectivity and intersubjectivity. Human existence has been illuminated as being in the world and basic structural features of human space and time have become manifest. Nevertheless the characterization of basic existential structures remains too broad and abstract. As noted in discussing Heidegger, there are aspects of his brilliant analysis which seem artificial and mistaken; these should be more carefully examined. In addition, concrete analysis of human existence in given situations is very much needed. The concrete analyses performed by the phenomenologists already studied are indications of the promise this method contains. The most heuristically valuable and exciting possibility comes from Binswanger's attempt to integrate phenomenology with empirical, scientific research and reflection. In the second part of this book what Binswanger started will be developed so as to enlarge, amplify, and make more precise insight into basic structures as well as into several common worlds of meaning. The primary focus will be upon the phenomenon of love and an exploration made into its primary meanings to human existence. Yet the meaning of love cannot be appreciated apart from a consideration of other fundamental existential possibilities; similarly the latter cannot be understood if divorced from the presence and cognitive power of love. Consequently the span of research includes both existence and love.

I am also particularly concerned to bring phenomenology and the social sciences together, not merely into dialogue but into collaboration; for I feel strongly that they need and complement each other. While the social sciences provide their special insight into given situations, phenomenology offers a framework within which to understand human phenom-

---

[1] Cf. the brilliant elaboration of a phenomenological critique of narrow empiricism and idealism by Merleau-Ponty, *Phenomenology of Perception*, pp. 23-56.

ena from the standpoint of the lived world. The philosopher Maurice Natanson has made the provocative suggestion that phenomenology provides precisely the form of philosophical *verstehen* needed for the pursuance of social sciences.[2] Binswanger had a similar idea and acted upon it. Phenomenology is able to see into and reliably reconstruct personal and social action. It perceives in a unique way the significance of action and experience, because it is able to provide a fundamental clarification of the basic worldly structures of meaning within which experience occurs. At the same time phenomenology needs the evidence, criticisms, and insights of the sciences; without such data and testing phenomenology stands in danger of developing into an artificial discipline, promulgating apodictic utterances divorced from concrete situations and incapable of existential verification. Husserl's call, "back to the things themselves," was an appeal to both sciences and philosophy to escape irresponsible arbitrariness; it is an appeal phenomenology of any variety must always attempt to heed.

In this chapter I shall focus upon the existential a priori of spatiality, building upon the initial insight of Heidegger. However, to move beyond his limited notion of spatiality, a clue from music is helpful. Music provides a model for refining our understanding of existential space. Furthermore the musical model suggests a way of combining phenomenological insights with those of social sciences. To use an auditory rather than a visual image of space makes it possible to bring the psychoanalytic notion of psychosexual development into the broader perspective of being in the world; at the same time the Freudian theory suggests in detail how one "makes" his world and how an adult world is constituted.

2.

Heidegger's analysis of space started from an awareness that existential space is not to be thought of geographically, as space "out there." In common parlance, the term "space" connotes magnitude, position, and

[2] M. Natanson, *Literature, Philosophy and the Social Sciences*, p. 166. The work of the late Alfred Schütz has been extremely helpful in developing and refining the concept of *verstehen*. See Natanson, *Literature*, pp. 161 ff.; also two essays by Schütz in Natanson, *Philosophy of the Social Sciences*, pp. 230-249, which showed how Weber went beyond behaviorism and pp. 302-346, which very perceptively revealed the value content embedded in every kind of fact. See also J. Lyons, *Psychology and the Measure of Man* which argues that phenomenology is necessary to gain insight into the other as a person. The important work of S. Strasser, *Phenomenology and the Human Sciences*, should also be considered.

relations between positions. Heidegger pointed out that this supposedly objective notion of space is secondary. Human existence is spatial; it is "in" the world. But a human being is fundamentally not in the world in the same way that objects are in space. Human existence is in the world in a creative and constitutive way; human being *in* the world constitutes a unique mode of historical space. Being *in* the world is not something about which man is concerned in the same way he is concerned about things at hand for practical use or things on hand to be analyzed and classified. Rather, his *in-ness* is itself constituted by a basic concern which structures the meanings that beings have for him. The spatializing of concern is an existential a priori; it precedes any other awareness man has of space, even though one frequently or usually ignores such awareness. The spatialization of this basic concern for my own being constitutes a foundation of my being in the world. This basic existential space is characterized furthermore by the dynamic structures of distancing and taking a direction. By distancing myself and taking a direction I make room for things. My world is one which makes room for beings, giving them significant places to be. In Heidegger's view, then, man is not primarily an object in space; he is a being whose existence spatializes itself through concern, a spatialization which sets the direction for the temporalizing of concern. Being *in* the world is to be directed toward historic possibilities in the structure of concern. The mode of man's concern will determine what possibilities he will make room for in his world.

Although Heidegger delineated some basic features of existential spatiality, his emphasis clearly was upon the temporality of being in the world. He strongly reacted against the traditional dichotomy of space and time, as well as the traditional mode of conceptualization which tends to reify reality by thinking primarily in spatial categories. The results of such traditional conceptualization have been extremely misleading, not merely with regard to our understanding of existence but even of the universe. We are now conscious that our customary mode of conceptualization in spatial categories is limited and artificial. The distinction between the spatializing tendency of Greek thought in contrast to the temporalistic, historically conscious mentality of Hebrew thought, for example, is now familiar so as to require no elaboration. The discovery by modern physics of the temporal dimension of space is another parallel to Heidegger's concern to uncover and understand the radically historical nature of Being. The danger is that there is now so much emphasis upon temporality and historicity that human space tends to get ignored. The few pages Heidegger devoted to spatiality is a case in point. Pure temporality is just as much an abstraction as pure spatiality. Certainly human space transcends physical, geometric space, but this should not be interpreted to mean that it does so by a transmutation into temporality. Man is a spatial creature both physically and existentially. It is necessary for phenomenology to explore more fully the notion of existential space; without a more adequate understanding of human space we shall eventually lose hold of the human world.

To demonstrate and illuminate the distinctive reality of existential space the phenomenon of music proves to be extremely helpful. A philosopher of music, Victor Zuckerkandl, has pointed out that music has mistakenly been considered to be a nonspatial art form. Of course musical sound does not occupy space in the way objects do. We cannot locate exactly the position of its boundaries, nor grasp and analyze it as we can tangible things. It seems to occur, as he says, "where the sun rises and sets, where birds fly past, where a shout sounds." This might seem to make music not merely into a purely temporal phenomenon but also into a subjective one; but clearly that is not the case. The sound of music does not arise within me. It arises "outside" of me and comes to me.[3] As a dynamically flowing phenomenon it is definitely temporal. Yet it would be ludicrous to deny that music has spatiality. When a tone strikes we say, "It is *there*." When five tones strike simultaneously we are aware that even more is there. We might even detect that one tone is an octave higher than the lowest tone. Here some kind of space is presupposed; but it is a spatiality which must be considered differently from that of visual objects, for it is transcendent to the space in which bodies have locations.[4]

[3] V. Zuckerkandl, *Sound and Symbol*, p. 268. An argument similar but in much briefer form was presented by Susanne Langer. She pointed out that music is a presentational rather than a discursive symbol: "music articulates forms which language cannot set forth" (*Philosophy in a New Key*, p. 189). She went on to elaborate that musical forms are much more congruent with human feelings than are the forms of language, so that "music can *reveal* the nature of feelings with a detail and truth that language cannot approach" (p. 191). If we are to reach a true understanding of the distinctive nature of human existence we must then pay greater attention to music; it brings to light what is all too easily obscured by words, because music is so much truer to feelings than are words. "Music is the myth of the inner life" (p. 199); yet like myth it is ambiguous. Music does not so much communicate as give us an insight as to how feelings go; it is one of the tasks of philosophy to make this insight articulate and as precise as possible. See also J. W. N. Sullivan, *Beethoven: His Spiritual Development*, for amplification of this view.

[4] Zuckerkandl, *op. cit.*, p. 270.

Several insights are to be gained from a consideration of the phenomenon of music. We are aware of a transcendent space which does not arise within me; it is transcendent space which encounters me, as a thought does. Thus it provides us with a different concept of space and also of transcendence. Hearing a tone I am aware of space, *not* an object in space. The tone is everywhere in an undivided space which contains tensions, rhythm, and meter, but not parts. "The space we hear is a space without places." [5] I encounter color as something in space and which is without; I encounter tone as something which *comes from* without. For the eye, color is caught in a moment, is located as "right there." For the ear, the tone comes from without and catches me. As a visual being I know that space is something which remains without; as a hearing being I know space as coming from without, as motion directed toward me, and which fills my life. Thus musical space is space which has become alive; it is not sound that has become alive in space. Musical space is flowing space; it is thoroughly dynamic, lacking the characteristics of optical space, having parts, three dimensions, etc. [6]

Though music or auditory space does not consist in positions and relations between positions as does visual space, it does have its own order. It is a space which is full; one tone occupies the whole space in which it sounds. Yet when a chord is struck more space is opened up; where previously there was one dynamic quality, now there is a multiplicity of dynamic qualities coming toward me. [7] As a series of chords is played we become aware of tonal motions of varying tensions constituting rhythm and meter. Thus we encounter a purely dynamic phenomenon which nevertheless constitutes both space and order. We also can say of it that it has depth, though not in terms of the distance of visual space; it has a placeless depth which surrounds and moves toward the hearer.

What Zuckerkandl makes clear is that seeing and hearing are two distinct modes of existence revealing to us two distinct characteristics of space, not two different spaces. Eye experience is an *experience of distance;* the space of auditory experience is a *participative experience.* Auditory space is not simply out there, but it comes from out there into me and through me. This space is not transcendent to space as such, but to space as the eye sees and the hand grasps, as geometry thinks and measures.

[5] *Ibid.,* p. 276.
[6] *Ibid.,* pp. 277 ff.
[7] *Ibid.,* p. 307.

Therefore the space as conceived by practical, visual life is not all space, but only one aspect of it. Even where no bodies are seen to move from place to place, there is still space; musical space is not empty but alive and full. The one who listens to music is aware of space differently from the one who forms his concepts primarily or exclusively by the eye and hand. Zuckerkandl's argument is that our concept of space must include the testimony of music.[8] This point is not totally new to American thought. William James also mentioned the importance of music as a way of opening us up more fully to the manifold dimensions of reality; as he put it, "music gives us ontological messages which non-musical criticism is unable to contradict, though it may laugh at our foolishness in minding them." [9] Whether it conveys ontological messages is debatable; but certainly music can make us aware of space which is transcendent to the eye and hand. This space is one which comes from without as a stream directed toward me in which nothing can be divided, except abstractly; it is a placeless, flowing space.[10] The space of music is not a primitive spatiality which should be superseded by or reduced to visual space. Only the dogmatic mind will insist upon such a limited conception. To understand existential space we must open our vision to spatiality which transcends the space of bodies and location. In this respect music opens doors that seem permanently shut to the eyes.

One of the characteristics of tonal or auditory space illuminated by Zuckerkandl is in contrast to Heidegger's characterization of existential spatiality which was obviously conceived largely with visual models. By investigating this characteristic more closely we shall be better prepared to understand the reality of interpersonal communication. As we have noted, the space revealed by the eye and also by concern is one of distance. The space of music, however, includes a special kind of movement, one which comes from without and penetrates my whole life. Thus musical space is primarily characterized by *interpenetration*—the interpenetration of notes in a chord, of chords in a melody, of sounds in us. This means that limits of space which are perceived visually are by no means absolute; auditory space transcends the limits of visual space. Musical space is one which obliterates the boundaries between my being and that of another being, the being of music. In the space of music two beings interpenetrate. In this space there

8 *Ibid.*, p. 292.
9 W. James, *The Varieties of Religious Experience*, p. 412.
10 V. Zuckerkandl, *op. cit.*, p. 336.

is no longer subject over against object but a form of encounter in which we become one.

Music will lead us to revise radically our thinking about spatial reality especially as it applies to the reality of communication and love. Taking music as an analogy, we can begin to understand the possibility underlying the claim to knowledge of other minds through direct participation. It might well be that so many philosophers have stumbled upon the rock of interpersonal knowledge and have been scandalized by it because their approach to reality was primarily visual; they could not move beyond the limits of space as visually conceived. As the sound of music transcends visual, spatial barriers, so indeed do the sounds of man speaking to man. The essence of the space of sound is not a "making room for" beings; it is better characterized as interpenetrating spatiality. This insight will later lead us to correct and enlarge Heidegger's one-sided scheme and to develop in the next chapter an awareness of the distinctive space and *world* of love.

We should not, however, absolutize the analogy. Even Zuckerkandl admits that music alone is not the only way of revealing this newly discovered aspect of space. Music discloses a mode of spatial being which is accessible through other channels, yet with more difficulty. Gestalt psychology has helped us to see the dynamic, flowing, interpenetrating character of reality; it taught us to see reality as *event*. As we unlearn our prejudices which restrict our perception, our experience of colors, for example, may be comparable to the hearing of sounds. An artist such as Cezanne can, through visual means, reveal the dynamic quality of a scene in such a way as to pull us into his scene so that we become a part of it. He enables us to encounter the scene as a living event in which we can participate. Thus his painting communicates a vision of alive, flowing, interpenetrating space not unlike that provided by music.[11] Nevertheless, music is a particularly significant symbol of reality; it has the power to illuminate one aspect which is usually obscure. It does not necessarily tell us something totally new; but it tells it better than most other events.

In music, in the event of sound and also in the event of personal communication we experience the world in a unique way. To fill out our picture of being in the world we must therefore *listen* to phenomena, which is probably one original insight underlying that tired and misused term "intuition." Being in the world becomes attuned to its unique mode

11 Cf. Zuckerkandl's similar discussion, *op. cit.*, pp. 338-346.

of being by listening as well as looking. Through music we discover that the old oppositions between space and time, subject and object, even past, present, and future break down. By listening we can hear a new mode of spatiality which is essentially dynamic, transcending the limits of visually conceived space. By listening to music we learn to perceive reality in terms of a unitary whole again, yet a whole which is always in process of historical becoming.

3.

Taking music as a symbol of existential transcendence we can better understand what is meant when we say that human beings are spatial beings. As a mere body I occupy space; but as a human being I also constitute a unique type of spatiality. My being here creates and takes space, alters and interpenetrates space, interprets and fulfills space. My being spatializes itself historically, like a melody. Music presents us with a viable symbol of existential space; as Bergson said, our personality is "the continuous melody of our inner life." [12] By emphasizing the spatiality of music we can more appropriately symbolize man's inner life; we may conceive of inner life history not as though enclosed in a body, as in space, but as itself spatial in an intentional and dynamic way. Human or historical spatiality does not refer primarily to bodily existence, though it definitely includes it. Man is in the world in a way which is analogous to music in its dynamic, interpenetrating wholeness. By listening to existence imaginatively rather than merely looking at it we shall better understand how it is for us to be in our world.

Though he did not use the analogy of music, Binswanger came upon a similar insight. In 1933 he published an essay dealing with the problem of space as this arises within psychopathology.[13] Binswanger here was already under the influence of Heidegger, but in a creative way which led him to emphasize numerous concrete aspects of man in his world. He, too, realized that different kinds of spatiality emerge whenever space is considered from an existential perspective; these can best be illuminated by phenomenology. The most obvious kind of space is that pertaining to the natural world, that is, oriented, physical space. What is striking about this space is its homogeneity; my body, for example, could be considered as an object

---

12 *Ibid.*, quoted, p. 142.
13 L. Binswanger, *Ausgewählte Vorträge*, II, pp. 174-225.

whose space might be occupied just as easily by some other object. What distinguishes objects from this spatial viewpoint is their location and not any qualitative differences. However when we consider space from an existential or historical viewpoint, we get a different picture. Kurt Goldstein's famous experiments with wounded veterans from the First World War showed clearly how people can have, for example, two kinds of existentially oriented space. Patients whose sense of space came from vision without the ability to move around differed considerably from those whose sense of space was kinesthetic, coming from movement without any vision. Goldstein's study showed that our sense of space arises not merely by looking at the world but also by moving through it. Optic space and kinesthetic space differ, though normally they are integrated; physical damage brings to light those differences which are usually obscured. Binswanger insisted that to understand another person it is imperative that we understand how he conceives space, not merely the space around him but also himself as a spatial being.[14] How one orients himself in the world will greatly affect what his conception of space is, and hence of himself as a spatial being.

Most suggestive is the kind of spatiality which Binswanger discussed at length and which he referred to as tonal space (der gestimmte Raum). This is a kind of space which we must listen to if we are to perceive it; for Binswanger the essential mode for hearing tonal space is feeling (das Gemüt).[15] Scheler had suggested that the heart could reveal the kind of space in which a person lived; a person sensing emptiness of space is suffering, for example, from an empty heart, the loss or lack of love. What is involved here is not introspective subjectivism but, rather, a listening to the heart (symbolically understood) which reveals the intentional structure of existential space. By concentrating on feeling Binswanger maintained that one could then come to "see" the person and his actual lived world. That is, feeling can reveal a very "objective," existential mode of being in the world. To Binswanger that world of mood and feeling, the tonal world, has its own temporality and spatiality. This is to say that there is a distinct form of human dynamics, a definite way of becoming spatial and temporal, which will only be distorted or lost from view if we approach it within a perspective restricted to physical and visual space. What he was suggesting was that any attempt to understand existence must investigate the particular spatiality of feeling.

Binswanger's illumination of tonal space was primarily designed to

14 *Ibid.*, pp. 180-190.
15 *Ibid.*, pp. 195 ff.

help one person understand the world of another. His suggestions are important and we shall return to them shortly. First, however, we might draw together a few points and move in a slightly different direction, one which brings together insights into space from phenomenology and psychoanalysis. Both in the study of music and in Binswanger's essay there was an emphasis upon listening to existence so as to understand it, rather than placing all one's conceptual criteria within visual boundaries. Listening to music, especially great music, involves more than just "tuning in" with one's ears. One also listens with one's feelings, imagination, and intelligence. One listens to another person in the same way; particularly important is that one listens to another with one's feelings. It is through feeling that one tunes in to the very heart of another's world. We can also say that by tuning in to our own feelings we discover how we have spatialized our world.

4.

Our own existential world space is constructed by "listening" rather than by looking. Heidegger's notion that one's world project arises from and in response to one's primordial feeling of being in the world might be interpreted in that way. In forming a world one's feelings precede one's vision; and these feelings give the basic shape within which one's visual perception of reality occurs and finds significance. If such is the case, then the Freudian concept of childhood development is seen to have new significance. Now it is possible to lift the Freudian scheme of psychosexual development out of a subjectivistic framework and see it as an illuminating sketch of the process of man's creating the primary world in which he lives and thinks.

We can follow up this possibility most easily by looking briefly at the theory of infantile sexuality advanced by Erik Erikson, who is also a Freudian revisionist and in some ways an American counterpart to Binswanger.[16] Erikson's theory is that a mode of behavior, particularly in the early stages of life, is correlative to a particular body zone.[17] Though his theory is an attempt to enlarge upon the traditional Freudian scheme, he has also

---

[16] Erikson expressed his theoretical aim as a search "for the proper place of the libido theory in the totality of human life" (*Childhood and Society*, p. 64). Like Binswanger he has sought to understand human phenomena within a genuinely historical framework; and like Binswanger his interests have led him to study philosophy, literature, religion, history, anthropology, as well as psychology and sociology.

[17] Erikson, *Childhood and Society*, pp. 52-53.

tried to demonstrate "the systematic relationship of the organ modes of pregenitality which establish the basic orientation that an organism and its parts can have to another organism and its parts and to the world of things." [18] He has found that a person's existential mode, and particularly his mode of spatiality, has a direct relationship to his awareness of a particular bodily zone. If we can assume that our world is formed primarily by listening with our feelings, then Erikson's theories based on long periods of observation and clinical experience throw new light on how particular spatial modes develop; at the same time his scheme, when set in an existential framework, not only takes on new meaning but opens up to us much significance of spatiality that we might otherwise miss. By setting his theories into an existential perspective we gain insight into the developmental process of human spatiality.

According to the Freudian scheme which Erikson pretty well follows, the mouth is the first body zone which provides the emerging person with a focus for a general life approach and outlook. During this oral stage the primary mode of behavior is one of incorporation. The infant's primary intentional structure is directed toward taking in food and sucking so as to attain satisfaction of tensions. Rather than use technical language or Latinized forms, such as incorporation, Erikson has suggested that this first existential mode of spatiality might best be designated by our English verb "to get." [19] The modality of "getting" is the first social mode which is learned. Indeed "getting" constitutes a primary intentional structure, and thus is a basic orientation to life. As existential concern evolves and thus spatializes itself, this primary spatiality is structured in terms of a concern to receive and accept satisfaction. Unless we choose to remain within an infantile world, historical development requires each of us to move "beyond the pleasure principle."

A second stage develops when the infant attempts to control his environment by taking a more active and direct approach to his world, such as biting with his teeth or grabbing with his hands. His eyes also learn to focus upon objects so that he can "take them in"; and his ears and hands develop in a similar way. This second stage of development Erikson refers to as the social modality of taking and holding. [20] This mode is extremely significant and I shall give it greater elaboration especially in Chapter 11.

[18] Ibid., p. 96.
[19] Ibid., pp. 72-75.
[20] Ibid., p. 77.

Important here is to note that an infant's existential spatiality is modified as his body develops. As he listens to the tensions and satisfactions of his body his sense of being in the world takes on new form and hence develops new structures of significance. During this second stage the child's approach to his world is definitely creative. He learns to take hold of himself and his world in his own historical way. At this point the little person senses a break with the maternal matrix with which he has been in complete unity.[21] Here arises further significance for his world, because he begins to develop notions of good and evil. He will sense the badness of himself or his mother as he experiences gnawing teeth, a withdrawing mother, and anxiety at being unable to control his anger or obtain the desired satisfaction and trust.

A third stage emerges which shifts the focus to another bodily zone having to do with elimination of waste products. Here the infant begins to define his entire world, particularly his space, in terms of yours and mine. His mode of spatiality now assumes another form, in terms of letting go and holding on.[22] As we shall consider much more in detail in chapters 12 and 13, how the child grows into this new mode depends to a large extent upon how successfully he passed through the previous stages. It is quite possible that a basic conflict emerging from within the development of the world of letting go and holding on may have a dominant effect upon one's entire approach to reality, which is the existential meaning underlying the misleading phrase "anal personality." One often takes unresolved conflicts of these early stages into the fourth stage of development in which the genitals become the particular body zone that is listened to most attentively. Of course if one must pay constant attention to an unresolved conflict from an earlier stage this complicates the listening project of the later stages.

These stages become increasingly difficult to characterize as development proceeds because of the incredible complexity of a given person's intentional structures. Yet we can frequently detect a particular mode, a distinct form of existential space, which is correlative to a body zone. Anyone at all observant of a young boy is aware of his distinctive mode of behavior; we say that he is constantly "into things." In Freudian language this means that the significant mode at this stage of development is phallic. The social modality of a young boy corresponds to his awareness of his

21 *Ibid.*, p. 79.
22 *Ibid.*, p. 82.

genitals. He is constantly "poking" into other people's interests, poking into their ears and minds by shouting and talking and intruding into their *Lebensraum* by obtrusive behavior. As Erikson points out, girls share in this rising ability toward locomotion and intrusive behavior, but they obviously lack the correlative bodily organ, which may cause them confusion.[23] Perhaps the evidence here is inconclusive, and any conclusions must be tentative. Yet one truly important aspect of Erikson's studies is the insight into the difference between the young girl's spatiality and that of a young boy's. This point is often overlooked by existentialists and phenomenologists. If existential space is a basic structure of concrete concern, then it is artificial to neglect sexual differentiation in the construction of existential worlds.

In a number of experiments Erikson demonstrated that "boys and girls are differentiated not only by differences in organs, capacities, and roles, but by a unique quality of experience." [24] In clinical experiments he discovered that boys consistently constructed space in a phallic modality. They built towers, turrets, steeples, etc. Girls, on the other hand, consistently constructed their space differently by building enclosed areas such as swimming pools, houses, rooms, and the like. Of course there were exceptions, but there was such a high degree of consistency as to indicate that perceptual patterns as well as existential spatiality emerge within a system of correlation between behavioral modes and body zones. Like Binswanger, Erikson has insisted that any particular form of spatiality must be interpreted in human rather than merely sexual or libidinal terms. High towers, for example, may represent a phallus. But what does a phallus mean in a particular historical situation? A large phallic symbol may often express the need to compensate for a doubt or fear of one's existential capacities.[25] Merely the presence of a phallic form of spatialization does not automatically reveal the meaning of it. What is important is to recognize "that the dominance of genital modes over the modalities of spatial organization reflects a profound difference in the sense of space in the two sexes." [26] As Erikson's studies of American Indian tribes further disclose, sexual patterns not only play an important role in an individual's development but also throw much light upon the differences that exist between cultures.[27]

[23] *Ibid.*, pp. 85-91.
[24] *Ibid.*, p. 91.
[25] *Ibid.*, p. 103.
[26] *Ibid.*, p. 106; cf. the relevant discussion in D. Bakan, *The Duality of Human Existence*, pp. 110-120.
[27] See Erikson, *Childhood and Society*, pp. 111-186.

As Wordsworth put it, the child is father of the man. To understand the complexity of his adult spatiality, a man must learn to listen again to the child in him. He must learn to recognize that his prescientific view of the world was formed primarily by listening to needs, tensions, and satisfactions, indeed a whole symphony of feelings which played a formative part in shaping his mode and picture of his own being in the world. Phenomenologists should give much more attention to Erikson's insights, especially in an attempt to understand human space. In his words, an individual's space-time "preserves the social topology of his childhood surroundings as well as the image of his own body, with its social connotations." [28]

To bring his insight into our existential framework we see that man is a dynamic, creative spatial being whose spatiality is set in numerous directions. On the basis of clinical evidence it would be ludicrous to suggest that man exists essentially in one form of intentionality. Human spatiality is often not a melody but a cacophony of getting, taking, grabbing, poking, manipulating, as well as making room for. Human being in the world is directed along various modes aimed at different possibilities of meaning which often do not easily interpenetrate one another. These possibilities include bodily satisfaction of various kinds, environmental control, social mobility, and others which we have not yet carefully considered. The intensity and weight, the significance any one direction has within the history of any individual varies according to his particular development, a history which definitely includes his sexuality.[29]

To be truly historical we must listen to the whole "continuous melody of our inner life," a melody which has its unique form of spatiality that is constantly taking on new patterns as well as being influenced by old ones. We must learn to listen to the whole of existence, which includes the various dimensions of sexual, somatic, psychic, social, cultural, and intimate existence. Admittedly I have been accentuating at this point the lower reg-

---

[28] *Ibid.*, p. 244.

[29] Merleau-Ponty also emphasized the dynamic spatiality of embodied existence; and he suggested the importance of considering the diversity of references (meanings) which arise because of the diversity of directions which constitute any given person's spatiality (*Phenomenology of Perception*, pp. 98-147 especially). As we become aware of various basic possibilities for meaning and how they emerge in a developmental pattern of growth, we shall learn to detect which forms precede others, which encourage and which inhibit the development of other forms, etc. A tremendous and largely unchartered area of research and understanding lies ahead for those who would continue investigation of psychological and sociological reality in a phenomenological way. Cf. also R. D. Laing, *The Divided Self*, ch. 4.

isters in the existential melody; but this is necessary because bodily zones have had too little attention paid to them in phenomenological literature. It is one thing philosophically to maintain that I am my body; it is another thing really to listen to it. The trend in phenomenology has been to disregard much data of scientists; that is something it simply cannot afford to do.[30] To use the image of music again, the phenomenon of existence does not consist in a pure and simple tone but in a melody comprised of chords; these chords consist of diverse tones which reverberate so as to open up new and different possibilities for experience. Existential possibilities are grounded in the sexual, somatic, psychic, cultural, social, and interpersonal dimensions of the world as we make it. Erikson has maintained that the goal of his approach is to see "the interpenetration of the biological, the cultural, and psychological." [31] To hear the whole phenomenon in the fullness of its interpenetrating modalities, a phenomenological approach which penetrates to the heart of existence is necessary. With existential phenomenology incorporating an interdisciplinary method, we may hope to gain a vision of the whole of man in his world of significance. At least so far a more precise view of the historicity of human space has emerged.

5.

Through feeling we have the primary clues to how we, as well as other persons, spatialize existence. Quoting a phrase from Goethe to the extent that our world and heaven shrink considerably when our heart quivers from fear in our breast, Binswanger suggested that our human world becomes revealed by taking such moods and feelings seriously.[32] As Goethe suggested, a fearful heart indicates a form of spatialization which is characterized by constriction. A fearful person's world becomes walled in. A person in despair lives in a world that has become empty, dark, and shriveled. In the experience of joy a person exists in a bright, expansive, exciting world. By listening to a person's moods and feelings we become aware not only of dynamic, intentionally oriented patterns of existence but also of colors, shades, and diversities of tempo in the lived world. These colors, shades, and tempos illuminate concrete possibilities of meaning that are to be found in the spatiality of a person.

[30] Cf. a similar position presented by Merleau-Ponty, "The Philosopher and Sociology," *Philosophy and the Social Sciences*, M. Natanson, ed., pp. 487-505.
[31] E. Erikson, *Childhood and Society*, p. 108.
[32] L. Binswanger, *Ausgewählte Vorträge*, II, pp. 200 ff.

Because it is so easy to misunderstand the existential point here, it must be emphasized that this is not a return to subjectivism or irrationalism. The phenomenology of existential space concentrates upon a fundamentally irreducible intentional structure of the lived world. The phenomenon of the lived world is an indivisible unity separated only by violent abstraction, which in our culture has unfortunately become a habit. This lived world, as we are coming to understand it, is not a thoroughly determined reality in which things reside and are moved about. It is a dynamic reality in process of being "made" by each human being as his historical existence unfolds within a given culture; as radically historical, it is indeterminate. Furthermore, being in the world is not a homogeneous reality; on the contrary, there are many different moments, each of which spatializes itself in a distinctive way, as the material provided by Erikson has made clear. Because man is essentially historical, we might say that these moments are time-spaces which are avenues toward meanings. There are, for example, time-spaces which we see as weird, fraught with danger, posing a possibility where we might be taken in or where we might lose our grip. There are other time-spaces where we see our existence as able to relax and feel at home. The lived world is the primordial fact in which all other facts and their significance emerge; it must be seen for what it is.

In attempting to understand others, it is helpful to study personal space phenomenologically in terms of how persons feel about their homes, that is, where "home" really is to them and what it means to them. "Home is where the heart is," a proverb has it. In much Christian devotional literature it has been said that to be with Christ is to be truly at home; any place without his presence is felt to be a separation from home, regardless of how many significant members of the family might be gathered around the old family hearth. Taking a cue from such religious literature, Binswanger suggested that the space of a person is structured around the real or approximate homes one finds in his world. In addition to possibilities already considered, existential space can be seen as distancing and taking direction with respect to arriving at and departing from, of going forward or away from home. When a loved one departs, one's space can become hollow, and turn from light to dark, and even bring one into confrontation with the possibility of death. The lover may feel, as Cole Porter put it, as though "every time we say good-bye, I die a little." In the same way one may not really feel at home in his own house until some unwanted guest finally makes his departure. In understanding the spatiality of another it is important to discover where and how he is at home in his world. Is he able to find a true home or is he constantly faced with the impossibility of being at home with anyone or in any place? When communication breaks down between persons or cultures, we often say: "We just do not live in the same world." This means that one history does not interpenetrate with another history; it suggests that one cannot recognize anything that looks like home in the world of the other. The other's world is all too strange, unsettled, signifying perhaps a waste land, a mad house, a terror chamber, or dangerous waters, but not a haven of trust, a promised land, a place to rest and be at peace.

In the phenomenon of schizophrenia we frequently discover a person who has spatialized his existence in such a way as to make no room for a home. A psychotic is often too busy making a world in which space is foreboding, from which he must escape or hide. A manic may be understood in terms of his history being structured by constant darting in and out of various spaces with his quick, scattered talk. We often characterize such a person as socially brash, curt, and rude. In reality he has no place in which to settle down; he is always running along on the periphery of significance. His mode of spatiality drives him to spring incessantly over the world, from place to place, moment to moment, never stopping long enough really to take anything in or to relax and be at home with anything or anyone.[33] Such phenomena reveal, as Binswanger discovered, that one aspect or direction of existence has become dominant to the extent that some basic possibilities have not been allowed to develop or to interpenetrate with the others. The psychotic mode of spatialization has been transformed from a melody into chaotic noise; the tones of his basic possibilities have not been allowed to interpenetrate with each other so that they clash together.[34] A psychotic has reduced his spatialization to one particular mode so as to simplify what to him is a thoroughly frightening world. Ironically this reduction does not bring about simplification; it produces unbearable confusion, fantastic turmoil, maddening inner riot. Even though the patient may be lying quietly in bed, he can get "carried away" by the chaos which penetrates his world. In contrast, a dancer who leaps through the air, turns, twists, jumps, touches numerous objects, embraces different people, hears the sound of horns, drums, the beating of his

[33] *Ibid.*, pp. 209 ff.
[34] For a powerful and brilliant insight into how psychosis can feel, see Hannah Green's, *I Never Promised You a Rose Garden.*

own heart, shouts and applause, may actually experience a very cohesive, integrated spatiality. In music it is not just the number of notes which determine the sound of the chord but, more important, their relation to each other and how they interpenetrate with each other. So it is with man and his possibilities. As we shall discover in more detail later, to achieve a flowing, alive, integrated sense of space which is historically cohesive through reciprocal interpenetration of past, present, and future, one must discover a home. To find a home means to find another person, for one is not really at home alone. An attentive phenomenology of existential space points to the space of interpersonal relations and in particular to the space of love.

8

The New World of Love

1. LOVE'S SPATIALITY

The lived world has diverse modes of space. To be in the world as a human being is not to be contained in a predetermined space; being in the world makes its own space in a way that is analogous to music. Existence spatializes itself in a dynamic, flowing stream of history that contains possibilities for significance which may harmoniously interpenetrate or jarringly reverberate against each other. Yet human space itself is not merely an individual's creation; the interaction involved in existential encounters is part of the givenness of human spatiality. The encounter with love is also decisive, in that it opens up not merely a mode of spatiality that is different from what we have so far considered; love opens up a whole new world. This insight dawns most dramatically when one falls in love. Lyrics of popular love songs portray the change in appearance of the lived world when one is lifted into the ecstasy of romance. A lover will confess to his beloved that he has not noticed bells ringing, buds bursting, birds soaring, and love singing everywhere—"until I met you!" The world symbolized by these words is quite a different world from that symbolized by Heidegger's paradigm of resolute being-unto-death. It would be erroneous to suppose that the phenomenon of romantic love is purely subjective. Quite obviously the spatiality of lovers is different from that of two courteous citizens. The latter will make room for each other on the sidewalk and give place to each other as they pass through a small doorway; but lovers will transcend the distance of this polite space by an embrace. The space constructed by the two citizens is public; each openly declares the separateness of the other and makes concessions to it. In an embrace lovers transcend concessions and separateness in complementarity that can never fully be observed by the public.

In this chapter we shall investigate the phenomenon of love, first in terms of its spatiality, then in terms of its temporality. We shall then be able to see more clearly the distinct world constituted by love and to distinguish that world from other basic existential possibilities. The method of this phenomenological investigation will be somewhat unorthodox; concentration will not be upon immediate experience but upon poetic self-expression of the experience of love. I shall focus upon romantic love, not because it is love's most sublime or most significant form, but because it is perhaps the most outstanding and hence the easiest to delineate. However, since it is sublime, possessing a very distinctive ecstatic form, its truth will hardly be best expressed in pedestrian observations and analysis. To express the meaning of the experience of romantic love requires brilliant imagination that is an integral part of genuine poetic expression. The English poet C. Day Lewis has made an important and pertinent point: "The poet is trying to make sense, poetic sense, out of his experiences. . . . [he] is usually not just putting truth into verse, as a dressmaker might build a dress round a model; he is discovering truth through verse." [1]

I take poetry very seriously, not in this respect as a literary critic, but as a phenomenologist investigating symbolic expressions of the basic meanings of a person's encounter with his world. Through attentiveness to the verse of a poet we can discover his world in the richness of its meaning, a richness which might easily be hidden unless illuminated by his imaginative expression. The truth which a poet discovers through his verse is there for us to receive and thus become truth for us. Through poetry, as through music, the power and meaning of a concrete existential encounter may penetrate and inform our own vision of reality. I have suggested that phenomenology and the social sciences should collaborate; it will become increasingly clear that existential phenomenology and art are also similar

[1] C. Day Lewis, quoted by C. A. Coulson, *Science and Christian Belief*, p. 99. The view expressed by Lewis is, of course, common in the world of arts and letters. That is not to say that it is infallible; it would be contested by numerous philosophical positions, starting perhaps with Plato. We cannot enter into the vast argument of aesthetics here, but must remain uncomfortably content with a position that might appear arbitrary or at least dubious to some. However, the poetry which we shall consider does discover and express important existential truth!

and should cooperate in our common endeavor to expand our awareness of human transcendence and the meaning of human life.

For a phenomenological pursuit of the meaning of love the work of Binswanger is helpful. He investigated the phenomenon of love, largely in its romantic form, and discovered a characteristic of its spatiality which we have already noticed pertains to music. The space of music has an unbounded, placeless character. Similarly love, as portrayed by poetic lovers, has a quality of boundlessness. In one of his letters the poet Rilke suggested that since two lovers will wish for and expect the very best for each other, they cannot commit the injustice of restricting each other's being; on the contrary, from their relationship will emerge reciprocal, unceasing space and freedom.[2] The exact quality of romantic love's experience may well be a relatively recent historical phenomenon as an outgrowth of courtly love;[3] however, its essential features are quite extensive. Certainly romantic love was not monopolized by the passionate nineteenth-century Germans whom Binswanger quoted so copiously; nor is it something which Hollywood has either monopolized or understood. The boundless character of love's spatiality was at least alluded to by Plato in his reference to the ecstatic madness of love; and it seems to be akin to aesthetic transport described long ago by Longinus. Other studies might well discover that the basic meaning of romance has at least been dimly known in numerous cultures. Our concern, however, is to focus upon and attempt to delineate its essential structures. John Donne aptly characterized the boundlessness discovered in the moment of love's ecstasy as "lovers' infinitenesse." The space of a loving encounter stretches endlessly in directions of joy and fulfillment. Because this area is usually smothered in the fog of sentimentalism, it is necessary for existential phenomenology to listen particularly carefully to the symbolic self-expressions of romantic love if it is to clear away the fog and bring in some light.

For our purposes we may select as a paradigm of romantic love the

[2] Cf. L. Binswanger, *Grundformen und Erkenntnis Menschlichen Daseins*, pp. 21-35, in which he discusses the nature of the spatiality of loving, interpersonal relationships. Though many points made in our discussion are similar to those of Binswanger's, my approach and the development of existential phenomenology are quite independent of his. The lines quoted from Rilke are to be found on p. 27, Binswanger, *op. cit.*

[3] The classic study in this field has been C. S. Lewis, *The Allegory of Love*. However, see also Denis de Rougemont, *Love in the Western World*. It will become obvious that my study of romantic love does not share in the disparaging view of romance that is to be found in the works of these writers; my view is more akin to that of Charles Williams.

lives and poetry of the Brownings. The tale of their romance is famous. A rather dashing, young, highly eligible bachelor who was becoming a much admired poet is mysteriously attracted by a slightly older, semi-invalid spinster who also writes poetry. In the drab repressive environment of her Victorian home he woos and wins her. They elope, are married, and settle in Florence. Soon thereafter Elizabeth presents Robert with a belated wedding gift, a small book of poems known as *Sonnets from the Portuguese* which she wrote for him. These poems express her love for him and as such present us with a marvelous testimony of the new world of love into which her romance and marriage had brought her:

> The face of all the world is changed, I think,
> Since first I heard the footsteps of thy soul
> Move still, oh, still, beside me, as they stole
> Betwixt me and the dreadful outer brink
> Of obvious death, where I, who thought to sink,
> Was caught up into love, and taught the whole
> Of life in a new rhythm. . . .
> The names of country, heaven, are changed away
> For where thou art or shalt be, there or here; . . . (VII)

By comparison her previous world was dreadful:

> Beloved, my Beloved, when I think
> That thou wast in the world a year ago,
> What time I sat alone here in the snow
> And saw no footprint, heard the silence sink
> No moment at thy voice, but, link by link,
> Went counting all my chains as if that so
> They never could fall off at any blow
> Struck by thy possible hand,—why, thus I drink
> Of life's great cup of wonder! (XX)

But that cold and lonely world of near death has been transcended by the new "wonder-full" reality of the other person known in love. In this new world visual spaces have been changed, given new names in terms of where he is, has been, or shall be. Distance is relative to his proximity, and life to his presence. The tempo of existence has learned a new rhythm. As she makes clear in the next poem, her formerly narrow world has expanded considerably because his love has overcome in her the constricting effect of fear.

> And yet, because thou overcomest so,
> Because thou art more noble and like a king,

> Thou canst prevail against my fears and fling
> Thy purple round me, till my heart shall grow
> Too close against thine heart henceforth to know
> How it shook when alone. . . .
> . . . If thou invite me forth
> I rise above abasement at the word.
> Make thy love larger to enlarge my worth. (xvi)

Here is a sense of finding a "brave, new world" through love, one which has connotations of boundlessness. This world manifests a new order of meaning: "Make thy love larger to enlarge my worth" suggests the creative and expansive power of love to reorder and thus heighten the value or meaning of human existence.

The ecstatic and heightening power of love calls to mind the religious symbol "heaven," which is a common term in much love poetry. The beloved is seen in terms of space which affords the greatest possible delight and satisfaction, such as expressed by Faust in Christopher Marlowe's *The Tragical History of Dr. Faustus*:

> Was this the face that launched a thousand ships,
> And burnt the topless towers of Ilium?
> Sweet Helen, make me immortal with a kiss.
>
> .   .   .   .
>
> Here will I dwell, for Heaven be in these lips,
> And all is dross that is not Helena.

Mrs. Browning invokes her beloved as though he is the Holy Spirit; the significance here is that life with him on earth is better than her expectation of an ethereal heaven. She chooses to exchange the one for the other in the confidence that she will be gaining the true heaven:

> Then love me, Love! look on me—breathe on me!
> As brighter ladies do not count it strange,
> For love, to give up acres and degree,
> I yield the grave for thy sake, and exchange
> My near sweet view of Heaven, for earth with thee! (xxiii)

Of course she is obviously referring to the fact that her health improved tremendously as a result of their mutual love; but in the context of the poems she is also declaring a newly discovered and chosen value. For the lived world of love is filled with beauty of color and sound, of light, joy, and hope, which was also beautifully portrayed in Edmund Spenser's

"Epithalamion." The relationship in which lovers dwell, their being "in love," is filled with brilliance. This new mode of being is also a haven of safety in which the interpenetrating lives have overcome the fears which arise in isolation, as Mrs. Browning made clear:

> Life to life—
> I lean upon thee, Dear, without alarm,
> And feel as safe as guarded by a charm
> Against the stab of worldings, who if rife
> Are weak to injure. (xxiv)

The space of love is a heaven of joy constituted by an interchange of presence, of personal interpenetration, which also is a strengthening power that makes one feel secure.

In the following sonnet she summarizes and states freshly the effects of love, transforming her isolated transcendence into one that is "safe, and strong, and glad."

> My own Belovéd, who hast lifted me
> From this drear flat of earth where I was thrown,
> And, in betwixt the languid ringlets, blown
> A life-breath, till the forehead hopefully
> Shines out again, as all the angels see,
> Before thy saving kiss! My own, my own,
> Who camest to me when the world was gone,
> And I who looked for only God, found *thee!*
> I find thee; I am safe, and strong, and glad.
> As one who stands in dewless asphodel
> Looks backward on the tedious time he had
> In the upper life,—so I, with bosom-swell,
> Make witness, here, between the good and bad,
> That Love, as strong as Death, retrieves as well. (xxvii)

Here the power of love to transform and transfigure human existence is strongly attested so that we have, as it were, living empirical data which interprets itself. Heidegger's hermeneutics of *Dasein* presented resolute being-unto-death as the authentic manner to appropriate the truth of human being. It is necessary for phenomenology to be hermeneutical, not merely because existence reaches forward into the future but also because it is constituted, as Marcel has said, by unfathomable mystery. Yet that mystery which lies "between the good and bad" can be illuminated. Mrs. Browning has been able to "make witness" to the creative power of love, which reveals its own reality as well as that of the lovers. Thus she is able to "let us in" on something of the new order of her world as reconstituted by love; and, as we have seen, it is a "heavenly world," a world in which she finds things she never saw before and better than those dreamed of.

Another quality of this heavenly world is that of ecstatic elevation. She had complained of bearing "a heavy heart . . . from year to year until I saw thy face." Until that time the natural joys of childhood had been repressed so that she began to lose the sense of "dance-time," by plodding with "long despairs" which had replaced early hopes. Not even God had been able to lift her from despondency. But by dropping her heavy heart into the "great deep being" of Robert, she found herself in a new environment "betwixt the stars and the unaccomplished fate." This quality of elevation points to a new form of transcendence, of ecstasy, which opened up to her a new dimension in existential reality. The following and well-known sonnet proceeds even further; her transcending love reveals a wholeness of existence that was otherwise obscure. Love carries her to the very limits of her possible being, giving her security, freedom, insight, and the hope of life unassailable even by death.

> How do I love thee? Let me count the ways.
> I love thee to the depth and breadth and height
> My soul can reach, when feeling out of sight
> For the ends of Being and ideal Grace.
> I love thee to the level of everyday's
> Most quiet need, by sun and candle-light.
> I love thee freely, as men strive for Right;
> I love thee purely, as they turn from Praise.
> I love thee with the passion put to use
> In my old griefs, and with my childhood's faith.
> I love thee with a love I seemed to lose
> With my lost saints,—I love thee with the breath,
> Smiles, tears, of all my life!—and, if God choose,
> I shall but love thee better after death. (XLIII)

Here the boundlessness of the space of love is expressed clearly and directly. This space is not mere diffusion of substance. It cannot be understood with a visual image but only as, perhaps, invisible energy or as the boundlessness of a sound. In the midst of the ordinary and practical everyday world a new spatial structure has sounded, one which cannot be located in any one particular spot because it interpenetrates all places and occasions. This dynamic, living, flowing space of love is characterized by interpenetration spatially but also temporally. In the phenomenon of boundless love she finds an interpenetration of past, present, and future. There is a recovery of a lost love of saints and the faith of childhood; but this is not a return to the past. Rather, past and present burst into the future, even "out of sight" to the very "ends of Being and ideal Grace." The moment of love is an integral space-time unit bringing into harmony her faith, hope, passion, and even "the breath, smiles, tears, of all my life." The phenomenon of love as Mrs. Browning has illuminated it is truly ecstatic, not only in a temporal sense but also in a spatial sense. Her whole space sings in the spatialization of love.

The new world of love is phenomenologically characterized by a form of spatiality which is distinct from that which comes to mind from a visual, physical viewpoint. Like music it especially has the qualities of dynamic, indivisible unity which seems to be boundless not merely in outreach but in terms of interpenetration. This phenomenon of interpenetration relates both to time and to other spatial modes; but the most obvious reality to which it applies is that of personal coinherence, the reciprocal, shared reality of genuine love. A boundary-less love constituted by reciprocity was suggested in the classic drama of romantic love, when Juliet said from her balcony to Romeo:

> My bounty is as boundless as the sea
> My love as deep; the more I give to thee,
> The more I have, for both are infinite.[4]

Though quotations of love poetry to demonstrate various points could likewise be infinite, we can find the essence of romantic love's space expressed in the adaptation of the Romeo and Juliet story in the contemporary musical, *West Side Story*. Stephen Sondheim's lyrics disclose the space of love, illuminating especially clearly the basic element of reciprocity, mutuality, loving coexistence, coinherence, call it what you will.

Toward the start of this musical drama the contemporary Romeo, named Tony, sings that his world will never be the same since he just kissed a girl named Maria, his Juliet. The two later sing a duet, a dialogue of praise, which brilliantly expresses the new outlook their world has taken since they have fallen in love.

Maria:
Only you, you're the only thing I see, forever.
In my eyes, in my words, and in everything I do,
Nothing else but you, ever.

[4] W. Shakespeare, *Romeo and Juliet*, Act II, Scene 2.

Tony:
And there's nothing for me, but Maria.
Every sight that I see is Maria.
Always you, everything I'll ever know,
Everywhere I'll go, you'll be.
. . . All the world is only you and me.

Maria and Tony:
Tonight, tonight, it all began tonight.
I saw you, and the world went away.
Tonight, tonight, there's only you tonight,
What you are, what you do, what you say.
For here you are; and what was just a world, is a star, tonight.

Tonight, tonight, the world is full of light,
With suns and moons all over the place.
Tonight, tonight, the world is wild and bright,
Going mad, shooting sparks into space.

Today the world was just an address, a place for me to live in, . . .
Yet here you are, and what was just a world, is a star tonight.

In the eyes of these lovers the old world has been left behind, and they
have entered a new world full of brightness, elevation, and total personification. It is an ecstatic world, transcending the ordinary, everyday world of
concern. The tragedy comes, of course, because they could not in fact leave
the old world; it still exists interpenetrating the new, even though they do
not recognize it. In the touching wedding scene they sing of their new life
which will be characterized by unity; they will be one hand, one heart, one
life, a union confirmed in their mutual exchange of vows. This union will
be so transcendently strong that even death cannot part them. Yet their
vision, their faith, their one life is shattered by what they in love tried to
deny and escape: death, which comes from the old, everyday world. It was
the unusual success of the Brownings to have allowed their love to interpenetrate with the other dimensions of being in the world. In this musical
drama the interpenetration of lovers is restricted to themselves; it is not
permitted to be incorporated and integrated into the old world.

Toward the end of the drama the lovers realize that their "heavenly"
love cannot exist in the space-time of their former existence. As they sense
the latter rushing in upon them to crush their love, they sing together a
song of eschatological hope: "somewhere there's a place for us," where
peace, quiet, and "open air wait for us." This space will merge with a new
temporality allowing "time to spare, time to look, time to care." As they

say, the achievement of this new space-time with its open freedom, safety, individual development, and mutual fulfillment requires that they "find a new way of living . . . a way of forgiving." Only by forgiving can their two alienated cultures be integrated. They then affirm a truth of love, that the attainment of their fulfilled life will become actualized only as they learn to share and depend upon each other: "Hold my hand, and we're half way there; hold my hand and I'll take you there, somehow, someday, somewhere." Tragically the bitter sting of death shatters this possibility. The truth which they have professed, however, is not totally fantastic or merely ideal. It is, rather, an existential possibility which this couple and other lovers have at least approximated, as they find life no longer confined in a world which is "just an address, a place for me to live in," but which is a world "wild and bright, going mad, shooting sparks into space." Here is revealed an existential structure that is a historical possibility, though one which is obscure from most other viewpoints, certainly those which are not attuned to love. When existence is marked by a heightened sense of dynamic, flowing, alive space and so thoroughly characterized by personal interpenetration, it is small wonder that song seems to be necessary to bring this truth into the light.

Romantic love is not the ultimate in human existence. It is, however, a very significant existential possibility and must be included in an attempt to understand human space. As we shall see in Chapter 13, this phenomenon of romantic love might best be understood within the perspective of human development, somewhat along the lines of Erikson's scheme. When we examine the viewpoint of Harry Stack Sullivan we shall discover an important adolescent phenomenon similar to romantic love in its basic effects though not necessarily including all the fireworks. Obviously if we are to see love as a basic structure of historical existence then the "heavenly heights" must be brought down to earth. In this respect Binswanger's use of the term "home" is helpful. He pointed out that the "heavenly feeling" associated with romantic love corresponds to the deepest sense of home.[5] When one is with another in mutual love one feels at home. Existence in the presence of one who is familiar, who really knows you and is near to you and for you, spatializes itself in the ecstasy of trust that transcends the constrictions of anxiety. Lovers say to each other: "My real home is where you are." In much social existence we feel ill at ease as we meet people who are basically strangers to us; when love elevates us to its own mode of

[5] L. Binswanger, *op. cit.*, pp. 72 ff.

transcendence beyond playing social roles, we feel at home with the other who was formerly a foreigner to the center of our world.

A phenomenology of love makes it increasingly evident that the space of being in love is radically distinct both from the space of ordinary visual conceptualization and from the Heideggerian picture of existential spatiality. Though Heidegger saw space dynamically, his individual's space was bounded by anxiety; in love these boundaries are overcome in a new structure of mutual trust. Awareness of the distinct spatiality of being in love presents us with a new concept of freedom, which will be expanded later. Freedom in terms of love is not to be understood in terms of the confrontation of nothingness which supposedly stimulates existence to stand forth as it truly is in the face of possible nonexistence. In love, freedom is discovered as a new openness in a mystery of coinherence that is constituted in part by the presence of the other. Boundless possibilities for personal existence emerge in love which were not *there* when the individual saw himself essentially in terms of his own goals. In love, the freedom of one individual interpenetrates with that of another individual. The result is not the sum of two parts; it is a new structure of human transcendence. Like two lines of notes which meet simultaneously, a new melody of man's inner life arises in which there are possibilities for development and meaning inconceivable in a monophonic context.

Binswanger insisted that when we consider personal existence we must recognize at least two basic modes. One is that of concern, which as Heidegger delineated it, may be radically singular; the other, as revealed by love, is the irreducible mode of dual existence. The spatiality of love's dual mode is, like polyphony, characterized by an apparently inexhaustible and manifold fullness. The space of love is never singular but is filled with the interpenetrating presence of the other. Freedom for expansion in meaning arises not from the confrontation of nothingness but out of the fullness that is discovered in the gift of presence. The entire Gestalt of love constitutes a spatiality in which individualistic conceptions about existence seem quite foreign. The love letters exchanged between the Brownings attested to a growing realization that the more they gave love to each other, the more there was to give; in love the boundaries of existence appeared to become increasingly wide, like the "lovers' infinitenesse" of which Donne spoke. If we persist in thinking strictly within an individualistic mode, such language emits sheer nebulosity; the meaning of lovers' testimonials becomes evident within the context of a dual mode of existence. This duality of existence implies a specific historical process in the new space-time unit of coinherence which constitutes a basic structure of human freedom and meaning. The task of phenomenology is to become aware of and to point out the various dynamics in the melody of life. This is very difficult to do; but the difficulty is no warrant either to give up the task or to attempt an overly simplified solution which fails to heed the tones in the upper registers.

Because of the overflowing, interpenetrating character of love's spatiality it is grossly misleading to portray love only as an individual's experience. In love a new aspect of intentionality has become evident. This intentional structure is not something *between* subject and object; rather, it is a form of existential transcendence which, like music, comprehensively involves the participatory interpenetration of lovers. Love as a self-revealing phenomenological agent has given its own witness to the spatial structure of loving interpersonal existence. It is a structure grounded in I-Thou. The *existential duality* of I-Thou is best understood in terms of the transcendent reality of *We*. The interpersonal phenomenon of *We*, as Binswanger pointed out, is the underlying dual reality which makes it possible for personal existence to discover that I belong where you are and that I *may be there* in the truest sense of the term *where you are there*.[6] The distinctive existential spatiality of love arises from this grounding principle of We. The common expressions of love, "I want to be where you are," and "Wherever you are, there is where I belong," are not inevitably fantastic notions, though admittedly fantasy may sometimes be involved. It is also possible to see expressions of love as authentic revelations of the coinherent reality of We, and of its unique form of spatiality. The space of real love is marked not by singularity but by *duality*. You and I in love have a common ground in the reality of We.

Binswanger argued consistently that the reality of We is not secondary, as though imposed upon a supposedly more basic reality of individual existence. He did not make use of Buber's term of an inborn Thou, which suggests a latent individual capacity to actualize a reality not yet present. Instead, Binswanger pointed to duality as an irreducible intentionality. Man basically exists in duality as well as in singularity. In fact it is only as an individual is grounded in the duality of a We that he finds a "place" for himself. To understand personal existence we cannot start with two separate individuals and then attempt to understand their union. It is

[6] *Ibid.*, p. 29.

imperative to begin with the reality of *we are* which discloses individuality emerging from within it. Love cannot be understood simply as an action between two subjects whose existence is reduced to the world of yours and mine; on the contrary, love reveals a unity of being, a totality. The melody of existence in love is a symphony in which different expressions interpenetrate so as to form a cohesive unity. Binswanger maintained that the unity of We is an existential *Urform,* a rudimentary structure of personal existence.[7]

Binswanger did not suggest how this *Urform* might arise; in Germanic fashion he merely proclaimed it was there. Yet he would not have accepted a common suggestion from sociology that the We-form pertains basically to social existence; and he definitely disagreed here with Freudian theory. Freud, like so many theorists before him, assumed that one's primary consciousness is of oneself; consciousness of others has been said to be secondary, such as a recognition of another as an object bringing pleasure or inducing frustration or pain. However, Freud's view has increasingly been recognized as part of the positivistic prejudice which permeated his environment; it does not accurately represent the facts. Obviously it is impossible to have complete certainty in this matter, but it seems likely that an infant is at first unable to distinguish himself from the mothering one. In his unformed consciousness some recognition dawns; and within an environment of consistent love the infant is aware of a reality of love which brings forth consciousness of otherness and then of himself. Experimental testing has suggested even that deprived of love an infant's physical dynamics will remain so undirected as to prohibit or retard the consciousness of others and the relationships he has with them. The emergence of anxiety and fear arising from the threatened loss or deprivation of the needed love stimulates consciousness of a break in the unity. The consciousness of self over against others arises from anxiety, along with the accompanying felt need for tenderness, the recovery of loving unity.[8] In other words, the nearly universal phenomenon of motherly love is the matrix from which personal consciousness arises; as such it forms a basic structure of human existence. This is not to say that later love is an attempt to return to mother, though that is certainly a possibility. A char-

[7] *Ibid.,* pp. 29-31.
[8] See the cogent argument along these lines by Ian Suttie, *The Origins of Love and Hate,* especially pp. 1-30. A similar position was worked out by Harry Stack Sullivan; see especially *The Interpersonal Theory of Psychiatry* as well as my discussion in Chapter 13.

acteristic feature of motherly love is symbiosis. The full duality of love, however, affirms the otherness of the Thou; this duality is a structure of reciprocal interdependence. The latter may be distinguished from the former, just as the intelligent sympathetic appreciation of Bach's music should be distinguished from an infant's delight at the sound of a shaking rattle. Yet there is no reason for refusing to recognize maternal love as a basis for the later discovery and fruition of adult, loving coexistence.

It is evident that Binswanger and Heidegger hardly refer to the same phenomenon when they use the term *Dasein*, because the basic characteristic of *Da*, the existential a priori, is differently conceived.[9] The difference is not restricted to variant conceptions of human space, but to the totality of the phenomenon of man. Binswanger rejected Heidegger's term "concern" (*Sorge*) as the most comprehensive or basic category to characterize existence. Heidegger maintained that *Dasein* is a relational being whose bearing in the world is structured by the modalities of concern such as feeling, understanding, and speaking. These basic forms of concern are directed upon beings in the world. The structure of intentionality is conceived in terms of existential openness to possibilities of being, either authentic or inauthentic. Yet this open concern in Heidegger's interpretation is rudimentarily a concern for oneself; it is my concern for my own being-in-the-world. To Binswanger this interpretation signifies that Heidegger's *Dasein* is not fully open to the whole world of existence but only to itself in the world. Hence Heidegger conceived of self in terms of *my* and *mine*. Binswanger discovered that love reveals an openness toward being which can only properly be designated as *our*.[10] What Binswanger attempted to show is that the selfhood of *us* is not derived from the self of you and me.

What is phenomenologically evident is that love is dynamically oriented in a structure that is different from that of a concerned individual. To be in love is to be open and oriented toward *our* possibilities. The

---

[9] This fact is apparently not recognized by Dr. Needleman. The very title he gave to *Being-in-the-World* suggests that he has not taken into consideration Binswanger's drastic overhauling of Heidegger as found in *Grundformen*. What is clear is that Binswanger rejected Heidegger's absolutization of care or concern. Needleman unfortunately concludes his lengthy discussion of the existential a priori in Binswanger "by noting that we have not changed our definition of the Existential A Priori as the concrete manifestation of the ontologically a priori structure of care" (*op. cit.*, p. 119). By failing to take into consideration Binswanger's most important contribution to existential phenomenology, Needleman's interpretation is misleading.

[10] L. Binswanger, *op. cit.*, p. 34.

world in love is no longer a place for you to be concerned about yourself and for me to be concerned about myself; it is a world in which we stand forth from that concern to abide in and for each other. It may be objected that this kind of talk does not sound very academic. Yet precisely the claim of existential phenomenology is that it moves philosophy out of the classroom to listen to the voice of existence speaking from the streets, the stage, the home, or wherever men testify to the existence which in fact they are. The testimony of love has borne witness that man is not merely or primarily an individual *en route* but that he is also a being who is at home with another. Love constitutes a new structure of existential space.

2. LOVE'S TEMPORALITY

To talk of existential space without at the same time making reference to existential time would grossly distort existential phenomena. Some mention of time has occurred in the previous discussion of space, enough to suggest that whatever was said of space has its counterpart in temporality. The human phenomenon is an integral whole of space-time. Heidegger's point that temporality itself is the clue to being is well taken; we approach the essence of human being by uncovering the roots of temporality, particularly as we move to an understanding of historicity. Yet to maintain balance it has been necessary for us to give far more attention to existential space and love's spatiality than to existential time and love's temporality. Only a brief review of human temporality and a short concentration upon the special characteristics of the time of love are necessary to illuminate the essence of this dimension of the human phenomenon. The brevity of this section should not mistakenly be interpreted as a sign of an unbalanced emphasis upon human space.

Heidegger demonstrated that existential time is to be understood in and for itself. Human existence frequently has been described and explained largely in terms derived from another area of reality; the kind of knowledge which emerges from such an approach is knowledge by comparison. The phenomenological appeal has been to get back to things in themselves, to hear human phenomena as they really are; phenomenology signifies an attempt to let existential phenomena speak for themselves. Heidegger's attempt to do so with respect to existential time was brilliantly successful. Existential time is not to be understood in terms of a succession of time periods in either a linear or a circular continuum. The dynamics of existential time are quite different from those of other beings, or at least different from the way that other beings have ordinarily been conceived. Hence existential time must be understood within a unique frame of reference. It has a special kind of intentionality which leads it to run ahead of itself into its future. The present is not a separate time period, but is constituted by the future and the past. The *future* is crucial in determining the meaning of a present. Inauthentic existence is dominated by a false future, one which has been molded and interpreted by the past. Inauthentic existence does not let the future really be. Thus man falls into an existential mode wherein his fullest possibilities have been refused, denied, and discarded. In authentic existence the mode of human temporality is ecstatic. Authentic temporal being is an ecstatic unity of past, present, and future, a unity which is running ahead into its own future. Repressed, fragmented, and fallen existence is overcome, as *Dasein* resolutely faces his ultimate possibility. A fragmented temporality is transcended by new integral wholeness. This integrated temporality, this ecstatic being unto oneself is more highly dynamic than fallen existence; for it has the character of being radically ahead of itself, running into a future which is already radically present, which, indeed, is even an integral part of one's past. Thus authentic existential temporality, as Heidegger illuminated it, is genuinely proleptic, charged with anticipation of a future which gives significance and direction to one's past-present being-in-the-world. In authentic resolution the fallenness of my facticity rises above itself to become true existence.

The image of music suggests the peculiar features of human time. Zuckerkandl argued at length that a visual measurement of time, by the clock, cannot be imposed upon music without destroying its unique form of existence. Especially is this true of melody.[11] If you close your eyes to listen to a melody you are aware of a dynamic, flowing, integral phenomenon. If you stop the music to analyze a part of it, you will have lost the melody. Experimental tests suggest that persons who are gripped by melody cannot pick it up immediately where it left off during an interruption. Only paper music has its parts. A melody is a dynamic whole with diversities of rhythm and meter. If you step away from it to analyze it, you have lost it. A melody does not consist of a succession of moments; it is itself a moment that has a fluid, dynamic duration. In music we have a Gestalt that is a symbol of existential time. Music helps us to listen anew

[11] Zuckerkandl, *op. cit.*, pp. 201-264.

to the phenomenon of man and to understand our unique space-time reality.

Existential time is like music. It does not occur in time; it is time. Existence temporalizes itself like a melody. Though there is before and after, yet existence is a whole in which before and after interpenetrate. Like music, existential temporality stands over and above standards of measurement which break it down into parts. No one has suggested this dynamic, flowing, alive essence of existential temporality better than Heidegger. Yet there is a difference between temporality in the structure of concern and in the structure of love. Mrs. Browning put her finger on it when she wrote:

> . . . love me for love's sake, that evermore
> Thou mayst love on, through love's eternity. (SONNET XIV)

The phrase "love's eternity" and ones similar to it redound through love poetry. It suggests a quality of time which definitely lifts existence above ordinary visual time concepts and above even the flow of time through the everyday world of concern. Binswanger also employed the term "eternity" to refer to the special ecstasy that appears in the phenomenon of love. He did not use it in any theological sense. Like the term "heaven," it is a poetic symbol which points to a special quality and a unique structure underlying the phenomenon of romantic love. It is time "beyond the slings and arrows of outrageous fortune," and it is beyond the boundaries of time in the singular structure of concern. Eternity does not belong to my being in the world for myself. In the temporality of love we find "the eternity of *Dasein* as *ours*, as an eternal *We*." [12] Eternity is the temporal correlate of the heaven of love's spatiality.

Though the term "heaven" suggests the "heights" as they are felt in the space of love, the term "home" is often more adequate to suggest the essence of love's spatiality. In a similar way the term "presence" may be more adequate than "eternity" to convey the most universal and basic structure of love's time.[13] "Presence" suggests an alteration in everyday temporality. Something *happens* when we encounter a particular person in a given situation. He is no longer just another being in the world along with me or over against me. Suddenly I sense his presence; it invades my space and time like an overpowering sound. As my own present is open to

[12] L. Binswanger, *Grundformen*, pp. 37 ff.
[13] Cf. *ibid.*, pp. 93 ff.

my past, which is no longer—and to my future, which is not yet—so, too, it may become open to the temporality of another person.[14] In a very special moment past and future seem to be fulfilled in a present that is grounded in the presence of another. Presence is a moment which transcends individualistic structures. I sense *his* presence; but it is a presence which fills *my* world and my time. When I receive his presence into my world, it is no longer his alone. It is a moment of *shared presence;* the moment belongs to *us.* There is something very familiar about it. Yet this familiarity is not of the order of the familiarity of my past or my future. It is familiar, yet new; it comes from without, yet makes itself known to me as though from within my own history, like a new song that seems to have come out of the past. Though this presence is an existential temporality, yet it is not marked by the anticipation of Heidegger's authentic individual. Rather, future expectations of fulfillment appear already to have been actualized. The presence of another in the moment of love constitutes a unique temporal ecstasy which cannot be reduced to temporal succession or to a proleptic being-unto-the-future. As Max Scheler put it, love is an uplifting or elevating action which carries man beyond his individual fate into a reality of personal fullness, into eternity.[15]

The phenomenology of love is still in its incipient stages, and much more attention needs to be given to the phenomenon of personal presence. Yet we can already see that the phenomenon of presence creates for existence a new moment of truth. The term "moment" has had great significance in existential literature. Kierkegaard referred to the moment as the paradox of God in time which one may enter through faith and thus become an authentic individual.[16] Heidegger also spoke of the moment as the ecstasy of the authentic individual when he transcends his fallenness and facticity and achieves the wholeness of his being through resolutely facing his own death.[17] Yet these interpretations simply do not portray man in his truth, at least not from a viewpoint which is aware of love. In Heidegger's scheme, as Binswanger put it, we see loving coexistence stand-

---

[14] Cf. M. Merleau-Ponty, *op. cit.*, p. 433. In speaking about interpersonal existence the concept of temporality is more appropriate than that of consciousness. When we think of consciousness we think of an isolated reality over against other consciousnesses; however, temporality naturally suggests the possibility of interpenetration, which is the hallmark of shared experiences. Cf. Marcel's discussion of presence, *The Philosophy of Existentialism*, pp. 36-46.

[15] M. Scheler, *Nachlass, op. cit.*, pp. 347-376.

[16] See especially S. Kierkegaard, *Philosophical Fragments.*

[17] M. Heidegger, *Sein und Zeit*, pp. 328, 338 ff.

ing freezing outside the doors of an isolated individual's existential proj-ect.[18] Man's authentic moment, when he uncovers the truth of his being, arrives when he discovers the loving presence of another affirming the whole of his own being in the world. The authentic moment of existence happens as one is open to and discovers the *presence* of another *in love*. Man becomes aware of his ownmost truth as he discovers the possibility of being a person in the fullness of love. The full truth of man emerges only when one confronts another in the dual mode of loving We.

The quality of the moment of love has the character of ecstatic dura-tion as opposed to mere succession. In mutual presence there is a newly discovered contrast, as Mrs. Browning put it, between the "Love that endures" and the "Life that disappears." [19] William Shakespeare said it in now-famous words:

> Let me not to the marriage of true minds
> Admit impediments. Love is not love
> Which alters when it alteration finds,
> Or bends with the remover to remove:
> O, no! it is an ever-fixèd mark,
> That looks on tempests and is never shaken;
> It is the star to every wandering bark,
> Whose worth's unknown, although his height be taken.
> Love's not Time's fool, though rosy lips and cheeks
> Within his bending sickle's compass come;
> Love alters not with his brief hours and weeks,
> But bears it out even to the edge of doom.
>   If this be error, and upon me proved,
>   I never writ, nor no man ever loved.[20]

The special durability of love here is what Marcel referred to when he spoke of love in terms of fidelity. Love is not an act upon somebody but a bond with him or her. To love another is to be committed to another being in such a way as to find oneself identified with him. The bond of love which "endures" is not meant to suggest an obdurate clinging to another or a fixation upon another but something quite different. One is, as we say, a "prisoner of love"; yet this should not, in the case of true love, signify a loss of creativity but, rather, a gain of it. It would be more accurate to speak of being "released by love" for participation in an exis-

[18] L. Binswanger, *op. cit.*, pp. 49-53.
[19] Sonnet XLI.
[20] Shakespeare, Sonnet 116.

tential possibility that transcends the narrow confines of isolated existence.[21] As Marcel said, this new quality of love which is characterized by endurance leads one to say to the beloved, "Thou, thou shalt not die." [22] Such language, if set in the perspective of visual space-time, would be ludicrous; yet it belongs to another order. The words are better set to poetry, as Mrs. Browning knew:

> Men could not part us with their worldly jars,
> Nor the seas change us, nor the tempests bend;
> Our hands would touch for all the mountain-bars:
> And, heaven being rolled between us at the end,
> We should but vow the faster for the stars. (11)

To say to a beloved: "You shall not die!" is first of all to refuse to consider the other person as an object. More profoundly it is to affirm the transcendent quality of a bond between two people which will persist creatively even though "rosy lips and cheeks within [Time's] bending sickle's compass come"; for, "love alters not with his brief hours and weeks, but bears it out even to the edge of doom."

In addition to the quality of existential duration there is in the moment of love another quality which can be denoted by the term *simultaneity*, which suggests its unique mode of ecstasy.[23] In individual existence running ahead of itself into the future there is the marked sense of anticipation. In the phenomenon of loving mutual presence there is a sense of having already arrived. In love, one comes home. Temporally speaking we have here an ecstatic mode which is neither closed to the future nor anticipating it, but one in which the appropriate future possibilities find instantaneous fulfillment. In love all time seems to be fulfilled in one moment. There is the sense of life coming to fruition "all at once"; or, as we say, one's dreams come true in an instant. This "all at once" quality gives to the phenomenon a heightened sense of the interpenetration of past, present, and future. It is a dramatic instant which cannot be measured in terms of clock time. As Nietzsche said, love thinks not on length

[21] See the still important essay by Gabriel Marcel, "On the Ontological Mystery," *The Philosophy of Existence*, pp. 9-46. Though written before his thought reached full maturity, Marcel's exploration of the mystery of presence as constituted and continued by creative fidelity, still deserves serious consideration.

[22] G. Marcel, *The Mystery of Being*, Vol. II, pp. 62, 153.

[23] Baron Friedrich von Hügel in *Eternal Life* suggested that even from a theological perspective "eternity" should be understood in terms of simultaneity.

but on the moment and eternity.[24] The characteristic of simultaneity is not, however, equally strong within the duration of the moment of love; it is rather like a strong chord struck at a climax of melodic progression, one which gives a peculiar intensity to the entire piece of music. The moment of simultaneity presents us with a new dynamic existential mode; it is not an existential project of anticipation into possible nothingness (*das Nichts*) but an arrival into a fullness that is truly ecstatic, which stands forth from succession and sheer individuality in the coinherent harmony of duality.

What the poets designate *eternity* is a quality of an existential moment, a special mode of existential transcendence. The character of this "eternal moment" is qualified not merely by an individual's act but by the presence of a Thou in the full reality of We. The illumination of presence makes it possible to understand the scope, rhythm, and tempo which mark any enduring love relationship. Though the phenomenon of love is an indivisible reality, like a melody it may have high and low points, moments of intensity and quiet, rich harmonies and sparseness. As the other's presence fades, the time in which one lives takes on different colors, tones, and significance, as it moves in another direction. No one said it better than Shakespeare:

> How like a winter hath my absence been
> From thee, the pleasure of the fleeting year!
> What freezings have I felt, what dark days seen!
> What old December's bareness every where!
> And yet this time removed was summer's time;
> The teeming autumn, big with rich increase,
> Bearing the wanton burden of the prime,
> Like widowed wombs after their lords' decease;
> Yet this abundant issue seemed to me
> But hope of orphans and unfathered fruit;
> For summer and his pleasures wait on thee,
> And, thou away, the very birds are mute:
> Or, if they sing, 'tis with so dull a cheer,
> That leaves look pale, dreading the winter's near.[25]

Distance and nearness, presence and absence cannot be measured simply in terms of physical proximity; human spatial and temporal terms must be understood within an existential context. Yet we are reminded by the

---

[24] "Liebe denkt nicht an Länge, sondern an Augenblick und Ewigkeit," Nietzsche; quoted in Binswanger, *op. cit.*, p. 44.

[25] Shakespeare, Sonnet 97.

poet that we cannot disregard the physical dimension as we attempt to understand existence and love. The full significance of love comes from the whole Gestalt of love, which certainly includes the physical presence of the beloved: "For summer and his pleasures wait on thee, And, thou away, the very birds are mute." In the phenomenon of love the whole of existence takes on new meaning which transcends all significance discerned from merely a visual-practical or individualistic outlook; yet the transcendence of love must interpenetrate with the other directions, or it will become false and be banished to fantasy. Love "throws" being in the world into a completely new light; the discovery of love, as Binswanger said, leads to a Copernican revolution in our understanding of man.[26] The light of love shows us a new world, constituted by structures bearing significance, which we can no longer afford to ignore so long as we harbor any hope of understanding the essence of personal existence.

3. THE DUALITY OF BEING IN LOVE

Thus far I have been adapting a Heideggerian type of existential analysis to focus upon the distinctive phenomenon of being in love. In doing so I have been guided in part by Binswanger's research. It is not surprising that Binswanger, a psychoanalyst, realized, in a way that Heidegger apparently did not, that man has a deep need to live in personal relationships with others; without love a person's historical venture through the world goes awry.[27] As a therapist who dealt regularly with seriously disturbed persons suffering acutely from the loss of trust and the breakdown of personal communication, he recognized that love plays a crucial role in authentic historical development. Following Binswanger's lead we have investigated love and have discovered that it creates a world constituted by forms of spatiality and temporality which simply cannot be fitted into a narrow existential scheme represented by Heidegger's authentic individual. Phenomenological research has sought to uncover the essence of existential transcendence; the phenomenology of love has provided a new perspective with which to view man as a whole and thus to understand essential

---

[26] L. Binswanger, *op. cit.*, p. 100.

[27] For a recent survey of psychological investigations into man's sociability drive or his impulse toward interpersonal relations, see Mark Abrahamson's *Interpersonal Accommodation*. The studies herein considered demonstrate almost conclusively that when individuals are forced in one way or another to live without an open and intimate exchange of affection and understanding with other persons, individual development is severely impaired.

structures of existence. From this point on I shall attempt to illuminate the meaning of love as a basic existential form, as an existential a priori, which man encounters as a historical possibility that must be realized for him to become truly human. From the perspective of love it becomes apparent that the main aim of human life is not to become oneself as an autonomous agent. Man's existential goal is to transcend his singular self by becoming a person in relation with others. The basic existential structure within which a human being becomes a person is loving coexistence.[28]

By listening to the poetic expressions of love we have heard existence sound a new melody of its inner life. Moving to the tune of love existence unfolds in a unique direction; that is, love provides existence with a unique intentional structure which is not readily apparent apart from the perspective of love. The history of this new structure is not directed exclusively for the sake of *my* existence; it is directed toward the fulfillment of *us*. In contrast to the direction of singular existence *en route* toward an individual achievement or the realization of oneself, the space of love is structured in terms of *being at home with another*: "The names of country, heaven, are changed away for where thou art or shalt be." This home-space is neither yours nor mine; it is ours. Because existence in love finds itself in a world where personal histories interpenetrate and complement each other, one has the sense of discovering unbounded and elevated space. The testimonies to such space will be falsified if interpreted in individualistic or subjectivistic terms; the discovery of unbounded space in love pertains to the awareness that *here*, in the world of love, I am no longer restricted to my own world and its individual possibilities. In love I am alive in a world that is constituted by a reciprocal exchange and mutual presence which opens up a horizon of vast new possibilities. The space of love is not

[28] David Bakan has presented an extremely enlightening psychological study of the roots of human existence. He maintains that there are two basic roots, self-assertive autonomy (which he refers to as agency) and interpersonal communion. See his *The Duality of Human Existence*. In his study duality refers to the two roots rather than to the union of two persons; what he refers to as communion I have called duality. As will become clear, there are more than two roots to existence; furthermore, the term "duality" is to be preferred to "communion" in that it suggests the origination of individuality from within communion. To oppose individuality and communion suggests that the former arises apart from the latter; phenomenological studies indicate otherwise. Professor Bakan's psychological study, however, wonderfully complements and reinforces a phenomenological approach. His focus is largely upon the gradual rise of agency in modern Western civilization; he is thereby able to detect the nature of the crisis which afflicts our times, in terms of the emergence of agency unmitigated by communion. Bakan's study is also especially relevant to an understanding of the roots of religion. It is quite possible that an entirely new approach to the phenomenology of religion could develop through the dialogue between Bakan's approach and our own.

subjective; it is *intersubjective*. The spatiality of love is characterized by duality.

Interpenetrating coexistence or personal coinherence is an essential element of love. The sculptor Auguste Rodin expressed this same insight powerfully in several of his works which portray love. For example, in his work "The Hand of God" two lovers are locked in an embrace so closely that at points it is impossible to distinguish clearly one body from the other. This work of art testifies that two beings tend to merge as they give themselves totally to one another in love. The two form a union, yet the union is more than physical. This sculpture symbolizes a spiritual or existential union. The lovers in union are like two melodic lines which have united to form a common space, thus producing a new reality which we call harmony.[29] As we must understand harmony in terms of a polyphonic rather than a monophonic structure, so we can understand being in love only in terms of its distinctive structure, *duality*.

In similar fashion the temporality of being in love is not to be understood simply as a melodic line running ahead of itself to completion. The temporal structure of personal existence is like a chord structure consisting of interpenetrating presences. In the ecstasy of romantic love a new quality is struck; existence is elevated into the eternity of interpersonal fulfillment. The essence of this *ecstasy* is one *of simultaneity in duration*, or *presence*. Such are the structural elements of the moment of love when it is grounded in mutual presence. In both its temporal and its spatial characteristics Binswanger has helped us to see that existence in love is constituted by a distinct form of intentionality, one which is not for the sake of one person but for the sake of *our* existence (*umwillen der Unsrigkeit des Daseins*).[30] In its romantic aspects love strikes the tones of heaven and eternity. Love in its more ordinary forms, whether between friends or in the family, constitutes a world of home and presence. The space of love as home and the time of love as presence are basic modalities to any human existence that claims to stand forth in the whole truth of being human.

At this point it is pertinent to elucidate one of the most distinctive contributions of existential phenomenology. This method is one which

---

[29] It is interesting that the full-blown emergence of romantic love occurred during the same cultural era in which there arose a new conception of music, from monophony to polyphony. How can one explain this coincidence? It might be that increasing awareness of this distinctive form of love demanded a new art form to symbolize it, to discover and express its truth. Certainly some of the composers of the High Middle Ages who broke away from plain chant to experiment with polyphony did so as much to express the meaning of courtly love as divine love.

[30] L. Binswanger, *Grundformen*, p. 59.

aims at opening up the phenomenon of man, not from the outside as though performed by a detached observer, but from within, from the viewpoint of a participant. The focus is upon inner life, but not in a subjectivistic or introspective sense. We would not expect to understand music by introspection; neither should we expect to understand man that way. To understand music we must let it encounter us, to come from without and through us until there is mutual participation of our two beings. In a similar way our particular endeavor to understand man focuses upon man in his meaningful encounters. One criticism to be made of other methods, many of which live on the borders of phenomenology, is that they do not grasp the full structure of *existential encounter*. Like Binswanger, I believe that Heidegger came closest to such a grasp and provided us with a framework which enables us to understand encounter as a whole, beyond the traditional cleavage of subject-object. Yet neither his nor the approaches of social science see the essence of "the being of loving encounter" (*das Sein der liebenden Begegnung*).[31] Phenomenologically it is crucial to distinguish basic modes of temporality and spatiality. This is also to suggest that phenomenology must illuminate the various modes of encounter in and through which man attains his truth. We must examine the encounter of man with the whole of his environment, where he both adapts himself to it and adapts it to his own needs and interests. In his world man encounters various existential possibilities which direct or dominate the course of his life. Especially important are interpersonal encounters. There are encounters with others with whom one conducts the business of life—people whom one is concerned to avoid or keep at a distance or to use, show respect, solicit support and recognition, offer assistance and encouragement, treat kindly or meanly, and so on. In addition to the several basic forms of encounter and the infinite patterns which their interaction and interpenetration may form within the structure of concerned being in the world, there is also the radically distinct encounter of those who love each other. This latter phenomenon is clearly recognizable to any who will look upon it with love; then they will see that the encounter of being in love has its own unique structure of duality. Binswanger wrote:

> The encounter of lovers in love . . . precisely spatializes the space of loving coexistence. That description of lovers in love is merely another expression for the special spatiality of love which consists of opening up

[31] *Ibid.*, p. 69.

and illuminating a We-space, the space of one another, of I and Thou. This encounter can "objectively" (*mitweltlich*) appear before us in a glance, a greeting, a word, a handshake, an act, a feeling, and even in a "fantasy" or "ideal"; and it can phenomenologically be experienced and illuminated. All the expressions (referring to such encounters) point to the fact that in this phenomenon a new world opens up, a world of We-in-love. This encounter, if it really is a loving encounter (or an encounter in love), cannot be repeated in a worldly sense of "once more"; for, as we already know, its very being is simultaneously not merely an already-having-been but also a being "for eternity," according to the temporal character of eternal duration.[32]

As existential phenomenology focuses upon the encounter of love or being in love, it requires us to reconsider Heidegger's restricted use of the terms "world" and "being-in-the-world"; for love opens up a new world. As Heidegger rightly pointed out, the primal world in which human existence unfolds is not a "place out there" where I have an address. The concept of a world out there is secondary to the lived world, the world as it engages me. World is first of all a transcendental, or better, an existential concept which refers to a basic structural dimension of human existence. Human existence is inseparable from world; I am being in the world. The world in an existential perspective both constitutes and is constituted by the total field of significance in which my existence takes its bearings (*Bewandtnis*) and according to which it charts its course toward meanings. The existential world is not something set out there which I happen to encounter somehow, one way or another, in the form of resistance. It is not a supposedly indifferent, objective world that I bump into if I don't watch where I am going. The existential world is *my* world, a structural element constituting my very own intentionality. The lived world is the field in which human transcendence discovers meaning. We imply this insight with the phrase "world of meaning."

This phenomenology of love has not repudiated a Heideggerian characterization of the world; yet love knows that human existence has a field in which to find its bearings which differs from that set by concern. In the encounter of love we discover that creative subjectivity belongs to *our* world; productive freedom emerges from reciprocal intersubjectivity. The world of love, freedom, and creativity cannot be reduced to the world of concern. The Heideggerian frame of reference, the being in the world of concern, is transcended by the basic existential reality of being in love. This

[32] *Ibid.*, pp. 82-83; my own relatively free translation.

love consists neither of I's nor Thou's separately, nor simply of individual acts for another individual; being in love is a dual reality of *we-are*. My true self will not come to light by focusing only upon the phenomenon of being in the world as directed toward *my own* authentic possibilities. As Binswanger suggested, to see the whole truth of man it is necessary to shift our perspective to the encompassing reality of We.[33] Love extends *beyond* my world. Its horizon constitutes the truly personal world. As such the horizon of the personal world is not something which I set by myself; it happens through me and comes to me as a gift from the other.

To place his insights in what he felt would be the appropriate relation to Heidegger's existential analysis, Binswanger coined a new term for human existence in terms of love. The full reality of man, he said, is not to be designated as spirit or as transcendence or even as being-in-the-world but as "being-in-the-world-and-beyond-the-world" (*In-der-Welt-über-die-Welt-hinaus-sein*).[34] The term "beyond" here obviously refers to the ecstatic quality of love's temporality—heaven and eternity—which gives to love a form of transcendence which "rises above" that already discovered in the phenomenon of concern. Yet the transcendence of love embraces being in the world; it does not properly leave it behind, for that would be a lovers' leap. Binswanger pointed to a special quality in the phenomenon of love which is implied by this term "beyond." As noted previously, Heidegger's solution to authentic existence in terms of resolute being-unto-death is essentially voluntaristic. The German term for transcendence, which both Heidegger and Binswanger played upon, is *übersteigen*, which means to climb up and over something. It connotes a physical form of ascending from one level to another or of stepping over hurdles in one's path. In any case, it demands a certain amount of exertion, whether it be through physical climbing or existential resolution. The ecstasy of love, however, is something which happens to you. You reach this phenomenon not by working up toward it but by letting it happen to you and carry you aloft. Suddenly or gradually you wake up to the fact that it has happened to you and that you are participating and alive in it. This form of transcendence is a mode of elevation which is like being carried away from one situation to another. Binswanger used the term *"Überschwung der Liebe* or *Überschwang,* which connotes being swung up into the heights.[35] The ecstasy

33 *Ibid.*, p. 71.
34 *Ibid.*, pp. 136 ff.
35 *Ibid.*, pp. 100 ff., 155 ff. et passim.

of love is something which happens to me as a gift; I am presented with it—with the gift of presence. Phenomenologically being in love is an ecstatic transport. The transport of love is not just an emotion, nor is it something like an exotic state of rapture or an intoxicated condition.[36] Though it reaches an extreme and particularly distinct expression in romantic love, transport or being-beyond-the-world is a characteristic of all genuine love. By being in love, persons are transported beyond the cares that become manifest in concerned being in the world.

Admittedly Binswanger's terminology is impossibly awkward; before attempting to arrive at a more satisfactory manner of expression, it is important to appreciate the truth he has uncovered. As we shall see, when one truly does not live beyond-the-world, when the world of love is not an open possibility and to some degree a presence, then the result is extremely unfortunate and under no circumstances could be considered to represent an authentic wholeness of existence. When the ecstatic reality of a true home beyond the world of concern (*die Überweltlichkeit der Heimat*) has disappeared or has become a fantasy, then one's existence is truly lost and swallowed up in the cares of this world.[37]

It should be clear that though Binswanger affirmed the special mode of love's transcendence, referring to it as beyond the world, yet he by no means implied that it is beyond form. The basic form or structure of being in love has been designated as duality. This term is meant to suggest the interpenetration of two worlds in the union that lovers experience through personal reciprocity and sharing. In an encounter with anxiety, one senses he has been thrown into the world; in the encounter of love, one becomes aware that his true being comes to him as a gift.[38] In contrast to an encounter with nothingness where one is forced to decide for one's destiny,

---

[36] The English term "transport" has unmistakable associations with the study of aesthetic transport in Longinus' *On the Sublime*. Its richer meaning was more helpfully attested by Thomas Aquinas when he wrote about interpersonal relations. In commenting upon the effects of love, Thomas affirmed that the phenomenon of mutual indwelling applies not only between God and the soul but also between those who love each other: "every love makes the beloved to be in the lover, and vice versa." Furthermore, the effect of love may produce an ecstasy whereby the individual is lifted beyond his natural apprehensive powers so as to be raised to higher knowledge (cf. *Summa Theologica*, II, 28). Unfortunately, Thomas was too bound to Aristotle to see that mutual indwelling is itself an ecstasy and thus provides a new source of knowledge that is common and natural to man, not something exceptional or supernatural. It is a sad and tragic comment that it has taken so long for our knowledge of man to probe this possibility and discover the world of meaning which lies behind it.

[37] Cf. Binswanger, *Grundformen*, p. 100.

[38] Cf. *ibid.*, pp. 95 ff. Marcel makes this same point emphatically.

in love one discovers a presence in which the whole of one's being is affirmed. Mrs. Browning expressed awareness of love's interpenetrating presence in SONNET XXI:

> . . . and yet I cannot rue
> The sin most, but the occasion—that we two
> Should for a moment stand unministered
> By a mutual presence. Ah, keep near and close,
> Thou dovelike help! and when my fears would rise,
> With thy broad heart serenely interpose.

The phenomenon of love in its fullness is structured by a mutual presence. The possibility of severance is there, and is to be dreaded. Being in love was recognized by her to be an interpenetrating reality so that all essential aspects of her existence were embraced, affirmed, and strengthened by it.

This interpenetrating mutual presence is a structural basis of the phenomenon of love and constitutes the horizon of meaning for truly personal existence. Binswanger maintained:

> The "mystery of love" will only be understood if one sees that the encounter of lovers in love, in which I and Thou are born as we-two, is only possible if *Dasein* is grounded in the reality of loving encounter. Only if it is grounded in this reality can we then see the world of love as opening up to us our lives as operating under a new principle.[39]

From this viewpoint we can say that man as a person is like a piece of music which simply is meant to play in harmony with other persons. If there is no harmony, no mutual interpenetration, then the intended chord structure, cadence, rhythm, and meter are tragically and mistakenly altered. If man is to escape the din of chaos which pounds through his life, then he must become aware of the basic personal structure in which the full melody of his life must be played out.

This personal structure is given to man, but it is given to be realized; the structure is historical. Certain events must occur for personal meaning to become actualized. We must stop thinking of human structures as finished products. Binswanger referred to the encounter of love not merely as an actual phenomenon but also as an a priori possibility; only because it is first the latter, can the former occur at all:

> Only because this is so is it possible for me to find and choose you, and you me. Whoever does not see that this phenomenon of finding and being found, and with it all the fullness and duration of love, is only possible

[39] *Ibid.*, p. 83; my own rather free translation.

strictly on the basis of the a priori possibility of loving encounter will neither be able to understand loving interpersonal relationships nor the other side of its "world" as opposed to that of concern.[40]

Binswanger rather dogmatically affirmed that man has what we might call a built-in encounter-structure (what he called an *Urbegegnung* and *Urmöglichkeit des Liebenden Begegnens*) that is specially designed to "house" love, without offering much evidence for the reality of it. I have previously suggested that the ground of this possibility is established in the earliest mother-child relationship. Binswanger himself pointed to the phenomenon of longing, so widely attested in poetic literature. In the expressions of deep longing for another being he detected not merely a physical or psychic desire but a feeling of being enticed and beckoned. That is, he viewed longing in terms of a possible interpersonal intentional structure. He maintained that the phenomenon of being drawn toward a beloved, even before an actual encounter occurred, cannot really be understood solely in terms of passionate desire, libidinal need, emotional instability, etc. The phenomenon of longing seen in the light of a basic possibility of loving encounter becomes the beckoning of one's own true self to find fulfillment in the reality of a loving we-are. As Buber said, all real living is encounter; Binswanger agreed with him that to find the fullness of being human one must encounter another as a person in the world of love.[41] As Binswanger saw it, man is the "born possibility" of a generalized We (*Wir-überhaupt*) whose task is to become this possibility concretely in a direct encounter of we-two (*Wir-beide*).[42] This view is essentially in agreement with Marcel's emphasis upon the existential reality of intersubjectivity as the true basis for creative subjectivity. In English literature a similar view is to be found in the perspective presented by the late Charles Williams. In this perspective, life begins with what he calls the first fact, *coinherence*. All of life, no less human life, is structured by coinherence. This is an order of interpenetration, of individual life converging with other individual life; but the particular insight is that the individual emerges from the

[40] *Ibid.*, p. 85; my translation.

[41] This is not intended to supplant or exclude the possibility that man's ultimate fulfillment comes only with a personal encounter with God. We must reiterate that our task here is to formulate an existential phenomenological view of man from a position which refrains from looking toward any possible ultimate meaning for man. It is the task of the theologian to deepen, clarify, and correct this phenomenology as he sees fit. Our task is not theology, though from an existential theological approach it might be seen as preparation for it.

[42] L. Binswanger, *op. cit.*, p. 86.

prior order of coinherence and not the other way around.[48] To affirm that personal coinherence is a basic structural possibility, part of the very givenness of man, is to insist that profound loving interpersonal relationships are not a pleasant addition to individual existence; rather, they are, to speak with reference to man's basic intentional structure, what man is in the world *for*.

Repeatedly the argument has come down on the fact that Heidegger's ontological construction which absolutized the structure of concern has failed to get at the full essence of human existence because it leaves out of account the heart of loving encounter, the basic structure of personal coinherence. There are at least two basic existential structures: concern and love, singularity and duality, transcendence for myself and transcendence for us-two. The encounter of love opens up a new form of existential intentionality, a new "world of meaning." If existence is to be considered in terms of openness, as Heidegger maintained, then it must also, both existentially and methodologically, be open to the *Urphenomenon* of being in love.

One's world is formed according to the kind and mode of one's encounters. The encounter of another in love presents a new possibility, a new dimension of meaning. The same old things are seen in a new light; they have a different meaning, because they are perceived from another perspective. The language of love in creative literature as well as in phenomenology has suggested that love is beyond the world, at least from one viewpoint. Yet this characterization is misleading. It was apparent to Mrs. Browning as well as to all who knew them both that she and her husband were two very unlike personalities. She admitted this from the start (SONNET III):

> Unlike are we, unlike, O princely Heart!
> Unlike our uses and our destinies.

For love to survive and flourish it is necessary to recognize the fact of duality, the special form of unity in love which does not overlook differences but affirms them. Apparently Mrs. Browning had to remind her husband that she could not be like him, that it was futile to try, and that it would kill love if she attempted to do so because it would destroy her.

---

[48] Cf. C. Williams, *The Descent of the Dove*, pp. 234 ff. See the relevant study of his writings, *The Theology of Romantic Love*, by Mary M. Shideler. The phenomenon of coinherence in the personal dimension is well illustrated in most of his seven novels, particularly *All Hallows' Eve* and *Descent into Hell*.

Love lifts lovers into a "higher reality" in which they find a new form of union through personal interpenetration or participation in the phenomenon of mutual presence, as she suggested in the following (SONNET XV):

> Accuse me not, beseech thee, that I wear
> Too calm and sad a face in front of thine;
> For we two look two ways, and cannot shine
> With the same sunlight on our brow and hair.
> On me thou lookest with no doubting care,
> As on a bee shut in a crystalline;
> Since sorrow hath shut me safe in love's divine,
> And to spread wing and fly in the outer air
> Were most impossible failure, if I strove
> To fail so. But I look on thee—on thee—
> Beholding, besides love, the end of love,
> Hearing oblivion beyond memory;
> As one who sits and gazes from above,
> Over the rivers to the bitter sea.

Two individuals who "look two ways," who have distinctly different personalities, who represent two quite separate private worlds, may nevertheless transcend these basic differences to find a genuine unity in love. In this unity the individuals appropriate personal fulfillment, "the end of love." From the outlook of love, existence appears different, takes on new significance. One sees life not merely from the vantage point of a historical past and present but a future of existential fulfillment, beholding oneself and the beloved in terms of "the end of love." The vision of love is also truly ecstatic; it reaches through past and present into the future and holds the whole of one's temporality in unity; even the deepest past is recovered and affirmed, "hearing oblivion beyond memory."

Any understanding and characterization of love should illuminate its own unique world. The world of love is not identical to the world of concern nor is it a smaller part of it. Both love and concern are basic modes in the primordial structure of being in the world. These modes are different and must be distinguished; sometimes they interpenetrate each other, but often they are in conflict or tension. By "falling" in love an individual "rises above" both his individualized world and also the common world of his society. If he allows love to fall into the world of concern and be swallowed by it, love dies; if he attempts to idealize the world of concern by viewing it solely with the emotion of love, tragedy is almost inevitable and authentic existence impossible. How the world of love is to be reconciled, at least in our understanding, to the world of concern will be more fully studied later. It is possible to suggest, however, that affirmation of the "worldly" character of love will lead to a re-examination of other fundamental aspects of the existential world in Heidegger's scheme. His characterizations of authenticity and inauthenticity must be questioned; furthermore, some existential modes which he labeled inauthentic might be seen to have a different significance from within the viewpoint of love.

A view of the basic existential modalities of feeling, understanding, and articulation or speaking changes when considered in the context of the love world. Feeling, for example, has its bearing not merely in terms of an individual's sensing his facticity, his being thrown into the world toward his possibilities. In the structure or world of love, feeling not merely reveals the facticity of being in love; it also constitutes interpersonal communication, as indicated by Scheler's phenomenology of sympathy (cf. Chapter 3). Feeling is a mode of communication; it not merely opens toward my possible being but opens a new world of creative exchange which otherwise was neither visible nor possible.[44] In a similar way love alters *existential understanding* by enlarging it. When understanding is viewed within a personal structure it includes awareness of an insight into not merely my existence both in terms of its authentic and inauthentic historicity but also of another's historicity and the present and possible meanings which are given in the *Gestalten* of love. As my understanding of another deepens, this changes not merely my own orientation but also has a radical effect upon the one whom I understand. Genuine interpersonal understanding affects both of us; it moves within the world of We-two.

The significance of articulation or what Heidegger referred to as speaking (*das Rede*) is also to be differently understood within the encounter of love. As was natural for a psychoanalyst, Binswanger gave much attention to the phenomenon of speaking. Though he realized its significance as a mode of self-expression, it is much more important to see speaking as an attempt at communication. The existentialists have maintained that authentic speech arises out of silence. Binswanger discovered that genuine personal dialogue arises from a silent recognition of the other as Thou. Only from within this perspective may its meaning be discerned.

---

44 The interpersonal intentionality is increasingly recognized in the field of psychotherapy, though the phenomenon is often referred to unfortunately as empathy. It is maintained by some American psychiatrists that empathy, which is defined as "the direct perception of another's emotional state," is the "persistent base for the human community and its communications." See for example Pearce and Newton, *The Conditions of Human Growth*, pp. 52-53.

To speak personally to another is to exchange mutual recognition. From a Heideggerian perspective phrases such as "How are you?" "Good to see you!" "What's new?" may appear to be mere small talk. The content of the ensuing discourse may seem trivial. Instead, however, what is more important is the nature of the relationship and the context within which they are spoken. To speak within the world of love is not primarily to discourse about something else for some ulterior purpose; often it is primarily to create, recognize, and reaffirm the reality of mutual presence. How much different is the significance of the question "How are you?" when arising in the context of a love relationship in contrast, say, to mere business relations or a medical examination. The language of love is not a kind of sign language in which words are used as arbitrary pointers to a distant reality which may be known only indirectly. Personal communication is genuinely symbolic. It creates the personal reality it is intended to express. It is speech which conveys effectively the presence of the person who utters the words to one who is open to receive them as intended. The language of love, of genuinely interpersonal dialogue, must be understood from within the whole encounter, the whole coinherent world in which the speech takes place.[45]

To have affirmed that love and concern constitute two distinct modes of transcendence is to maintain that the full man, man in his truth, exists basically in at least two different worlds. The boundaries of one are set by loneliness and anxiety; the boundaries of the other reach into the infinity of eternity and heaven. The world of concern, at least for the time being, we may designate as *singularity*. The world of loving interpersonal relationship has been denoted quite properly as *duality*. As we have seen, the testimony of love witnesses to a world that is structured by a distinct form of community, the personal duality of We. This duality is characterized by a unity marked not by the spatial merger of two liquids but more like tonal interpenetration. Henceforth a person must always understand himself and be understood in terms of interpenetrating relationships with the others. Again, Mrs. Browning was able to express these several important insights briefly and effectively (SONNET VI):

> Go from me. Yet I feel that I shall stand
> Henceforward in thy shadow. Nevermore
> Alone upon the threshold of my door

[45] Cf. L. Binswanger, *op. cit.*, pp. 196-218; see also his essays "Zum Problem von Sprache und Denken" and "Über Sprache und Denken," *Ausgewählte Vorträge und Aufsätze*, Vol. II, pp. 308-362.

> Of individual life, shall I command
> The uses of my soul, nor lift my hand
> Serenely in the sunshine as before,
> Without the sense of that which I forbore—
> Thy touch upon the palm. The widest land
> Doom takes to part us, leaves thy heart in mine
> With pulses that beat double. What I do
> And what I dream include thee, as the wine
> Must taste of its own grapes. And when I sue
> God for myself, He hears that name of thine,
> And sees within my eyes the tears of two.

As is the way with lovers, her individual life had been altered, nevermore to "command the uses of my soul" without an awareness of the coinherent reality of the other. In the world of love, one is not the sole maker of one's own destiny, for one is creatively faithful also to the destiny of the other. There is no space which is out of reach of the other's presence: "I shall stand henceforth in thy shadow." The heart of one's existence sounds with a dual beat. Even one's dreams and the encounter with God include the presence of the other. Such is the reality of genuine personal coinherence, which constitutes the foundation of truly personal existence. Only when a man is born in the world of love can he become a person, a man in truth.

English literature has made magnificent testimony to the reality of loving coinherence, not merely in the modern era represented by authors such as the Brownings and Charles Williams but also in previous generations by writers such as Shakespeare and John Donne. It was the latter who affirmed that "no man is an island," and who celebrated the special union of love in which two hearts are joined. This special mode of union, he maintained, provided unlimited boundaries for human growth and fulfillment. Loving coinherence operates according to a principle of exchange, in which one gives himself fully to the other; but here one gains everything, losing nothing. As he put it in his famous sonnet "Lovers Infinitenesse":

> Loves riddles are, that though thy heart depart
> It stays at home, and thou with losing savest it:
> But wee will have a way more liberall,
> Than changing hearts, to joyne them, so wee shall
> Be One, and one another's All.

The question must be faced, however, as to whether or not this way of love truly is "a way more liberall," one which is in truth the path of genuine existential freedom. Does not my "giving in" to love cost me my freedom? If in the exchange of love I am to lose myself, in what sense does *my* self ever get returned and fulfilled? Is it possible truly to be a free man and to be fully in love, or do the two exclude each other, as popular bachelor jokes often suggest? It will be our task in the following chapter to explore more carefully the apparently paradoxical relationship between freedom and love.

9

Freedom, Love, and Play

1. DIFFERENT MODES OF FREEDOM

Though existential thinking is as diverse as the disparate mentalities who prosecute it, nevertheless there is at least a unifying theme which runs like a red thread through its breadth and length. This theme is a notion of existence in terms of freedom. The literature of Existentialism provides strong testimony to human freedom. From Kierkegaard onward, existential thinkers have protested against an objectivist spirit in thought which would make man a pawn of deterministic forces, be they of an ideal or material consistency. One of the most moving appeals for human freedom was made by Sartre in his play *The Flies,* where the protagonist, Orestes, renounces both religious and social traditions which have kept men in subjection. Orestes is a paradigm of existential man who has discovered his freedom emerging as out of the blue, beckoning him to turn his back on situations and theories which would deny or reduce his uniqueness and to be free for himself, free to forge his unique destiny. The consistent affirmation and exploration of transcendence forms but another aspect of the existential witness to man's freedom. To speak of existential transcendence is to point to man's "rising above" complete determinism. Since Husserl we have become increasingly aware of the constitutive nature of consciousness; indeed we have recovered an insight into the constitutive function of existence as a whole. In the light of existential phenomenology, man is a being who himself constitutes his experience. Man is not merely a determined being, entirely constituted by less than human elements; he is also a self-determining being. The challenge of existential thinking emerges to awaken man to his possibilities of freedom. With limited awareness man is fallen from his true being, fallen from freedom. The search for the basic structures of human existence is an attempt to enlarge awareness by illuminating possibilities for the expression of human freedom. It has become clear that many common assumptions and conceptions repudiate freedom or at least ignore crucial aspects of it. Some beliefs keep man enslaved to the forces of nature and society and even deceptive forces of his own mind. To dismiss as illusory the problem of human freedom is to perpetuate darkness and thus betray the most human possibilities of existence. Man is born to be free. Existential phenomenology is part of a movement which seeks to bring human freedom into the light so that existence might find the freedom to be itself.

In existential thinking there are, however, diverse theories about freedom. In attempting to elucidate freedom, it will be best to dispel certain beliefs associated with the concept. Much traditional discourse about freedom has centered in a discussion of the will; advocates of freedom have asserted that there is a particular faculty in man which can escape the determining forces of environment, heredity, and even sin. Both modern psychology and philosophy quite properly avoid discussion of the hypothetical "free will." Certainly phenomenology rejects the highly dubious traditional bifurcation of intelligence and will; indeed it opposes any tendency to partition existence.[1] We should also reject as misleading and too narrow, a concept of freedom which sees it largely or exclusively in terms of a deliberate choice. The implications of any such theory suggest that man's freedom is sporadic, emerging only when one makes an act of the will. Phenomenology has made clear that the whole man, being-in-the-world, is to be understood in terms of freedom. Freedom applies to man in relation to powers and possibilities, not merely to isolated parts or acts of his existence. Furthermore, the whole man is *engaged* in a situation; thus human freedom cannot properly be regarded as existing apart from the world. The traditional view of free will, particularly in much Roman Catholic theology emerging from the Middle Ages as well as in much popular thought, has often failed to appreciate man's worldly involvement;

[1] See John Wild, *Existence and the World of Freedom*, especially chapters 6 and 7, for an extensive criticism of a traditional notion of freedom which centers it in a particular act of the will, divorcing freedom from man's understanding. As Wild makes very clear, the phenomenological approach has uncovered the ground of freedom in the understanding.

hence it has tended to ignore the relative and ambiguous character of freedom.[2] Absolutistic notions of freedom are unwarranted, whether espoused in the past, or in the writings of existentialists such as Jean-Paul Sartre, or in the popular mind as implied by the common assertion: I am free to do what I want. To maintain any notion of freedom which fails to acknowledge the limitations and restrictions pertaining to being in the world is to entertain oneself with gross delusions.[3] The only freedom that man knows is a conditioned, worldly freedom.

To speak of human freedom is to point to the whole phenomenon of existential transcendence as being in the world. To be free as a man means to be free in the world, to be engaged in a particular situation in a creative way. Freedom is a constitutive element in the human encounter with the world. Yet this encounter is dialectical. Being in the world is grounded upon a facticity that includes both my creative self and whatever my creativity has to work with and through. Man is not in the world by his own free choice; he is *thrown* into the world. Or to speak from the perspective of love, man is *given* being in the world. Man is given freedom in a situation, which means to be given limited freedom. Man is a shaper of destiny, but he is also a product of it. There are forces external and internal, natural and unconscious, historical and social which influence and determine man's being in ways of which he is scarcely aware. We must fully acknowledge the numerous determining factors which operate within our total situation. Binswanger wrote that "freedom consists in the commitment of the *Dasein* to its thrownness as such, non-freedom in denying it autocratically and violating it on the basis of an Extravagant ideal." [4] In the process of illuminating basic existential structures we have rejected both absolute causality and absolute freedom. There is no freedom without a specific situation; there is no field of significance without limitations. Yet there is no truly human situation without freedom; to eliminate freedom is to annihilate humanity.[5]

---

2 Cf. the criticism of the Catholic tradition by Father Remy Kwant, *Phenomenology of Social Existence*, pp. 48 ff.

3 It is interesting to notice that the notion of unconditioned freedom which is frequently associated with some forms of Christian theology is rejected as a demonic temptation in the Synoptic Gospels. In refusing to succumb to the temptation to change rocks to bread and to jump with impunity from the top of the temple, Jesus gave testimony to the conditionedness of creaturely life which man must learn to accept. God has not apparently made us "free as the birds" but to become free as men. See the Gospel of Matthew 4:1-11.

4 Binswanger, *Being-in-the-World*, p. 321.

5 Cf. Erich Fromm's interesting discussion of freedom and determinism in *The Heart of Man*, pp. 115-150.

Through phenomenological analysis we have come to perceive a human situation in terms of its intentional structure; thus freedom is to be understood within the intentionality of being in the world. Freedom gears itself to a given situation; it expresses itself in various modes called out by the specific situation and the given moment. As an individual develops he manifests a variety of free expressions, particularly as he spatializes and temporalizes his existence toward his own most possibilities. Man has a wide variety of possibilities, some of which may preclude or inhibit others. The realization of every possibility involves some freedom.

This is not to say, however, that every realization is authentic. Though a possibility be human, it may not be appropriate to one's stage of development; or it may be such as to preclude the realization of a fundamentally more significant possibility. The question of decision emerges at the point when one must choose which mode of freedom he prefers to follow. As the term implies, to make a decision is "to cut oneself off" from certain possibilities so as to be directed toward the attainment of others. It is not so much a matter of having or not having freedom but of choosing the kind and extent of freedom. Every act of being in the world is an act of freedom, but that in itself does not necessarily make it an authentic act; on the contrary, an act of freedom might in fact be the repudiation of authenticity or even the denial of existence itself. As Kierkegaard indicated, despair is a distinctly human phenomenon; as such, it is a form of freedom which ultimately, however, is self-defeating. Despair is a form of spiritual sickness which leads to the disintegration of one's being.[6] The same can be said of other existential modes such as cynicism and nihilism which are rightly understood as human threats to freedom. To change the direction of freedom does not require that one supposedly leap out of a particular situation. To appropriate greater freedom requires being engaged in one's given situation and becoming aware of the possible significance that may be uncovered there. This growth of awareness is stimulated by insight into the creative ground of existence which sees that I am responsible for realizing that significance. The increase of freedom demands awareness of my unique being in a given situation and with this an insight into the possibilities for life and death which are open to me.

To speak of freedom as being engaged in a situation brings it more clearly into view as a basic element of human encounter. Man is given a world, and he also constitutes the world in which his being unfolds. His entire worldly being is constructed by his world-encounters. As he develops

[6] S. Kierkegaard, *The Sickness unto Death.*

he increasingly determines how he encounters the world and the specific kind of significance it has for him. His encounters with possibilities are spatialized and temporalized, are historicized in his own unique way.[7] No one else encounters the world for him; no one else's history is identical to his own. In an existential framework, encounter is not to be understood as a meeting between a predetermined subject and a predetermined object. Existential encounter is primarily an outgoing historical process directed toward possibilities which in turn give direction to existence; it is only within a particular historical direction that we encounter significance. By understanding freedom within the framework of encounter we see it not primarily as a being-released-from restrictions but as a being-directed-toward possibilities. Rudimentary human freedom thus involves being oriented and being aware of one's orientation so as to make sense of one's encounters. Authentic freedom is man's encounter with those possibilities which give him the opportunity to be most fully human. To become truly human is to enact one's freedom so as to rise above fragmented existence with its distorted meanings toward a historical destiny of fulfillment and wholeness. To achieve the historical ecstasy in which the process of existence most completely attains an interpenetrating integration of the most fundamental possibilities pertaining to being in the world is to realize freedom most authentically.

It is now apparent that freedom is not to be thought of as something which man has either as a faculty or as a possession. As Marcel has put it, man is not born free; he is to become free. Man's freedom is to be won. Freedom is not a finished product; it is a dynamic process. Man does not bring it with him into the world; he is in the world to realize freedom by living it out. As an existential reality, freedom is thoroughly historical. To be free means to be open historically to the reality that one encounters; and this includes being open to one's historical possibilities. As one discovers basic possibilities one begins to uncover the truth of man. Thus in an existential perspective *freedom* and *truth* converge.[8] There is constantly the danger that I shall misuse my freedom and adopt a modality which closes rather than opens me toward my fullest possibilities. To close the

---

[7] Cf. the discussion of freedom by Merleau-Ponty in *Perception, op. cit.*, pp. 434-456. To my mind this is one of the most impressive and adequate treatises on the nature of human freedom to be found anywhere.

[8] Perhaps this is what Kierkegaard was getting at with his notion that truth is subjectivity; for *how* I am in the world determines *what* truth I shall apprehend and appropriate. See his *Concluding Unscientific Postscript*, pp. 169-224.

doors to basic possibilities is at once to narrow freedom and to shrink the truth. To live out freedom is to become continually engaged in a dialectical situation; to become free in the truth requires one to sustain the tension of possible directions. The winning of freedom demands increased awareness of possibilities as these emerge from within the facticity of a given situation. To become free as men requires us first of all to see and hear the truth of being in the world, to be open to it that it may make its claim felt upon us. Genuine freedom is constituted by openness to existential possibility, which in turn demands my response. Freedom can only become true if I pursue the meaning it offers me. To be free is to be open for historic encounter, which involves being open to the truth and open for responsible engagement. Freedom at its best is inseparable from responsible commitment in a given situation to the fullest possibilities of being human in truth. To run away from an encounter with a basic possibility of being in the world is to lose one's freedom; such actions bury one's humanity. As Freud attempted to point out with his theory of the death-wish, we attend our own funerals regularly.

To gain a vision of freedom as existential openness in a situation is to move toward the insight that freedom and love converge. To be truly free involves being open to another and directed toward the genuine possibility of being with him in the reality of We. Our experience of encounters with others may make us suspicious of this possibility. There are obviously modes of being with others which stifle freedom by robbing us of genuine possibilities for adventure, discovery, pleasure, tranquillity, and so forth. But is this true of love? Does not love require that you give up your independence as a free man? Has not the language of love, in the family especially, indicated that individuals must sacrifice themselves for the good of others? Does not love bind you to another or to a group so that individual ecstasy is precluded or greatly diminished? We have seen that love is a bond. Is it not a common experience that this bond ties you down so that you are not free to roam, to find new possibilities, to let your spirit soar to unfound heights? What freedom is left for the man bound in love but to allow his eye and mind to wander? Has he not turned in his freedom to obtain the security of bondage? Can we speak truthfully about freedom, freedom in its grandest aspects, within the world of love? If so, then we must examine the phenomena carefully with the awareness that many of our attitudes and much of the language of ordinary life imply that freedom and love really do not converge. However let us admit at the start that much of what passes under the name of love is false; and false love corrupts and diminishes freedom.

To begin, let us reject the notion of freedom in terms of an entirely free choice of limitless possibilities. Freedom is always within a given situation and thus is bound to the possibilities which emerge within it. One is never totally free to do what he wants. One must become free; and this requires becoming aware of possibilities. In the phenomenon of human freedom there is a constant interaction between self and world; it is impossible to distinguish clearly between what is given by the situation and what by the individual or group. The task of phenomenology is not to try to establish cause and effect; it is to consider and understand possibilities. Free encounter is constituted by numerous factors in the total *Gestalt* of being in the world, including project and prospects, openness, choice, and the very essential element of opportunity. As we have seen, existential encounter is not fundamentally a phenomenon of resistance, a kind of bumping into the world as it stands in one's way. The basic mode of encounter in terms of being in the world is a form of open communication. To encounter the world is to become aware of it, and to enter creatively into a process of being informed and giving form. The human world of encounter is thus a world of freedom, a confrontation with existential possibilities. To become free in truth involves an understanding of those possibilities which promise to provide a person with the significance most appropriate to his unique historical being; further, it involves becoming directed toward their realization.

We have discovered that encountering another person presents a particularly significant possibility for communication. This form of encounter also communicates a basic meaning of existence insofar as it reveals the essential structure of duality. To encounter another person in love discloses the possible meaning of being human in terms of personal coinherence. The meaning of any encounter does not lie beyond its situation in the realm of logic but emerges within the situation as genuine possibilities are appropriated, sought, ignored, or rejected. Being in love is a genuine possibility opening up a new world for us. Unless we decide to reject that world or unless that possibility finds no opportunity to encounter us, then the truth of that world remains open. Apart from the world of love the full truth of man cannot be uncovered, especially the truth of his freedom. In the encounter of love I not only discover the possibility of exercising my freedom to become a person; I also become aware that human *freedom* is not merely *mine* but *ours*. The human freedom of couples and groups must also be recognized. Tony and Maria, in *West Side Story*, did not primarily seek individual freedom; they longed for the freedom to become truly one—one heart, one hand, one life. As an elementary existential structure of meaning, *duality is a basic mode of freedom*. Much of the danger to and tension in love arises from the conflict between duality's freedom and that of singularity and society.

It is also possible to encounter another person within the referential framework of concern. This mode of encounter may involve sharing a common world, which is nevertheless to be distinguished from the world of love. The encounter of another person in the structure of concern is legitimate; indeed it is necessary to do so even with one you love. Marriage, for example, represents a total merger between love and concern. However, one way of encountering another person with concern is to meet him essentially as a foreign object. This possibility is all too human and familiar, and will be examined more carefully later. What is most important at this point is to distinguish between modes of freedom in our relations with others. As an individual I am free to care for another as an individual. Yet there is also the possibility of realizing a new kind of freedom which belongs to the two of us. There is in fact considerable evidence to indicate that the freedom emerging in love's duality is essential for full development of individual freedom.[9]

The question with regard to love and freedom is not: Shall I be free or be bound to another? but: What mode of freedom shall I express? As for my being with others, it is not a question of whether I shall be with them or not; human being is essentially being-with. What is basic to our contest for freedom is *how* I shall be with others. Yet the question cannot be put so simply. For another question is vitally important: How shall *we* be *with each other*? How shall *we* express *our* freedom? As psychoanalysis has so clearly shown, the mode of being with others is not a direction which is

[9] Clinical studies have shown that the absence of love in young children leads to or involves the breakdown in the natural communication between self and world. This breakdown then entails a tremendous loss of freedom, as in schizophrenia. A child suffering an impairment in his ego is not open to his situation; rather, he is fixated upon something in the past. He is not free to communicate within his situation except indirectly. Frequently in very young infants there can be noted what Erik Erikson denotes as a deficiency in "sending power"; but as he also makes clear, a breakdown in communication is more often a result of a deficiency of love. Thus, clinically, the suggestion comes forth strongly that genuine freedom without love is impossible. Cf. *Childhood and Society*, p. 207 et passim.

entirely up to me. How I encounter others is also determined by how others encounter me. Though it is impossible to say how much is determined and how much is up to me, at least as a historical being I must recognize the highly influential temporality of my past. There are often factors of my having been with certain people which restrict or inhibit my freedom now. It is commonly assumed that other people prevent me from exercising my freedom. Of course this is true; someone may stand in my way. Yet it is also true that a serious barrier to freedom emerges from the fact that certain persons have *not* stood in my way to support and encourage me. The absence of positive personal relationships throws each of us open to dreadful anxiety. As we shall see in Chapter 12, the nearest and greatest obstacle to freedom is our anxiety, our encounter with raw nothingness. It is not essentially the other person who meets me in love who constitutes the primary threat to my freedom. Hell is not so much other people but our inability to share in a mutual presence. Thus we become tightly bound by the dark and chaotic forces of anxiety. Man's fear of losing his freedom is only one aspect of a very complex phenomenon. Man is also, and all too often, afraid of his freedom, particularly the freedom to exist within the infinite boundaries of love; thus he seeks to escape from it.[10]

Psychoanalysts and existentialists have uncovered a universal fear of freedom. Albert Camus described this fear as a very basic factor in the human condition. In his novel, *The Fall*, the narrator, an ex-lawyer who habituates a bar, spoke despairingly of his former delight in freedom, which had turned sour with his awareness of its ambiguities and burdens. As he said,

> Once upon a time, I was always talking of freedom. At breakfast I used to spread it on my toast, I used to chew it all day long, and in company my breath was delightfully redolent of freedom. With that key word I would bludgeon whoever contradicted me; I made it serve my desires and my power. I used to whisper it in bed in the ear of my sleeping mates and it helped to drop them.[11]

As he discovered, his freedom could be a way of achieving certain satisfaction, though usually at the expense of someone else's freedom and the loss of truth. Within such a perspective, however, freedom ceased to be a

10 Cf. the now classic study by Erich Fromm, *The Fear of Freedom* or *Escape from Freedom* and also his more recent *The Heart of Man*.
11 A. Camus, *The Fall*, pp. 131-132.

delight; it became drudgery to protect it, execute it, and keep it from the annihilating clutches of others. Freedom, as the narrator continued, is really not a reward or a decoration, but a chore; it is a

> long distance race, quite solitary and very exhausting. . . . Alone in a forbidding room, alone in the prisoner's box before the judges, and alone to decide in face of oneself or in the face of other's judgment. At the end of all freedom is a court sentence; that's why freedom is too heavy to bear, especially when you're down with a fever, or are distressed, or love nobody.[12]

In the act of choosing a possibility one can sense his isolation and also his guilt. From such a perspective, to be free is not to gain release but to receive a sentence. As such we are indeed condemned to be free. The protagonist of this novel came to realize that he was afraid of his freedom. He also became certain that people really do not want freedom. That is why they invent such dreadful rules by which to live, so as to keep themselves in the safety of slavery.[13]

The probing, penetrating insight of this literary artist reveals the sometimes dreadful and burdensome dimension of human freedom. Man is frequently frightened by confronting the greatness of his freedom. It beckons forth his whole being; yet he faces the darkness of the unknown. But is this unknown an openness to authentic possibilities or to the negation of all possibilities? Does it beckon to fulfillment or death? To solidarity or solitary existence? The communication may not be sufficiently clear to say what it means. The greatness and mystery are too much for him. Thus man is often a compromiser, choosing little freedoms for trivial possibilities as cheap compensation for authentic freedom which he is too frightened to pursue. Especially in moments of weakness, when one senses acutely his isolation and vulnerability, freedom appears to be unbearable. In that situation man's only choice may be not to choose. By not choosing, one stays safe and alone. Yet such a man is really a stranger to *our* world. He drifts through life without a direction known to us. His world does not establish communications with ours. The private world of his freedom is often so weird as to call forth constant suspicion and uneasiness among those who encounter him, making all the more impossible a breakthrough

---

[12] *Ibid.*, p. 133.
[13] *Ibid.*, pp. 133-137. A similar argument is presented in the celebrated chapter "The Grand Inquisitor," in Dostoevsky's *The Brothers Karamazov*.

of understanding.[14] Yet to be truly human, man must choose the freedom which so often frightens him. But how?

We are beginning to see that freedom reaches more deeply into the being of man than other approaches have led us to suspect. Freedom is an essential character of the totality of human existence no matter how it expresses itself. Furthermore, freedom is grounded in the intentional structure of man, particularly in terms of its openness toward possibilities and hence meanings. In the intentionally directed structure of his being, man encounters possibilities which confront him with both promise and anxiety. Aware particularly of the latter, man becomes afraid of his freedom and feels guilty for his failures to become free. Man is that freedom which is aware of itself as a great possibility and which is also aware of the seeming impossibility of reaching greatness and dignity. In his fear man often declares the vision of greatness to be a fantasy. With fearful freedom man spins deceptions about himself. In the web of history he is caught and hanged by his own deceptions. Yet there is another aspect to this perspective which was suggested in the quotation above. Freedom, Camus's protagonist said, is too heavy to bear when you're down, especially if you "love nobody." The phenomenology of love suggests that such is precisely the case. In the transcendence of love I am lifted up above the weights of my own cares. The transport of love elevates one's being beyond the sentence placed upon it by mere singularity. Love can open existence to a new world; it thus gives existence new power to achieve new meanings. Love gives man the power to be free and the freedom to become whole.

The mistake of so much discussion of freedom has been to observe it only from a singular perspective. But freedom pertains at least as fully to being with others in love as to being for oneself. Freedom applies to the whole phenomenon of man, not just the individual or singular aspect. Earlier we noted that man was a shaper of his destiny. That is a phrase which has been gravely misunderstood and misused, because it often is meant to denote individuals rather than communities. But couples and societies forge human destiny. Cultures are not mere products of the past; if so, there would never have been any change and nothing like history as we know it. Change within historical and cultural development occurs to some extent through social action of men and women who together discover the power to direct history toward some meanings and away from others. Cultural change, and hence freedom, is definitely a corporate phe-

14 Cf. A. Camus's brilliant portrayal in *The Stranger*.

nomenon. Emile Durkheim in particular has illuminated the reality of corporate freedom even though his positivistic background led him consistently to deny freedom in terms of individuality. From his sociological perspective he discovered that in and through society a way is opened to man to uncover, express, affirm, and sustain genuinely human meanings. Durkheim pointed out that as a being with others, acting with them in a common world, man becomes free, transcending his materialistic limitations.[15] Man is born into the world with others in an intentional structure that is *for* them; as man has acted corporately with and for others he has made history and shaped his destiny.

A true act of freedom can be within and through a group just as truly as it can be apart from or in opposition to others. Social encounter is a basic structure of freedom. The same is true of the encounter of love. As we shall discover in the phenomenology of play, love itself is a basic form of freedom and provides a person with the *Lebensraum* to be free as an individual. Indeed, freedom for the fullest human possibilities, or for authentic existence, must be grounded on love. If the dread of freedom issues from man's encounter with anxiety as both psychoanalysts and existentialists indicate, then the solution in favor of greater freedom cannot come from voluntaristic exertion but only as a free gift of love which transports one into a new world beyond the terror of anxiety. The fear of freedom is not necessarily fear of all freedom but only of certain aspects of it. Seen from the perspective of love, fear may be a healthy sign, warning man that he must not attempt to stand all alone in his course through life.

When it is seen as "all mine," freedom can be a burden. Yet when it is realized that there is also the *freedom which is ours,* freedom can represent an open door to joy and personal fulfillment. Man needs to discover the freedom for two to be one in the new world of love; otherwise he will not truly become happy. Persons in love romp, skip, and sing their ways through their world. They are not lonely long-distance runners moving

---

[15] See, for example, his eloquent statements in this regard in *The Elementary Forms of the Religious Life*, p. 307 et passim. Though Durkheim went to extremes by emphasizing freedom as so collective that it could only be understood as a social phenomenon, he nevertheless uncovered one basic aspect of it which individualistic interpretations are wont to ignore. For a penetrating study into Durkheim's uncovering of freedom as social action, see Talcott Parsons, *The Structure of Social Action*. See also E. Durkheim, *Essays on Sociology and Philosophy*. For a phenomenological appreciation of freedom from within a social perspective, see R. C. Kwant, *Phenomenology of Social Existence*.

through the dark; they are sailing on bright clouds. The freedom of love is not imprisoned by worldly cares; it does not trudge under sentence through the world. Love often disports itself freely in the world; it is a mode of encounter between human beings with possibilities which call forth their joy and laughter. The boundlessness of love gives man room in his world to rejoice. The fullest expansion of personal freedom happens in the world of love, not by running away from it. Of course there is a freedom within love which gives to existence the seriousness of responsible fidelity; but love also inspires the levity of genuine playfulness. For greater insight into the relationship between love and freedom a phenomenology of play is instructive.

2. PLAY: A BASIC HUMAN STRUCTURE INVOLVING LOVE AND FREEDOM

Why do people play? What does it mean to them? It is increasingly being realized that play is a significant form of behavior. Yet it is a phenomenon which puzzles and confounds many who study it, as evidenced by a general inability to define it. What is play? From an adult point of view it would appear to be the opposite of work. It is a mode of being in the world whereby the workaday world with its sense of gravity is left behind. In the moment of play the serious cause-effect order of work is forgotten as one finds a freedom beyond the confinements of ordinary concerns. Play is definitely a form of freedom, a mode of transcendence, a genuine existential possibility. Yet it has rarely been understood as such. Many older psychological theories have attempted to explain play in terms of energy. It has been seen to be the result of an exuberance of energy; or, in the opposite direction, it has been viewed as a compensating form of behavior when one is not up to really serious work. Some theories have considered play to be a kind of pre-exercise, a preparatory behavior to work wherein one learns to develop new skills. Many theories of play have seen it in terms of observed effects without focusing upon the actual content of it. Current psychological approaches have shifted from mere observation of effects which were then combined with hypotheses regarding inferred causes to empirical studies of the actual play of children.

One of the most illustrious modern theories is that put forth by Jean Piaget, in which play is seen as part of the whole of infantile dynamics. As he studied children at play he concluded that play is a stage in a child's thinking about reality. He postulated two basic existential modes. One is to adapt reality to fit into what one already knows; the other is to adapt oneself to what is encountered. An infant's play begins when he has become somewhat familiar with his environment; and his play continues to be behavior directed toward that which is familiar. Accordingly, play is behavior which bends reality to what the individual already knows. It is behavior closely associated with dreams and fantasy. In Piaget's theory, play will tend to drop out as one progresses toward consistent adaptation to reality. Yet because it continues to bring pleasure and serves the purpose of learning to adapt to new situations or to find compensations for unfulfilled longings, an element of play will be found in adults.[16] Aside from the naïve naturalistic presuppositions, which have been exposed and challenged in preceding chapters, this kind of approach fails to distinguish the various possibilities of play which can be seen from an existential viewpoint. It does not see play from its own frame of reference but from a supposedly adult world of work. Thus it fails to see play in its actual situation as a form of existential encounter, which is to say, a specific mode of freedom.

Much more illuminative of the significance of play is the multi-directional approach of Erik Erikson. He also focused upon the play of children, particularly the play of disturbed children; and he, too, studied it primarily as a phenomenon within childhood development. Yet he has insisted that play is much more than a way of finding refuge from very new aspects of reality or of seeking pleasure; indeed, he has maintained, it is an essential and constructive mode of behavior. Like Sigmund Freud, and even more his daughter Anna, Erikson sees children's play as a way of dealing with anxiety by attempting to decrease and eventually dissolve it.[17] Yet a shortcoming of a strictly Freudian approach was that it concentrated upon the phenomenon of a solitary child's acting out his fears and wishes; his play was seen to be a dramatic concretization of his fantasy. Erikson has studied children's play in terms of its specific situations, and he has discovered that there are various forms of play, the unique meaning of which must be uncovered in each situation.[18] He found that a child frequently enters into play with a precarious sense of his own time-space, and that play gives him an opportunity to develop his own field of significance,

[16] See the study of play by J. Barnard Gilmore, "Play: A Special Behavior," in *Current Research in Motivation*, R. N. Haber, ed. Also J. Piaget, *Play, Dreams, and Imitation in Childhood.*

[17] See Anna Freud, *The Ego and the Mechanisms of Defense*, and Erikson, *Childhood and Society*, pp. 216-217.

[18] Erikson, *Childhood*, p. 219.

his own world.[19] Erikson's particular theory is that play is a function of the ego to synchronize his bodily and social processes; it is part of the struggle to achieve a sense of identity. Much children's play expresses the need of an ego to master various areas of life where he senses himself to be wanting, that is, where he confronts anxiety.[20] A neurotic individual is one who falls prey to overidentification with certain limited aspects of his situation; his play is often a way of breaking loose to find his own identity. Erikson's definition of play is limited because it is too centered upon childhood in anxious situations; he proposed the theory that "the child's play is the infantile form of the human ability to deal with experience by creating model situations and to master reality by experiment and planning."[21] Though restricted in scope, Erikson has made a valuable suggestion; his theory implies that play is a mode of creating a world. Before focusing upon play and love, it is first necessary to view play as a mode of freedom. It will best be seen as a distinct form of encounter, of existential transcendence; and as such it must be seen not from a detached observational viewpoint but through participation which reaches into and opens up its intentional structure as it really is.[22]

The classic work by Johan Huizinga, *Homo Ludens*, which sees play as an essentially indispensable mode of human existence is extremely helpful at this point. Huizinga moved far beyond the view of play as infantile or juvenile activity because he concentrated upon play as a cultural rather than as a merely individual phenomenon. As a cultural historian he was aware that any attempt to understand man as a cultural being which left play out of account would be hopelessly jejune. Inspired by Plato's eloquent statement that play is that form of activity in which man most nearly approaches the similitude of the gods,[23] Huizinga argued that play is a deep cultural phenomenon upon which man's highest spiritual accomplish-

---

19 *Ibid.*, pp. 100 ff., 220.

20 *Ibid.*, p. 211.

21 *Ibid.*, p. 222.

22 A healthy complement to Erikson's views are those put forth by George Herbert Mead. Mead saw the process of maturation as that of an individual acquiring a fully integrated social nature by a process of internal organization of social attitudes. He realized that much children's play involves taking roles of other persons, which is the child's way of organizing the attitudes of others and assimilating them within a whole experimental field. Again my criticism is that this perceptive theory sees only one aspect of play and needs to be set within an existential framework so that the phenomenon of play can be understood in all its rich and vital complexity. See Mead, *The Social Psychology of George Herbert Mead*, pp. 227-233 especially.

23 Johan Huizinga, *Homo Ludens*, pp. 211-212.

ments are based. Life to be human must be lived as play. Though eschewing neat definitions of play, he nevertheless concentrated upon the specific content of play as it has arisen in numerous cultures, both primitive and highly civilized, and he found within it certain basic factors.[24] Though we might challenge some of the fine points of his study, there are basic structures here which can be agreed upon. First, play is seen as an act of freedom, as freedom expressing itself. Second, this freedom consists in stepping outside ordinary life in the workaday world; its significance is not to be found there, but is to be discovered within its own intentional structure. Third, as distinct from ordinary life in the world it is constituted by its own form of encounter and so charts a unique direction in the world and creates its own space-time reality. Finally, though it divorces itself from the common world of work, it nevertheless can create another form of common world such as indicated by the term "a play community." To clarify its unique intentional order, we should point out that play has two universal functions; one function is to *contest for* something, while the second is to *represent* something.[25] His detailed historical study substantiates that often play is freedom geared toward the appropriation of important existential significance. Play can be a primary way to encounter meaningful existential possibilities. In a contest man seeks to excel others, so as to be considered better; thus he seeks to be honored and esteemed, to achieve prestigious existence.[26] Play provides man with a way to establish his identity with dignity. Cheating is a foul crime in the play world because it breaks down the intentional structure, the special order and value sought for in play.

As a basic form of existence, play in Huizinga's view is linked to man's need to live in beauty.[27] Whether such a need can be demonstrated is questionable. Yet he substantiated play as a creative form of encountering the world, one which makes the significance of a man's being in the world more apparent to him. It is through "playing that society expresses its interpretation of life and the world." [28] Culture is not merely based on play; rather, culture plays itself out through us as we attempt to express how we feel about being in the world and where we think the truth of our existence lies. Play begins with childhood; and, he insisted, that "really to

[24] Cf. *ibid.*, p. 13.
[25] *Ibid.*
[26] *Ibid.*, p. 50.
[27] *Ibid.*, p. 63.
[28] *Ibid.*, p. 46.

play, a man must play like a child." That is, he must fully engage himself in this particular mode of being in the world.[29] Yet the childlike character of play should not lead, as in some theories, to its disparagement; for play is an essential factor in the whole cultural process. In summarizing his study, he wrote:

> It has not been difficult to show that a certain play-factor was extremely active all through the cultural process and that it produces many of the fundamental forms of social life. The spirit of playful competition is, as a social impulse, older than culture itself and pervades all life like a veritable ferment. Ritual grew up in sacred play; poetry was born in play and nourished on play; music and dancing were pure play. Wisdom and philosophy found expression in words and forms derived from religious contests. The rules of warfare, the conventions of noble living were built upon play-patterns. We have to conclude, therefore, that civilization is, in its earliest phases, played. It does not come *from* play like a babe detaching itself from the womb; it arises *in* and *as* play, and never leaves it.[30]

Like major thinkers already considered, Huizinga also felt that contemporary civilization faces a crisis. His theory suggests that the cause is to be discovered not in a breakdown of reason but in modern man's misunderstanding and disparagement of play. As civilization grows more complex it becomes more serious and assigns a secondary place to playing.[31] In our era we have lost much of the spirit of play and engage in pursuits which are similar to it but really constitute false play. Play is often regarded as less than dignified, as in the phrase "playing around." Indeed a contemporary psychoanalytic interpretation of play has been presented in terms of a game theory which sees the playing of games from a purely negative viewpoint, as a "basically dishonest" form of interpersonal behavior.[32]

Illuminating play as a basic form of existential encounter, one which expresses a genuine form of freedom, helps us to see the play phenomenon as it really is, in terms of its essential meaning. It also indicates play to be a

[29] *Ibid.*, p. 199.
[30] *Ibid.*, p. 173.
[31] *Ibid.*, p. 75. Cf. S. Langer's suggestions that play is a primary mode of symbolization, *Philosophy in a New Key*, pp. 120-129.
[32] See Eric Berne, *Games People Play*. This author's theory is that "a game is an ongoing series of complementary ulterior transactions progressing to a well defined, predictable outcome. . . . a series of moves with a snare, or 'gimmick.'" Thus they are moves interposed between our possibilities of obtaining genuine interpersonal relations and authentic cultural expressions. It is highly regrettable that this author does not see games from the positive viewpoint of play as presented by Huizinga or Mead.

form of transcendence which sounds remarkably similar to love. Play is a form of being in the world which is nevertheless beyond the world of concern; like love it is often a form of existential transport. Certainly play is a realization of genuine human freedom, not merely as an individual but also as a social and cultural phenomenon. Play is a historical phenomenon in the full existential sense of that term. Yet how is it related to love, if at all? We shall see the relation more clearly if we ask the question: How is it possible for man really to play, fully to engage himself creatively in play?

At this point pertinent insight comes from another Swiss psychiatrist, Gustav Bally, who made a study of freedom as play. Bally has emphasized that freedom is not a possession of man; it is a dynamic process of becoming.[33] Freedom also has its boundaries; and its meaning is to be discovered in terms of the extent of its boundaries. Thus we should consider freedom not merely in terms of what man is free *from* but what he is free *for*; or perhaps better expressed, what he is free *toward*. First let us recognize that play is a different form of activity from ordinary behavior. This is noticeable even in animals. Animal behavior seems to be largely under the domination of instincts directed toward specific objects. Yet when animals, particularly young animals, have received sufficient nourishment and are sure of security, a new behavior appears which is not aimed at the procuring of some external object. Rather, this behavior seems to end where it begins; it has no immediate aim other than itself. Such behavior is termed "play." [34] Man is in this respect different from animals, in that his play does not occur on the periphery of his involvement in the world. Rather, man plays his whole life, and his play has to do with his search for a sense of historical identity in a human world.[35] Play is essential to him if he is to gain a perspective of the world of genuine human possibilities. If inner forces prevent him from playing and thus from finding significance spontaneously, human development is severely retarded and/or distorted. A child must find the play room in which to grow to be a man; and as a man he must continually play so as to discover and formulate the significance of his being in the world. In play man engages himself totally in his world and thus may recover an awareness of his wholeness. A task of

---

[33] Gustav Bally, *Vom Ursprung und von den Grenzen der Freiheit: Eine Deutung des Spiels bei Tier und Mensch*, pp. 5 ff.

[34] *Ibid.*, p. 59.

[35] *Ibid.*, pp. 67-74. I have given more extensive consideration to the phenomenon of play in an article, "Creative Existence: Play as a Pathway to Personal Freedom and Community," *Humanitas*, Vol. V (Spring, 1969).

society is to keep man open to his genuine possibilities. Man needs the openness of the freedom which arises within play so as to lead his life within the world rather than to be led through it by anxiety, pressures, and deceptions.[36] Because play as freedom is a primary form of openness it provides man with a constant source of new ways to develop, new ways to discover himself, new ways of encountering genuine existential significance.

Man as being in the world is also engaged in problematic situations. As he confronts his freedom he is aware of his limitations and the possibility of his nonexistence. Thus the awareness of freedom as an isolated individual is a process which threatens to constrict the boundaries of freedom. Man stands in a world bounded by dark shadows of failure and death. One task of playing man is to learn to play while standing on the very boundaries of his freedom. Yet how is this possible? To face the naked horror of possible nonexistence leads man to be serious, to face his death resolutely or to escape from the fearful specter of his existential possibilities. Yet in the phenomenon of play there may be a presentiment of a reality which is beyond merely individual possibilities. It may be a presentiment of God, as Bally suggested; [37] or it may be the feeling that one is at home in the world with another being who addresses him as Thou. Bally discovered that as animals must have a sense of security really to play, so men must have a sense of being loved. In the heart of man's freedom there is a longing for loving encounter in which one's freedom will be acknowledged and affirmed. In order to play most creatively one needs to develop a sense of trust not merely in himself or in the other, but basically in the world which opens before him. This is precisely what the world of love provides; *love gives man a home in which it is safe to play.*[38]

Quite similar to Bally, Binswanger discovered that renewed freedom arises from the gift of love rather than from a confrontation with anxiety. As clinical studies indicate, a strong dose of anxiety will paralyze a child, preventing him from playing.[39] Play is one way of overcoming relatively mild forms of anxiety; but in confronting such anxiety the child needs to

[36] *Ibid.*, p. 76.
[37] *Ibid.*, pp. 103 ff.
[38] From within this perspective one can come to see an important possibility of significance for the liturgy, particularly the Eucharist. If the Eucharist is discovered to be a form of play within the arena of divine love, it provides the participants with a world of love in which their freedom is affirmed in the presence of Love. It is a sad commentary on so much Western liturgy that it so lacks a deeply playful element in which love and freedom may converge and grow.
[39] See both Gilmore and Erikson, *op. cit.*

find trust in himself by virtue of being trusted. In adults Binswanger discovered essentially the same facts. In psychotherapy the doctor confronts often massive anxiety which imprisons the patient; the latter finds his liberation through the love of a therapist who communicates presence and makes the patient feel at home in his world. Whereas Heidegger's analysis of existence maintained that freedom emerged as a freedom toward one's ground as one faced his own negation of being, Binswanger found that freedom emerges within the boundaries of love.[40] The ground upon which human freedom emerges is neither that of the isolated self nor that of the social self, but it is the ground of loving duality, the personal reality of We. Human freedom arises within boundaries, and needs a definite space in which to play itself out. Phenomenological investigations indicate that *the playground of freedom is love*. Real love is not a force which imprisons a person. It is a gift of trust; love is like an embrace which affirms the significance of the individual and the importance of becoming himself in a common world. Freedom does not die in love; it is born there. As the boundaries within the household of love are infinite, so the space of love gives room ample enough for freedom to express itself playfully in historical growth toward man's fullest possibilities. The time of love is a gift which enables freedom to rise above the constrictions of a dominating past or a confining present into the ecstatic fullness of presence.

Further insight into the meaning of play as a form of freedom grounded in love will continue to emerge from phenomenological investigations of forms of play within the structure of interpersonal relations. The emphasis of so many play studies has been on an isolated individual. Even in terms of individual behavior we have seen play as a mode of world-making which includes a world with others. Yet we shall understand play's significance better when we focus upon the world-making phenomenon of people playing together, which is surely the richest and happiest form of play. As people play together in sports, in the arts, and in love we discover a paradigm of interpersonal freedom creating its own meaningful boundaries. Playing together provides an opportunity for limitless expansion of the boundaries of freedom; and it is a form of communication which opens us up to an infinite personal world where our wholeness is affirmed. Play as genuine communication which opens up freedom to new possibilities can clearly be seen in much play of children among themselves or with their

[40] Ludwig Binswanger, *Grundformen und Erkenntnis Menschlichen Daseins*, pp. 139-142.

parents. A small child calling, "Daddy, come and play with me," is making a bid for an encounter in a new world of play, a world grounded in love and open to possibilities for existence not possible when one is alone. Playing together the child and parent may construct a common world which is not fantasy or subjective; it is the world of love in which they find a limitless home and an open moment of time in which to become themselves together. Like romantic love this can be a moment which sparkles with merry laughter. The play of love can produce frolicking freedom as it actualizes a new world of intimacy.

Such may also be the case in the phenomenon of love-play. In the play between lovers a time of trust is established where they can speak intimately. In playful caresses they define a common space in which they become sure of each other. Their histories interpenetrate in mutual presence as they come to feel at home with each other. In true love-play the difference between love and any attempt at seduction becomes clear. The latter is an effort to possess another, which would rob the other of his or her freedom. Love, on the other hand, reaffirms the unique being of the other so as to continue in the special moment of loving encounter. The "moment" lasts as long as within reciprocal presence each other's freedom is affirmed. Once the freedom of the other is downgraded or denied, the game of love is over, and a perverse game of suppressing authentic existence ensues.

To play with another within the bounds of love is to give another courage to be himself. As we are well aware, playing with loved ones, where we feel at home, often inspires us to very individual actions. We do things, sometimes silly or daring things, that we would never do in front of strangers. Our spirits and bodies soar in play as we jump, skip, kick up our heels, or swing through the air. Play in love is the most spontaneous of activities, the most unpredictable, the freest mode of existence. The poet Schiller was more right than perhaps he suspected when he wrote: *Der Mensch ist nur Mensch wenn er spielt* ("Man is only fully a man when he plays"). To stop playing is not to grow up; it is to cease living authentically as a human being. Man is by nature a playing creature. When playing he is not being like an animal; rather, he is most like himself, as man is meant to be. To speak again in terms of intentionality, play is what man is made for. In play, as it is grounded in love, man reaches into his fullest possibilities as an individual sustained and liberated by another in a truly personal world. In this modern era which still suffers from a hangover of the Puritan suspicion that somewhere someone might be having a good time and in which the ethic of work has been absolutized as that activity wherein man proves his worth, we are dangerously close to losing our awareness of the vital importance of play for authentic existence. To become human, to find the meaning of life as persons we must learn to play, not merely alone but to play together in the ecstatic, boundless, carefree, riotous world of love. Play is not an optional activity to be reserved for occasional moments of leisure, as though these are moments of escape from the real business of living. When man forgets how to play with others then he surely finds himself condemned to freedom, a freedom which is a distortion of human life. As Zorba the Greek told us, a man must have a little madness or else he will not be free.[41] The madness that is essential is constituted by the transport of love, the dual reality of We, and is attained as persons are inspired to dance together, to laugh together, to play together until their hearts are content.[42]

[41] N. Kazantzakis, *Zorba the Greek*, pp. 300-301.

[42] A strong argument for the essential place of playful, imaginative love in the development of man in society has been put forth by Herbert Marcuse in his *Eros and Civilization*. Marcuse also argues against the exaltation of what Freud called the performance principle; he looks forward to a culture in which men will regain genuine "forms of freedom and happiness" (p. 148 passim). Unfortunately, his notion of play is infantile and his view of love adolescently erotic.

10

The Transcendence and the Fall of Love

1. CONSCIENCE, FIDELITY, AND THE SEARCH FOR IDENTITY IN TERMS OF DUALITY

Thus far phenomenology has illuminated freedom as existential openness toward genuine historical possibilities. Man is not a predetermined sociophysical product; neither is his freedom a predetermined quantity. Man is truly born to be free. His being in the world is constituted by various modes of historical encounter which open up possibilities for both the increase and the loss of freedom. Man's history is played out in at least two basic modalities; for man's freedom to become authentic, both possibilities must be encountered with understanding, affirmation, and integrating actualization. To speak of authenticity brings this study clearly into the field of ethics. Reconsideration of the nature of the good life and particularly of personal morality in light of phenomenological research is not, however, a possibility which we can fully or responsibly prosecute in this book. Yet several factors can be elucidated in our effort to understand basic human structures from the perspective of love, which in turn will be useful to those who are more proficient and knowledgeable in the area of moral philosophy and ethics. Certainly a trustworthy insight into conscience is imperative to all who seek to understand what is involved in authentically responsible existence. In this chapter the inner voice of personal morality (conscience) will be considered from within the historical perspective of duality; this in turn will lead to a consideration of responsibility in terms of fidelity to conscience. More dialogue between phenomenology and the social sciences will emerge as the analysis moves to examine a related phenomenon, referred to as the search for identity. Finally, common obstacles which inhibit and distort a faithful historical development of existence in love will be elucidated.

Heidegger provided an unusual and profound interpretation of conscience. Though affirming existence as freedom in the world, he also stressed that man is fallen and therefore must discover authenticity in a decisive moment. This moment of authentic temporality occurs when *Dasein* proleptically realizes and affirms his wholeness in an ecstasy which arises as he faces his own death. Heidegger was saying that to become authentic, man must realize his historicity in an eschatological sense, anticipating his end. In this moment of anticipation, one's whole being stretches before him as an integral, temporal whole. As one becomes aware of one's own most possibilities in this ecstatic moment and directs his basic concern toward their realization in an act of resolute affirmation, one transcends his fallenness into authentic historicity. According to Heidegger, it is in this moment where one confronts his own most possibilities that one discovers his *true* conscience. Conscience is the *call* from one's authentic future to become one's true self. To become aware of your authentic conscience is to be addressed by your true self.[1]

Heidegger's consistent intention was to see the whole phenomenon of man in the most appropriate perspective. From his existential perspective a traditional and highly Scholastic definition of conscience as a special function of the mind "making moral judgments" appears to be myopic. Furthermore, Heidegger's interpretation enables us to be reasonably critical of both theological and psychoanalytic theories which have emphasized what is essentially a bad conscience. Too frequently conscience is viewed as the internalization of repressive external authority, such as the positive law or the voice of one's parents. Thus conceived, conscience is essentially an inner voice which says, "Behave! You *shall not* follow your own inclinations!" To Heidegger the primary phenomenon of conscience is not an encounter with the authority of others but with Being. This encounter involves one's own whole being; and the effect of an encounter with one's true conscience is liberating. The voice of conscience does not lay down rules but calls the individual *to be*. Its basic message is: Become what you are![2] The existential conscience does not arise from an encounter with a

---

[1] Heidegger, *Sein und Zeit*, pp. 267-301 (*Being and Time*, pp. 312-348).
[2] Though I shall follow in the main Heidegger's positive orientation, some defense

heteronomous precept, but within silence. In a moment of deep silence, Being beckons the individual to authenticity. Here the individual also becomes aware of his fallenness, as well as the guilt which lies upon him as a fallen being. Thus, as *Dasein* becomes aware of possible authentic existence, he also becomes aware of his inevitably guilty conscience; yet he becomes free to transform his life. This call of conscience is not something that an individual can easily will into existence. It breaks through in a moment of understanding when one becomes aware of himself as a unique temporal being thrown into the world toward authenticity. The voice of conscience, if heeded, will then lead the individual toward authentic resolution, toward his true self. To respond to conscience in an authentic way requires that a man hold fast to his truth; it demands complete fidelity to himself. Conscience calls me to be true to myself, and so to turn from pseudo-existence.

Within the purview of a phenomenology of love various existential aspects pertaining to conscience, fidelity, and the moral life appear rather differently. Binswanger agreed to Heidegger's emphasis that conscience be understood as an "inner voice" calling one to historical possibilities. Yet within the reality of duality, the call of conscience is neither an inner voice commanding social conformity as in Freud's view nor a proleptic anticipation of a singular self. In love, conscience is constituted by an address of a Thou to me, as a Thou beckoning me to discover the fullest possibilities of existence in the personal world of We. It is a call to find authenticity in personal relations, in loving duality.[3] A new view of conscience seen through the eyes of love was also suggested by Mrs. Browning (SONNET X):

> And when I say at need
> *I love thee* . . . mark! . . . *I love thee*—in thy sight
> I stand transfigured, glorified aright,
> With conscience of the new rays that proceed
> Out of my face towards thine.

of traditional thinking about conscience is in order. In moral theology conscience was often referred to by *conscientia*, which is an acquired knowledge enabling man's mind to make moral judgments. But there is another element, particularly strong in the Anglican tradition, which emphasizes the connative element of conscience, *synteresis*. The first element is frequently associated with a bad conscience, but *synteresis* is much like Heidegger's emphasis upon the positive call to become what you are meant to be. (Cf. H. R. McAdoo, *The Structure of Caroline Moral Theology*, pp. 64-97.) As for the narrow view of psychoanalysis, this has also been expanded by such writers as Erich Fromm. He distinguishes between the authoritarian conscience, which is Freud's Superego, and a humanistic conscience, which is the inner call within man to become his true self, much along the lines suggested by Heidegger. (See E. Fromm, *Man for Himself*, pp. 141-172.)

[3] Binswanger, *Grundformen*, p. 93.

Love had given her a new conscience, an awareness not merely that she was loved but that through love she had become a new being, "glorified aright," as she was meant to be. Love affirmed and enlightened her truest possibilities as a personal being; and in the response of her conscience she has answered the love: ". . . mark! . . . I love thee . . . ." Her new conscience in love was not merely knowledge of being addressed; it was a knowledge of new directions and dimensions in personal existence. In love one awakens to the full possibilities of becoming a person. Heidegger's interpretation of the existential conscience failed to account significantly for the intersubjective nature of conscience within love. Intersubjective duality constitutes the structure for the unique form of knowledge which conscience possesses in love. If one does not perceive the existential structure of love, he inevitably fails to appreciate the new knowledge of existence which love offers.

Heidegger saw fidelity as another basic characteristic of authentic existence, as a distinctive structural component of resolute being-unto-death. To be authentically faithful, he said, is to be true to the manifestation of Being apprehended in the moment of authentic historical ecstasy. Thus, to be authentically faithful means being true to your conscience. To be sure, fidelity pertains to the truth of existential transcendence; but my truth as a personal being exceeds the possibility of my singular being in the world. Fidelity to my truth includes loyalty to you who have shown me who I am; and at the same time fidelity is owed to your truth as I behold and reveal it to you. Thus fidelity in love is not a one-way street; it is basically reciprocal. Though lovers may say to each other: "Be true to yourself; for as you are true to yourself, you are true to me," yet this is not to be taken in the same vein as the fatuous platitude spoken by Polonius: ". . . to thine own self be true, . . . Thou canst not then be false to any man." The self as it emerges in love is seen to be a dual self. Personal existence includes the interpenetrating, *personal self* of We-two in which the individual selves of you and me arise and gain significance. Consequently personal fidelity is authentically directed to you *and* me within the larger self of We.

The effect of fidelity in an open interpersonal structure is to enlarge freedom, not to curb it. The greater the faith between us the greater the possibility of the genuine independence of you and me.[4] Personal fidelity is basically not an act of exclusion in which I deny my possibilities for your sake, or ignore yours for my sake. Fidelity is primarily a personal affirma-

[4] Cf. *ibid.*, p. 125. Reference must also be made to the brilliant elucidation of this phenomenon by Marcel, particularly in his discussions of "creative fidelity."

tion of freedom for both of us. In being faithful one knows he must be true to freedom. Yet the greatest freedom is not an individual possession; it is an intersubjective reality. To be true to freedom is to be faithful to the world of freedom, not some single part of it. The full truth of personal freedom is best seen from within the world of love. In the moment of love two persons meet each other as free agents; yet each is not free to do as he or she pleases. In love they must continue faithful to freedom; he cannot be faithless to her freedom, nor she to his, without being faithless to the new possibility of becoming whole and free in the duality of We-two. Fidelity to freedom involves being faithful to the full scope of freedom discovered by conscience in the new world of love. What one realizes in this perspective is that merely individual freedom is a restricted, undeveloped aspect of free existence in the truth. There is the greater freedom of communal existence. Only in love can an individual's freedom be saved from suppression in this larger communal world; for in the loving encounter there is a dual affirmation of each other as well as an affirmation of life together. For us to be free and stand in the truth, it is necessary for us both to be faithful; only as both of us are faithful to the truth of each other is the freedom of each secure. Personal freedom without faithfulness is impossible.

From the perspective of love, conscience is discovered to be an exceedingly complex phenomenon. It includes a primary awareness of oneself in terms of basic possibilities along with an inner call to direct oneself toward their attainment. Yet the voice of conscience is not usually, if ever, a clear unambiguous call to a simple possibility for your own existence. Conscience may have several legitimate voices. One may call you toward shaping a world distinctly your own; yet simultaneously you may hear a call to develop a common world. Conscience demands you to be faithful to your own truth but also to the truth of the other. To be true to one and false to the other is to betray freedom. Such is often the dilemma of conscience; only love offers a solution in which to be true to both appeals.

The tension within a conscience sensitive to the personal world is basic; but it is a tension particularly acute during adolescence. Erik Erikson has pointed out that the problem of conscience and fidelity becomes central in the adolescent's groping search for some significant sense of self. It is essential that he find some self-knowledge and develop fidelity to it so that he may gain the necessary strength to move ahead into adulthood; otherwise he may spend his life fighting what is primarily an adolescent battle for self-identity. In this historical epoch of his development the person is keenly aware of changes of all sorts—bodily, sexual, mental, social, and personal. As a juvenile he has developed basic skills which enable him to establish who he is in a given context. With the onrush of new possibilities he experiences an identity crisis wherein he is unsure of his capacities and possibilities, both social and individual. In this time of upheaval he often desperately is in search of something to be true to. Hamlet is a paradigm of an adolescent torn by the problem of fidelity. He constantly questions his own faithfulness to his late father and to himself, not merely as a son but as an independent self. He is plagued by the faithlessness of his mother, his uncle, and then his friends. Fidelity becomes such an obsession with him that he even confronts the actors with the problem, telling them to be faithful to their roles. To find fidelity to one's truth is a crucial aspect in the search for identity, for a unity of personality which is marked by historical continuity. In much adolescent flaunting of society we can see this search for a sense of identity combined with a developing sense of fidelity to a unique self which is threatened by pressures toward social conformity. Yet it is impossible really to seek the identity of a self which is not at the same time recognized by at least others who are significant. Self-identity is one aspect of an encounter with others. To know who you are, you need to be recognized. The adolescent must discover fidelity, not simply or primarily to you or to me, but to you and me, to oneself within the larger self of the personal and social worlds. In short, it is particularly crucial for the adolescent to be in love so as to discover his true identity as a person.

The insight from a social-science approach into the meaning of and the tension between fidelity to self and to others becomes clearer when brought into partnership with a phenomenological approach. As both the social sciences and existential phenomenology indicate, an exclusive emphasis upon the claims of conscience in terms of fidelity to one's individual possibilities is a dangerous absolutization, one which is particularly troublesome during adolescence. The adult as well as the adolescent must discover that fidelity is a power of being, a virtue, which only truly develops within the reality of loving coexistence.[5] At its deepest level the call of the self to

---

[5] See E. Erikson, "Youth: Fidelity and Diversity," *Daedalus*, Vol. 91, No. 1 (Winter, 1962), pp. 5-27. Erikson also raises the question if it is not possible that some great philosophers have absolutized their adolescent problems. "Is it not probable," he asks, "and in fact demonstrable that among the most passionate ideologists

itself is of a dual nature. As such, conscience presents a multiple form of address: "Be true to yourself:—be true to me!—be true to us, to our possibility for individual and corporate existence!" There is consistent evidence of the reciprocal nature of the personal world, of the reality of We-two, which shows that each self is finally to be understood within the framework of the We-self.[6] The double reference of fidelity and self must constantly be borne in mind in considering the language of lovers as they express awareness of each self's possibilities. This was expressed by Robert Browning when he wrote to his wife in a letter: "This I say of me, but think of you, love." [7] The "riddle of love" is that when I speak of me, I mean you also; that when I speak of us as a unity I mean also you and me individually. In the reality of love, true fidelity to myself is fidelity to you, for it is at the same time fidelity to you in the coinherent reality of intersubjectivity. Conscience is distorted if it is seen exclusively either as a call to fidelity to one's individual self or as fidelity to another's claim upon me.

The phenomenological insight into the coinherent reality of personal selves has relevance to a consideration of the moral life of adolescents as well as other persons. Problems of morality arise from the possibility of becoming authentically human. If such possibilities were closed off, moral life would be finished. Individual possibilities are basic; but increasingly it is being realized that existence is radically social and personal.[8] The self is not born whole; it grows through encounter with a world of others. The lived world consists of various existential directions in terms of various basic modes of encounter. Encounter with others, not primarily in terms of resistance, of meeting them over against us, but in terms of sharing a common world with a reciprocal outlook and an agreed-upon course of action is crucial. Phenomenology and the social sciences agree that "the self and society are twin born" in the process of existential development.[9] Only as we see the self within the human world with others do we ap-

there are unreconstructed adolescents, transmitting to their ideas the proud moment of their transient ego recovery, of their temporary victory over forces of existence and history, but also the pathology of their deepest isolation, the defensiveness of their forever adolescing egos—and their fear of the calm of adulthood?"

6 Binswanger, *Grundformen*, p. 71.
7 *Ibid.*, quoted p. 78.
8 This point is made at length by R. C. Kwant, *Phenomenology of Social Existence.*
9 See the comparison between Buber and Mead on this point by Paul E. Pfuetze, *Self, Society, Existence*, pp. 350 f.

proach the full dimension of the moral self as implied in the phenomenon of conscience and fidelity.[10]

From an existential approach conscience is heard to be the voice of self; but the self is not a simple entity. The self is variously structured in terms of basic possible encounters which include the private, personal, and social modes of being in the world. From the viewpoint of love, the call of conscience is received as an address coming from a Thou, beckoning me into authentically personal existence.[11] The outlook of existential phenomenology thus suggests that the popular ethic of self-realization suffers from gross myopia by exalting the individual over communal self-realization. The realization of the individual self is not a goal in itself but rather, within the bounds of love, comes as a gift. To seek at all costs to realize one's individual self will result in the loss of freedom for genuine personal encounter. To set one's direction in the world primarily in terms of self-realization and self-definition becomes a form of imprisonment in a world which is emptied of spontaneous and mutual personal encounter. Only as one opens his individual self to the risk and mystery of personal encounter does the possibility arise of finding the freedom and significance which persons so earnestly seek, especially with the onset of adolescence.[12] The realization of the truly personal self is not an individual accomplishment but a free gift of love.

Our existential perspective sees conscience basically not as an organ or function of man but as a call of existence to itself to become what it is meant to be. "Become what you are! Be yourself!" is really a call to transcend the self which you now are. Yet the question arises within a phenomenological perspective: Who makes that address? and, Which self is addressed? [13] Conscience is an inner voice evoking human freedom, but

[10] This point is made very forcefully in Pfuetze's study of the approaches to the self as a social reality in the thought of Buber and Mead; see especially Pfuetze, *op. cit.*, pp. 229-287. Further consideration of adolescents and love is given in Chapter 13.

[11] The emphasis upon the underlying personal nature of conscience is especially strong in many forms of contemporary Christian theology. See as one example Pfuetze, and Josef Goldbrunner, who represents a Roman Catholic position. Goldbrunner stresses that conscience is not an organ in man or a function ("mind making moral judgments," etc.), but is basically a person being actuated by the call of others in personal and social encounters. Conscience rightly arises out of the relationship of love, and it is here that a person is awakened to the will of God. (*Cure of Mind and Cure of Soul*, pp. 102 ff.)

[12] Cf. the similar view in Binswanger, *Grundformen*, p. 130.

[13] The concept of plurality of selves as proposed by such eminent Americans as William James, G. H. Mead, and Gordon Allport is probably familiar enough to require no further elaboration here.

the self of human freedom is not basically isolated or private. In the phenomenon of love we have seen the call of conscience emerging from an intersubjective reality, an address issued from a loving Thou who affirms and evokes my own most possibilities. The free, responsible, personal self is one who is open to others and who attentively participates in the dual reality of We.

With good insight, psychoanalysis stressed conscience as an inner voice issuing from others. If we resist adopting negative and individualistic prejudices implicit in Freudian conceptualizations of conscience, we can see that conscience can speak affirmatively even though it arises within the intersubjective reality. Orthodox psychoanalytic theories put all their stress upon conscience as a suppressive voice of external authority. Revisionists such as Erich Fromm have emphasized the positive, humanistic side of conscience, yet continue to view it within an individualistic perspective. The individualistic bias is perhaps a reaction against social theorists such as Durkheim and Mead, who have attempted to substantiate the basically social nature of man and his social conscience by arguing for a collective conscience and a social self respectively.[14] Individualistic theories of conscience have argued that the social approach often fails to account for the individual's response to his conscience to challenge and shape the social order which begets him. In fact both approaches are necessary.

A phenomenological analysis of conscience, by focusing upon love, reveals much of the complexity embedded in conscience, fidelity, and the moral life. Conscience in its healthy or authentic modes is a call or a pull toward an objective reality of existential possibility. It is a call to become a self. Yet there are a variety of selves arising from the multiple forms of basic existential encounter. As indicated through phenomenology, man lives in a plurality of worlds, including at least the personal, the social (Mitwelt), and the private (Eigenwelt).[15] Each world constitutes a different self, a different mode of encounter, a different form of transcendence, a uniquely constituted space-time, a variant mode of freedom toward significant existential possibilities. In the fullest perspective conscience does not consist of a single voice but several, which becomes obvious whenever we

14 See Bibliography, including Parsons' study of Durkheim in *Structure of Social Action* and Pfuetze's study of Mead, *op. cit.*

15 The influence of William James is not to go unmentioned. See, e.g., his view of a pluralistic universe in *The Varieties of Religious Experience*, p. 120, and chs. 18-20. Cf. also J. Wild, *Existence and the World of Freedom*, pp. 5-18. See the next chapter for an elaboration of the "social" world.

consider a serious and genuine conflict of conscience. The real problem of conscience does not simply involve a choice between a good and a bad, or between a proper self and an evil self; rather, a decision must often be made as to which among several legitimate "calls" to respond. The right choice involves frequently setting a direction toward only one of several legitimate modes of meaningful encounter.

The deepest and most essential voice within the phenomenon of conscience emerges from within the dual reality of We. It is a call to an individual to become a truly personal self. The fullness of this vocation is felt not by one alone but by two.[16] In the reality of loving coexistence conscience is personal; and as one aspect of personal being it has basically a reciprocal nature. It is not the dictatorial voice of parents and society commanding one to curb individual spontaneity and creativity. In the phenomenon of love, conscience does not speak as a summons to be on the alert. It is not so much a call from a distant future but an address from an interpenetrating presence urging those in love to be aware of their mutual home in the midst of their individual homelessness in a dark and broken world. The voice of conscience in love is a breakthrough of deeply personal communication, from silence into awareness. It is a voice of encouragement to play freely and creatively within the boundaries of love. It is a beckoning to individuals caught up in the fleeting discursiveness of private and practical histories to enter into an open interpersonal exchange in the moment of mutual presence. And it is a call to be faithful to this exchange, to sustain an open responsiveness to the incalculable duration of the moment of love. To be faithful to conscience in love is to be true to this basic mode of existence; indeed it is a promise to live for the truth of existence as revealed in loving encounter.

To speak the truth about conscience, it would be false to suggest that conscience is usually a call of love. In the political world it is more often a demand for justice. What existential phenomenology has attempted to demonstrate is that the call of love is a basic possibility, not an inevitable or everyday reality. Conscience as a call of existence to itself is a call to discover man in truth, as Binswanger put it; the proper response entails awareness of the basic possibilities so as to become ready to hear the call

---

[16] This is particularly true in the cases of extraordinary religious courage. Luther's bold, "Here I stand, I can do no other," is often interpreted as his courageous isolation from most of the rest of society and the Church. However, this must be seen in light of the whole thrust of Luther's theology, which is to affirm that in faith man never stands alone, but that he stands with Christ in every place of faithful affirmation.

and to respond to it when it comes, when the encounter emerges from within personal history. Though one possibility is an address in and to love, experience as well as the insights provided by social sciences and creative writers make us painfully aware that existence is caught in a web of conflicting voices; and the confusion increases during periods of significant change. The full reality of conscience seen from an existential-phenomenological viewpoint reveals tension as existence is pulled toward numerous possibilities in its plurality of existential worlds. Consequently, we must be wary of seeking peace within conscience. The search for an easy and quiet conscience is not necessarily a longing for the fullness of life but may really be for death. It would appear that a man completely at peace with his conscience is one who has achieved peace at the price of putting several basic possibilities to sleep. In certain situations it may be necessary to suppress basic possibilities. It might be less than wise to keep oneself wide open for the possibility of romantic love while in the situation of war combat, an adventurous mission to Antarctica, a prison, or a monastery. However, the function of existential phenomenology is to point out basic existential possibilities and the actual or probable results if one responds to them; it is the task of ethics to argue for the rightness or wrongness of following or cultivating a particular mode of encounter within the perspective of an accepted world view. Not only are there various legitimate voices of conscience, but within any particular mode of encounter there are numerous possibilities for false calls to unrealistic or harmful modes of existence. Yet even if one were to rise above all the false voices, even then authentic conscience would not be a pull in a single direction.

An authentic conscience is marked by the phenomenon of convergence of different possibilities. Here again the analogy of music is helpful. The full sound of authentic conscience is not a single tone, certainly not a lullaby, but a harmoniously structured melody where divergent tones which exist in tension with others nevertheless interpenetrate to form an exciting, integral whole, moving us to respond with our whole existence toward achieving our truth, our real identities. Although phenomenologically we become aware of the overflowing nature of love which gives the individual being in the world new boundaries and new possibilities for meaningful freedom, yet the tide of love does not extinguish the distinct sense of self. As Binswanger pointed out, though the lover is aware of and faithful to the fullness of the moment of love, of mutual presence, yet he is cognizant also of a loneliness (*Einsamkeit*) which balances and gives tension to the experienced togetherness (*Zweisamkeit*).[17] This loneliness is not the dreadful isolation which his phenomenology also brilliantly illumined, especially in studies of schizophrenia; it is a loneliness such as that known in moments of solitude wherein one reflects upon what one has received in the shared moment of love. Thus this loneliness is an encounter with a special form of distance. It is not distance over-against another as an object. It is not a sign of withdrawal from the beloved or a mark of incomplete fidelity. It is an awareness of the distance which is necessary for an encounter to occur at all. Love endures as an encounter. It does not develop into a form of mutual absorption or the immersion of one person into the other. Loving encounter, as Buber and Marcel have so emphatically and repeatedly stressed, is a mutually creative action in which the otherness of the beloved is discovered and affirmed within the infinite boundaries of the unity of love. As the term "duality" is meant to suggest, loving encounter is simultaneously the union of two and a differentiation of two persons in the new world of love. Awareness of and fidelity to this distance is also necessary to maintain the creativity of the union. Without distance the encounter becomes mutual submersion, and the personal world becomes dull and flat, a secure but stodgy mode of being-together; the possibility of creative duality is thus transformed into stolid together-ness where the distinctive identity of two persons is diminished.

The sense of loneliness in love is markedly different from that emerging from outside the boundaries of love; an awareness of severe separation is what Binswanger characterized as existence become a naked horror.[18] Loneliness in love is endurable because it converges with a sense of the omnipresence of the beloved. Love poetry frequently speaks of a personification of all reality in terms of the beloved: "You are my all." "I see you in every tree and cloud and bush." "In every passing face I see the sweetness of your smile." Such typically romantic language expresses the felt interpenetration of the Thou in all one's existential directions, while at the same time recognizing existential differentiation. The personal world is experienced as interpenetrating the other existential worlds. According to Binswanger the penetration of Thou, seeing all reality through the eyes of a particular I-Thou relationship, signifies the highwater mark of existence, wherein the world of concern is raised to the world of love.[19] Just how

[17] Binswanger, *Grundformen*, pp. 131-134.
[18] *Ibid.*, p. 445.
[19] *Ibid.*, pp. 76-77.

love may interpenetrate all spheres of the lived world is something which remains to be seen. Certainly here we find an important area for further phenomenological research. Romantic love at least has certain enticements which would, if followed, lead existence to absolutize this one form to the detriment of other legitimate possibilities and hence of existential truth. Existence needs love, even romantic love, so as to become aware of its richness and the fullness of its possible meaning and freedom. But love also needs intelligence and a certain amount of cool analysis to illuminate existence if we are to be faithful to the whole and thus avoid sham imitations and threats to the life of personal being.

2. ENEMIES OF LOVE

To discover those aspects in which love's existence is jeopardized we are tremendously indebted to creative literature and social sciences, psychoanalysis in particular. The latter has clearly revealed monstrosities of behavior which masquerade as love and which have frequently suffocated love and existence. The contemporary conscience has nearly inexhaustible and invaluable resources to enlighten it as to how man is inhuman to man often in the name of love. To endorse love in truth we must be fully aware not only of the transcendence of love but also, as Binswanger put it, the fall of love, the possibilities for its distortion and destruction. In speaking of the fall and possible death of love we can again concentrate on the phenomenon of romantic love. Much will apply to other modes of love; yet further research and reflection are needed.

In considering the fall of love, Binswanger pointed to recurring possibilities which arise in extremely varied forms.[20] The quality of authentic loving existence is a balanced convergence, a mode of interpenetration between an I and a Thou, of individual selves and a corporate personal self. In romantic love especially, however, there is the possibility, the temptation, toward fanaticism; and fanaticism marks the destruction of love as well as of freedom.[21] Fanaticism can occur in various modes, yet in every form of it, existence falls into enthrallment and slavery. One form of fanaticism is to deny or ignore all other reality, a frequent basis for dramatic tragedies. Another is to absolutize the sexual aspect of romantic love, so as to see sexual fulfillment as man's basic need and the goal of love. But

20 *Ibid.*, pp. 160-167.
21 See the interesting comparison between fanaticism and devotion by John Wild, *Existence and the World of Freedom*, pp. 167-176.

to resort to sexualism is to see love within a pragmatic structure, which is to make of it something to be used by an individual for his own private ends.[22] The contemporary sex craze tends to reduce love to an entirely foreign world of taking where it cannot find a home. Love transcends the space-time of getting and taking, whereas mere sex establishes meaning through getting and taking possession, pleasures, etc. Relationships which are preponderantly or exclusively sexual are not personal but possessive; they do not realize the freedom or the meaning of love.

Another fallen form of love is to be found in much love mysticism where the beloved is deified. When the beloved really becomes your All, then love is vainly attempting to go beyond the boundaries of being in the world and is no longer open to the unique yet limited otherness of the beloved. Many popular views of romantic love fail to consider the worldliness and historicity of love. One of the most penetrating students of romantic love, the late Charles Williams, made the point that a common but deadly temptation of romantic love is to consider itself everlasting. It thinks of its particular moment of grace as one which will endure in this world and beyond without interruption. Yet in the universal experience of romantic love the bright flashes of heaven fade away. Dante's vision of Beatrice was incredibly brilliant, inconceivably rich, reflecting the glories and treasures of heaven itself; but even that moment faded. As Williams suggested, the romantic moments must be allowed to die so as to force man's intellect and will to action.[23] To speak of allowing love to die when we have referred to love's eternity will at first appear to be confusing. But romantic love must be transformed into a love which is more enduring and complete. Phenomenologically we can suggest that romantic love, for all its height, has little depth or breadth. If its moment of eternity is absolutized and kept aloft, so that a couple's love is not allowed to interpenetrate with the whole of their existence, then it has in fact been excluded from life in this world. Thus its freedom is transmuted into fanaticism. Such fanaticism breeds unintelligent sentimentalism, which surely marks the fall if not the death of love.

To treat romantic love in an idolatrous manner is closely related to

---

[22] For a brisk, thorough, and judicious treatment of sex within a personal perspective, and one which is particularly well attuned to university students, see R. F. Hettlinger, *Living with Sex: The Student's Dilemma.*

[23] The points referred to as made by Charles Williams are found repeatedly in his extraordinary novels, his studies of Dante, and his theology. Many of his points are handily summarized by Mary McDermott Shideler, *The Theology of Romantic Love: A study in the writings of Charles Williams;* see especially pp. 113-211.

another way of destroying it. A second temptation is to regard romantic love as sufficient in itself to give man authenticity. This view regards romantic love not merely as the pinnacle but as the sole essence of existential transcendence. If one has had a romantic affair, supposedly one has reached the summit of life. This temptation also moves in the direction of isolating a romantic love from the rest of existence, not allowing it to interpenetrate with other authentic possibilities. To use our analogy of height, romantic love must be allowed to take root in the world or it will lose its historicity and be set adrift in sheer subjectivity, like the lovers Paolo and Francesca whom Dante portrayed in the second circle of hell, endlessly adrift in the monotonous mutual submission to passion. Each form of absolutization is a way of regarding love ultimately as a personal possession. To consider love as one's possession is the foundation for jealousy and envy which destroy love. To seek to possess the beloved as one's own is a denial of interpersonal exchange, of receiving and giving, of reciprocal freedom.

There are many enemies of love, but the most basic is man's unwillingness or inability to be open for an encounter of mutual presence. Being in the world is "fallen" from authenticity and has lost its sense of direction toward the truth of personal existence. Love opens a way for the discovery as well as the creation of authentic communion and freedom simultaneously. Yet men are afraid of love, and in their fear build walls that foreclose the possibility. Or, having received love, they are tempted to regard it as a private possession; thus they force love into a cramped world where it cannot thrive and where it will eventually die. As Williams put it, exchange, not possession, is of the essence of love. One must sacrifice possession and control, or else kill love. The dynamics of interpersonal exchange involve unmerited, spontaneous receiving and giving in the openness and interpenetration of being in love.[24] Each fallen form of love has its own determinates, and its own temporal and spatial forms, just as fallen existence portrayed by Heidegger. Basically, however, the fall of love in each case amounts to a mutation of the I-Thou form to an I-It relationship, where the other is considered an object to be possessed, be it by adoration or tyranny. This mutation closes the freedom which is born in love. If the

---

[24] See also the excellent, literate, and somewhat phenomenological study by Dom Aelred Watkin, *The Enemies of Love*, which portrays beautifully the possible meaning of romantic love between a young boy and girl from a theological as well as a humanistic viewpoint. Cf. also W. Trobisch's touching account of a young African couple in *I Loved a Girl*.

principle of personal exchange is disregarded, the person becomes an autonomous self, self-willed and closed to an encounter with others.

In such a situation, love often becomes transformed into hatred. Hatred is an obvious enemy of love, but it is not the principal one. Hatred is rightly understood as often arising out of a lack of the true boundary set by love.[25] Where I cannot encounter love, I am desperately homeless, which causes me to feel fury and anxiety. With an untrue love I cannot find my true home. Hatred emerges not against a true Thou but against a Thou which has become a him or a her to me. It is energy directed not only against an object but against the lack of a Thou and a lack of possible loving encounter. Hatred is often the longing for love turned against itself through disappointment. If in its search for genuine reciprocity with another person the longing for love attaches itself upon an ersatz object, it will inevitably revolt or dissipate into disinterest. In the latter instance we may find the muted hatred of cynicism, whereas in the former instances we find outright hostility. Hatred is a distortion of the energy of love now directed toward life as viewed in a world of objects; as such it is a sign of the death of oneself stemming from a radical fall of love. Hatred is extremely dangerous not merely to love but to existence. Where love sees persons, hatred is blind to them; love leads to fulfillment, whereas hatred aims to destroy life. Through phenomenological analysis we are aware that behind hatred is the temptation to consider another and even love itself as an object. To reify love or existence, to make it part of one's experience as a possession, is to bury it. The world of love stands in constant jeopardy that man will attempt to reduce it to another world, that he will fail to appreciate its unique form of transcendence and thus attempt to interpret it in terms borrowed from a foreign sphere, one in which there really is neither time nor space for love to exist. That world in which love lies fallen is universal; it is the world inhabited by each of us.

From a phenomenological approach the enemies of existence in love appear to be different from those of other perspectives; existential phenomenology uncovers the ground from which the more obvious enemies grow. Our discovery has been that love itself is often its worst enemy when it allows itself to fall into a world project which would reify it, even though with the noble intentions of paying it the highest honor. We have also

---

[25] Cf. *ibid.*, p. 165, and even more so Binswanger's case histories. For a similar view of hatred arising out of the lack and frustration of love see Ian Suttie, *The Origins of Love and Hate*. See also C. Williams' novel, *Descent into Hell*.

arrived at insight into the meaning of hatred, which will enable us better to understand and conquer it. It seems clear that one of the most deadly enemies of love and hence of personal existence is man's own attempt to live autonomously. Because of the dual nature of man and the plurality of his worlds, it is sheer suicide to assert one's autonomy. To attempt to stand exclusively on one's own ground, to make all decisions by oneself and for oneself, is not to reach maturity, as some theorists would lead us to suppose. To assert one's existential autonomy would be a move in the direction of a horrible solitary confinement where one becomes increasingly out of tune and out of touch with the common life of humanity.[26]

The final enemy of love is generally regarded to be death itself. Yet where death is final from the viewpoint of an object world or that of singular existence, there is a quality in the reality of loving coexistence which endures in spite of "the life that disappears." "Never say of me that

[26] My criticism is somewhat directed against Binswanger as well as numerous philosophers and even psychiatrists. One would expect that Binswanger would share Buber and Marcel's vehement and trenchant criticisms of autonomy as a life goal. Such is not the case. (See Sadler, *Ludwig Binswanger's Existential Phenomenology*, pp. 187-203, for a much fuller discussion of this matter.) Binswanger felt that Heidegger's grounded individual had as much to be said for him as for the dual ground of loving encounter. He proceeded to examine varied types of literature to determine the nature of an individual ground of being which is distinct from that of being in love. Does not, for example, the language of self-love suggest an individual ground? An investigation of the writings of Augustine and numerous Christian love mystics led him to the judicious conclusion that self-love is a misnomer. To love oneself in God is really to love the act of God's love. In more mundane ways, the love of self really refers to high regard for objective good; it does not imply the structure of mutual presence. (Binswanger, *op. cit.*, pp. 391-404.) He would agree with the judgment of William James that love is not really the right word to refer to the vital concern we all have for the bare principle of our existence. (W. James, *Principles of Psychology*, Vol. I, p. 323.) In further examination Binswanger discovered that language about love of self when in the context of inner conflict, where we attempt to decide which is our true self which is to be served, is also misleading. What is at stake here is a conflict of roles. (Binswanger, *op. cit.*, pp. 434-435.) Though he stands firmly opposed to any anthropology which maintains absolute individualism or egotism, yet he holds out for a being-toward-one's-unique-ground (*Sein zum Grunde*) which falls outside the boundaries of love (*ibid.*, pp. 194-196; 457-468). In doing so he resorts to the language of mystery similar to that used by Jaspers and at times upholds the solitary individual advocated by Heidegger and Kierkegaard, which his phenomenology logically leads him to castigate. In what is one of his least illuminating and most confusing discussions he seems to have made an unhealthy compromise with man's natural egocentricity. His hero in this section is of all people H. G. Wells! By rejecting any sort of theological answer to the question of man's meaning, Binswanger may have discovered unwittingly a problem which phenomenology cannot answer. From a standpoint of Christian theology the search for one's ground does not end in the mystery of oneself but, rather, points to the ultimate ground of all being. The ground of individuality is not mine but His. In the experience of grace one is aware of being grounded in a Reality which gives to one the capacity for freedom; but this ground is not separate from that of duality. This, too, is love.

I am dead," wrote Robert Browning to his wife. This is not to be interpreted necessarily as fanciful thinking or as an arrogant unwillingness to refuse inevitability. It is like the language of Marcel quoted earlier, which says to the beloved, "You shall not die." This language is meant to indicate that the world of love cannot be reduced to the world of subject-object where death is total loss. If the meaning of existence cannot be found in that secondary world, surely the meaning of death is not to be located there. As Marcel has emphasized repeatedly, there is undeniably a sense in which the beloved person who dies is yet a presence for us, who remains with us not as an idea but within the personal structure of our existence. Only a metaphysic which insists that the body entirely circumscribes man will legitimately maintain that physical death is the total end of the love world and personal existence. Death faced by one who senses the presence of loved ones has a different meaning from death faced in isolation. The death of the beloved is often felt as an extreme but not total loss; for in some way the beloved continues to be a presence in a way which so far defies explication. Such an experience was movingly expressed by Robert Burns:

> Ye banks, and braes, and streams around
>   The castle o' Montgomery,
> Green be your woods, and fair your flowers,
>   Your waters never drumlie!
> There simmer first unfauld her robes,
>   And there the langest tarry;
> For there I took the last fareweel
>   O' my sweet Highland Mary.
>
> How sweetly bloomed the gay green birk,
>   How rich the hawthorn's blossom,
> As underneath their fragrant shaed
>   I clasped her to my bosom!
> The golden hours on angel wings
>   Flew o'er me and my dearie;
> For dear to me as light and life
>   Was my sweet Highland Mary.
>
> Wi' mony a vow and locked embrace
>   Our parting was fu' tender;
> And, pledging aft to meet again,
>   We tore oursels asunder;
> But oh! fell death's untimely frost,
>   That nipt my flower sae early!

Now green's the sod, and cauld's the clay,
   That wraps my Highland Mary!

O pale, pale now, those rosy lips,
   I aft have kissed sae fondly!
And closed for aye the sparkling glance,
   That dwelt on me sae kindly!
And mouldering now in silent dust,
   That heart that lo'ed me dearly—
But still within my bosom's core
   Shall live my Highland Mary.

Unless or until we have conclusive evidence to the contrary, we have no warrant to surmise that the presence felt in the heart is sheer fantasy, and we have great reason for further phenomenological investigations.

We have learned that love, especially romantic love, must never absolutize itself and must never think that it is everlasting. Romantic love must be transformed and men must die. For man to find his truth he must learn with humility to accept his finitude and the inevitable fact of death. And yet in the phenomenon of love the being of the beloved in some way seems to transcend the grip of death, at least in terms of the continuing sense of her presence carried in the heart of her lover. Religious teaching is necessary to give death a meaning such as might point to the possibility of fulfillment in a mode of transcendence and communion not apparent in this world. Yet much religious teaching and the insights of phenomenology can agree that the meaning of life is not to be found by preparing for death, nor is it to be realized by attempting to escape or postpone death. The greatest enemy to life as well as to love is not death. Man's worst enemy is himself; and man most jeopardizes his chances of realizing the greatest possible meaning, freedom, and happiness because of his faulty misunderstanding and misuse of love.

11

A *Phenomenology* of the *World* of *Social Existence*

1. UNCOVERING THE WORLD OF SOCIAL EXISTENCE

Thus far our existential phenomenology has illuminated two basic possibilities of human existence. One possibility or mode of existence is singularity; the other is that of loving coexistence or duality. Though these two modes are distinct, they are not totally separate. The individual self and the personal or interpersonal self are twin born. Even twins, however, are born successively, not simultaneously; from our phenomenological vision we have seen that the individual self is called into existence through the beckoning voice of a Thou. It is from within the reality of We that a person gains true awareness of the personal meaning of his being in the world. From the point of view of singularity, existence within the transport of love appears to be beyond the world. Yet being in love is truly being in a world, one which is constituted by its own unique space-time structure. We have spoken of man living in various worlds in the sense of being directed toward various possibilities of meaning arising out of specific forms of encounter. The total structure of human existence is being in the world, but the lived world has a variety of possible meanings. The world is not a single intentional structure. It does not indicate merely one basic form of transcendence which can be either authentic or inauthentic. Within the totality of the lived world there are lesser worlds structured by the intentional direction a human being is set upon in his encounter with a particular situation. These lesser worlds are systems of reference structured in terms of how man takes his bearings in the totality of his lived world.

241

What I am advocating is a kind of pluralism within an existential phenomenological approach which sees man essentially as a historical being whose worldly existence is constituted by divergent basic structures of meaning. From the perspective of the world of concern, the world of love may seem foolish; from the viewpoint of the world of love, the world of concern may appear dull, drab, even dead. From an individual outlook a warm, brilliantly colorful summer day may inspire one to ecstatic self-expression; yet that same day, seen from the eyes of the lover who acutely senses the absence of his beloved, may seem like an endless stretch of bleak winter. An encounter with a large, foreign city by oneself may arouse anxiety, produce a presentiment of dark uncanniness, and appear as the last place in the world to find a home; yet that same city approached with a loved one may appear as a dazzling, unlimited playground for love and creative growth. Each of us lives in at least two basic worlds within our total world structure. That is an objective fact of our subjectivity. Our being in the world assumes different forms of transcendence, opens up to diverse possibilities of meaning, is characterized by essentially different intentional structures. Yet these worlds, though distinct, usually interpenetrate within the fundamental world of existence.[1]

In the next chapter I shall focus upon extremely unfortunate existence where a person's divergent worlds do not converge but remain isolated. The existence in which the world of love is nearly or entirely excluded from the world of concern is often clinically diagnosed as schizophrenia. To live in radically separate, thoroughly compartmentalized worlds is to suffer a radically fallen existence; it is to live in a broken world. The private

[1] John Wild has also implied a pluralistic approach to the understanding of the lived world, particularly because he emphasized that human being as both historical and free lives in a world which is essentially open. He follows the position proposed by William James, who was opposed to the dogmatic spirit he found in metaphysics. Pluralism was an alternative approach to understanding reality, particularly experience. While I have much in common with this kind of pluralism, yet my meaning is different. Wild repeatedly contrasts two kinds of worlds—the scientific or objective world and the lived world. Again like James there is the conflict between two approaches to life; one by way of experience, the other by way of a restricted kind of experience associated with a laboratory. But this war of worlds, as Wild puts it, actually uses the world in two different senses; one is existential, the other supposedly scientific. I am proposing that pluralism refers to the basic lived world. Man lives in various worlds according to the mode of his basic encounters. It seems that only within this perspective can there really be a possibility of dialogue between philosophy and science. Wild's "war" seems to be insoluble, except for a treaty in which the sciences succumb to philosophy in an unconditional surrender. See Wild, *Existence and the World of Freedom*, especially pp. 5-18, 66-97.

world of genuine self-regard (*Eigenwelt*) has a definite place within the personal world of love; it is evoked and sustained by it. The coinherent reality of We is properly all-embracing. When a man rejects that embrace and chooses to stand all alone, to isolate the world of love from the rest of his worldly being, he has used his freedom to undo itself by foreclosing genuine possibilities of existential integration.

Though we have illuminated two basic possibilities, being unto oneself or self-realization and being in love, it is obvious that no one of us stands completely in those worlds all or most of the time. Though our over-all existential structure may be grounded in loving duality as well as directed toward genuine individuation, yet everyday life is also structured by other concerns having to do with ordinary relationships with others in the public world. These relations are not deeply I-Thou; but without further phenomenological analysis they cannot be classified as merely the I-It relationships of fallen, inauthentic existence. What needs to be investigated are ordinary forms of association and those aspects of life which are by far the most frequent and which demand our attention, even if they are not the bearers of our most important existential meanings.[2] This mode of existence is the world of social existence (*Mitwelt*), public life, or what we might designate as *secular* existence, here employed in the sense of being distinct from essentially personal and private existence rather than as the opposite of the sacred. In advance it should be noted that what follows are merely first steps in an area that demands extensive exploration and reflection.[3]

[2] Harvey Cox rightly questioned the misuse of I-Thou categories which in Buber's scheme would appear to be the only alternative to I-It relations with others. Cox suggested that we need to develop a sense of I-You or somewhat personal impersonal relations, which is very much in line with the aim in this chapter. See *The Secular City*, pp. 48-49.

[3] Father Remy Kwant has written an entire book which proposes to be a *Phenomenology of Social Existence*. This is a clearly stated, unnecessarily repetitious attack upon an individualistic approach to the understanding of human existence. His argument is that man cannot be understood merely as an individual. Individualism in all varieties fails to see that the whole fabric of human existence is social: "the entire pursuit of our manhood, all our human activities, are social" (p. 60). The social dimension of existence is like a second nature to man, from which he is inseparable (p. 127). Especially is it important to consider the social dimension when we consider the human world: "Every genuinely human activity is interwoven with an orderly field of worldly meaning. But such a field of meaning is at our disposal only through others, through society" (p. 68). The entire aspect of human existence participating in a common world understood as a social reality is scarcely touched upon in my own limited study; and the reader is encouraged to study Fr. Kwant's work. However, it should be noted that the title is misleading. It is difficult to see how this work is really phenomenology.

2. A DISTINCT INTENTIONAL STRUCTURE OF SOCIAL EXISTENCE

As a start let us look briefly at Binswanger's phenomenology of social existence in the mode of everyday life. Whereas for Heidegger everyday existence (*Alltäglichkeit*) is a fallen mode, for Binswanger it is just the average and ordinary without any pejorative connotations. Though Heidegger's ontological evaluation could be right, Binswanger was not interested in making such a judgment, at least not until the full reality of being in the world had become manifest.[4] He did, however, appreciate Heidegger's insight that the everyday mode of existence often conceals possibilities of transcendence. It can easily happen, for example, that ordinary social relationships can become absolutized so that one is blind to the true reality of loving duality. Yet the primary task in the phenomenology of personal existence is to see the full structure of intentionality and imaginatively to intuit the various existential meanings emerging from within it. It must be stressed that an interpretation or judgment as to the ultimacy of any meanings is not the work of phenomenology but of theology.[5] Binswanger, as we have noted, was attempting to remain theologically neutral; his commitment which shaped his interpretation was to a priori possibilities, not to their ultimate meanings. As such he has helped to uncover much that otherwise lay concealed.

As we focus and reflect upon our everyday mode of being in the world we become aware that we often relate to our situation in a functional manner. We are concerned, as Heidegger said, with things as utensils. Or to use Marcel's language, ordinary existence is largely played out on the level of having rather than of being. Things are there at hand to be grasped, analyzed, used, enjoyed, or disposed of. Even another person does not ordinarily appear directly to me as a unique historical, personal existence but as somebody who may help me to accomplish a set task or who might stand in my way. For me to function satisfactorily, it is important to know and be able to predict how he will function, especially if he occupies

Rather, it might be more accurately classified as a first step toward a phenomenology, a kind of preliminary *epoché* which clears away the prejudice of individualism. One of the major challenges to phenomenology is to enlarge our insight into and deepen our understanding of the basic meanings of social existence as this is being explored and uncovered by sociologists.

4 Binswanger, *Grundformen*, pp. 270-271.

5 Cf. the suggestive article by Gibson Winter, "Theology and Social Science," in *The Scope of Theology*, Daniel Jenkins, ed., pp. 174-198.

an important role in my situation. We should be cognizant of this everyday functional mode of operation without disparaging it. However, within a utilitarian framework individuals and groups stand outside the boundaries of loving duality. Hopefully, duality may interpenetrate this functional perspective; but if the encounter of I-Thou is forced into a pragmatically purposeful intentional structure, the underlying unity of We may be obliterated. Certainly the full meaning of duality will not be discovered in this intentional modality.

This pragmatic, functional mode of being in the world with others appears to be constituted by the particular form of being in the world that we have already designated as *taking*.[6] Binswanger called it the "as structure" (*Als-Struktur*) of existence, in the sense that you appear to me *as* someone who plays a particular role in society. It is a form of worldliness in which the world stands between you and me. You are over there in the world, and I can observe how you behave. You perform a certain role, and as I take it in I become aware of what is called your personality. This *as* structure is grounded in a definite distance between you and me and things, a form of distance that is quite distinct from the distance discovered in loving duality. This mode of taking refers to relations with other personalities as well as to things at hand.[7] I take my clothes and put them on in the morning and take them off in the evening. I take in food for nourishment and enjoyment. I take a short trip to engage in employment which will provide me with take-home pay to take a vacation; and I might even take you along. Man is a functioning organism who relates to his environment by diverse ways of taking.

Erikson's study of human behavior in terms of zones and modes is also relevant. Erikson suggested that we can understand a total mode of existence as it is centered around a particular body zone in relation to its environment. The earliest existential modes are in terms of getting, taking, holding, intruding, or being on the make. Thus in the development of an individual from his earliest perceived response to his environment we observe varieties of a basic mode which falls within a general classification of *taking*. Man constructs a human world in terms of this form of encounter. He takes things in his hands to use them. He takes things into his mouth to chew them. He can take things into his arms and hold them. He

---

[6] Cf. Binswanger, *Grundformen*, p. 273. See also the discussion of spatiality in Chapter 7, above. The analysis and images, unless otherwise noted, are my own and should not be blamed on Binswanger.

[7] Cf. *ibid.*, pp. 274-289.

can take another person by the hand, by the ear, or even by the neck. Each of these functions points to a definite mode of transcendence, constituting a distinct form of human meaning. Mere description of man's taking hold of various aspects of his situation will not, however, reveal the meaning of it. A phenomenology which acknowledges a definite existential or intentional structure in human encounters is needed to accomplish that.

The discovery of this mode of being in the world throws new light on our understanding of man, beginning with the nature of ordinary perception. One form of taking which is clearly an existential mode is the act of sensory perception, whereby man "captures" a particular scene through the medium of his senses. Ordinary language clearly reflects this. We stand on a mountaintop and with our eyes take in the extent and beauty of the view. Our body is gripped by the cold air. Our ears pick up the sounds of the wind. Our nose takes in the aroma of pines. Psychology has helped us to realize that perception of our environing world is an act of the total man, not primarily or exclusively something done by the eyes. Bodily zones such as the mouth, the sexual organs, the limbs, indeed the total bodily condition are basic modes for learning and evaluating the nature of human experience. The totality of man as a bodily being in the world functions in the act of environmental perception. Yet the bodily process is certainly not the final source of significance. Sensory perception is an intentional act, participating in a referential process directed toward meanings. It is one form of existential transcendence, one definite mode of being in the world. It is a mistake to suppose that all perception must be understood within one particular intentional structure. The phenomenon of knowing in love is not a form of taking. All human existence cannot be reduced to the ways in which men take things in.[8] There is the frequent tendency in psychological theories of personality, as Binswanger pointed out, that would force human existence into this one particular mode; from there it is but a short step to considering social relations as merely an extension of the way in which we relate to our nonpersonal environment. Any science or philosophy which claims to grasp the whole man by assembling his various parts and functions that have been conceived from detached, nonparticipatory observation has succumbed to the illusion that the mode of taking is the only basic structure of perception and of existence.

The structure of taking, whether it be social or environmental, involves a peculiar form of spatiality. This spatiality is characterized by a

8 Cf. *ibid.*, pp. 290-300.

specific mode of existential distance. Binswanger suggested that this distance is structured by proximate *accessibility* and *attachment.*[9] It is neither spatialization which makes room for beings in which to find their meanings nor the space of a trustful home but, rather, of concern that moves to overcome distance so as to establish an attachment, to get hold of something. The corresponding mode of temporality here is a special mode of *attentiveness.* This attentiveness is the temporal expression of a concern to make sure that what is desired is taken in as opportunity presents itself; it is an attentiveness that aims not to let the object escape, to get out of hand. This temporality is not characterized by presence; yet it is not the fallen temporality of distractedness analyzed by Heidegger. Time in the public world is measured, calculated, and agreed upon by society; this is time which has been externalized so that it can be taken in hand. Man is often meaningfully oriented in the world in terms of setting a direction geared toward taking action to acquire a goal, which may be obtained if one is attentive to the temporal distance between desire and achievement. For most practical purposes man lives in this public space-time. He takes stock of his time by the clock or calendar to determine whether his time is being well spent or wasted. Time in the world of taking is probably the easiest mode of temporality for people in our pragmatically oriented culture to understand. We can agree upon how much time it takes to get something done, just as we can concur upon the accessibility a thing or goal has in terms of its distance to our present situation. Social existence with others in a public world is largely constituted by the existential mode of taking. This is a necessary and legitimate form of encounter; but it is not the only foundation of existential meaning.

Though the structure of taking applies to both the natural and the social environment, it should be obvious that the intentional structure of this encounter is much more complex with respect to people than it is with things. Much of the specific meaning of taking is partially derived from the way what we meet offers resistance to the act of taking. Particularly with respect to complex forms of life it is important to recognize not merely that an organism performs functions; it is also a bearer of functions. To understand the encounter, it is necessary, as Teilhard de Chardin suggested, somehow to get at the "within of things." [10] This is even more true

9 *Ibid.,* pp. 301-302.
10 Teilhard de Chardin, *The Phenomenon of Man,* pp. 53-67. This suggestion should not be misconstrued to mean an uncritical acceptance of all aspects of Teilhard's notion of "within."

with respect to any attempt to understand the meaning of an encounter between persons on the level of taking. A strictly objective description will not reveal the existential dimension. What complicates social encounters particularly is not only the manifold ways of taking which may function simultaneously. What must be considered is not merely the particular mode of our taking another person but also the way in which the other person resists or permits us to take him. In addition we must be aware that as we take, we are also being taken.

Consider the possibility of taking another person by the ear. This may be literal or figurative: "Friends, Romans, countrymen, lend me your ears." The difference in meaning is not primarily in the mode of taking, the one being physical, the other mental. Much meaning depends upon what kind of impression is made. A teacher can literally get the ear of his pupil to make an impression, usually momentary and negative; or he can figuratively gain the ear of his pupil and make an indelible and lifelong impression that will help to shape the young person's entire world. In the former instance we see a form of taking which is largely external, a hand grabbing an ear; in the latter, more social, modality an impression is made not upon a part but upon a whole. The teacher makes an impression upon *someone*, upon *him*, not upon his ear or his feelings, or his mind alone. Here a new factor is introduced into the encounter of taking. The extent to which I reach the whole of the other is dependent upon the other as well as upon me; in attempting to understand this phenomenon, the other's viewpoint and response must be considered as well as my own outlook and behavior. It is obvious, then, that in the social modality we have to do with a form of reciprocal taking which is not to be understood from a singular approach. Taking of another person includes a certain amount of mutual involvement in each other's world. Thus the mode of social taking must be understood as an existential phenomenon comprising various dimensions of facts and meanings.[11]

In the phenomenon of taking another and making an impression as sketched above it becomes evident that public, social existence may approach or even interpenetrate the world of love. As I suggest in Chapter 13, a goal of mature personal existence is to allow the special quality of love to permeate as widely and deeply as possible the basic structures of the lived world. If that happens, then mere social intercourse, for example, can mean much more than living up to expected formalities; it can also be an

[11] Cf. Binswanger, *Grundformen*, pp. 305-307.

expression of love. A simple public greeting can have a variety of meanings, depending upon how the encounter is structured. Interpenetrating social existence with love is a high aim of human life. A reverse direction is also possible and represents a constant threat. In romantic love, for example, it is all too easy to slip from loving encounter into the mode of taking. In erotic moments, when emotions and passions are aroused, one's partner may reveal vulnerability. One's attention may be diverted to this vulnerability, which in turn offers the possibility of manipulation and possession. Various devices, such as looks, words, and gestures, may be used to discover where the other is weakest. Then may begin intrigues, cool calculation, and all sorts of cunning attempts to conquer and control. In passion, fear, or longing the other may be caught, seduced, and controlled. As Binswanger suggested, the incentive of mere erotic passion is blind to the Thou of the other.[12] Ordinary language suggests a common insight into the danger of transforming personal encounter into the structure of taking. In the act of making love, it is sometimes said that one of the partners is *made*. The phrase indicates that one of the partners has been taken advantage of. When personal existence is shoved into the intentional structure of taking, relationships occur on the level of instrumentality. The other is treated as an instrument to be had, controlled, and perhaps enjoyed. In a situation of pure taking there may be some sharing in a world held in common, but full personal freedom has been repudiated.

According to Binswanger much psychology unfortunately thinks of man primarily in terms of his vulnerability, the possibility of his being taken. Man is often conceived as a creature of impressionability, as a creature of drive and affect whose life can be taken over by tension and desire.[13] An individual who is conceived essentially as an instrument under the control of various factors is man the victim—the victim of those aspects of life where he "can be had." Man's personality often is calculated in terms of how he can be caught. This way of conceiving man is at least as old as Machiavelli, and it is still as false to the creative human possibilities of life. Human freedom is not an instrument that can be manipulated without destroying it. When a free man is treated merely as an instrument then basic possibilities for personal creativity are excluded from both theory and practice. Max Weber pointed out that through the rise and

---

[12] Cf. *ibid.*, pp. 308-312.
[13] *Ibid.*, pp. 314-316. Erikson and others have suggested that psychoanalysis is more a study of what man suffers from experience than what he does with it.

expansion of rationalism there has developed in the modern world a generalized instrumentalization of life. Though we today enjoy the benefits from the increasingly successful technical control of both natural and social environment, we stand in jeopardy that the importance of a technical grasp of reality may be grossly exaggerated. When that happens we then tend to subscribe to the cynical faith that what cannot be had is either nonexistent or not worth considering.

Binswanger's endeavor to develop an anthropological view of the structure of ordinary life has helped us to realize the necessity of using varied approaches to perceive and understand human phenomena. Coming from a background of psychology he had focused upon dynamic characteristics of the personality such as affect or varying intensities of libido. Though physical syndromes had to be studied as such, he realized they were not to be explicated merely in terms of the organism itself. While considering some aspect of the individual by which he has been or might be taken (conceived and controlled), one must realize that the origin, for example, of a particular affect or drive which has held him to a certain course of development does not lie in the organism alone. Rather, an affect emerges from within a situation of interaction. The possibility for an affect lies not only in the organism, but also within the situation; furthermore, its significance is not understandable apart from human freedom in its capacity to exist in and to transcend the mode of taking and being taken. Binswanger thus proposed an ecological approach to personality and existence, by which he meant something very similar to the multi-directional approach advocated by Erik Erikson.

Existential phenomenology seeks to expand this position for further research. The phenomenological approach which seeks to discover, analyze, and understand basic human structures points to an interdisciplinary method as being the most adequate one from which to understand social existence and personality. Various means of attack are requisite to uncover the complexity of taking the world in and being taken by it. A responsible approach to man in his public existence with his environing world must include at least sociological, psychological, and historical studies. Yet for an understanding of the whole man these disciplines need the larger framework of existential phenomenology which will provide a frame of reference for both investigation and interpretation. In other words our understanding of man must begin with insight into the fact of transcendence; one should not suppose that he may arrive there merely by observing the taking mode of being in the world.

A responsible existential phenomenology must counter the opinion expressed in much existentialist literature that all forms of social or public existence are inauthentic. Specifically with respect to possible relations with others, there are positively meaningful ways of taking people. If I take an interest in someone or take him seriously or take him at his word I am not attempting to manipulate, impress, or dominate him. There are forms of taking in which the individual freedom of each of us is recognized and even affirmed. If I take you at your word, I am acknowledging the integrity of your particular being in the world; and at the same time I profess my trust in our relationship and my dependence upon your intentions and actions. When two persons meet and take each other at their word, they seal a bond between them; but the bond does not have the duration that love does. In this moment there is an approximation of love, but the distinctive ecstasy of being in love is not present. To trust another because of his reputation or to take him at his word is to act on the basis of knowledge. However, the knowledge learned from love comes through a direct personal participation in the common world of duality. The knowledge I have of you by taking your word is inferential, rather than through an I-Thou encounter.[14] I cannot live freely if I cannot take people for granted in the social world of existence; but if I merely take one I love for granted, the relationship of love deteriorates. I may take an interest in another person and learn to help that person solve a problem or achieve a goal; but so long as the relationship exists on this social level, the other is for me a he or she, not a Thou. To take an interest is to show concern for aspects of another's personal development. It is not through concern but in love that I really meet another in his or her wholeness. Though social existence may not reach the creative heights of radical individuality or love, it nevertheless constitutes an indispensable structure for distinctively human life.

Existential phenomenology has uncovered social or secular existence as a genuine mode of being human with others. However, to subsume all human existence with others under the category of social existence is a mistake typical of juveniles and schizophrenics who identify themselves and others totally in terms of reputations. This amounts to a reduction of personal existence to the impersonal mode of him, her, and they, eliminating the basic modes of I, Thou, and a loving We. That reduction absolutizes one particular form of distance encountered in relation to others. Such an absolutization results in a total breakdown of trust, which is

[14] Cf. *ibid.*, pp. 326 ff. and pp. 377-380 ff.

vitally important to all forms of existence; and it is an action which debilitates the existential conscience. Certainly the tension felt by the conscience is most frequently not a result of facing a choice between a right and a wrong on the same level of existence but involves being faithful to several possibilities at once. The voice of conscience within love calls a person to be faithful to himself and to the other; but conscience within social existence also makes a claim upon an individual to be true to his word, to live up to his name which others have counted upon. The question of right action is not simply to be a Thou to another; it also involves modes of taking and being taken. To consider morality and conscience as having to do solely with social existence is to betray love; but to consider morality and conscience to pertain only to the world of love is to ignore one mode of being in the world without which there could be no personal existence.[15]

3. THE MEANING OF SECULARIZATION IN LIGHT OF THE INTENTIONAL STRUCTURE OF TAKING

Though personal existence may be stifled if all major aims and values are reduced to those of man's public life with others, nevertheless it should be apparent that the common existentialist wholesale repudiation of everyday social existence is unwarranted. Binswanger has been particularly helpful in uncovering a primary structure of meaning in which ordinary and routine relationships with others occur. Following his insight it becomes evident that the specific mode of everyday being in the world can be understood, at least in large part, within the existential structure of *taking*. I exist in the world by taking things; taking is no less than another existential a priori in which I find life meaningful. Though it may have a pejorative connotation

---

15 Cf. *ibid.*, pp. 352-357 ff. Here I take issue with two one-sided positions. First, I disagree with Binswanger, who separated love and morality. Following Nietzsche he also declared that love is "beyond good and evil." The previous phenomenology would render that statement as nonsense, pure and simple. It would seem that Binswanger was guilty of oversimplifying morality and ethics, putting it all on one plane or in one form of encounter. As I have suggested, morality applies to the whole world, which includes the triple worlds of individuality, duality, and social existence. This would also suggest that the currently fashionable situation ethics of Christian theology which advocate love and the personal world as the basic solution to moral problems is equally guilty of reductionism. A phenomenological approach to human existence is increasingly aware of the vast complexity of man's transcendence, of his varied basic forms of intentionality; thus it may be considered to be in opposition to if not a form of repudiation of any methods which are guilty of false or precipitous simplifications.

as a structure within which I relate to other people, taking is also a legitimate and meaningful way in which I relate to others in our common life. Thus it becomes possible to detect the meaning of many social encounters by focusing upon the intentional structure of taking and attempting to determine how this mode is related to singularity and duality in a given situation.[16] Furthermore it becomes apparent that the fundamental a priori of concern as delineated by Heidegger has much more relevance to everyday existence than to the worlds of creative individuality and duality. I take things into consideration, take care of them, or take an interest in people because I am concerned about them. Concern reaches out to take hold of meaning; but as I create a new world through play or meet another in love, it is necessary to let go, to cease being concerned and trying to take, and to open to the surprise of something new which transcends the objects of concern.

The illumination of the intentional structure of social existence has relevance to the issue of secularization which is widely discussed today, especially in the field of religious sociology. It is said that our era has been undergoing a process of secularization. In contradistinction to secularism, which is an absolutization of some cultural form, secularization refers in part to a historical process in which men break loose from the hold of religious ideologies and religious institutions.[17] Secularization has been given a positive interpretation even by leading theologians; it has been seen to be a movement which makes man aware of his individual freedom and his responsibility in creating authentic historicity.[18] From this perspective secularization may be seen as the background for an existentialist affirmation of freedom. The secularist mentality celebrates human freedom and is concerned about shaping history; yet the secularist framework within which human life is interpreted is too narrow.

The secular man considers himself freed from sacred ideas and institutions; he is now able to devote his full attention to what is going on in the

[16] Cf. *ibid.*, pp. 341 ff.

[17] See, e.g., Gibson Winter, *The New Creation as Metropolis*, pp. 35-43. The phenomenology of secularization will throw much theological interpretation into a new light. A sharp distinction between the religious and the secular is really superficial and misleading. What current theologians rightly protest is that a particular "secular" modality, as emerging from the Middle Ages, was absolutized and taken to be essentially infallible, as instituted by God himself and therefore sacrosanct. What is meant by a secular approach to reality is basically an open approach to the nature and meaning of secular, everyday existence. In this respect, the new theology and phenomenology have much in common.

[18] *Ibid.*, p. 59.

world. Secularization is considered a release from the bondage of religious ideology which did not appreciate or emphasize historical existence nearly enough. As a free man, the secularist is no longer magically enthralled by mysterious powers, nor is he ontologically concerned to understand the essence of a thing. The secularized man is basically a pragmatist; he thinks not in terms of gods or essences but in terms of functions.[19] He tends to ask the same question of a theory as he does of a machine: Will it work? Much modern theology has presented a serious and worthwhile interpretation of the process of secularization. Unfortunately, some of it gives the impression that the whole structure of historicity can be understood and appreciated from a secularist viewpoint. From the theologically neutral vantage point of existential phenomenology, to establish secular existence as the criterion for interpreting the whole of human life would be extremely unfortunate. Though secularization has undoubtedly brought men new freedom in some areas, it has also jeopardized other forms of freedom which may be more important to creative personal existence.

Phenomenological reflection upon secularization indicates that much of so-called secular existence falls within the intentional structure of taking. Harvey Cox, a theologian who rejoices in the new secularization of life, claimed that secularization marks a change in the way men grasp and understand their lives; it is a way of losing religious and quasi-religious understanding and of dispelling closed world systems.[20] Both his language and his analysis of secularization evince the intentional structure of taking. In terms of secular ideology we find the language of grasping and letting go. In everyday secular life, man is primarily concerned to engage in history with a mentality of instrumentality. How does it work? How can I take it, shape it, direct it, get it to work for me? Cox rightly affirms the goodness in this existential mode as he points to an increase of freedom; but it is freedom within only one possible modality. He seems to over-emphasize its goodness and its totality. To say of Albert Camus and John F. Kennedy that they symbolized the buoyant reasonableness and "calm sense of assurance which characterize the best in our epoch" [21] overlooks their anguished search for meaning beyond strictly secular existence, beyond this limited way of being in the world. Pragmatic man can find

19 Harvey Cox, *The Secular City*, pp. 60-65. See also Mircea Eliade, *The Sacred and the Profane*, ch. 4.
20 *Ibid.*, pp. 1-2.
21 *Ibid.*, p. 78.

honest delight in a functional process; this is a rightful and basic part of his life as a man. But he does not find his home there. As Camus so brilliantly depicted in his novels, secular man is anxious and afraid; he is suspicious of others and even of himself. Secular man is both fascinated and terrified by the unknown. He wills to possess it, to take it into his experience, to make it work for him; yet he is aware that it does not belong to him and that his attempt to make it his possession might be fatal. From an instrumental viewpoint, secular man has been amazingly successful at enlarging the circumference of his domination. He has increased his capacity to lay hold of large areas of life; yet he is nevertheless still in the grip of potentially paralyzing fear. As long as he persists in living in a one-dimensional world, which is to be understood essentially in terms of function and possession, he will be a prisoner of the fear of losing his hold on the world and on life itself.

There are various ways of interpreting the deep and prevalent fear found in secular existence. It may be taken as a stage man is passing through before he comes of age and gains the mastery of the universe. It might be seen as a basic enemy to man's ongoing accomplishments, as in the famous words of Franklin D. Roosevelt: "We have nothing to fear but fear itself." On the other hand, phenomenology indicates that it might also be interpreted as a healthy pointer to a basic existential world beyond that which is structured by the encounters of taking and being taken. Fear is a transmutation of basic anxiety by which the latter becomes attached to an object. Anxiety operates in a different intentional world than fear, as we shall see in Chapter 12. Fear is most appropriate to the world in which things are taken, where even life is taken. This is the secular world. Fear can be debilitating; but it can be healthy if it calls the secular world into question. Fear can just as well lead secular man to a discovery of his full historical being by pointing to his need to recover deep, personal trust. Thus within a personal perspective fear can be dealt with creatively so as to enlarge the full scope of human freedom. Freedom in the secular world of taking is only one form of freedom. If through fear a man absolutizes his secular existence, he is closing doors to basic existential meanings that are grounded in singularity and duality. In his security through secular mastery, man becomes a prisoner within the narrow confines of the pragmatic and profane world. If secularization is to lead man into freer understanding of historical existence, then it must be recognized that historical categories such as fear have deeply human meanings which point to the existential matrix of loving interpersonal relations. As Gibson Winter so rightly put it, "historical man is the man who finds himself freed to answer responsibly for his identity in the world; he knows that his answer to the meaning of being in the world is bound up with the interpersonal world which mediates this identity to him." [22] Certainly fear is an enemy to the enjoyment of man's freedom. But if secular man runs away from it or drowns it out through sedatives or frenetic activity without really listening to what it might be saying about the nature of his world, then he may well be imprisoning his historical freedom within a world that basically cannot distinguish between the history of a man and the history of a machine. Without the secular world a man cannot live; within only the secular a man is not truly a person.

The everyday, secular mode of social existence is a legitimate, necessary but restricted form of being in the world. It has its own distinct space-time structure, with its own distinct meanings. Binswanger denoted this world as *discursive*, to be distinguished from singular and dual. By designating existence as discursive he meant to suggest that the mode of taking operates in a cause-effect structure, going from one thing to another in its concern for how things function.[23] It would be proper to speak of this modality as fallen if, for example, lovers ceased to live in mutual presence and regarded each other in terms of taking and having, as in the cases of possessive, symbiotic love or seduction. Such behavior distorts love, because it takes love out of its proper world and thrusts it into another world where it is deprived of its own authentic meaning. Or one could speak of fallenness if one's self-regard has been reduced to a concern for how one is

22 G. Winter, *New Creation*, p. 109. In the context of this important book, Winter maintains that the task of theology is to engage in deeply historical reflection upon the whole process of human existence. Theology must be open to the meanings of secular existence; but it must also become aware that basic historical meanings of life come from other dimensions than that of instrumentality. The specific task of theology is to help men become open to the deepest dimension of historical existence, to summon them toward "their real future," toward the ultimate meaning of human existence which is the New Mankind, the life in Christ (see pp. 59-72). With this thoroughly historical approach—historical understood in an existential manner—theology and existential phenomenology have much in common; a dialogue between them seems natural and certainly promising of rich insights. My point here to those who would carry on a theological enterprise along an existential vein, is that man's real future, the direction of his whole existence, is not to be identified with any one particular intentional avenue. The lived world of experience has several basic directions, several existential a priori, all of which must be taken into account if one is to make any sense about ultimate meanings of existence. The *secular world* is *not* the *most historical* dimension of existence.

23 Binswanger, *Grundformen*, pp. 341-350.

functioning in the world where all is take or be taken, as in hypochondria. Otherwise, this world, consisting of its own existential spatiality and temporality, must be appreciated. Heidegger's portrayal of everyday existence as *das Man*, the anonymous, shallow, functional individual is certainly a possibility for each of us. Indeed many astute observers of our own era have suggested that with our increasingly functionalistic approach, man stands in jeopardy of losing himself, consumed by lack of awareness and decision in the irresolute drifting toward power, pleasure, and security. Yet even in the mode of secularity one can assume historical responsibility for oneself and others. Here one is a member of society wherein he can exercise responsibility creatively and courageously; here, too, one has a distinct name (reputation and personality) which bears genuine worth. Certainly in secular existence one knows pain, courage, and satisfaction issuing from decisions and actions toward legitimate meanings that are important for individuals and the society as a whole. In Binswanger's view the discursive mode of existence moved between the extremes of total existential fallenness such as portrayed by Heidegger and of ebullient existence in the transport of love.[24] Binswanger suggested that Heidegger's portrayal of everyday existence is more applicable to schizophrenia than ordinary secular existence; of course Binswanger recognized an uncomfortable prevalence of schizophrenic symptoms in much of contemporary life. However one decides on that score, it seems evident that secularization marks the increase of freedom in one, but only one, basic mode of human transcendence wherein man can discover and realize authentic existential meanings.

4. TOWARD A PHENOMENOLOGY OF SOCIAL INTERSUBJECTIVITY

At this point we have uncovered *three* distinct and positive ways of being with others: communion with another in duality; creative self-awareness or differentiation in the encounter with others; and functional relationships of secular existence. Yet we have not accounted for the full phenomenon of social existence particularly as this has been uncovered and interpreted by sociologists and anthropologists in the last sixty years. The world of love includes romance, family, and friends; but intimate, personal intersubjectivity is hardly identical with society as a corporate existential reality. Neither does a phenomenology of *taking* uncover the full transcendence of our existence in society. Phenomenology has found it difficult to move beyond

[24] *Ibid.*, p. 343.

individual subjectivity and interpersonal relationships, partially because it is often still in the grips of individualism but also because it has not paid sufficient attention to the data of social scientists. In this section I shall suggest an area that needs much more phenomenological research, and indicate at least one relevant purpose toward which this research may be directed. In the final section I shall attempt to sketch out the kind of relationship phenomenology and the social sciences might best develop.

While Freud was humiliating man's egoism by revealing unconscious urges and unresolved inner conflicts which drive men through history, another decisive blow was being struck to individualistic pride by the French sociologist Emile Durkheim. Ironically enough, Freud's analysis of determining factors nevertheless affirmed man's freedom and made us more aware of human dignity; the same is true for Durkheim's theories. Durkheim's investigations into various social phenomena, and particularly the breakdown of common social values and meanings, led him to the discovery of the deeply social nature of man. In his view man is only truly human to the extent that he is genuinely social. In pointing out the social nature of man Durkheim was not merely reiterating the platitude that man lives in society with others; rather, he was emphasizing that *society lives in man*. Society is a transcendent reality constituted by freedom and meaning; as a participant in society an individual comes to a realization of what it means to be human, particularly as he becomes aware of basic values which hold the social fabric together. Durkheim rejected all forms of intellectualism which attend to ideas rather than to concrete reality in the pursuit of knowledge. Yet most significantly he criticized narrow empiricism, in a way which brings him close to the borders of phenomenology; he attacked narrow empiricism because it fails to account for the creative operation of intelligence in man's encounter with his world. His notion of intelligence, however, is more social than individual, as reflected in his basic term *conscience collective*. In his own way Durkheim confronted the mysterious and provocative phenomenon which has also held our attention: How is it possible for a human being to have a world at all? The answer he gave, based on extensive reflection on the nature of society, was a devastating critique to all forms of individualism.[25] Durkheim came to the conclusion

25 It is not surprising that Durkheim has often not been very popular in America, especially with religious sociologists who feel strong kinship with Kierkegaard, Nietzsche, or other individualistic heroes. To criticize intellectualism fits in well with our pragmatic mentality, and to tear apart narrow empiricism will be received like a sermon which supposedly all believe but few bother to practice. But to demolish individualism

that man's growing awareness of himself as a human being is not a result of individual ingenuity; the phenomenon of self-awareness is inherently rooted in the a priori reality of society. By growing up in society the individual acquires basic mental categories which enable him to understand himself as a moral being and to function in a responsible and successful manner. In Durkheim's view transcendence, more specifically man's capacity to perceive and structure a distinctly human world, is not fundamentally an individual phenomenon but a social one. It is not man as an individual agent who can transcend the conditioning factors of environment, but man as society. As he wrote of each man in his classic study of religion:

> There are two beings in him: an individual being which has its foundations in the organism and the circle of whose activities is therefore strictly limited, and a social being which represents the highest reality in the intellectual and moral order that we can know by observation—I mean society.[26]

Admittedly Durkheim carried his interpretation to extremes, failing to recognize man's capacity to act individually in a way which is fully consonant with his highest reality. As it has often been pointed out, Durkheim did not allow for the genuine possibility of an individual's challenging and transcending his society by altering basic categories through unusual insight and understanding. In this particular work in which the social nature of man is stated so strongly he was concerned to discover the sociological basis for knowledge and to understand the role religion apparently plays in symbolic self-expression and the maintenance of social cohesiveness. He was working with a new insight which he did not comfortably understand, one which he formulated repetitiously. He was trying to make clear that

is nearly to kill God. Of all the *isms* which America denounces—communism, socialism, materialism, fascism, totalitarianism, etc.—this *ism* remains enshrined in the mythology of American history, is lauded in the eloquence of our statesmen, and lives vigorously at the center of unwritten creeds of the American way of life, which have had no less influence on our sociologists than on any of the rest of us.

[26] E. Durkheim, *The Elementary Forms of the Religious Life*, p. 29. The point is made repeatedly and is expanded throughout this very significant work. See also T. Parsons *Structures of Social Action*, chs. 9-12, and also E. Tiryakian, *Sociologism and Existentialism*. The latter has seen the close parallels between Durkheim's and an existential approach, particularly as Durkheim sought to uncover and understand social action. In conclusion to his interesting study Tiryakian makes the provocative suggestion that an "existential sociology" needs to be developed (pp. 165 ff.). Though it is not entirely clear what he is advocating, the general aim is thoroughly in line with my own intention to develop a phenomenology of social existence as well as a dialogue between phenomenology and the social sciences.

the social dimension in man cannot be fully appreciated when it is seen from an individualistic perspective, such as the common view which starts with the individual and then moves in the direction of his life with others in society. Rather, he was saying, we must start with the original unity of the social phenomenon and understand it as a human factor, especially in terms of creativity and cohesiveness. Society works creatively within the individual, enabling his awareness to develop in such a way as to bring him to a realization of his distinctively human world wherein he finds his experiences meaningful.

In America George Herbert Mead, to name another representative social scientist whose thought in this respect moved along similar lines, emphasized that the self is not primarily an individual entity but is a thoroughly social being. Man's adjustment to his world is always mediated through his particular society or culture, which means that his society is operative in his deepest self-understanding and in his basic formulations of a meaningful framework of existence. The effect of society upon the formation of one's distinctive existential perspective can be observed at a very early age, particularly in the play of young children. A child's play may be seen as his way of appropriating the organized social attitudes of his particular group or community. He thus learns to think of himself in terms of his social relationships and to integrate social roles and values into his own perspective.[27] One's history includes the development of a social self which is an integral factor of one's being in the world.

We must realize that the social is an emergent level which must be given full consideration in our attempt to understand existential history. Furthermore, we must learn to consider man's basic possibilities, and not merely his particular problems, as outgrowths of his peculiar social, religious, and economic institutions; the particular forms of man's basic possibilities are to a large extent manifestations of his culture. Thus we must come to appreciate society, and in particular human culture, as a fundamental mode of being in the world, which so far has been considered

[27] *The Social Psychology of George Herbert Mead*, A. Straus, ed., pp. 227-236 et passim. See also the study by P. Pfuetze, *Self, Society, Existence: Human Nature and Dialogue in the Thought of George Herbert Mead and Martin Buber*. In a way that Durkheim did not, Mead emphasized both aspects of the self's relation to society, that is, the way an individual takes hold of society and changes it as well as the way he is taken hold of by society in terms of role formation and sense of self which develop through society's participation in the individual. This first aspect I have referred to in our delineation of *taking*; but the latter phenomenon does not account for the full extent of social existence, particularly not in terms of social intersubjectivity as discovered in human culture and true communities.

largely in individual and interpersonal terms. Our phenomenology of love has revealed the fact of interpersonal coinherence wherein individuals discover communion. However, a growing body of knowledge from the social sciences is making more evident the fact that man's creative encounter with the world in a uniquely human manner is a result of social coinherence. Furthermore, social coinherence may develop into another form of communion denoted by the term *community*. Certainly without a phenomenological approach to society as an existential reality we shall hardly reach a full understanding of man's "second nature," his culture. In addition, without such an approach one has little chance of achieving a phenomenological understanding of religion, which is a deeply social phenomenon.[28] Too much phenomenological interpretation is guilty of what Bronislaw Malinowski would have referred to as a one-dimensional operation in that it does not take into account the full scope of the social dimension of existence.[29] As some sociologists appear to be moving toward an existential sociology, so phenomenology must now concentrate upon human communities and human culture.

[28] It would require a book in itself to develop an existential phenomenology of religion. Certainly this is a task which needs doing. Most phenomenology of religion, such as presented by eminent figures as Otto, van der Leeuw, Eliade, and Dumery, is, it seems to me, much too abstract; I would suggest that the reason is partially because the concept of phenomenology used or implied by these authors is Husserlian, and often with a very idealistic stamp on it. Though their abstract images of the essence of religious experience are sometimes helpful for methodological distinctions between alternative approaches to or interpretations of reality, these same formal essences of religion frequently stand in the way of an attempt to gain insight into and understanding of a particular, concrete religious encounter. They also tend to lead to a highly artificial and dangerously facile interpretation of contemporary "secular" life. It might be that one aspect of the "death of God" movement is a rejection of the unreal image of religious experience presented by much phenomenology of religion. Another reason for the artificiality of much phenomenology of religion is because the concrete life of the *community* has not been the focus of research.

[29] B. Malinowski, *Magic, Science and Religion*, pp. 239-245. Quite early in his career Malinowski expressed his keen insight into the social dimension not merely of religious beliefs but of human existence as such. As a student of culture Malinowski has been responsible for opening up to many social scientists the depth and dynamics of the social as a living phenomenon; and he encouraged what often looks like an existential approach, one which aims at entering the experience of a foreign culture so as to see its world from the inside. See also *Man and Culture: An Evaluation of the Work of Bronislaw Malinowski*, R. Firth, ed. Strangely enough, Malinowski dissociated himself from Durkheim's views and occasionally in strong language attacked them; however, it is now recognized that he did not really see how close his own views were to those of the latter. For an essay which brings the two together see P. Bohannan, "Conscience Collective and Culture," *Essays on Sociology and Philosophy*, E. Durkheim, ed. by K. Wolff, pp. 77-95. A collection of essays which is a classic expression of many American social scientists' understanding of the social dimension in personality is *Personality in Nature, Society, and Culture*, 2nd revised ed., C. Kluckhohn, H. A. Murray, and D. M. Schneider, eds.

One way in which a phenomenology of the social intersubjectivity may be developed is to investigate the social construction of the lived world, which thus far has been too exclusively the concern of the sociology of knowledge.[30] Another particularly important aspect of the phenomenology of social existence would be to concentrate upon the particular space-time of given cultures, including our own. In this era of increased international tension and cross-cultural contacts we are acutely aware that another society or culture represents a lived world surprisingly different from our own. The pioneering typological studies of Max Weber have illustrated the possibility of delineating a particular culture in a way that is similar to the study of individual personality types. Yet its keen awareness of existential structures, its sensitivity to human transcendence, and its emphasis upon imaginative participation in the phenomenon of a lived world should make existential phenomenology even better suited to reach insight and understanding in this area. I can here merely suggest the nature of numerous relevant projects, taking African culture as an example.

It is common knowledge that Africa is in a process of fantastic transition, one which is not primarily political, though this is perhaps what is most obvious. The transition involves a revolution that is deeply economic and even more deeply social. The Africans have frequently maintained that the Westerner fails to understand the nature of the transition because he does not understand the heart of the African. Unfortunately the African himself is suffering from a divided heart, and one of his most acute problems is that of self-identity. Is he a true African or has he sold his birthright to the West so as to accumulate and enjoy Western technology and affluence? Those of us who want to understand the African's personal dilemma in this uncertain transitional period must come to understand the African mentality from the inside. The native African coming from a community that is largely agricultural and tribal has thoroughly different thought patterns from those of us in a highly technical, urbanized culture. What is this African tribal mentality like? How does the native African who is not yet dominated by the influence of Western society see the world?

An attempt to gain access to this African *primal vision*, as John Taylor has so aptly called it, will require something of a phenomenological reduc-

---

[30] A handy, albeit dated review of the German approach to the sociology of knowledge is K. Mannheim, *Ideology and Utopia*. A more recent study is by P. Berger and T. Luckmann, *The Social Construction of Reality*, which is a systematic rather than historical essay in the sociology of knowledge.

tion on our part. We must first overcome our Western culture prejudices; we need to realize that though the African native is uninformed about many matters which are part and parcel of our culture, he is by no means less intelligent or less informed than we are about many things, including existence itself. With reference to the latter, Taylor has pointed out that the African's understanding of himself and others is at least as keen as our own, only it does not originate with an individualistic bias:

> Any attempt to look upon the world through African eyes must involve this adventure of the imagination whereby we abandon our image of a man whose complex identity is encased within a shell of his physical being, and allow ourselves instead to visualize a centrifugal self-hood, equally complex, interpermeating other selves in a relationship in which subject and object are no longer distinguishable. "I think, therefore I am" is replaced by "I participate, therefore I am." [31]

The African thus starts with an understanding of the world which is rooted in a deep awareness of his social nature. Many African sayings articulate this awareness, such as: "Man is no palm nut, self-contained" and "The Spirit of man is without boundaries." [32] This deep sense of the self's participation in others is definitely fostered by the geographical arrangement of the tribe. The tribal huts arranged around the hut of the chief who represents the community adds to the perception that each one lives within the orbit of other members of the tribe. The world is in fact thought of concentrically, with outsiders sometimes viewed as existing on the very perimeter of the world. The social context of the African has thus been a creative as well as a conditioning influence upon his self-understanding, upon the formation of his world in which he finds life meaningful; the same, of course, must be said about us. Since the African's world is differently constructed from ours he will see his hopes as well as his threats and problems quite differently from the way we do. For example, as Taylor puts it:

> Because of the different "myth" of human nature in which each lives, the European represses the things in himself that he is afraid of, the African projects them. The European is on guard against the self he has battened down in his own mind; the African is on guard against the self he has externalized into the world around him.[33]

[31] J. Taylor, *The Primal Vision*, pp. 49-50.
[32] *Ibid.*, quoted, pp. 43, 56.
[33] *Ibid.*, p. 176. My own brief sojourn in East Africa confirms the insights of Taylor; and Africans I have asked have expressed admiration of this study of the African

The African's self-understanding arises within his world and cannot be properly illuminated or appreciated apart from that rudimentary historical context. His world is spatialized differently from ours. Space to Westerners is land which we cut up, parcel out, buy, and sell; to us space is basically property, be it on this earth or out among the planets. Space is something to be staked out; we want to know who has a claim to it. The African sense of space frequently emerges from within a tribal perspective; that is, he understands space in terms of the relationships within the tribe and of his group with other tribes. A large part of the frustration experienced by demographers and map-makers from the West was due to the difficulty of applying our spatial concepts to a people whose relationship to the earth was quite different. The African's understanding of space was rooted in social relationships and group memberships; and he acted accordingly, often unable to comprehend the abstract, artificial boundaries which had been drawn by someone from another world.[34] Anyone who has lived with Africans is also aware that they have quite a different sense of time from that which dominates Westerners. Their lived world and its history has a distinct and definite structure which can be studied and understood; this fact of social intersubjectivity need not be relegated to the sidelines of whimsical speculation. One service which existential phenomenology may render to our contemporary situation is that it can provide a way of exposing at least some of the forces of prejudice and provincialism operative in our world and of opening up a pathway to genuine cross cultural insight, respect, and understanding.[35]

5. EXISTENTIAL PHENOMENOLOGY AND SOCIAL SCIENCE

Existential phenomenology as we have come to understand it is the illumination of meanings. Meanings in the context of our analysis primarily signify basic existential possibilities. To seek to uncover the meaning of existence as possibility is to ask which direction it is moving along. Where

mentality. Paul Bohannan's *Africa and Africans*, though along quite different lines, presents similar interesting and pertinent insights into the African way of encountering reality. For an illuminating study of Africa from the viewpoint of the Christian Church's attempts to understand it and be helpful, see D. Kitagawa, *Africa in Transition*.

[34] Cf. P. Bohannan, *Africa and Africans*, p. 175 et passim.

[35] Existential phenomenology might also be well equipped to achieve the general aspirations expressed by Harry Stack Sullivan in one of his most eloquent articles entitled "Towards a Psychiatry of Peoples," *The Interpersonal Theory of Psychiatry*, pp. 367-384.

is it going? This leads to the question of where it has come from and how it has got there. To focus upon existence in terms of its directions is to take a fully historical approach, which we have come to realize is the most appropriate manner of opening up the reality of human freedom. As we have seen, freedom is not primarily an act of decision, a cutting away from something toward something else. Being in the world is freedom; yet as historical being, freedom is in the process of becoming. Man is meant to be free in and for the basic possibilities of being fully human. What our phenomenology especially has revealed is the reality of freedom within the world of love. We have also seen how the meaning of love is in tension with both secular and individual existence, each of which represents other possible directions of freedom. Itself a mode of freedom, phenomenology may properly be considered as a vital expression of and search for basic human freedom. Its aim is to expand and clarify man's vision of himself in terms of the full scope of existential possibilities which emerge from within the basic intentional structures (worlds) of distinctly human being.[36]

Social sciences also represent ways of seeing and understanding human freedom; but their focus is upon restricted areas of freedom, and hence restricted areas of meaning. It is all too frequently suggested that philosophy deals with man in terms of freedom whereas the sciences focus upon those characteristics which determine man's freedom. Insofar as science attempts to sort out factors within a cause-and-effect scheme so as to explain the present and predict the future, there is some truth here. Natural science especially has often been restricted to a world that is viewed as already determined, though contemporary physics makes even this judgment tentative and incomplete. Social sciences, however, do not fall into the same classification as do the natural sciences; they do not inhabit exclusively the world of the natural sciences. In a significant contribution in the endeavor to relate phenomenology and the social sciences, Stephan Strasser demonstrated that the social sciences, or what he calls the human sciences, emerge from the lived world of experience (*Lebenswelt*), as does phenomenology. Neither of them is pure description. Both involve definite existential interpretation, since they both focus upon human freedom directed toward possible meanings.[37] As mentioned earlier with reference to Weber, the social scientist is concerned with meanings. Such was obviously

[36] Cf. the interesting discussion of the relation between philosophy and human freedom by J. Wild, *Existence and the World of Freedom*, pp. 120-135.

[37] See the long discussion of this issue by S. Strasser, *Phenomenology and the Human Sciences*, pp. 65-242.

true also of Freud, whom we may consider to be a representative of psychology as a social science; the same applies to Dilthey, who may represent the historian. Each of these three traditions within the social sciences emphasizes the aim of entering experience so as to discover and interpret its meanings. Their common aim is not mere knowledge but understanding (*verstehen*). These disciplines are similar enough to be grouped together as social sciences but different enough from phenomenology so as to be kept distinct.

Both social sciences and phenomenology are concerned with experience, not just the behavior of organisms. Furthermore, they are aware that experience is not an isolated subjective phenomenon but occurs in a world with others. The lived world of experience involves sharing in a common world; its meanings are discovered through participation in the world of others. Interpenetration is a basic fact of experience; it also provides the basis for understanding others and communicating with them. To understand and communicate something about the meaning of any given social-historical existence, its (his, her, their) experience must be entered. Weber and Dilthey's notion of *verstehen* as well as the technique requisite for psychoanalytic understanding require some form of participant observation. To observe and gain knowledge of another's experience, one must be a participant in it; to understand experience one must see it from the inside. The old distinction between philosophy as a mode of participation and the sciences as a mode of detachment breaks down here.

Involvement is a key term in both social sciences and existential phenomenology. By concentrating upon experience, both approaches have to do with human freedom, which is a structural element of all genuinely human experience. Yet here we may discover a basic difference. While both approaches concentrate upon what we might call a life situation, existential phenomenology is concerned to reveal particular meanings of a situation in terms of the whole scope of basic existential possibilities. The social sciences situational concentrate upon those factors which human freedom has to work with, and particularly those factors which seem to lead existence down one direction rather than another. Furthermore, the social sciences are especially concerned to detect those influences of the past which have been particularly significant in the formation of man's freedom.[38] The phenomenology of social existence in terms of the world of

---

[38] E. Erikson in "Psychological Reality and Historical Reality," *Insight and Responsibility*, pp. 161-215 makes the interesting point that the focus of psychoanalysis

taking suggests that social sciences are particularly adept at bringing into focus the details of this particular human world. Social sciences point out and analyze especially well how individuals, groups and cultural units are taken hold of and acted upon by a given society and are brought into a common social or public world. They indicate how individuals and social units interact, and how they are taken in by various forces in the social and natural environments. They show how individuals and groups take hold of necessity and chance to forge new patterns for meaningful action. Such studies definitely help us toward understanding the secular meaning of human freedom. Phenomenology, however, illuminates the framework of being in the world in its wholeness in terms of basic possibilities for meaningful freedom. As such it sets a frame of reference within which the insights of social sciences can find broader and more existential meaning than if restricted to the secular world. Existential phenomenology is attuned to participate in and open up the distinct world of love, which may interpenetrate social existence, but is nevertheless a world of its own; it is also attuned to reveal the meanings of genuine singularity. Social sciences study one essential dimension of human existence, one basic direction it must take; but they do not enter into the heart of love or the depths of solitude, even though they may at times press hard upon those borders. Social sciences take an interest in human existence; they do not, as a science, approach it within a truly *personal* framework. They may reveal, for example, how one aspect of human freedom may place a roadblock in front of love; but they cannot tell us of the meaning that may lie beyond the barrier.[39]

In summary I suggest that the social sciences will best concentrate upon and interpret social existence in a manner which is particularly ap-

is upon man's inactivity, his being acted upon, which in turn illuminates determining forces of his particular historicity.

[39] Gibson Winter has proposed that the task of social sciences is to investigate the basic structures of society. They may also perform the very important function of pointing out historical patterns which either tend to express or hinder the meanings appropriate to love. See his essay "Theology and Social Science," *The Scope of Theology*, D. Jenkins, ed., pp. 174-198. Milton Yinger has also recently attempted to formulate a theoretical basis for social sciences which will give structure to a thoroughly interdisciplinary approach to human existence. See his *Toward a Field Theory of Behavior*. He maintains that social scientists are looking for basic patterns in individual development and social process. In doing so they discover what Yinger refers to as smaller systems of variables and larger systems of variables. The various systems which may be grouped as basic patterns are nevertheless within the secular world of taking. What an interdisciplinary approach needs is the broad framework of phenomenology in which the basic meanings of experience may appear.

propriate to that mode of being in the world. They will not as such reveal the full extent of *personal existence* and *existential meaning* and should in themselves not be expected to do so. Existential phenomenology will be of particular assistance to do that. Since social scientists happen to be personal beings and since what they study is basically grounded in personal being in the world, their approach will inevitably include a tendency to overlap and interpenetrate with existential phenomenology. An absolutely clear-cut distinction between social sciences and existential phenomenology is probably impossible. Both methods are forms of radical empiricism centered in distinctively human experience, both emphasize the basic role of understanding in illuminating this experience, and both are themselves expressions of human freedom aimed at understanding freedom so as to enlarge it.[40] Existential phenomenology provides a basis for understanding existence from numerous points of view, each of them valid. While existential phenomenology will provide a framework and basis for the social sciences, it needs data from the sciences and other resources for continuing insight and understanding. I am not suggesting that phenomenology be elevated above the sciences; it is to be hoped that that kind of arrogance is now a matter of the past. Rather, my point has been to present existential phenomenology as one existential encounter among others which is particularly well suited to discover human meanings. Only as existential phenomenology engages in dialogue with existence itself through imaginative reflection and the disciplined study of scientifically procured data will it grow in insight and understanding and move forward toward the full truth of human existence.[41]

[40] One of the most egregious inconsistencies of Freud's determinism was that the aim of therapy was to liberate an individual from the unconscious past so as to become a rationally responsible self-determining being. If he had taken his determinism all that seriously, he would have precluded the possibility of psychotherapy before ever beginning.

[41] Cf. the position worked out by S. Strasser, *op. cit.*, especially pp. 245-313. He conceives of phenomenology as a dialectical process, which would seem to bring phenomenology back to Hegel. However, he makes a very important qualification. By dialectical he means specifically a form of personal communication. We might then say that phenomenology must proceed dialogically rather than dialectically.

12

Anxiety's Threat to Personal Existence

1. PREFACE

A human being stands forth in his world facing several fundamental possibilities. Through existential phenomenology it has been possible to discover the nature of some of these possibilities. Much of the glory and the misery of human life consists in the attempt to realize basic possibilities and thereby appropriate life's most significant meanings. A man can struggle to discover and shape his unique singular identity, enjoy communion within personal relationships, achieve harmonious and just social relationships, forge symbols with which to express his feelings and communicate his insights, and construct devices whereby he can domesticate nature and make his environment a home for society; all these are hallmarks of human freedom. Yet a man may suffer the agony of discovering some basic possibilities in conflict with others. The worlds in which a man lives are sometimes or often at war with each other; the melody of his life may become a cacophony. By developing efficiency in taking hold of situations, a man may find that he is squeezing the vitality out of his intimate relationships. Or by idolizing intimate personal relationships he may find that he is vulnerable to the onslaught of social and environmental forces which he might otherwise have controlled had he been responsible in those areas. To achieve a richly meaningful human life is a challenge to man to keep himself and his relationships open to the historical possibilities of basic existential structures and to seek the authentic realization of each fundamental possibility. From the vantage point of love it appears that man's

269

existence must be grounded in loving duality if he is to become a person in truth. In the pursuit of the truth about human being, in the development of historic and personal continuity, in the formation of free community, love is indispensable. The crisis of our age is not so much that life is so little loved; our dilemma is that love is so little understood it is being crowded out by other concerns and allowed to play only a minor role in the formation of the human world. A major significance of a phenomenology of love is that it helps us to understand the world of love and to appreciate its power and meaning.

Though many of the dangers attendant to the development of truly personal existence have been illuminated, the most severe threat to the history of man's world needs to be exposed and phenomenologically considered. From the standpoint of personal existence anxiety threatens to thwart and pervert every basic possibility of authentic existence. The phenomenon of anxiety is as universal as love; it reaches deeply into the lived world of each of us. Like love, we have paid it too little attention. In this chapter I shall focus upon the phenomenon of anxiety and attempt to discover its meaning, particularly with reference to personal existence. Tremendous insight into anxiety is to be found in the writings of the two psychiatrists examined in this chapter; their positions, which are amazingly similar, support and complement each other. Making much use of work done by others, we can bring an understanding of anxiety into the perspective of love and personal existence, and thereby detect another basic possibility which confronts every man.

2. HARRY STACK SULLIVAN'S UNDERSTANDING OF ANXIETY

Harry Stack Sullivan (1892–1949) was regarded as one of the most empirical of psychoanalytic theorists.[1] Perhaps more than anyone in America he enlarged our understanding of the decisive role anxiety performs in everyday experience and particularly in mental illness. Erikson expressed a conviction commonplace among psychoanalysts who have been enlightened by Sullivan, when he wrote that a psychotherapist "deals, above all, with *human anxiety*." [2] One of Sullivan's great insights was that bizarre schizophrenic expressions are not beyond understanding but represent, at least to some extent, attempts on the sufferer's part to communicate his

[1] Cf. Clara Thompson, *Psychoanalysis: Evolution and Development*, p. 211.
[2] E. Erikson, *Childhood and Society*, p. 25.

horrifying experiences.[3] It disturbed him that psychiatrists could copiously apply labels to bizarre phenomena; yet when you looked for the data alleged for using the label they were often not to be found. He complained that there was too much emphasis placed upon descriptive diagnosis and not nearly enough attention given to actually understanding and assisting the patient.[4] Like Binswanger he had turned toward Freud's method as a way of understanding a suffering patient in terms of inner dynamic patterns; yet he, too, came to realize that Freud had made the mistake of assuming manifold unconscious mechanisms without giving sufficient attention to the actual encounter of one person with another.[5] Sullivan was convinced that the detached role of a psychoanalyst as advocated by Freud was not really necessary or beneficial to the patient. In contrast he came to be famous for emphasizing participant observation. The psychiatrist, he said, must participate fully in the personal field of the one whom he is attempting to observe and cure.[6] For Sullivan, therapy consists essentially in interpersonal events. Through his open participation with patients in their peculiar worlds, Sullivan encountered massive anxiety. Eventually he guessed that anxiety, rather than repression of libido or neurological impairment, had a great deal to do with the patient's problems. By focusing upon anxiety he began to study the development of an individual in relation with his environment and especially with significant other people. He discovered through clinical experience as well as by inference from later developments observed in patients that anxiety reaches far back into the very beginning when, as he was wont to put it, a little animal becomes a person.[7]

Though remaining within a tradition which was relatively on the side of Freud, Sullivan actually created a revolution within psychoanalysis as great as that caused by Binswanger. Like the latter, he insisted that the primary factor behind mental disturbance is a uniquely human phenomenon and not a somatic or even a psychic mechanism. He insisted that mental illnesses arise out of life experiences; though there may be a genetic basis, it has not been proved, nor does it appear to be the most significant factor.[8] To restrict oneself to internal problems is to miss the source of the

[3] H. S. Sullivan, *The Interpersonal Theory of Psychiatry*, p. 327.
[4] Sullivan, *Clinical Studies in Psychiatry*, p. 194.
[5] *Ibid.*, pp. 65-66 et passim.
[6] Sullivan, *Interpersonal Theory*, pp. 13-14.
[7] *Ibid.*, pp. 114-119; see also p. 68.
[8] Sullivan, *Clinical Studies*, p. 359 et passim.

worst ones, which is in interpersonal relations. Thus he turned the attention of social scientists to the study of man in his distinctively human aspects. In doing so he emphasized the universal phenomenon of anxiety which threatens to rob man of his humanity by destroying his freedom to be personal. His approach, so similar to Binswanger's, was an attempt to catch sight of the basic patterns of human experience, particularly as these are shaped by anxiety. For him anxiety is so important that with a grasp of the concept you are able to follow the whole of his system; without it you will understand neither his theory of personality nor any human being, for that matter.

According to Sullivan anxiety is a symptom, or an experience, or what we might call an encounter, of any threat to the security, the well-being, the very existence of an individual; as such it calls into being or into increased alertness a system of defense.[9] He offered numerous definitions as to what actually constitutes anxiety, but these are all oblique. One reason for lack of a clear, immediate grasp is that anxiety does not appear to be a meaningful phenomenon but poses as a threat to possible meanings. It is "a disjunctive or disintegrative tendency" occurring specifically within interpersonal relations. As such it operates against the integrative tendency, which is man's creative being in the world toward the realization of his own most possibilities, or what he sometimes referred to as man's drive toward appropriate human living.[10] As a disjunctive process, anxiety works negatively upon all the basic patterns of creative development, but especially upon man's relation with others. It is "an outstanding ingredient in breaking up interpersonal situations, which otherwise would be useful in the satisfaction of the needs of the person concerned." [11] Similar to Augustine's doctrine of evil as nonbeing, anxiety for Sullivan in itself is meaningless, in that it is a power that breaks down the intentional structure of human existence in which meaning is embedded. Yet the effects of its power are poignantly meaningful. To experience anxiety is, in contrast to other experiences, not to learn any positive particular information; rather, anxiety hits like a "severe blow on the head." [12] Especially if it is sudden and severe, it will prohibit "any clear prehension, or understanding, of the immediate situation." [13]

[9] Ibid., p. 56.
[10] Sullivan, Interpersonal Theory, pp. 95, 373. I have adapted Sullivan's wording to make it clearer how similar his approach is to that of existential phenomenology.
[11] Ibid.
[12] Ibid., p. 152.
[13] Ibid., p. 160.

As a psychiatrist he was particularly concerned to map out those areas of disjunctive forces which restrict awareness and cause an unnecessary blockage of interpersonal relationships as well as creative human development.[14] His method of description, especially when it pertains to anxiety, is particularly moving; he informs the reader how it can feel to be terrorized and struck dumb with anxiety, indicating Sullivan's own deep participation in such an experience. Yet he primarily sought to describe objectively observable human patterns from a distance. Thus his method is one which stands at the edge of the fullness of experience rather than at its core, where phenomenology originates. Though he wants to emphasize "that which is essentially human—the utterly vital role of interpersonal relations," [15] his stance is basically within what I have referred to as the social mode of existence. Consequently his method makes use frequently of hypothetical and foreign abstractions which are imposed upon experience so that its information can be taken in, classified, and calculated. All this is terribly helpful and important, but it needs the larger existential frame of reference wherein the fuller meaning of human experience may be discovered and interpreted. Though he emphasized the need for participation to get close to the subject to be observed, he also upheld an impersonal distance needed for the task: "We will not study people as such, but what they do, and what can be fairly safely inferred as to why they do it." [16] Thus his knowledge was often largely inferential, rather than following the phenomenological lead to return to existential meaning directly.

By concentrating upon anxiety as the primary factor in schizophrenia Sullivan was nevertheless led to focus not merely upon what people do, but upon experience. He in turn devised a unique developmental theory of experience which takes anxiety into account. Anxiety is not an entity in itself but a threatening ingredient in experience. By experience Sullivan had in mind the inner component of a human event, not merely the occurrence of it. Experience is a distinctively human phenomenon; as such it is not to be explained either in terms of so-called instincts or external forces. The most essential experience is in the interpersonal sphere where one becomes most distinctively human.[17] This experience in Sullivan's view is

---

[14] *Ibid.*, p. 376. For a brief and extremely compelling presentation of Sullivan's approach and its relevance to concrete world history, see his essay "Towards a Psychiatry of Peoples," pp. 367-384 in this same volume.

[15] *Ibid.*, p. 242.

[16] *Ibid.*, p. 26.

[17] *Ibid.*, pp. 19-26.

man's encountering his world with and through others. Sullivan insisted that experience is the primary way in which we have information about anything. He repudiated, as does existential phenomenology, the view that knowledge arises primarily either in sensation or in ratiocination. "What we have in our minds begins in experience," he said.[18] To translate this into phenomenological language, the lived world is the rudimentary basis upon which our knowledge and the criterion of knowledge and judgment are founded. As he came to consider the totality of experience as the locus of our knowledge and understanding, Sullivan began to suspect that anxiety plays a crucial factor in existential knowledge, which in fact it does.

Having posited the primacy of experience Sullivan went on to indicate three basic forms of it. The first, what he calls the *prototaxic* mode, is the crudest, earliest, simplest, and most abundant form of experience. The prototaxic mode of experience originates as the infant first encounters the world, but it continues throughout life to be a basic experiential form. Since experience is cognitive, its form of perception and knowledge consists in what he called prehension.[19] His understanding of prehension is similar to existential insight into the intentional nature of feeling or prescience, though Sullivan stressed that feeling is largely characterized by particular bodily zones, similar to the position of Erikson studied previously.[20] This additional insight from the social sciences is extremely important. For certainly knowledge is dependent upon the mode of its reception. If we are to take feelings seriously as means of communication, it is essential to discover which feelings in particular in a given situation are acting as the media of communication with our world. As valuable as this contribution is to phenomenology, nevertheless Sullivan's elaboration on the nature of experience needs some drastic overhauling.

Having maintained that feelings are the primary form of experience, he unfortunately went on to declare that experience is basically of tensions and needs, energy transformations, and anxiety.[21] This led him to posit a highly reductionistic scheme of basic human goals. These goals were stated to be satisfaction from tensions and security from anxiety.[22] Phenomenology has consistently affirmed that experience as well as life goals are constituted in terms of meanings. Sullivan's rather positivistic characterization of

18 *Ibid.*, p. 28.
19 *Ibid.*, pp. 29, 76.
20 *Ibid.*, pp. 29, 280.
21 *Ibid.*, pp. 35-36.
22 Sullivan, *Clinical Studies*, p. 10.

experience would seem to leave meanings out of account, or see them as some secondary aspect. Fortunately, like Freud, he was not entirely predictable. Sullivan also emphasized that human dynamics can only be understood if first of all you bear in mind their goals.[23] As though he were schooled by early advocates of the intentionality of experience, Sullivan regularly emphasized that "one's actions, however they may impress the observer, are most importantly defined by what they are 'intended for'— that is, they are determined by the general pattern of motivation that is involved, by what is significant to the person concerned, quite irrespective of any impressions an observer may have."[24] The exact interpretation of that sentence depends, of course, on what Sullivan understood when he used the term "motivation." Though he was sometimes apparently ensconced within a physicalist fortification, he was actually vehemently opposed to an over-all physicalist framework for understanding experience precisely because it was blind to distinctively human significance. He vigorously stressed that perception is always the perception of significance. One perceives not isolated things but patterns, which in themselves carry significance. One perceives signs; the significance, the signs, are not something added to a human being and his perception; at the very core of his experience "the person has the sign."[25]

So Sullivan in his theory was inconsistent; not unlike Freud he attempted to fit his penetrating insights into distinctively human life within a physicalist model that simply cannot do them justice. Yet he himself affirmed that human experience unfolds in terms of "referential processes," and that these significant processes are not necessarily verbal. Most experience occurs with a wordless thinking. It is questionable, if not irrelevant and nonsensical, to segregate significant experience from insignificant experience, or the symbolic from the nonsymbolic, especially where perception is concerned.[26] From this perspective we can agree that experience is always and essentially intentionally structured, and that as perception it is directed toward significance. In Sullivan's language, experience is engaged in reading the signs in the field; that is, being in the world is always an encounter with meaning.

The importance of anxiety becomes apparent in the earliest stages of experience. According to Sullivan's inference, the first learning occurs as

[23] *Ibid.*, pp. 6-9.
[24] Sullivan, *Interpersonal Theory*, p. 68.
[25] *Ibid.*, pp. 82-83, 101.
[26] Cf. *ibid.*, pp. 185-186.

the infant reads the signs of anxiety.[27] Though the infant has the obvious needs for food, liquid, sleep, air, warmth, and freedom of movement, he also has a basic need for tenderness, which is a form of interpersonal cooperation. Tenderness is the tension called out in the mothering one by the manifest needs of the infant. This tension is a "need" for contact and as such arises from within a communal experience, not from within a physico-chemical universe.[28] The tension of anxiety also arises within the mothering one's presence. Part of what the child apprehends is the *good* mother, the one who responds to his tensions and provides satisfactions. Yet he is also aware of the *real* mother who in turn prehends the infant and her responsibilities toward it, her feelings about it and herself, especially her feelings of inadequacy.[29] So anxiety enters the scene and makes the situation of tension seeking satisfaction quite complicated. In its primary modes anxiety has nothing specific about it, and the infant has no capacity for its relief. There is in his mind no object or action which may be associated with overcoming it. Thus anxiety overwhelms him, bringing him near a state of unrecognized horror. Consequently it becomes imperative for him to develop some sort of security or freedom from further attacks of anxiety. As Sullivan made clear, anxiety is induced by another person who is extremely necessary in one's life. At first it is not manageable; and furthermore it is in opposition to one's other needs and the groping for tenderness. As such it might seem to be an instructive ingredient in experience. On the contrary, however, anxiety here is so dreadful, so overpowering, that it cuts off awareness of the past and the future, nearly obliterating foresight.[30] In existential terms we might say that anxiety shatters existential temporality, which includes one's cognitive being unto his own truth.

Thus from the very beginning there is a basic conflict between the tension or tendency to develop a positive mode of being in the world and anxiety which threatens this existence so drastically as to alter its development. In Sullivan's scheme tensions are essentially integrating tendencies in the sense that they aim to integrate within the individual and his

27 *Ibid.*, p. 121.

28 *Ibid.*, pp. 40, 59. Sullivan did not want to call tenderness a need, for he wanted to reserve the term "need" for physicochemical requirements of life (p. 39). Thus he used the term "tension," which can apply both to personal as well as to physical needs. Unfortunately, with this shift of terms he has made the human seem more physical and the latter more human and the entire experience more confusing than is necessary.

29 *Ibid.*, p. 113.

30 *Ibid.*, pp. 42-44.

experience a situation which is necessary and appropriate to the satisfaction of a need. Anxiety is a disintegrative tendency that closes the individual off to those elements in the situation which are most threatening.[31] Since anxiety arises within a communal experience, anxiety is particularly damaging to the interpersonal situation, leading one to escape from or avoid that which he needs most: genuine tenderness.

In response to the dynamics of both integrative and disintegrative tendencies the individual develops his personality. He fashions his own distinctive mode of being in the world as he encounters the polar forces of love and anxiety. The dynamic tendencies of experience begin to develop basic patterns, which Sullivan referred to as dynamisms. A dynamism is an abstraction which is meant to refer to "the relatively enduring pattern of energy transformations which recurrently characterize the organism in its duration as a living organism."[32] What he means here is very similar to Binswanger's basic forms of human existence. For as Sullivan maintained, these dynamisms are "universal human equipment, sometimes represented almost entirely in dreadful distortions of loving, but still universal."[33] As "relatively enduring patterns" they are human, not physical; that is, they are postnatal, existential possibilities, not psychosomatic potentialities. Yet an obvious difference between Sullivan's dynamisms and Binswanger's forms is that dynamisms can be conceived as pertaining to particular zones of the body, such as oral or anal dynamisms, as well as to the total subject engaged in an interpersonal field.[34] As essentially integrating tendencies the dynamisms are basically positive. Yet the presence of anxiety in experience causes unfortunate but defensive dynamisms to develop which are meant to protect one from the onslaught of anxiety. The over-all dynamism aimed to achieve and maintain security he called the self-system, and it is an unfortunate part of the total personality.[35]

In early experience the infant is aware of the mothering one and her awareness of and concern for the infant. There is, then, a kind of mutual awareness which provides the basis for recognition of both self and others as well as of the particular kind of relationship between them. As the mother cares for the infant the latter is at times aware of anxiety which gradually tends to become attached to a certain aspect of the relationship.

[31] *Ibid.*, pp. 93-95.
[32] *Ibid.*, p. 103.
[33] *Ibid.*, p. 305.
[34] *Ibid.*, p. 280.
[35] *Ibid.*, pp. 164 ff.

The infant identifies this aspect as that part of his personality which is the *not-me*, in contradistinction to the *good-me*, who is caressed, and the *bad-me*, who is spanked for recognizably naughty behavior.[36] The dynamism of the self-system attempts to block out of awareness that aspect of the personality which apparently brings about anxiety, that is, the not-me. Since the self-system operates entirely under the impetus of anxiety, "anxiety is responsible for a great part of the inadequate, inefficient, unduly rigid, or otherwise unfortunate performances of people," especially what comes to a psychiatrist for attention.[37] The unfortunate result of restricted awareness, distorted perception, and unnatural relationships arises because "the sudden occurrence of severe anxiety practically prohibits any clear prehension, or understanding of, the immediate situation." [38]

Experience is structured along the lines of anxiety gradients; those experiences where the least evidence of anxiety is felt will be freest to be open to the new situation. Where anxiety is felt to be crouching at the door, the blinds are closed and the doors are shut to the givenness of the situation. Here the second basic form of experience emerges, which Sullivan referred to as the *parataxic* mode; this term represents Sullivan's revision of Freud's concept of projection. Parataxic experience is ruled by anxiety so that aspects of what is encountered simply are not seen to exist. There is a blank spot, the not-me, which is too dreadful even to allow into the horizon of consciousness. The not-me is the terrifying nightmare of life which must be avoided at all costs. Dynamisms as integrating tendencies are basically directed toward significance, which is to a large extent interpreted by the situation itself; that is, the dynamism includes signs.[39] Here, however, the significance does not come from an open encounter with a new situation; it is imposed upon the situation as a matter of security measures. Fear, for example, is a perception of a potentially threatening aspect in an actual situation; it may be a recognition of something unknown. In parataxic distortion, the threat to existence is imposed upon the situation under the imperative of the self-system in its role of avoiding anxiety. Thus the parataxic mode is a distortion of the authentic possibilities for learning, relationship, and maturation. As a practicing psychiatrist Sullivan focused largely upon this second universal and highly unfortunate experiential form.

36 Cf. *ibid.*, p. 145.
37 *Ibid.*, p. 160.
38 *Ibid.* and ff.
39 *Ibid.*, p. 109.

In terms of authenticity or personal maturation the self-system is quite undesirable; indeed, according to disciples of Sullivan, the goal not merely of therapy but of life is so to expand the self-system that it becomes practically disposed of within a fully integrated personality.[40] Yet in the realistic purview of Sullivan, the self-system does serve a positive function, in that anxiety can never be completely eradicated. Because the growing individual evinces such a dynamism within his interpersonal environment, he is able to learn how to avoid or minimize the incidents of anxiety and thus learn to live securely with the significant persons in his world.[41] The primary and positive function of the self-system is to reduce the disjunctive tension of anxiety, so as to free the person for creative encounter.[42]

In recognizing the slightly positive role of the parataxic mode, Sullivan thus pointed to the third and most mature manner of experience, the *syntaxic* mode of experience. Whereas the self-system operates according to what he calls *selective inattention*, whereby the individual suspends awareness of the actual situation and perceives only what is safe to perceive in ways which will least endanger one's security,[43] in the syntaxic mode there is open recognition and genuine communication.[44] "Selective inattention is the classic means by which we do not profit from experience which falls within the area of our particular handicap," [45] whereas in the syntaxic mode there is mutual learning and mutual maturation. It is here that one breaks loose from a purely subjectivistic interpretation of experience. The latter consists of the imposition of a rigid criterion as a security measure. Healthy syntaxic experience is constituted by an open awareness of life whereby one's knowledge through experience finds *consensual validation*. Genuine learning and the emergence of an integrated personality come about as one's awareness of himself in the world finds validation from those persons who are most significant. It is a thesis of the interpersonal theory of personality that "the crux of acquired defects in later functioning

[40] J. Pearce and S. Newton, *The Conditions of Human Growth*, pp. 156-157.
[41] Sullivan, *Interpersonal Theory*, p. 165.
[42] It is clear that Sullivan's self-system in part embodies several Freudian concepts such as the Super-ego, the mechanisms of the Unconscious such as repression and suppression, etc. Like Binswanger he increasingly felt that Freud's way of talking was much too mechanistic and tended to partition unnecessarily the human unity of experience. Also it is patently clear that Sullivan emphasized the dynamics of interpersonal relations which he felt Freud left nearly out of account with his consistent stress on instincts and libido.
[43] Cf. *ibid.*, pp. 169 ff., 319.
[44] *Ibid.*, p. 183.
[45] Sullivan, *Clinical Studies*, p. 50.

lies in the inadequate representation of those functions" which are directly dependent upon an initial validation of their significance by the mothering person.[46] On the other hand, the strength of the personality also emerges with syntaxic experience with the mother and other significant persons. The syntaxical mode is the most desirable for personal existence, consisting as it does in consensual validation. The latter amounts to mutual recognition of discovered meaning; the I discovers who he is in truth as he is recognized and affirmed by a Thou. Important as this mode is, nevertheless Sullivan has very little more to contribute to our understanding of it. He concentrated upon understanding parataxic distortions. In this respect Binswanger's contribution is complementary and important, because he stressed the necessity of seeing the fullness of existence in its most personal form before trying to understand fractured versions of it.

Sullivan's extremely significant contribution has been to point out that we rarely grasp the highly important factor of anxiety, because we are too busily engaged in our own security operations. We all too easily fall into a rut of unconscious prejudice toward the infinite world of values and meanings. By spending our energy building up and defending the supposedly anxiety-proof shelters of a self-system we become extraordinarily resistant to change by experience, because the self-system by its nature tends to escape all aspects of experience which are incongruous with our current personality organization and functional activity.[47] That becomes our way of growing old; it is our way of dying to experience, a process which begins in infancy. Though one goal in life is to expand the self-system, which means to take in experience which might otherwise be blotted out by selective inattention, nevertheless the everyday mode of being in the world remains curiously insensitive to the whole of experience. Mental disorders include nothing novel to human equipment; rather, they represent either an increasingly strong hold by the self-system upon the total personality so as to choke the life out of it, or they are a sign of a breakdown of the self-system so that one is overwhelmed and torn apart by anxiety. Like Binswanger, Sullivan saw mental disorder basically as "an inadequate and inappropriate way of living with other people and with one's personifications." [48] Thus the insights to be gleaned from sympathetic studies of mental disorder pertain not only to particularly unfortunate individuals but to the real and

---

46 Pearce and Newton, *op. cit.*, p. 84.
47 Sullivan, *Interpersonal Theory*, pp. 190 ff.
48 *Ibid.*, p. 208.

manifold threats confronting each one of us as our being in the world is struck by and attempts to deal with the disintegrative power of anxiety.[49]

3. BINSWANGER'S EXISTENTIAL ANALYSIS OF ANXIETY

To turn now to Binswanger's understanding of anxiety, my main purpose is not to compare their points of identity but to bring their approaches into juxtaposition so that our understanding of universal human phenomena such as anxiety and interpersonal relations may grow. We can also, at the same time, appreciate the differences between both the two men and the two approaches. Sullivan obviously was primarily concerned to engage in therapy for the greatest possible benefit to patients. To do so he realized that he had to move beyond symptoms to significance. This required that he participate in a supposedly meaningless experience of a disturbed patient, so that he could himself pick up through feeling the sense within the apparent nonsense of it. To facilitate analysis and understanding as well as to protect oneself from the barrage of anxiety, it is necessary to have some conceptual scheme to recognize fairly recurrent patterns which bring about distorted perceptions, judgments, and behavior. Sullivan's personality theory originated from this attempt to be more successful therapeutically. It was designed to be a working procedure, not a grand philosophy; yet his personality theory approaches, without quite reaching, a magnificent full-scale anthropology.

Binswanger also started out to develop an operative psychology; but his interest in turn shifted toward philosophical anthropology. He realized, and in this he was surely right, that psychology or sociology or history presupposes some basic understanding and interpretation of the meaning

---

[49] In his *The Courage To Be*, Paul Tillich made a distinction between existential and neurotic or pathological anxiety (cf. pp. 40-63). In view of both Sullivan and Binswanger's studies this distinction appears questionable. Both of the latter talk about existential or human anxiety in every aspect of their writings. If there is a difference it is in degree not kind. The distinction by Tillich might in the long run be spurious. It could breed a kind of Pharisaic self-righteousness in those who proudly affirm that their anxiety is deeply existential and not at all pathological or undesirable from the standpoint of either mental health or Christian theology. And it could easily be a way for theologians to rationalize their personal problems as signs of spiritual depth. I suspect that both Sullivan and Binswanger would agree with Bonhoeffer that the world, to say nothing of the Church, has had quite enough celebrated emphasis upon man's problems, needs, and conflicts from which supposedly only the gospel can deliver him. To identify the extremely unpleasant aspects of human life as the most existential is just downright morbid. (Cf. the criticism by Dietrich Bonhoeffer, *Letters and Papers from Prison*, pp. 114, 115.)

of human existence. Thus his aim in this respect was to develop what he called existential knowledge (*Daseinserkenntnis*), by which he meant awareness of and insight into the meaning of the basic forms of human existence and, in addition, of the relatively common forms of their interaction in terms of integration and disintegration. Thus his interest was to discover the ground of experience, what with Heidegger he came to call being in the world. The means of reaching this ground was through participation; but the method was not to be equated with the social sciences, as it was in Sullivan's view. It includes insightful participation not merely in the mode of social intercourse and the public life but also in the ecstasies of loving coexistence and solitude. Because man lives in a plurality of worlds, we must be prepared to realize that there are various approaches to him. The truth we discover about man depends upon our mode of access to him. Phenomenology attempts to get at the truth of man in his wholeness, which means that it must listen to the manifold voices as they witness to loving duality, singularity, and the relatively impersonal being in the world with others. As Kierkegaard indicated that the plunge of faith was the only way really to know God, so love demands that one be caught up in its heights to behold its truth. Yet this intimate personal knowledge is not the only authentic or important knowledge about man. As there is knowledge of man which can come only as a free gift through the modality of love, so there is also knowledge of being in the world which is obtained through more detached observation. Even here, however, one takes part in the experience, at least to some extent, so as to take in information before sorting it out and classifying it. The full process of existential knowledge requires not the assimilation of one mode into another but a dialectical process of interpenetration between love and concern, between phenomenology and the social sciences.[50]

We have seen something of this dialogue occurring within Binswanger himself. As a practicing psychiatrist he became frustrated with Husserl's notion of phenomenology as a process of pure ideation. Though stimulated by the notion of intentionality, he came to regard the process of knowledge as one of communication between man and his world. Thus he came to envisage the most basic form of knowledge about human existence in terms of personal communication, an insight shared by numerous psychoanalysts though not explicitly stated in their theories. His phenomenology helped him to develop a clearer awareness of existential phenomena, while

[50] Cf. Binswanger, *Grundformen*, pp. 499-565.

in turn his openness to phenomena as well as knowledge of them gleaned from other approaches helped to correct, modify, and expand his phenomenology. In this way phenomenology quite rightly is seen to be in the service of reason. Yet reason, as it is served, is expanded, or at least our understanding of it is.

Human reason includes feeling, intuition, and imagination, which are essential components of the phenomenon of love. Binswanger proposed that intuition, a term so important in phenomenology, be understood as a personal phenomenon in terms of a loving thinking or loving imagination. In doing so he was inspired by Dilthey's attempt to reconcile the sciences and history through the concept of understanding (*verstehen*). The insight which emerged from Binswanger's clinical experiences and reflection was that the fullest existential understanding of personal existence is based upon an intuitive grasp of the wholeness of human being as this is presented in the moment of love. From the starting point of loving imagination one could then focus upon a particular *Gestalt*, or encounter, and execute an analysis that would yield a diversity of knowledge about particular moments of being in the world. Such knowledge is both truly existential and scientific; it includes the insights from the social sciences within the encompassing framework of loving imagination.[51] It was also imperative for Binswanger that this knowledge be not merely theoretical but also concrete and practical; for the initial impetus for seeking it was better to help the patients in his clinic. He was moved by daily encounters with suffering human beings to develop a new kind of understanding that would serve as a basis for personal understanding and communication. So he conceived of existential knowledge not as an act of judgment, such as categorization, diagnosis, and such, but more basically as a knowledge which answered the question: How does it stand with man, and in particular, this man? Thus he developed a form of knowledge that sought the truth of subjectivity in the full scope of intersubjective existence.

The formulation and concrete application of his anthropological psychology he called *Daseinsanalysis* or *existential analysis*.[52] This in itself is

---

[51] Cf. *ibid.*, pp. 591-698.

[52] Medard Boss has also adopted the term "Daseinsanalysis." See his exposition in *Psychoanalysis and Daseinsanalysis*. Boss, however, has committed himself to Heidegger's ontology and has labeled Binswanger's attempt to be radically existential a reversion to subjectivism. I have discussed already the interrelations between these three thinkers. Throughout the above book, Boss emphasizes *ad infinitum* that Daseinsanalysis is open to experience as it happens, that the therapist is open to the world of the patient, that healthy existence must be open to all existential possibilities, etc. Obviously the key

an existential mode wherein it becomes possible to view the whole of
existence, to see the whole person as being in the world with others. Yet
existential analysis is also a means of uniting the social sciences, particularly
psychology, with phenomenology so as to understand human phenomena
which have not properly been understood in the past, if they have been
understood at all. Because Binswanger was clinically oriented he felt it was
permissible to remain merely within an existential framework without
pushing into the ontological discussion raised by Heidegger. He kept focusing upon concrete existential relations, striving always to penetrate to their
essential existential meaning without regard for supposedly deeper ontological meanings. His existential analysis seeks to illuminate not some ontological content of experience but the universal and particular patterns of a
particular being in the world.[53] We shall best grasp the contribution and

word is "open." But criteria to distinguish various kinds of openness are lacking. From
his earliest to his latest writings Boss has tended toward if not outrightly opted for a
form of monism. Originally it was a monism of libidinous energy, which developed
into the monism of Being à la Heidegger, to an Indian interpretation of the unity of
Being along the lines of "Atman and Brahman are one." Boss has consistently been so
intent upon perceiving being when he examines bizarre behavior that he tends to
overlook the destructive forces in conflict with man's innate drive toward health. It is
not surprising that sympathetic psychoanalysts on the continent as well as in America
are uneasy with his broad classifications and sweeping generalizations. They rightly
miss an appreciation of the complexities and force of existential conflict and the careful
attention to facts which the art of healing and the science of social existence demand.
It is no more accurate to consider Boss and Binswanger as essentially the same than it
would be to lump together indiscriminately as existentialists Sartre and Marcel or
Jaspers and Heidegger. Similarity of interest in no way implies identity.

  [53] One of Binswanger's articles on this subject may be found in English, "The
Existential Analysis School of Thought," in *Existence, op. cit.*, pp. 191-213. Throughout this discussion I use the term "existential analysis" to refer to the approach represented by Binswanger and not to the theory associated with the Viennese psychiatrist,
Viktor Frankl. The distinction is obvious in German; the former is *Daseinsanalyse*
whereas the latter is *Existenzanalyse*. Frankl's theory essentially is not pertinent to our
enterprise. Frankl's writings are generally in the genre of popular moral philosophy;
indeed, they have been used as such in Austrian high schools. His chief contribution
has been to call attention to the fact that man must be understood as a creature who
needs meaning to live. His Logotherapy provides a therapeutic procedure to help disturbed people find a meaningful life. Religiously minded people will find classic themes
such as the meaning of suffering appearing throughout his writings in secular vestments.
Equally significant are numerous insights from Scheler which Frankl has incorporated
into his own theories. However, Frankl is actually a prephenomenological philosopher
with no apparent awareness of existential intentionality. Thus his discussion of meaning
is still within the old dichotomy of subject and object. Probably his most important
work, and one which contains the bulk of nearly all his subsequent writings, was his
first book, *The Doctor and the Soul*. It is a moving testimony rendered to psychiatry
to consider the spiritual dimension of man. This testimony carries the weight of
Frankl's own experience in Nazi concentration camps where he was subjected to a
consistent dehumanizing process. For a brief summary of his position see my translation
of his article listed in the Bibliography. See also his personal account *From Death Camp
to Existentialism*.

mode of operation of his existential analysis if we turn specifically to Binswanger's study of anxiety and its role in the phenomenon of schizophrenia.

Binswanger approached schizophrenia first of all as a human phenomenon and saw it within the basic perspective of human existence before a classification of sick or healthy has been made. Thus he was able to understand schizophrenia as an existential form, as an unfortunate mode of being in the world. Like Sullivan he looked to the experience of being in the world and detected an existential process which disturbs the basic structure of human life. Furthermore, he was able to chart four stages in the development of severe schizophrenia which we can briefly map out.[54] The first stage in the life history which becomes schizophrenic is what he referred to as the breakdown of the consistency of experience. Similar to Sullivan's parataxic distortion, he means that what is learned is inconsistent with what is actually encountered. There is the refusal simply to let things be in themselves. Unlike a revolutionary, who will not tolerate things to be as they are because he is too attentive to how imperfect the situation is, the budding schizophrenic is unable to let things be because he is anxious. An inconsequential factor enters his experience which has the effect of cleaving the basic unity of being in the world with others. Anxiety is like an arrow which drives deep, splitting the growing tree of human life to its roots. This breakdown in the natural order of life as Binswanger depicts it is similar to Sullivan's concept of the schizophrenic dynamism of dissociation whereby the self's means of dealing with conflict is to separate from awareness a significant portion of experience.[55]

From this experience of inconsistency follows a second stage in which existential possibilities are divided into rigid alternatives; and a set framework of either/or is established. On the one hand, for example, there may appear a high-flown ideal which is inappropriate to the totality of one's experience. On the other hand, there is the possibility of an encounter with a nightmare of a life, the naked horror, the terrible abyss of anxiety or what Sullivan has called the not-me.[56] The individual stakes his entire being in the world upon maintaining this rigid stance, keeping the two alternative possibilities completely separate. For example, in his famous case of Ellen West, this patient had a high-flown ideal of becoming thin.

[54] See Binswanger's introduction to *Schizophrenie;* an English translation of the introduction fortunately is now available in *Being-in-the-World*, pp. 249-264. The page citations in this chapter, for the convenience of the reader, will refer to the translation.
[55] *Ibid.*, p. 252; cf. Sullivan, *Clinical Studies*, p. 6.
[56] *Ibid.*, p. 252.

The alternative possible mode of existence, one which constantly oppressed her, was becoming obese. She exhibited classic symptoms of an obsessional dynamism, alternating between stuffing food into herself and then starving herself. Her compulsions came not from simple alternatives of obesity or thinness, but from the fact that she had given her bodiliness existential roles which it simply could not bear.[57] Without an existential framework the full significance of her symptoms are lost on us. In the case of Jürg Zünd, which we shall consider in detail later, we find a similar phenomenon, except that here the social mode of existence was forced to provide a meaning that really must only be sought in the interpersonal sphere of love. Again existence was split into alternate possibilities, which entailed one of them being required to provide meaning which should rightly be borne by the other that has been detached from one's world. Obsession is basically an adjustive process in which the individual is given over to a substitute meaning and becomes chained to it, because he feels an imperative to avoid the anxiety associated with that mode of experience where the truly satisfying meaning is to be found. To be imprisoned in this set of unsatisfactory and hence constantly frustrating alternatives is really to be fallen into the world.

This phenomenon of acute fallenness, or what Binswanger also referred to as *mundanization*, is well illustrated in his case of Lola Voss.[58] The German term for mundanization is *Verweltlichung*. We might also speak of it as total *secularization*, in the sense that the secular world is so absolutized that the existential meanings from the personal world of love are shut out. Lola Voss was also a person driven by anxiety, who exhibited first obsessional compulsions which developed gradually into full-blown paranoia. Her basic intentional structure was severed, and she maintained the unfortunate ideal which was to be left entirely alone by the world of other people, to let no one really get close to her. As in all schizophrenia studied by Binswanger her existence was radically threatened by anxiety. It compelled her to formulate a world which would protect her from the imminent invasion of anxiety. Such a mode of existence, however, is in reality like walking on thin ice, where existence needs artificial props to maintain some kind of stance and where there is a constant fear of falling, plunging, sinking into the terrible. Her actions to an outsider would seem ridiculous and bizarre, but in reality they were attempts to protect herself

---

[57] *Ibid.*, p. 256; see also Binswanger, "The Case of Ellen West," *Existence*, pp. 237-364.
[58] Binswanger, *Being-in-the-World*, pp. 266-340.

from being thrown into the whirl of inauthentic possibilities and eventual annihilation by chaos.[59] Her attempt at self-protection was an exercise of freedom which in fact was tantamount to the denial of her full historical continuity; thus, it was the choice of unfreedom. She was constantly possessed by the overpowering fear of a sudden eruption of uncanniness. Her existence was not moving forward into freedom but was bound hard and fast by this unfortunate model which held her a prisoner to the very world she feared and wanted to escape. Her compulsion was her attempt to read the signs of the world so as to avoid contact with the dreadful. This compulsion kept awake her memories of dreadful areas of experience that in turn became associated with persons and objects. These were to be avoided at all costs. The association was actually a kind of identification whereby the dreadful memories entered certain persons and things. Hence she had a terrifying feeling whenever she was in their presence. And always she was aware that in her world the dreadful might appear at any moment. As Binswanger pointed out, this severe existential anxiety arises only where love, which gives existence a home and shelter, has disappeared. Thus we discover here a new form of spatialization in which distance as known in the security of trust is overcome, and one faces the constant threat of the invasion of the dreadful.[60] Historical space is transformed into mundane space, whereby authentic historical possibilities constituted by responsible freedom have been displaced by a compulsive entanglement in external affairs and circumstances of a world that has been dehistoricized through the domination of fate. In the study of Jürg Zünd we shall see even more clearly an example of the imprisonment of freedom by the fall into thoroughly secular, social existence.

The existential process of mundanization as well as that of high-flown, extravagant existence are examples of how existence can transform anxiety by projecting it as fear into one's immediate world. The actual situation becomes a horrible shell, concealing threats to one's being, which in turn demand that an individual constantly hide behind a mask. This phenomenon helps to make clear the third stage in the schizophrenic process which Binswanger described as the process of concealment. Having severed existence into two completely isolated alternative possibilities the individual feels an imperative to cover up the dreadful aspect of his existence.[61] Like Sullivan's not-me, this possibility simply does not exist as one's own, as

---

[59] *Ibid.*, pp. 290-291.
[60] *Ibid.*, pp. 297-300.
[61] *Ibid.*, p. 258.

long as the dissociative process is successful in keeping it out of reach of conscious awareness. Yet there is the ever-present possibility of a sudden breakthrough of overpowering anxiety or what Binswanger referred to as a naked horror. This is a horror which anticipates the existential structure's being obliterated, where one is reduced to the nightmare of sheer chaos. The pretense maintained to deny this possibility then leads a person to concentrate upon all kinds of irrelevant matters in the immediate present. Here we find an even more drastic fallenness of temporality. In the case of Lola Voss, she lost the continuity of a genuine future and of her actual past by living in a mere present, jumping from one now to the next now, with one worry after another. This was her particular attempt to conceal from herself the dreadful possibility of an encounter with the naked horror by establishing a permanent foothold in the everyday world of concern. She did so by worrying, bargaining, caring about all manner of inconsequential things, such as whether her clothes might have been touched by a certain suspected person in the hospital. Though a defense against the naked horror is maintained, there is played out the tragedy that existential anxiety has cut the patient off from her deepest roots, from her own unique truth. The real misfortune is not that irrelevant matters are given so much attention but that, as Sullivan once said, "the significant is not attended to." [62]

The energy required in maintaining the rigid set of alternatives and concealing the dreadful possibility is immense. Usually a fourth stage ensues wherein a person's existence is worn away by tensions. This occurs because the person cannot find a way out of his imprisonment and wears himself out; or because at last he gives in to a temptation to give up his attempt to maintain alternatives and submits to the threatening forces. This action leads him into a complete retreat from the common world. With Lola Voss the compulsions gave way to a thoroughgoing sense of persecution, which meant that her existence was held fast by a model that interpreted every experience as a breakthrough of inimical forces.[63] She felt unable to remain compulsive; worn out by this mode, she went completely mad. According to Binswanger, a thoroughgoing persecution complex is significant not because of its bizarre content but because it illustrates how a given individual has submitted to that aspect of his particular world which had been so intensely denied. Lola Voss had tried to keep

[62] Sullivan, *Clinical Studies*, p. 43.
[63] Binswanger, Introduction, *Being-in-the-World*, pp. 258-262.

herself aloof from the world and its hold; finally she resigned herself to that which she most dreaded, surrendering herself to the very power of others which she consistently had viewed as demonic. This last fall marked the total breakdown of her ability to decide, to establish alternatives, and hence a withdrawal of her creative being in the world.[64] In other words, she submitted to the antinomic tension which she had established in the first and second stages of her illness. Thus she became what Binswanger called a "burned-out crater," an existence consumed by anxiety.[65] When existential anxiety becomes so severe, as in this case, a person's ability to be creatively attuned to the world is lost. As such existential anxiety represents "not life-fire and life-warmth, but an opposing principle—chilling and destructive—the principle of death. To this extent, but only to this extent, one may rightly say that any anxiety is anxiety about death." [66] Her surrender to a world of hostile ambiance marks the final stage of mundanization wherein one particular world has overwhelmed her existence to such an extent that there is no longer any genuine self. It is a world that bears no more traces of the world of love and trust, where the world of authentic selfhood has been obliterated, and in which all genuine freedom has been consumed. It is in this existential frame of reference that we can begin to *understand* autistic thinking and to see the *reasons for* it and *in* it, which for so long has baffled and bewildered psychiatry as well as the rest of mankind.[67]

Similar to Binswanger, Sullivan also saw schizophrenia not primarily as an illness but as an unfortunate form of existence. It is "an attempt to cope with what is essentially a failure at being human—a failure at being anything that one could respect as worth being." [68] To become schizophrenic is not to cease to be human, but it is like stumbling into a new universe, a new world which is marked by fantastic urgency to get something established. The schizophrenic suffers the unceasing fear of becoming nothingness, of finding his self collapse totally. The frequently intense urgency in their worlds might best be understood as an expression of their burning interest in becoming again full human beings, or at least in finding a world in which there is peace.[69] When a mild schizophrenia develops

---

[64] *Ibid.*, p. 263.
[65] *Ibid.*, p. 337.
[66] *Ibid.*, p. 322.
[67] Cf. *Ibid.*, pp. 336-339.
[68] Sullivan, *Clinical Studies*, p. 185.
[69] *Ibid.*, pp. 316-320.

into paranoia we see an individual facing his world with danger flags flying and all guns ready to shoot. Such an individual has transferred to others the blame for all his faults and especially for the lack of what he needs most, intimacy.[70] Sullivan also saw that paranoia constitutes a world in which love has collapsed, wherein the schizophrenic feels especially persecuted by everybody from whom he wants warmth and trust. From this perspective the frequent association of homosexuality and paranoia can be understood, though the two should not be confused or identified. As Sullivan pointed out, the beginning of a sense of persecution starts long before the emergence of the lust dynamism.[71] Every paranoid has previously been schizophrenic for a while; he has lived in a world of crude, disjointed referential processes. Advanced stages of schizophrenia are characterized by the breaking down of the self-system which has lost control of awareness so that the individual is overwhelmed by those extremely primitive and dissociated parts of the personality which had thus far been concealed from one's attention.[72] Homosexuality can signify an attempt to establish relations with others which will bolster the self system and protect it from collapse.

In a manner similar to Binswanger, Sullivan insisted that the doctor must establish a personal relationship with every patient so as to reintroduce into his personality a sense of trust, dependability, and solidity.[73] Both agree that the schizophrenic has lost considerable freedom, particularly in the most personal spheres of life. In Sullivan's words, a schizophrenic is driven by the whip of anxiety and suffers constantly from that horrible nightmare in which every person is suspect. What will the next person be like? he asks at each moment. Certainly Sullivan has greatly increased our awareness of the interrelations of dynamisms that lead to schizophrenia, and he has opened a way for us to understand many unfortunate forms of existence.

Binswanger concentrated on just a few specific cases; in a way quite similar to the psychologist Gordon Allport, he preferred to concentrate on the patterns of one individual at a time, rather than to provide us with a vast array of insights into a wide variety of dynamic possibilities. Yet his existential frame of reference enables us to make the most sense of the observations and intuitions provided by Sullivan. Through phenomenology

70 *Ibid.*, pp. 89, 145, 158.
71 *Ibid.*, pp. 150 ff.
72 *Ibid.*, pp. 24 ff.
73 *Ibid.*, pp. 363-364.

we can enter the world of the schizophrenic enough to begin at least to understand how it really goes with him. Both approaches far exceed the outlook of the general background from which they emerged. To say that madness consists in the breakdown of logic, as a purely descriptive method often does, adds nothing to our understanding of it. Actually madness signifies not a breakdown in logic but merely in the logic of our restricted everyday world. To suggest that mental disturbance is constituted by fantasy or by the loss of reality is less than helpful and far from the truth. Binswanger's existential analysis has provided a way of understanding autistic existence by setting its symptoms and dynamic patterns within the human framework which is common to us all; he has thus provided a unique mode of understanding so that a bridge of therapeutic communication can be established. Sullivan's successful therapy with schizophrenics encouraged him to construct a theory which would account for it. However, his system of dynamisms, for example, does not bring us into the schizophrenic world. If the reader of his theories feels that they do, it is because his imagination is filling in the existential reality in the same way that Sullivan's obviously did when he worked with his patients. It was the achievement of Binswanger to bring the intuitive imagination which underlies all genuine communication into the light and to let it reveal the meaning of those basic dynamic structures of existence within which both fortunate and unfortunate forms find their places.

4. THREE COMMON FORMS OF UNFORTUNATE EXISTENCE
   AND THE CASE OF JÜRG ZÜND

Before proceeding to an examination of one particular case it will be helpful briefly to consider Binswanger's important study of three forms of existence which certainly are not basic structures but which are extremely common in the worlds of schizophrenia as well as in our own. These forms can be characterized by the common terms "high-flown" or "extravagant" (*Verstiegenheit*), "eccentric" or "perverse" (*Verschrobenheit*), and "affected" (*Manieriertheit*).[74] Each form has its own peculiar and quite historical essence, which it is the purpose of his study to illuminate in a scientific way. His purpose here was to expand the scope of existential knowledge. Specifically he aimed at seeing these phenomena not as schizophrenic symptoms but as relatively universal existential modes of being in

[74] See Binswanger, *Drei Formen Missglückten Daseins*.

the world, which unfortunately curtail human freedom. In contrast to authentic modes these are unfortunate because they stand in the way of genuine existential fullness.[75] Each represents a dead-end avenue, marking the end of a basic possibility, a stand-still in the history of being in the world. Binswanger's aim here was phenomenological; he sought to uncover the essence of each of the three existential modes. By so doing he would understand the "reasons" for the behavior often diagnosed as schizophrenic, which is to say, he would understand its meaning.

The first and all too brief study is of what he designated "high-flown." [76] The German word suggests a climber who has gone too high up the mountain and has become stuck on a ridge; he can neither rise higher nor can he come back down onto common ground. Ibsen's master builder is a good example; religious case studies are particularly rich in evidence of this unfortunate existential mode. High-flown existence involves being caught in a particular set of alternatives in which there is a discrepancy between goals and experience, between aspiration and actual possibility. In this sense, high-flown existence is truly extravagant; to maintain an ideal it pays a price which existence simply cannot afford. The stubbornness manifest in people who have "fallen" into this modality can be understood as indicating that in their high-flown existence they have become caught on one rung of the ladder leading to spiritual heights; they dare not move from that rung for fear of falling off the ladder entirely and being caught up in chaos. Psychotherapy should attempt to help the person regain a view of the whole scope of his being in the world and to climb down from his imprisoning pinnacle so as to become free to be fully human, to be open to the wide range of possibilities that belong to authentic existence. Unfortunately this study, so promising in insight, is so short as to contain not much more than a hint of what is involved. If Binswanger's phenomenology sketches roughly the meaningful portrait of high-flown existence, we are acutely aware that the details and color must be filled in by the social sciences. Taken as it is, it requires a great deal of imagination to make the picture come to life.

A second form of unfortunate existence is more fully drawn, which Binswanger called "eccentric" or "perverse." Again the connotation of the German term suggests unusual stubbornness, as though a person has bored

[75] Ibid., pp. ix-x, p. 91. For a more detailed examination of these studies see Sadler, Ludwig Binswanger's Existential Phenomenology, pp. 290-310.

[76] Fortunately this study is now also in English, though regrettably the key term has been translated as "extravagant." See Being-in-the-World, pp. 342-349.

crookedly into his world so as to become stuck in a peculiar way like a screw that has become jammed. In English we often say of such people that they are twisted, off the beam, out of line, queer, askew, cracked, screwballs, etc. Binswanger's examination of the colloquial language used of such existential modes led him to see that this existence had become caught in the secular world of taking. All the terms originate from the secular sphere of *Homo faber.* The individual is spoken of as an instrument or piece of machinery which has gone askew. Certainly he is seen to be less than personal.[77] A phenomenological investigation more clearly reveals that the world of this perverse eccentric is understood by the individual himself in terms of instrumentality that is out of line, has jumped the track, or been caught in a rut. Consequently he finds it impossible to confront another human being directly as a person. His personal encounters must be oblique, as he meets persons in his world where all beings have become things at hand.[78] The framework of time and space is almost entirely structured so that their meanings are encountered in terms of taking, turning, twisting, and being twisted. It should be no wonder that when we meet such people and engage in conversation with them we have the feeling that our meanings are being turned around. If we are really to communicate with a perverse eccentric it is necessary to look into his world as we receive his words. By traveling along on his unhappy track, it may be possible to reach the community in which personal communication is grounded.[79]

The third unfortunate form we might refer to as affectation or more precisely as a mode dominated by affected mannerism. Similar to the last mode, the term "mannerism" suggests the insight behind ordinary language that this form of existence is striking, unusual, strange, deviant, and eccentric because it has been wrongly handled.[80] This form represents a fall into the discursive mode of taking and being taken, but it also implies a similarity with high-flown existence. Affected manners are not authentic; they are inappropriate to the situation, and as such represent not a response but actions toward an ideal which are forced, unnatural, manufac-

---

[77] Binswanger, *Drei Formen,* pp. 23-30.
[78] Cf. *ibid.,* pp. 64-67.
[79] Cf. *ibid.,* p. 89. See also the moving account of extensive psychotherapy with an adolescent whose language falls into the pattern illuminated by Binswanger and whose therapist heard behind the very mechanical jargon a genuine desire to enter a common world of mutual exchange and trust, in Beulah Parker's *My Language Is Me.*
[80] *Ibid.,* pp. 92-93. The French word *manier* from which our term is derived refers to manual contact, handling.

tured, and artificial. There is a great distance between good manners which the situation calls for and mannerisms which are pretentious.[81] Binswanger began his phenomenological investigation first by examining and pointing out that other attempts to understand mannerism, particularly those found in psychiatric literature, fall far short because they do not see the world in which mannerism is an event and a way of life.[82] The common assumption that mannerism is primarily a device to attract attention completely misses the target. The case of Jürg Zünd (see pp. 300ff.), which is a paradigm of mannerism, will help us to see into its world and to understand the reasons behind it.

An examination of the phenomenon of mannerism in the aesthetic realm is illuminating. There is something forced about mannerism in art, just as colloquial language indicates something forced, willed, and stilted in existential mannerisms. In both instances industry accomplishes more than creativity allows. There is the dominance of technique over natural growth. Mannerism is not a style indicative of strength but an attempt at concealment of a felt deficiency of one's own creative powers by imitating the recognized greatness of some other artist. Mannerism develops when there is a loss of confidence in one's own creative ground combined with an earnest striving toward an ideal that really belongs to another.[83] The opposite of mannerism's artificiality and affectation is growth. In the particular affected mannerism in art as in the general mode of existential mannerism, we encounter existence which apparently has lost its own roots and where consequently creativity cannot flourish. The affected person withers in his self-imposed artificial atmosphere. We miss the grace and charm of the naturally responsive person, for in mannerism the individual has taken on a role which is a substitute for growth. In advanced forms of schizophrenia the task of imitation is so debilitating that often the patient becomes incapable of performing any but the most routine functions.

By understanding mannerism phenomenologically within the framework of being in the world and bearing in mind the splintering effect of anxiety, it becomes possible to see why an individual adopts this particular mode. As in the case of Jürg Zünd, what leads to mannerism is a deep awareness of homelessness. Feeling unsure of his home and without roots he was overpowered by anxiety which led to radical doubt and despair. In

81 *Ibid.*, p. 95.
82 *Ibid.*, pp. 99-110.
83 *Ibid.*, pp. 160-162.

order not to sink utterly into chaos, into the horror of meaningless existence where the intentional structure has been shattered, he took in hand childhood idols, patterns, roles which would enable him to wear a mask. By always wearing a mask which was a copy of others' life styles, particularly those of the upper classes, he sought to conceal his anxiety and make a place for himself in some world. The existential ground of mannerism is thus the loss of confidence in one's own world.[84] Anxiety encountered in all aspects of one's being in the world is the driving power behind the industrious art of imitation. It is an attempt to find support in someone's else's strength.

Phenomenology should question the common existentialist claim that anxiety is the heart of authentic self-development. Rather, it seems that anxiety may push the individual to conceal anxiety from himself and others by adopting an ideal image and frenetically attempting to imitate it. We feel the hidden dynamics underlying pretense when we sense that there is something unnatural or artificial about affected behavior. In contrast to the ersatz independence which is achieved through the life style of affected mannerism, genuine independence emerges through creative encounter with the styles of others, receiving from them, being nourished by them, and encouraged by them to be original. As Marcel has repeatedly demonstrated, creativity in art as in life is grounded upon fidelity; and creative fidelity is quite different from slavish imitation.

The attempt to cope with anxiety such as in the phenomenon of affected mannerism does have some positive meaning. Though mannerism arises from the breakdown in confidence, yet it tends to ward off, at least momentarily, the threat of the naked horror of annihilation, though at the price of severing one's being in the world from its roots, from its own ground of creativity. Jürg Zünd held anxiety at bay by affecting the mannerism of high-class society in his social relations and the mannerisms of a superior artist in his music. The tragedy was that he could not relate himself genuinely to people nor could he continue with his performances on the piano. The artificial supports which propped up his being in the world kept him standing but prevented him from moving forward toward his own historical fulfillment. Mannerism was an expression of freedom in that it was his own choice; but it was a barrier to the freedom to develop authentic existential possibilities.[85] His freedom became dominated by a

84 *Ibid.*, pp. 163-168.
85 *Ibid.*, p. 170.

general type of orientation and behavior. Yet at least he did not go totally mad nor did he commit suicide, which are two other prominent alternatives. All three of these unfortunate forms maintain existence, but actually all of them are extravagant, paying, for minimal freedom, the price of authentic existence.

From the vantage point of a phenomenology of these three forms we reach a clearer understanding of the character of fallenness. The power of anxiety presses existence to the limits. If it finds no strength in itself and its relations with others, if it lacks the basic trust required to affirm being in the world as openness toward full existential historicity, then it falls into a particular mode which is not intended to reach fulfillment but merely to stay alive. This, to Binswanger, really signifies the meaning of inauthenticity. In the mode of mannerism the individual clearly has become *das Man;* he has identified himself with a mask and with the role of showing this false face in public. Such a person has fallen into the public image. As long as he maintains this existential mode he is separate from any community of love. His communications are not heart to heart but run along on the surface. He is constantly playing a game, putting on a show, keeping up pretenses to himself and others. In this phenomenon we do not find either loving community or true singularity. Having lost touch with his own ground, the center of his personality, he has become hung up on an ideal created by someone else. He is the prisoner of a foreign image. His fate is that he shapes his destiny according to a pseudo-independence. He is not openly responsive in any encounter. His existence is enclosed in his own self-deception that attempts to conceal his shame, his anxiety, his weakness. Though he may delight in his success at imitating his ideal in dress, speech, and behavior of various kinds, yet the earnestness of his endeavors is tinged with a haunting despair which he must deny.[86] In moments of weakness and in sleep, signs of the controlling power become evident.

There is a rigidity in mannerism which usually is classified as compulsiveness. Existential phenomenology, however, makes clear that this compulsiveness actually refers to an imprisonment in this particular mode of being in the world. By trying to keep up pretenses one cannot relax as though on his own ground. He must constantly be on the alert, always thinking about his mask, whether it is on properly. Is his behavior corresponding to his image? Is he playing the role properly? These questions

[86] Cf. *ibid.*, p. 180. It should be pointed out that though the main suggestions here are taken from Binswanger, the development is my own. For a critical exposition of Binswanger see my previous study of him, *op. cit.*

constantly run through his mind no matter what the situation calls for. For fear of being discovered as other than his ideal, he cannot for a moment forget the role he has chosen to play. The tragedy is that his roles prevent him from opening up as a person in interpersonal relations, even if he has chosen to play the role of a grand person, be it civic leader, doctor, teacher, or priest. From this viewpoint we can better understand the common assumption that the compulsive, affected individual is self-centered. Self-centeredness actually is a misnomer here. On the contrary, the center of his being has passed out of his horizon. Rather, he is in the desperate situation of having to clutch an ideal, an artificial mode of existence, a mask, an idol. He has little time or energy left to think about anything else.

Phenomenology has little by little been opening up the temporality of this terribly significant and prevalent mode of human existence. Binswanger characterized the temporality of mannerism as expectation (*Gewärtigung*).[87] By this he meant that such a person lives in constant expectation of imminent danger; he is constantly on the alert. His temporality has a fixed quality about it. It has the same structure whether he is crossing through busy traffic, appearing on stage, sitting in an audience, or conferring with a colleague. Every present situation forces him to adopt his generalized self-image. Every future moment will be like the present, which is a repetition of every past moment. When a human being falls into affected mannerism he has committed himself to know in advance what to expect. He will interpret the world, every situation, every encounter, all his possibilities in terms of maintaining this artificial image, of serving his idol. It is small wonder that he is often plagued with boredom, with the sickening feeling of monotony. Similarly it is no surprise that he often seeks to escape with a plethora of diversions, which nevertheless offer little satisfaction; for everything is basically the same. Consequently, he never knows the full meaning of a genuine present. He cannot receive the presence of another because he is too busily engaged trying to convince himself and the other that he is someone who essentially he is not. His future is consumed by a past that has become stereotyped and is imposed upon every moment. And every moment is lighted up with a warning signal which tells him to be on the alert, to maintain the false identity, to hold onto his reputation, which has become the prison of his being. The temporality of this mode of being in the world throbs with tension and pressure, with deathly earnest, doubt, despair, and often the absence of genuine humor and grace. It is human time become harnessed to a lifeless

[87] *Ibid.*, p. 182.

foreign idol. Yet in certain cultures where formalism prevails, such a person will be recognized as one of the group, part of the gang, a model citizen who plays the game according to the rules, or even the representative of orthodoxy.

The essence of mannerism's spatiality has also come to light. Certainly the space of mannerism is not wide open; on the contrary, it is characterized by an oppressive closeness, what Binswanger has referred to as the nearness of push and shove (*Druck und Stoss*).[88] As his time is urgent, so the affected individual's space threatens to close in on him. He is constantly pressured by the world, which is always getting too close. He must always put on an act so as not to attract attention; he dares not increase closeness, but will keep everything at a distance, because somewhere lurking out there is the possibility of an encounter with the naked horror. He may escape to the most remote regions of the earth; nevertheless, in his world he has fallen into the spatiality of strictly social existence. Distance is in terms of accessibility and attachment, not in terms of singularity's making room for beings in which to be free, nor in terms of love's being at home and making another be at home. The space of mannerism is always handled in essentially the same way to serve the same purpose. It is not free, flowing space, but space which is always under surveillance. He must always keep his hands on it for fear of its getting out of his control.

High-flown existence falls onto a high ridge where there is the enormous disproportion between the heights of aspiration and the plains of experience. Perverse eccentricity falls into a rutted world in which every encounter is somehow crooked. The whole world is askew and is stubbornly kept that way. Affected mannerism falls into forced handling of existence, which constantly attempts to make it conform to an inappropriate pattern, to an ideal of the past or of one segment of society. Each of these three unfortunate forms of being in the world can be rightly understood as modes of fallenness. They signify often brave but nevertheless regrettable attempts to be human. As fallen from their ground and away from their authentic future, such existence maintains life but stultifies growth, not only its own but also that of others who come within reach. That is the unfortunate meaning of much mental sickness; according to Binswanger it is proper from this perspective to consider such existence as sick.[89]

[88] *Ibid.*, p. 183.
[89] *Ibid.*, p. 184.

These forms often appear also as cultural phenomena, characteristic of groups of people, or even of an entire era. It might be more useful to further phenomenological research if we continue to regard these phenomena as modes of fallenness into particular versions of the social world of taking, a world which takes on exaggerated importance at the expense of the worlds of individuality and loving coexistence. Whenever a society or any part of it elevates the public world over individuality and love, it upholds world images which represent fallen existence. It makes much sense to see cultural phenomena as social forms of being in the world, some of which are unfortunate from the full viewpoint of the basic possibilities of existence. By studying individuals who are particularly fallen into certain patterns, we may bring to light unfortunate tendencies and characteristics not merely of our individual selves but also of the culture in which our worlds are born. The greatest heuristic value of these studies may prove to be in the help they offer to the scarcely developed phenomenology of cultures and societies. Equally important in this respect would be a phenomenology of fortunate social existence.

Needless to say, these special studies illuminate more aspects of the human world than were uncovered in a phenomenology of basic forms alone. They further substantiate my suggestion that being in the world is to be understood pluralistically. In these unfortunate forms we discover clefts in the worldliness of each person. The split of schizophrenia is not just in a personality but in the whole world of a particular being. In healthy existence the world is rightly directed toward several basic possibilities of meaning that struggle against each other yet interpenetrate. In spiritual illness the world is divided, and existence submits to one worldly mode. We can now understand the apparent contradiction, for example, in mannerism, where on the one hand we discover awkwardness, clumsiness, stiffness, and pathos, while on the other hand we find in obvious evidence ebullient expressiveness, ceaseless activity, and frivolous daintiness. Whereas other approaches draw our attention to unusual behavior but reach conclusions about its meaning from inferences, Binswanger's contribution has been to let the phenomena stand forth in their own light, revealing how they work for good and for ill. He has helped us to understand how such unfortunate forms of existence nevertheless represent a last-ditch stand for survival. Without seeing the potentially creative good in such phenomena, he could scarcely have helped patients suffering in these modes. By helping us to see both the signs of life and freedom in these disjointed worlds, he points beyond them to an authentic personal world. Only as we see these worlds as unfortunate modifications in the basic structure of being in the world can we hope really to reach out in freedom to establish communication with another and give him hope to discover meaning that lies beyond the grasp of anxiety.

In this chapter we have been focusing upon the phenomenon of anxiety, seeking not merely to discover its widespread presence and devastating effects upon human life, but to gain insight into and understanding of various forms existence may have as it encounters anxiety. High-flown, eccentric, and affected existence are three fairly common forms man falls into in his battle with anxiety. A classic study of one particular existential world under attack of anxiety is Binswanger's case of Jürg Zünd.[90] His analysis reveals not merely the world of this human being but also demonstrates how phenomenology and the social sciences cooperated to reach understanding. Like the patient in the famous case of Ellen West, Jürg Zünd had few symptoms specifically indicating schizophrenia. Consequently, various doctors had made diverse diagnoses; each had sensed that something was out of order but had not been able to pin it down. Since the symptoms gave little indication of what was actually wrong with the patient, existential analysis had the challenging opportunity to understand and clarify the reasons for unusual behavior, and more, to understand the person who suffered. Unlike Ellen West, whose lack of contact with others led her to overburden her body with meaning it could never provide, Jürg Zünd apparently was extremely caught up in society. He certainly could not be classified as one who had lost awareness of others. On the contrary, he was acutely aware of other people and particularly of their social class. He was also aware that he had a life problem, though he was unaware of the reasons for it. These factors did not indicate autistic thinking, which is a prime signal of schizophrenia. Jürg was a strange man with several notable eccentricities who at the age of thirty-seven presented himself at the clinic to receive treatment. Because of his oddness, it was difficult at first to establish sympathy. Thus it was all the more imperative to use existential analysis by which this person could be understood in terms of its unique being in the world.

To begin his research, Binswanger regularly acquired all the various data which could be derived from various tests and interviews with the patient and, if possible, the family. Binswanger was fairly certain that

90 See Binswanger, *Schizophrenie*, pp. 193-288.

heredity was a factor in schizophrenia, in that bodily constitution at least predisposed a person to this illness. In tracing Jürg's life history, it was discovered that a paternal uncle had been a catatonic. Jürg himself was constitutionally weak and at the age of five had suffered an acute attack of bronchitis. In early childhood he also had an unforgettable dream about decapitation which continued to plague him. His father, a musician, was a polite but meek man; his mother was a stormy, emotional, overly-protective, and intelligent woman. Both parents had been constantly anxious about their son. They always watched over him, never allowing him to play with other children on the street. Early in life he felt he was different, especially so when he was the only boy who was dressed in an overly long jacket, wore long hair, and had yellow buttons on his shoes. Between the time he entered primary school at the age of seven until he left it at the age of twelve, he suffered from the conflict between his parents and his schoolmates who always teased him. About this time he found pleasure and some security in the company of his maternal grandfather and an aunt and uncle who lived on the lower floor of their house. But the gulf between his own family and the rest of the world widened, especially after he heard a maid remark that his parents were considered to be strange and proud, not like normal folks.[91] Small wonder that Jürg felt exposed much of the time in public view. He often felt undressed or transparent, and attempted to hide one way or another.

Upon entering adolescence his anxiety increased and in particular was associated with masturbation, which he had read produced harmful effects. Formerly he had felt superior to girls; now he developed an inferiority complex. By the time he was eighteen depressions were characteristic of his personality. He was extremely self-conscious. He was afraid as he entered a classroom that he would attract attention to himself. His battle with anxiety affected his study program. After just barely passing a first set of examinations at one university, when he started in at another university he developed such phobias that he could not even attend lectures until two semesters had passed. It took four years before he gradually relaxed and took part in student life. He felt extremely inhibited with others so that he could not act naturally with them. As he walked down the street he was constantly plagued with the question: What kind of impression am I making on people? Am I accepted? Do they like me? Feelings of inferiority developed during self-interrogation. As a consequence of his embarrass-

[91] *Ibid.*, pp. 195-196.

ment, his gestures and manners became more peculiar than ever. He would often not remove his coat in class, for fear of making a movement that might suggest he was degenerate. He was afraid that by walking down the street he would attract attention by his gait and bearing, and that his suspected vulgar, inappropriate interest in other people might become apparent. So in his attempt to become inconspicuous he could not make any movement which was half-way natural. With each step he swung first one shoulder forward, then the other; and he so swang his arms that his intention to avoid attention had just the opposite effect. His anxious feeling that he was cutting quite a figure as he walked down the street was only too well founded. The reasons for his mannerisms, however, certainly were not to attract attention. At the age of twenty-three he suffered such anxiety about becoming disgraced that he decided to move to still another city to pursue his studies. Finding comfort and security with wealthy relatives there, he was able in five years to complete his studies; and subsequently he even earned a doctorate.

He could not, however, remain employed. He considered earning a living as a concert pianist. He was quite talented and played well; but he was such a perfectionist that he could not face the possibility of playing in front of others. Eventually he returned home to live with his father and aunt, where he found his situation overwhelmingly depressing. He spent his time doing nothing. He got up late, lay around the entire day, only went out after dark, never associated with anyone, and carried on no correspondence. His affairs were in great disorder, and his increasing sense of inhibition prevented him from straightening them out. When sedatives failed to help, he decided to present himself at Binswanger's clinic and enter the sanitarium. While there he was observed to be sometimes demanding, unreasonable, and mendacious but usually he was modest, likable, and considerate of other patients.[92] No definite schizophrenic symptoms were evident, yet Binswanger suspected that some form of schizophrenia was present.

One of his most prominent symptoms could easily be misinterpreted by the inferential method of psychoanalysis. Jürg was very conscious of strong sexual feelings which in turn made him feel anxious. Particularly he was terrified of the possibility of having an erection while in polite society. Ordinarily this fear would be interpreted along the lines of an Oedipus complex and repressed libido. Binswanger noticed, however, that he was

[92] *Ibid.*, p. 202.

sexually attracted to various types of women and often in strange situations. Once he had been strongly attracted to a woman over seventy. She was of high society, and Binswanger observed that Jürg's sexual attraction was not responsive to sexual appeal but to the social class of the particular women. His fear of having an erection was really a manifestation of a deeply felt disgrace anxiety that was akin to his feeling of inferiority and lack of confidence. Actually he felt nausea at times about his own weak and insipid existence. To cover up his anxiety and lack of confidence he adopted mannerisms of brusk actions and haughty speech. This behavior only kept him more separate than ever from people, so that he felt increasing opposition to society. At times he felt so uncomfortable that he desperately sought to disappear into the anonymity of the masses. Yet he chose to identify not with the commoners but with the upper classes, even though he felt that he had some vulgar interests. Consequently his mannerisms were an attempt to put on a mask so as to conceal his embarrassing vulgar side and to create a favorable impression among the right people. Unfortunately his trenchant anxiety of shame and disgrace only led him to reveal what he most wanted to conceal, that he did not truly belong to any social world. His fear of having an erection was definitely a form of his disgrace anxiety. If it were noticed that he had an erection in polite society, he would surely be recognized for what he suspected he was in reality, a member of the vulgar masses. Within the purview of existential analysis it is possible to understand this complex phenomenon with its noticeable sexual traits as an expression of a deep feeling of social inferiority arising from the rudimentary cleavage in experience and the establishing of alternatives. Jürg passed through his world feeling that there was no real space for him on the planet, that he was nothing more than a mangy sheep. It is not hard to understand why he felt observed as he walked along the streets and why when he noticed people talking or laughing he believed that he was the subject of conversation and the butt of their jokes. Binswanger's analysis also pointed out that his feeling of having unusual interest in people was deceptive. He really was not interested in persons but in what people said, hoping and fearing that whatever was said concerned him.[93]

His disgrace anxiety (*Blamageangst*) also became apparent in other fantasies in which he anticipated an irreparable catastrophe, a sudden loss of status, respect, and position. He also was anxious lest he suffer an overpowering fear of death. His mannerisms of speech dramatized his

[93] *Ibid.*, p. 207.

anxiety. "I have been forced off the springboard of normal life." "I have outlived my own death." "I have taken upon myself the anxiety of the whole world." [94] His feeling of standing in opposition to others led him to surmise that others lived in a world different from his, and that they had plotted in a conspiracy against him because they would not reveal to him their secret of finding normality. Consequently he was always on the alert.[95] He felt that something essential had been withheld from him. The feeling of being in opposition to others, living in a world separated by an unbridgeable abyss between their worlds, increased to the point where he could not even sit down to dinner with others without feeling that something dreadful would befall him. In addition to his unbearable anxieties he also suffered symptoms of hypochondria, such as headaches, loss of energy, feeling the ebbing away of sexual vitality, etc. He was also tormented by a sense of smell, related apparently to his early decapitation dream. And he was anxious because he felt that his thinking no longer took hold in reality. Consequently, he much preferred to think in cold abstract terms, since practical, personal, concrete life was so distasteful, threatening, and seemingly impossible.

It is apparent that his entire life had become an unbearable torment. In his constant encounter with anxiety he increasingly lost any firm sense of self-identity. He tended in turn to seek for anonymity, not as Ellen West, who tried to waste away to nothing, but by becoming immersed in the masses. His unconscious aim was to force his painful ego into the narrowest possible limits so that others would no longer notice that he had been branded as a queer fellow. Yet here again there was ambivalence, for at the same time his individuality called out for recognition and fulfillment. His ambivalence and problems in this respect are illuminated by a project he had during the First World War. As a volunteer he believed he could escape from his painful ego by getting caught up in the spirit of a cause which transcended him and through which he might lose his life. He would then escape his painful identity; no one could point a finger at him, because he would not exist any more as an individual. He would be immersed in the cause and then in death. Yet by sacrificing himself in this way he believed he would purchase honor and redeem his lost individuality. Binswanger pointed out how abstract and impersonal his sense of self was. He conceived of himself as a coin which could be given to a cause in

[94] *Drei Formen*, p. 115.
[95] *Schizophrenie*, p. 208.

exchange for honor.[96] Jürg forced his existence into the narrow straits of utilization, into the discursive world of taking and being taken.

Most of the data and observations thus far have been culled from an approach which falls into the broad category of the social sciences. We have yet to illuminate Jürg's existential world, to see how his life was lived and why it took the form it did. We are fully aware that his existence was marked by extreme sensitivity and vulnerability to the hostile forces of anxiety which he encountered in nearly every corner of his world.[97] He could not get away from these forces nor from himself, though he tried both repeatedly. In fact he constantly, excessively reflected about his condition. His compulsion was an inability to be open to think about something else, to encounter the world without having the encounter dominated by his prejudice. The concept of repression does not aid our understanding here. There was hardly any repression; on the contrary, he was extremely conscious of and tormented by his world. His sensitivity and vulnerability disclose his world as one which pressed in upon him. Everything was too close, things as well as people. He bumped into all sorts of things and was anxious lest moving entities might bump into him. In order to hold the world at a distance so as to keep it from pressing in upon him, he devalued much that he would otherwise have prized. His world became inhospitable, threatening, strange, and fallen.[98] His manner of degrading the world was not merely to adopt a haughty attitude but in particular to think in highly abstract terms. By reverting to generalizations and abstractions he reduced experiences and beings to generalized types. His manner of perception became highly abstract; he was constantly arranging his world in symmetrical patterns, giving it an artificial order. By throwing the world into abstraction, he himself became an abstraction, a generalized type for which ordinary language has a treasury rich in descriptive labels.

Jürg's life was marked by social contact, and it was not devoid of sexual encounters. Analysis indicated, however, that there was little evidence of the dual mode of existence, of a loving We. He seemed not to have known the gift of grace that comes from loving encounter. There was no sign of deep personal trust, no hope for creative personal fullness. There

---

[96] *Ibid.*, p. 211.

[97] Binswanger also administered Rorschach and free-association tests which substantiated existential insights into the nature of Jürg's world. Rorschach tests especially indicated his sense of vulnerability in terms of his body and also his sense of temporal urgency, having to be always on the alert. (*Schizophrenie*, pp. 220-222.)

[98] *Schizophrenie*, pp. 223-226.

was scarcely any awareness of the possibility of the ecstasy of a loving We in which an individual finds his living space to be a home and his history to be integrated and affirmed in the mutual presence of love. There was hardly any indication of loving imagination or of the security of love which inspires carefree play and which fosters the discovery of truth, beauty, and goodness. Only in music was he able to free himself briefly from his secular imprisonment. The ecstasy of music, however, lacked the firm foundation of a loving Thou, so that his existence found no personal ground upon which to stand. He could find no roots so as to grow into freedom. In every encounter the possibilities for loving encounter had shriveled up.

We discover here an overgrowth of impersonal social intercourse with others. Discursiveness reigned in his relations with things, other people, and himself. It is not accurate to say there was no trace at all of love of community. Binswanger saw a slight glimmer of the light of love in his childhood longing to find security in his mother's love and of his appreciation for the little security he experienced with his relations downstairs.[99] But longing that finds only lack sours into hatred, envy, and a general disparagement of the whole of life. The lack of love put a seal of desecration and profanation upon the whole world. To devalue the world places one in the constant presence of hostile forces, so that anxiety is often raised to the heightened power we associate with the demonic. In Jürg's case the result of devaluation from not finding a home in the world was to transform the world by laments, complaints, flight, hostility, and occasionally self-destructive raging over his wounds caused supposedly by the cold heartlessness of others. In place of loving encounter emerged the constant battle with the finite forms of taking and being taken. Eventually his defiant freedom was taken into submission by that narrow world. Instead of a loving home, his existential space was the space of always being on the alert, always raising the anxious question: Who goes there? In lieu of the simultaneity and duration of loving presence there was ceaseless hovering in momentary danger. Time was an endless string of danger signals. Rather than growing in open responsiveness, this existence was marked by compulsion, suspicion, mistrust, envy, hostility, depression, and despair. Without the spirit of play, it became hard, brittle, and formal. He had encountered all too soon in life the dissonance of existence when worlds are at odds, and he did not find any possibility of reconciliation. He was aware of the wound, and his life history carried a strain of longing for reconciliation

99 *Ibid.*, pp. 231 ff.

within his world. But eventually his hopes foundered, as his existence hit on the rocks of longing too long unfulfilled.

We have come to *understand* his existence as a being in the world which is almost exclusively confined to the particular form of worldliness designated as the secular world of taking. In this particular mode a person can be very impressionable. He can be taken by the ear or at his weak point, where he is most sensitive. Jürg's sensitivity constituted exaggerated impressionability. He was overly influenced by his immediate environment in the negative sense that he felt it pressing in upon him. Thus he felt and was subjected to critical observation, ridicule, and the domination of others' opinions. Because there was no inner strength of singularity or loving duality the hold of this world became tighter and more extensive. He was increasingly unable to escape from the pressure of any situation, to meet it with resolution or to rise above it with the additional strength of loving coinherence.[100]

We can push further in our understanding of his unfortunate existence and also those high-flown, eccentric, and affected existential forms, all of which pertained to his lived world, by realizing that Jürg had lived in three worlds which did not interpenetrate. These worlds represented constant possibilities to him, but he could never bring them together. One world was the vulgar world of the streets, where as a youth he had been teased, though on occasion he had been a daredevil there. The second was the world of his parents, the upstairs world which was overprotective, demanding, out of the ordinary, and unsettling. In this world his tempestuous and often unreasonable mother dominated him. It was from this world that he emerged in odd clothing which caused him to feel exposed. His home life was so uncomfortable that he actually preferred the world of the streets. But because his parents caused him to look and feel so odd, his preference was mixed with an oppressive need to hide from others. The third world was constituted by his relatives downstairs, where he had at times felt security. Here were people who were not considered queer; on the contrary, they were very highly thought of. His uncle had been dapper and had taken him on walks during which he would encourage escapades. Here was a new, enticing world which had in it traces of charm and security. When his father had discovered about the uncle's influence and the escapades there was "hell on earth" for Jürg. He was nowhere at home. That is the basic meaning of the original rent in his experience. His being

[100] Cf. *ibid.*, p. 233.

in the world was not aimed at three authentic possibilities; it was torn into three worlds, each of which fell within the world of secular, social existence. His secular existence was not only split three ways; it was greatly overloaded, expected to render meaning which did not belong to it.

Consequently the time and space, the whole history of Jürg Zünd was radically affected. What individuality he had was not an expression of creative strength. His life had become a mirror, in which his expressions reflected the impressions that others had made upon him, especially high-class society, with which he finally identified as much as he could. This identity, however, was in constant opposition to the undisciplined world of the streets and the parents' world. Jürg's high-flown ideal of upper-class society was only one factor in his unfortunate existence. For as he attempted to identify fully with the ideal, he also needed to deny his other identities. But he could not entirely divorce himself from those other two worlds. Though they also were cast in the social modality, each of them was a sign of a basic possibility which he had not found open. The world of the street beckoned in terms of individual freedom; it promised an opportunity to cut loose and to be completely singular. The world of the parents beckoned as a potential home and community of love. As an adult Jürg sought strenuously to escape from those two worlds. If only he could have seen them as symbols of basic possibilities which he had not yet encountered, his history could well have been radically different.

The task of psychotherapy as Binswanger saw it was to help the patient see beyond the restricted war-torn world in which he lived toward authentic possibilities pertaining to being in the world. Elsewhere he wrote:

> What we call psychotherapy is basically no more than an attempt to bring the patient to a point where he can "see" the manner in which the totality of human existence or "being-in-the-world" is structured and to see at which of its junctures he has overreached himself.[101]

Since most of us are trained to be psychotherapists, this might just pass as an interesting formulation. However, it can also well serve with some slight adaptations as a description of existential phenomenology. We are concerned to see the way in which the totality of being in the world is structured; and since few of us can consider ourselves to have attained authenticity, we are also concerned to discover at which points certain

101 Binswanger, *Being-in-the-World*, p. 348.

structures have overreached themselves in our lives and in those whom we encounter.

In the world of Jürg Zünd there were structures which had far overreached themselves and others which had hardly a chance to open up and come into the light of day. A pattern began to develop early, and there was nothing to offset or balance it. Having been a sickly child it is not surprising that his world seemed strangely hard, made of foreign material which constantly pushed against him and to which he was easily vulnerable. The natural development of many possibilities was deterred or prevented by his world designed in terms of push and shove, where he was always being pushed around and pressured by his entire environment. He was a soccerball of oppressive forces—dreams, hostile groups, individuals, things, talk, illness, stares, and so on. To master these forces would require a superman. He felt that the raging power within would not be sufficient to break the hold of that opposing world if he let it explode. So he followed the commonly accepted pattern of the way of least resistance. Since the whole world represented potential areas of attack he decided to flatten out these areas through abstract thinking, reducing all encounters to general types. Another way to avoid attack was by hiding behind a mask. From early childhood his world had been seen in terms of pain and the avoidance of pain. To dispel the pain he allowed his being to fall into an unfortunate form of worldliness. Here there was no room for natural growth. Space was threatened, vulnerable, pressed in upon, always in sight and within easy reach of inimical powers. The tragic ambivalence of his existence pulsed like a turbulent sound: "Live! Hide! Hide! Perhaps, live."

We have concentrated upon the fallen spatiality of his world. It was just as apparent that his temporality was fallen. In the temporality of authentic singularity and duality we have discovered moments of ecstatic unity. Especially in love the present embraces the past and the future as the whole of existence is affirmed in the measureless moment of mutual presence. Here, however, time was fragmented. Jürg's temporality was characterized by urgency and abruptness. Each moment could present him with a shove, an attack. This very minute he might be discovered or exposed. Enemies lurk in all vicinities. For this reason no time can be lost. Always he had to maintain an alert, to be ready to jump to the defense, to be sure that pretenses were always maintained. In this world his existence was overpowered by each mere present. His temporality was splintered into urgent nows. Yet underlying this fractured time was a firm grip of the past which determined that each present shall contain the same narrow possibilities as the last. In traditional psychoanalysis this grip of the past upon the present was referred to as the unconscious, which has been reinterpreted existentially. Instead of seeing events against a backdrop of love, all that transpired for him was set against a stream of social intercourse that carried eyes which were always upon him. In his history there was no time for love, and so no time for authentic play, peace, or joy. Nor was his time individualized. It had been taken over by the opinion of others. It had been made to serve the type of personality which he had anxiously chosen to become.

In the world of Jürg Zünd, said Binswanger, we find the personification of *das Man*. He was given to abstraction, even when thinking about himself. He ceased to appear as a growing being even to himself. His world became an object world. He thought not in terms of "life" but of things. He was constantly dependent upon talk and the idlest chatter, dominated by frivolous curiosity, and caught in inescapable ambiguity of meaning.[102] One consistent meaning became the master of his world, and that was the possibility that at each moment he might be caught, exposed, hurt, and destroyed. Such a world was naturally conceived in terms of warfare, for he was aware of himself as a victim in constant danger of recurrent invasion from the enemy. His solution was not to fight, however, but to put on a mask of composure and take things in hand. He did so by seizing the world in standardized abstractions and forcing the life out of it. What was so noticeable about his world is that it was homogeneous. In a fallen world, conversation is essentially about the same old thing; for the new, which brings with it the possibility of danger, is ruthlessly kept out of sight as much as possible and almost entirely out of mind. This is the framework within which the existential meanings of ritualism, formalism, mannerisms, conservativism, etc., can become evident.

There were similarities between Jürg and a genius as there are between autistic behavior and actions of a truly original man. Binswanger pointed out, however, that the genius is open to what is new; he is objective in the sense of being openly responsive to the givenness of history. The cause of his suffering is often that what he sees lives in him, becomes alive in his world. Jürg's suffering, like that of other schizophrenics, was brought about through the lived contradiction of isolation and oppressive closeness. He thereby became enclosed in his subjectivity. Jürg was not open to the possibility of being a full human being and so he did not grow outward in

[102] *Ibid.*, pp. 242 ff.

that direction. His existence went off the track, and he was bound to the past, cut off from the future. Aware of his distress, he did not find the strength or the opportunity to alter his life situation. He sought to escape, to fly into a nirvana of the anonymous masses. Instead, he fell and became submerged in a world which no longer belonged to him but to unfriendly others. As a last effort at self-preservation he elected madness. Unfortunately this step was not toward salvation but away from the healing power of community and love.[103]

In the study of Jürg Zünd there were observed feelings of shame, disgrace, guilt, punishment, mistrust, suspicion, envy, hatred, and all sorts of unusual behavior which had something to do with these feelings. The ordinary procedure in psychopathology would have been to ask which factors were primary and to proceed to classify this person accordingly. Binswanger's existential analysis has asked instead: How are we to understand a being who manifests these particular features? With an awareness of the ground structure of existence as being in the world directed toward basic possibilities and with imagination combined with careful observation and analysis, it was possible to see these phenomena in their lived context and to understand the meaning of this unfortunate mode of existence. It has become evident that the latter signified a roadblock to the possibility of becoming truly personal; yet we can also appreciate that it represented an effort to save the self from total decline, to hold off at least momentarily the threat of complete annihilation which an encounter with massive anxiety poses.[104] It was apparent, too, that this unfortunate form of existence marked a fall of freedom into a predetermined world where basic existential structures are molded according to rigid abstractions. The case of Jürg Zünd does more than reflect the peculiar development of one unique historical existence; it throws light upon the fallen existence of each one of us. As did he, each of us stands in the world vulnerable to attacks of anxiety; without the courage of individual commitment and the strength of love, anxiety may drive us so hard into the narrow world of taking that we become lost in it.

This book began in search of the meaning of human transcendence. Existential phenomenology has revealed much of that meaning, particularly in terms of basic possibilities for the authentic realization of human freedom. Through an analysis of anxiety from within the perspective of

103 Cf. *ibid.*, p. 254.
104 Cf. *ibid.*, pp. 250-259.

love, we have seen the possibility of a radical fall of transcendence and the loss of freedom. When a human being is not borne by love and friendship, and when he cannot temporalize himself in an authentic singular mode as an original individual, anxiety will push him into the world which allows him only the opportunity to take and be taken.[105] In this world man falls into a constant repetition of one basic form of encounter. This is the meaning of another existential possibility, that of *total secularization*, or what Binswanger referred to as mundanization. It still represents a mode of freedom, but one which dominates existence so that it can no longer be open to the freedom of love and of creative individuality. The real power behind its history is not the beckoning possibility of expanding freedom but the menace of anxiety. Because of an underlying terror and fright, which must at all costs be concealed, all encounters are forced into predetermined patterns. In this mode of existence many cherished aspects of life are debunked, ridiculed, and rejected. To be fallen into a totally secularized world is not to be clear-eyed and objective. One may become cunningly perceptive, detecting new ways to take advantage of situations so as to control the outcome of developments; but one cannot from this modality gain the distance to see the true meaning of personal encounters or genuinely creative expression. To submit completely to the totally secular world as a means of warding off anxiety means to become closed to the mysterious presence of a Thou; it means to exist with a great emptiness where love should dwell. To live under the attack of anxiety exposes every man to a *fourth* basic possibility of being in the world: *fallenness*. Especially as personal values are debased, one's existence becomes a being-fallen in the world.[106] The only way to transcend this fall and to become directed toward authentic personal existence is to encounter love somewhere along the stages of life's way, a love which leads a man beyond the terror of anxiety into the peace of being at home with the mystery of freedom and intersubjectivity.

105 Cf. *ibid.*, pp. 260, 481 et passim.
106 Cf. *ibid.*, p. 261.

13

❦

The Meaning of Love in the Stages on Life's Way

1. THE PROMISE OF A NEW HUMANISM

It has been said before that man stands on the brink of a brave new world, but perhaps never have the words had such profound significance as they do today. It is man's nature to make a world; more than ever before man is making his world change. The contemporary transformation is so rapid and so radical that the term "evolution" is inadequate to convey what man is producing and experiencing. There is no doubt that the historical process of secularization combined with the increase of technical knowledge and skills as well as the development of urbanization has brought man into a new era. With the proliferation of knowledge and the acceleration of technical efficiency, man has discovered countless ways to change and improve his environment, reshape society, alter basic modes of behavior, transform values and morals, invent new forms of expression and communication, in short, to refashion his entire world. In many ways man today is doing things that formerly were considered to be prerogatives of the gods. Modern man is not unaware of his spectacular feats; he spends fortunes in advertising and world fairs to applaud human accomplishments. Yet the signs of the times are not entirely auspicious. Some eminent students of man have warned of probable if not imminent disaster. Many existentialist witnesses to the human condition have moaned like Cassandra about the tragic consequences of modern life, particularly with respect to the rise of technocracy as man becomes absorbed in technical achievements.[1] Perhaps

[1] As much as I admire Gabriel Marcel, even he has succumbed to this myth; cf. his *Man against Humanity*, which outdoes Heidegger's evaluation of everyday life.

recent developments have a tragic aspect; at least they spell the end of many things men have held dear, including traditional ways of life. Yet alarmist predictions about man's condition can be myopic and unwarranted.

Though this phenomenology of existence and love has not shared the dire predictions to be found in much existential literature, nevertheless it has emerged in a situation where crisis has been felt. This study has in common with optimistic views of man a deep awareness of human freedom while at the same time being fully cognizant of many factors which limit and challenge freedom. Modern man is increasingly aware through social and cultural change of his ability to overcome obstacles and to operate with considerable success incredibly complex machines as well as vast economic, social, and political systems. While delighting in our capacity for invention, many of us are becoming conscious that increased secular freedom has also provided us with "the elbowroom to lay hold of our destiny as men." [2] As one senses that he has "come of age" in a new world, he often begins to realize his awesome responsibility to forge not merely new products and systems but a destiny which will make his activities worthwhile. One aspect of the modern crisis is that there is great uncertainty about where freedom leads and what human destiny is or is meant to be. A serious flaw in much modern life is not that we are insufficiently liberated from the past but that with all our knowledge we are so little aware of human potentialities. We have discovered ingenious ways to demonstrate our capacity to be clever; we are still far from becoming wise. One astute observer has remarked that modern men have learned "to grow up healthily without reaching personal maturity, to live well but without purpose, to invent ingeniously without aim, and to kill grandiosely without need." [3] Reflection upon our world will make us aware not merely of vast potential freedom but also of much freedom grossly misspent. The challenge to human freedom in this as in any era is to reach a trustworthy insight into what it means to grow up and become distinctively human as individuals and in our relationships with others.

Among theological writers, Berdyaev, Tillich, and even Buber have sounded an unbalanced alarm at our technological world. It is heartening to see a swing in the other direction as in the writings of Bonhoeffer, Winter, Cox, and others, a direction which is to some extent in line with phenomenological insight into existential meaning.

2 Myron Bloy, "The Christian Function in a Technological Culture," *The Christian Century*, Feb. 23, 1966; pp. 231-234. See also his thoughtful book, *The Crisis of Cultural Change*.

3 Erik Erikson, *Insight and Responsibility*, p. 227.

Modern man looks for a bright future, but he has become confused about his identity as a person. Having questioned traditional criteria for evaluating and guiding human life, one wonders if there are any norms which can be trusted. Aware of the opportunity to shape a meaningful world many are nevertheless perplexed about the meaning of human life. There are many factors which have contributed to the contemporary crisis in man's understanding of himself, but surely one of the most crucial has to do with our ignorance about and our neglect of love. Many will espouse love as a great virtue, but frequently one is embarrassed to mention it in responsible discussions. Love has often been buried in sentimentality, beclouded by rhetoric, or shriveled up through abstractions. Increased virtuosity of pragmatic accomplishments and stupendous challenges of radical social upheaval have tended to make love appear to be an ideal reality belonging to a world apart from everyday life. It is thought to happen "only in the movies."

One value of existential phenomenology is that it has helped to uncover the reality and the meaning of love. With this approach it is possible to become aware of the basic structures of human existence. By so doing a criterion or norm for understanding human life begins to emerge. To become authentically human does not mean to become successfully productive, or thoroughly secular, or completely autonomous, or radically socialized. The chief task of human life is to become personal; and the ground of personal existence is loving duality. Through secularization man has become liberated from many forces which curbed his freedom to become a productive individual agent. Yet the freedom to be an individual is neither the only nor the most significant mode of human transcendence. The ideal of human life, however, is not to suppress one form of freedom in favor of another, but to foster the interpenetration of the basic intentional structures of freedom. This phenomenology has revealed love to be an intentional structure man cannot afford to ignore so long as he has any hope of fulfilling his freedom. If modern culture fails to appreciate and foster love, our world cannot become progressively and authentically human. The primary form of personal freedom is constituted by the possibility of being one with others in creative duality. Without love man can neither be himself nor discover the truth of his personal destiny.

The existential phenomenology of love has brought the whole of human existence into new light. Within the perspective of love it is possible to appreciate significant forms of existence which might otherwise be slighted, such as romance, play, and everyday practical-social existence. It also helps to correct our cultural bias which is prone to perceive reality in an overly individualistic and extremely visual manner. Furthermore, it enables us to reassess numerous phenomena; in particular the illumination of the devastating force of anxiety should put to silence much existential nonsense about anxiety's supposedly creative power. The source of personal creativity is not anxiety but love. Without love man's ingenuity will inevitably be aligned with security operations designed to avoid situations where severe anxiety is likely to be encountered. The phenomenology of existence and love claims to offer trustworthy insight into basic human structures so that we can understand the fundamental possibilities inherent in human destiny. As such, this existential phenomenology points toward a new humanism, founded on love, in which the meaning and value of personal existence is appreciated and where love is looked to as a true guide for shaping history.

In this penultimate chapter I shall bring phenomenology and social sciences into further collaboration in the attempt to see more concretely what love means to the full history of human life. Love is not an occasional moment but an enduring structure of human existence, though one which has often become obscure. It has been said that modern man has been so intent upon becoming an individual that he has neglected intimate relationships with others and lost sight of their importance. Yet more than ever man has the freedom and leisure to love, and to follow love in pursuit of the truth about human existence. There is still the suspicion, however, that really mature worldly wisdom must be kept separate from the supposedly weak passion of love. As that very modern man, Francis Bacon, wrote:

> You may observe, that amongst all the great and worthy persons whereof the memory remaineth, either ancient or recent, there is not one that hath been transported to the mad degree of love; which shows that great spirits and great business keep out this weak passion. . . . For there was never proud man thought so absurdly well of himself as the lover doth of the person loved; and therefore it was well said, "That it is impossible to love and be wise." [4]

In contrast to widespread uncertainty about the actual significance of love with respect to the development of authentic existence and insight, it is becoming evident in some quarters that love is the cornerstone of wis-

---

[4] Francis Bacon, "Of Love," *Essays.*

dom.[5] If we are to be wisely guided by our insights into the fundamental meaning of love, it will be necessary to discover more precisely what the world of love means to the major stages of human development. By bringing insights from various other perspectives into this phenomenological focus upon existence in love, it is just possible that we might advance in wisdom and move at least one step closer to a truly human destiny.

2. LOVE IN THE EARLY YEARS

While phenomenology has concentrated upon the significance of love for adults, psychoanalysis has emphasized its importance for human development, beginning with infancy. Psychoanalytic insight needs to be incorporated into phenomenological understanding. Our history is obviously under way in the infant; the infant, too, is being in the world. He, too, has a capacity to perceive, through prehension or feeling, the facticity of himself with others and how others feel toward him. Learning and personality structure, in fact our whole world, evolve through a process of consensual validation. The infant learns to identify what is mutually recognized by the parent. When the infant detects anxiety in the mothering one, the result is a formation of a security system that forms the basis for defective learning in the future wherever anxiety is encountered or suspected. As the infant develops his personality by identifying his good-me with the good mother, he also is constructing a world with an increasingly thick defense system so as to avoid the possible interaction between the bad mother and the bad-me. Thus his early world horizon is constricted by the possibility of falling into the naked horror, which is the origin of the dynamism of paranoia. Without real tenderness, without parental love to strengthen the little person's budding independence, the infant begins to shape and confront his unique world with serious handicaps.[6] One hopes that in this early relationship the infant begins to learn the fact of mutuality which will be of immense significance and a constant source of strength to him during his development toward maturity. In mutuality he will find the power to transcend the agonizing rent in his world introduced by anxiety. It may be

[5] In the prosaic carefulness of the language of social sciences this insight is expressed so: "Respect is the core of the process of validation" (Pearce and Newton, *The Conditions of Human Growth*, p. 20).

[6] Cf. the discussion by Pearce and Newton, *op. cit.*, pp. 70–82 ff. They bring together the working insights of Sullivan with those of other and later workers in this field. See also the classic study of early childhood by Erik Erikson, *Childhood and Society*.

surprising to everyone but loving mothers and attentive fathers to learn that an infant is aware of mutual interaction and recognition. This *fact* "of the mutuality of adult and baby," as Erikson puts it, is "the original source of hope" and trust; [7] it is the gift of helping a little person feel at home in this world.

With basic trust in the fact of being in the world gathered from this primal relationship, the little person is strengthened to move forward into the next stage of development. Without it he may *never* find the courage to face directly the task of becoming truly human. He may spend much of his time turning aside from his destiny. Man is constantly absolutizing particular areas of his life, as in moralism, ecclesiasticism, rationalism, formalism, historicism, scientism, and even secularism. He identifies himself with his own abstractions in a compulsive way. "All of this," as Erikson points out, "has its psychological basis—namely, the individual's determination never to meet his childhood anxiety face to face again, and his superstitious apprehension lest a glance at the infantile origins of his thoughts and schemes may destroy his single-minded stamina." [8]

Admittedly what has been lost in one stage, such as trust, *might be* recovered in a later one. Few psychologists today accept the exclusive emphasis placed upon early childhood by traditional Freudians. Nevertheless, sympathetic and honest insight into our relationships with the very young is important. Even the very young need to be given the trust to encounter life openly, to find creatively their own unique historicity as free human beings. Too easily we think of love as purely an adult phenomenon. We must be aware that if it is the foundation for truly personal existence, it is thoroughly historical. To become *historically* aware requires that we gain insight into the reality and meaning of love at each stage on life's way, which involves recognition of our need for love at each developmental epoch. Though mature love will have different qualities and characteristics from love known in infancy, the origin of mature love will be found in the sense of mutual presence in the relationship between parent and infant. In the same way the origins of men's rage and hate may also be found in the

---

[7] E. Erikson, *Insight and Responsibility*, p. 231; cf. also the study by F. J. J. Buytendijk, *Das Menschliche: Wege zu seinem Verständnis*, which points out that though the infant response has analogies with that of animals, nevertheless the infant reveals a definitely personal response to the expression of motherly love. The mother-child relation, he argues, is truly an interpersonal encounter, the basis for the expanding freedom, possibilities, and meanings which are open to man in his life with others.

[8] E. Erikson, *Childhood and Society*, p. 404.

early relationships they suffered with their parents.[9] In our modern era we have learned a great deal about early development; and we have learned not to stunt a child's growth through labor and not to repress natural curiosity and expression through the infliction of guilt feelings. We must also learn not to stunt creative personal relationship or a child's "growing spirit by making him the victim of our anxieties." [10]

The love which is necessary for the child in the earliest stages of life does not imply that loving parents spoil a child or encourage him to become egocentric. Whether he is infant, adolescent, or adult, a person needs the liberating and encouraging power of love; without it, his probabilities for developing positively meaningful relationships with others will be seriously reduced.[11] Without love man is anxious to take what he can get; he cannot really relax in a world where he lacks the home and presence of love. The fruit of love for a little person will be a healthy sense of self-esteem, or what has often been meant by the misleading term "self-love." This sense of self-esteem is indispensable for personal growth, and it is easily distinguished from pride. Sullivan has usefully pointed out that pride is a dynamism which functions to conceal insecurity with one's past experience. Pride is a fictitious self-appraisal to cover up personal inadequacy. It

[9] Cf. the penetrating study by I. D. Suttie, *The Origins of Love and Hate*.

[10] E. Erikson, "Growth and Crises of the Healthy Personality," *Personality in Nature, Society, and Culture*, C. Kluckhohn and H. A. Murray, eds., pp. 185-225. Further evidence of the tremendous significance to be found in the early mother-child relationship has been presented by Dr. Herbert Hendin in his *Suicide and Scandinavia*. Both Sweden and Denmark have very high suicide rates. By using a clinical method, interviewing patients who had unsuccessfully attempted suicide as well as normal individuals in the same society, he discovered that the framework which made suicide a meaningful alternative was provided by the early mother-child relationship. In Sweden the extremely early separation of mother from infant is a source of great anxiety which underlies the "typical" Swede's preoccupation with death and his tremendous drive toward success; excessive tension or failure in the latter leads easily into the former. Bergman's films and Dag Hammarskjöld's diary are both good examples of what Dr. Hendin refers to. In Denmark there is the opposite characteristic in the mother-child relation; there is overdependency, which breeds anxiety relative to independence. Death is frequently thought of as a way of remaining dependent, by "joining the beloved in heaven." Interestingly enough Norway, which has a quite different typical pattern of mother-child relationships has a very low rate of suicide. Both Hendin and Erikson, whom Hendin criticizes for inadequate methodology, emphasize the relationship between cultural patterns and psychodynamic development.

[11] Cf. Sullivan, "Towards a Psychiatry of Peoples," *The Interpersonal Theory of Psychiatry*, p. 371. To sense the power and relevance of Sullivan's amazing insight into human beings, there is no single writing of his that I know of which will provide these more movingly and easily. Elsewhere in this volume Sullivan points out that if the child does not receive the love he craves, a disintegrative pattern will emerge, such as we see in malevolent children (pp. 201-216).

is an operation designed to prevent a frontal attack of anxiety upon a particularly vulnerable area.[12] Binswanger's study of three forms of unfortunate existence phenomenologically illuminated various distortions of basic human structures through pride. High-flown, eccentric, and affected persons manifest pride to conceal anxiety. From the perspective of love, a source of danger to authentic personal development lies not so much with pride but with the failure to acquire and maintain self-esteem. When that good spirit leaves a man, at least seven evil ones come to take its place; and one of those is pride.

While highlighting the meaning of love for the earliest stage of personal development, it should not be overlooked that these love relationships are also meaningful to the historical development of the parents. In the mutual exchange of love, parents discover an extension of the meaning of being a person. Not only does the parent gain a deeper sense of self-esteem, he or she develops a distinctive identity and discovers more about what it can mean to be human. A man learns something about masculinity as he becomes aware that he is a father; a woman finds new significance pertaining to femininity as she is conscious of her being in the world as a mother. And parents discover even more their duality in the union of love. In the mutuality of the love relationship between parents and children each person grows in understanding and gains inner strength for creative growth. One discovers also the important truth that one's full personal identity does not issue primarily from individual initiative but comes as a gift. The adult finds security and identity as he is recognized in love by one who calls him "Dad," who calls her "Mom." A child can give his parents the grace and courage to be more fully human, to be freer to expand their horizons of meaning, to be open and ready to discover the world of love more often with increasingly more people.[13]

3. FIRST LOVE: THE CHUM

The little person passes through childhood into the juvenile era. Provided he has received sufficient love to allow an easy development of a self-system which can provide him with enough security so that he is not overtaken by dissociation or frightened into withdrawal, the juvenile will begin to develop skills that give him satisfaction of tensions, a sense of accomplish-

12 Sullivan, *Clinical Studies in Psychiatry*, pp. 117-124.
13 Cf. E. Erikson, *Insight and Responsibility*, p. 232.

ment, and thus increased security through the approval of others. The juvenile forms a distinctive world as he learns to focus his attention in such a way as to ward off anxiety and to augment his competence both as an individual and as a member of several groups. The juvenile can often find considerable harmony in his life as various existential possibilities interpenetrate in his world. Because the juvenile may achieve considerable security as well as increasing satisfaction, these may be relatively easy years.

However, a change begins to occur as the juvenile enters the stage of preadolescence; and according to the interpersonal relations theory of psychiatry, this change is terribly important. It is marked by a radical shift in orientation through the development of a new type of interest. Typically, juvenile interest is concentrated upon one's individual accomplishments in achievements; the juvenile is interested in competition, cooperation, and compromise. Now there develops a new kind of interest in another human being which marks the beginning of a more developed form of reciprocal love. At this point the fortunate young person finds a chum, one usually of the same sex, who becomes a friend of the greatest importance. What matters now is not what I should do to get what I want but what I should do to contribute to the happiness of or to support the prestige of my chum.[14] As Sullivan pointed out, this love is not really sexual. We must learn that intimacy and sex are not inseparable. In the chum relationship there exists tremendous intimacy, involving such closeness as to afford two people consensual validation of "all components of personal worth." [15] Here a foreshadowing of genuinely mature experience becomes evident, which is experience in the *syntaxic* mode. The vibrant and open communication in this relationship is marked by what Sullivan called "collaboration," in contrast to juvenile relationships of cooperation and compromise. Juvenile relationships presuppose considerable distance, such as is spatialized in the world of taking in impersonal associations.

A new interpersonal structure develops in the chum relationship. Sullivan also referred to it as the W*e* structure: "When we collaborate, it is a matter of w*e*." [16] This change marks a highly significant adjustment to one's being in the world with others; for it involves a dynamic historical process that is structured by more and more mutual satisfactions and meanings. What Sullivan has in fact discovered is that even before adoles-

[14] Sullivan, *The Interpersonal Theory of Psychiatry*, pp. 245 ff.
[15] *Ibid.*, p. 246.
[16] *Ibid.*, p. 246 fn.

cent romantic love, two young persons can enter and mutually shape the new world of loving We. Entering this new world with a chum has enormous significance. As for the barriers to personal freedom erected by the self-system, this experience provides a way in which previous handicaps may be overcome. Though the self-system is relatively set in the early stages, yet on the threshold of a new stage it may more easily become open to the influence of new experiences. In this way it can undergo radical change. Forms of inadequate living may be overcome through the insight and trust that emerge especially in the chum relationship. Sullivan wrote:

> Because one draws so close to another, because one is newly capable of seeing oneself through the other's eyes, the preadolescent phase of personality development is especially significant in correcting autistic, fantastic ideas about oneself or others. . . . [The] development of this phase of personality is of incredible importance in saving a good many rather seriously handicapped people from otherwise inevitable serious mental disorder.[17]

It is to be hoped that the preadolescent will find a chum with whom he can be as intimate as possible, one to whom he can relate all his very private notions and crazy ideas, his dreams, fantasies, hopes, interests, fears, etc. In the same way he will receive the most intimate revelations of his chum's own peculiar notions, hopes, dreams, interests, as well as his crazy ideas. This intimate sharing is a miraculously natural means of clearing away many ideas about oneself and other people which would be barriers to mature growth and communication. Personal maturity and real communication emerge from within the We structure that this early intimacy does so much to establish. On the other hand, if the encounter of chumship does not occur, the individual may never get beyond the juvenile stage. According to Doctors Pearce and Newton, "if there has been no experience of chumship in a person's life, he cannot conceive of values beyond the juvenile mode. He never discovers that individuals matter." [18]

One of the reasons why chumship is so important is that it is probably the first experience of love which is thoroughly reciprocal and mutual. The space of love in the We-world with parents differs from that of the We-world of the chum. In the love experienced with parents, there is mutuality and interpenetration; yet the child occupies a position of subordination.

17 *Ibid.*, p. 248.
18 Pearce and Newton, *op. cit.*, p. 108.

The young person will rightly feel that he has to get out from under the potentially overpowering parental world. He discovers distance from his parents as he develops independent self-awareness; but the boundaries of this distance are extremely finite. In the chum the infinitely expanding boundaries of personal existence are rediscovered. With a chum the young person can maintain the necessary distance from the parental world and at the same time rediscover and recreate personal closeness. In the chum relationship he can be independently himself while at the same time living for another who has become extremely significant. This closeness helps to diminish his anxiety created by the increasing distance between himself and his parents; in this new intimacy the young person begins to discover that his true *home* is mobile, not a fixed place. Within the structure of chumship he finds a new possibility for meaningful freedom in a world with an expanding horizon. Though he may dress, talk, and act just like his chum, yet in the dawning world of love he has chosen to be in the world that way, regardless of what his parents think. He is no longer only free *under* his parents; he becomes free *with* another on an equal basis.

Phenomenology helps to reveal more clearly the existential meaning of this youthful relationship, as an encounter wherein the new being of We-two gives a powerful assist to the development of personal freedom and security. However, Sullivan has pointed out that in addition to the delightful discovery of a new sort of We relationship, for the first time the young person may also encounter what can properly be called *loneliness*. At this stage of development we uncover another universal dynamism. Loneliness is also a basic existential possibility; as such it is a tremendously significant factor for motivating existence and is a principal reason for a good amount of human behavior. Strangely enough, loneliness is frequently overlooked as a motivating power. Sullivan suggested that perhaps one reason why motivational studies spent so much time on trivial matters and no time on loneliness is because loneliness is so powerful that it practically baffles clear recall.[19] There are intimations of loneliness in childhood; but the child's world still exists largely within the framework of the parent's world. The child will feel lonely, but this distance is not that of total separation. Underneath there is the bond with his parents. What terrifies him is to have this bond threatened with anxiety, with chaotic destruction. This anxiety threatening total isolation and destruction leads him to construct massive security operations. He will often do this by keeping people other

[19] Sullivan, *Interpersonal Theory*, pp. 261-262.

than his parents at great distance. In preadolescence the full-blown phenomenon of loneliness hits with a driving force. In the moment of loneliness the young person cannot tolerate the feeling that he is all alone in the world. The impact of this force is sometimes so strong as to incite a person to tear down security operations at the risk of encountering great anxiety just so as to find a chum. If he finds the possibility of a chum concretized, he may overcome the disintegrative patterns of the self-system by opening himself to integration with another. From this stage onward loneliness is a crucial factor in the dynamics of living. It is an existential possibility which can be more terrifying than anxiety and which can only be understood and overcome within the world of love.

4. LOVE IN THE ADOLESCENT WORLD

The encounter of chumship opens the preadolescent to a world which beckons with the bright, warm intimacy of love and at the same time holds the possible threat of the cold, dark horror of loneliness. Soon after entering this larger world the young person encounters an even more drastic transformation, a crisis of such proportions that it may rightly be considered world shaking. He or she enters adolescence; and like it or not, ready or not, tremendous transformations occur. The adolescent finds himself or herself becoming the center of what Erikson has aptly called a major identity crisis.[20] The little girl suddenly looks like a young woman and is gratuitously treated by adult men with great deference. Just who is she, anyway? The little boy has outgrown his father and needs a shave. Former neighbors and friends of the family will call and say: "Who are you? Oh, for heaven's sake, I didn't recognize you." Chances are the adolescent does not really recognize himself. He has lost some juvenile skills and lost interest in others. However, he may find he is able to perform feats he recently hardly dreamed of accomplishing. Yet he may also find that he is too awkward to walk comfortably across the room to sharpen his pencil. As a competitive juvenile he had long sought attention. Now he is deluged with attention for which he is unprepared and much of which is not exactly flattering. Coming or going he is exceedingly self-conscious. And in every direction he turns he is challenged. He must develop new skills, new virtues and responsibilities, new knowledge, and new relationships. In our

[20] As a demonstration of what the identity crisis involves and particularly what it involves in a great young man, see Erikson's masterful study, *Young Man Luther*.

culture he lives in an era where a previous style of adolescence is vanishing. Now preadolescence is extending forward at the same time that adult responsibilities are descending, especially through increasingly democratic procedures in schools, churches, clubs, jobs, and community activities. The adolescent does not feel that he is sailing into his new world; he knows that he has been *thrown* into it. Being projected through life, his historical identity is confused. He is vaguely aware of a past which he and his peers are hurriedly trying to forget, while sentimental and domineering adults persist in reminding him of it. At the same time he is forced to consider his future, while he is trying to cope with a present which hardly seems to have arrived. All is change. His body is changing, his voice is changing, his relationships are changing, his interest in sex is explosively changing. His entire world is rapidly changing and becoming excitingly, frighteningly new.

In the midst of this world revolution called adolescence, the meaning of love is extremely important and also drastically confused. With special credit being due to the effective proliferation of mass media of communication, sex is thrown at the adolescent in most places, at most times, in every imaginable guise. What does sex mean? The adolescents, particularly those who politely play the role in interviews of typical "youth of today," reflectively confess that sex should mean something like love. "You shouldn't do it unless you really love each other." That judgment in the context of our common world is as naïve as the adults who rig the interviews or conferences so that it comes out that way. What is more obvious is that love has come to mean something like sex. We cannot pretend to be on the verge of probing all the significant meanings of love in the adolescent world, but phenomenology will furnish insight into basic phenomena so as to further our understanding.

We should begin with an awareness that those beings in the world whom we refer to as adolescents live in worlds just as complex and meaningful as our own. Their lives are intentionally structured so as to be directed toward a plurality of meanings, the most significant of which is to become persons in loving relationships with others. To distinguish sex from love in terms of meaningful dynamics, it will be helpful to follow Sullivan and in place of sex use the term *lust*, by which is meant merely "the felt aspect of the genital drive." [21] Lust is a dynamism, a basic existential form, which is conspicuously underpinned by a maturing development in the

[21] Sullivan, *Interpersonal Theory*, p. 295.

psycho-biological organism at the time of puberty. Its goal, especially in the male, is the release of tension as well as achievement of extraordinary satisfaction. It is to be distinguished from the need for intimacy, which is specifically a personal dynamism intended toward mutual presence and exchange. Yet in a given individual in a particular situation these dynamisms are extremely difficult to separate.[22] Yet both phenomenology and social science here agree that "the need for intimacy in its highest manifestations is unquestionably love—and while love has been many things to many people, the common denominator pertains to interpersonal intimacy," and not to the release of libidinal tension.[23]

To understand the world of an adolescent as well as to help with its peculiar problems, one must realize that there is no necessary connection between intimacy and lust. The adolescent is confronted with at least three basic needs, according to Sullivan, which often become radically dissociated. He has a need for personal security, which is a craving for the freedom from anxiety. He has a recognizable need for intimacy, particularly if he has previously experienced genuine collaboration with another. And finally he has a newly felt need for the satisfaction of lust. In the midst of radical transformation the world of the adolescent involves a "ubiquitous collision" between various needs or meanings, particularly collisions between one's lust dynamism and his need for security.[24]

One of the great misfortunes of adolescents is the separation of lust from the need for interpersonal relations. There is the frequent distinction made among males between the good girls you would want to marry, thus achieving approval (security) from parents and society, and the bad girls with whom you can covertly experience the satisfaction of lust. This solution, however, is not satisfactory, because it does not provide the intimacy one also seeks. In turn, intimacy might be sought by reverting to preadolescent chumships. You go off with the boys, where you can relax and be yourself. The next best thing might be double-dating with your best friend where you prove to each other that you are really men. In some situations one attempts to escape the conflict between needs for security and lust satisfaction by turning to homosexuality for intimacy; this of course is satisfactory to security only where a culture condones such a solution or where there is effective concealment. And of course one may become aware that as a solution it conflicts with the ground of sexuality.

22 *Ibid.*, pp. 280-292.
23 *Ibid.*, p. 292.
24 *Ibid.*, p. 266.

In other words, adolescents try to respond to a much wider world of possibilities than they are used to; frequently their solutions to conflict are in terms of segregating basic existential meanings from each other, following the path of rigid alternatives that can lead to drastically unfortunate existence. This segregation of meanings may lead, for example, to the unfortunate search for the ideal woman while finding satisfaction with less than ideal women as a lustful Don Juan, which reduces personal relationships to the world of taking and being taken; or one may revert, like Walter Mitty, to perpetual reverie. Fantasizing about ideal companions is likely to prevent a person from stepping outside his private world to encounter directly and openly persons of the opposite sex. These collisions of meaningful needs or world possibilities may be the principal motives, the underlying reasons for the prevalence of mutual support-and-protection societies (clubs), homosexual play, and autosexual behavior at this stage.[25] During adolescence a person naturally develops from isophilic relationships to heterophilic relationships, according to Sullivan. That is, one moves from seeking intimacy with another of the same sex to developing a deep interest in achieving intimacy with a person who is truly other, so much so that even the sexual gender is radically different. Barriers thrown up by anxiety, however, may drive the person back to an infantile autophilic relationship with his own body, as an expression of being rebuffed. Or he may revert to isophilic relationships, convinced that all members of the opposite sex, those persons who are not like himself, are essentially bad.[26] The problems which center around sex do not constitute purely or primarily a sexual problem. They happen in the collisions of directions toward meaning; these conflicts are felt acutely at this historical period of rapid transformation and potential personal growth as world collisions. As Sullivan observed, it is a mistake to think that one can solve personality problems by tinkering with sex life. It is more interesting and helpful to focus upon why a person has chosen, perhaps unwittingly, to focus upon this aspect of life as his particular problem.[27] To put this in phenomenological terms, it is more helpful and revealing to investigate the world in which

---

[25] Cf. *ibid.*, pp. 270-276.

[26] *Ibid.*, pp. 292, 275.

[27] *Ibid.*, p. 295. Sullivan offered here very straightforward advice to therapists: "Thus let me warn my fellow psychiatrists: If you want to do psychiatry that can well be crowded into a lifetime, see if you can't find something besides the sexual problem in the strangers that come to you for help. . . . You may notice that there is a slight difference here between my views and some of the views that have been circulated in historic times" (p. 296). For thoughtful discussion of adolescent problems involving sex, see R. F. Hettlinger, *Living with Sex.*

the problem arises. In this way we may come to a trustworthy understanding of the significance of the problem in the context of its world.

It should be clear that though they can be distinguished, a dissociation of lust from intimacy is not desirable, however universal the fact of it may be. From a phenomenological viewpoint, it is possible to uncover the personal meaning of lust. It may be understood as a dynamic directing of being in the world toward another person who is biologically, psychologically, as well as personally, different, a being who may be confronted and respected not as a replica of oneself but as a mysterious freedom with whom one can enter a new personal world of mutual presence.[28] It is possible, as our previous phenomenological investigations into romantic love demonstrated, for lust and intimacy to transcend collision and mutually to interpenetrate within the reality of loving duality. In the dark, foreboding world of mutual hostility and suspicion, Romeo and Juliet, Tony and Maria found a world full of light, joy, and trust. As adolescents are being pushed out of their homes, it is possible for them to find themselves at home with another in love. As they are being internally fractured by the confusing overlapping of their own historical eras, there is the possibility of finding with another a sense of historical identity in a moment marked by genuine presence. As the pressures of future responsibilities intimidate their increasing sense of freedom, they may be fortunate enough to find the moment of transport in which personal meaning and worth are mutually discovered and affirmed. From this perspective of loving duality their radically transformed worlds of individuality and secular responsibility are given reassuring validation and meaningful order. If adolescence is to be understood as an enormous identity crisis, it should also be understood that within a genuine loving relationship with another who is truly Other the individual may find his identity, his awareness of historical continuity or, as Heidegger put it, his authentic historical ecstasy. One's sense of identity even in adolescence comes as a gift from within a historical encounter with another. I know who I am when the one I love calls me to become my true self in the transcendent world of We. This fact of

---

28 Cf. the view of Vladimir Solovyev, *The Meaning of Love.* He advanced the provocative notion of sexual dynamics as an agent of spiritual well-being, driving man out of his isolated pride into direct confrontation with another being who is recognized as just as worthy as oneself of love. Sex, from this viewpoint, is a kind of dynamic impulse in man to discover his unity with another person and so overcome the fall of pride into alienated isolation; cf. also E. Lampert's theology of sex, *The Divine Realm,* pp. 92-99.

finding identity as an act of grace has tremendous relevance to the attitude and behavior of adults who are to guide adolescents to personal maturity as well as to the adolescents themselves. It also has relevance to our understanding of bodiliness.

There has been a long history of dissension and confusion over what has been called the mind-body problem. In existential phenomenology it has become clear that one is neither a mind nor a body. I am a *bodily being in the world*. The consistent existential affirmation has been: "I am my body" as opposed to "I have a body." Yet this affirmation does not tell the whole story, which is patently clear to any adolescent. He *has* a body about which he may be proud, embarrassed, curious, and frequently tense. He is terribly conscious that he is not simply to be identified with his body; in fact, he's usually self-conscious of *It*. He or she will take off almost all clothing to parade It around, or cover It with perfectly outlandish costumes. One's body is something one takes in hand, examines, admires, covers up, tries to ignore, puzzles about, and adorns. Furthermore, another person *has* a body. And if that person happens to belong to the opposite sex and has a particularly attractive body, a young male may feel acutely that he wants to have It for his own, at least for a long enough duration from which to derive satisfaction of the lust dynamism. When love and lust interpenetrate, however, the other's body *is* inseparable from the person. In love the body becomes not a thing to be taken but a being to be respected and loved.

In the encounter of love, each individual of a couple finds through mutual caressing a new sense of identity. Here one says: "I am my body. You are your body. I love all of you. All of me is loved." In the encounter of love the real meaning of bodiliness is revealed.[29] In a secular encounter I am aware that my body is something which can be taken; another can take my hand, my arm, my ear, catch my eye, etc. Yet in the embrace of love it is not my body which is taken but *me* as a person who is met, touched, loved. In the phenomenon of love one is given an identity that integrates and affirms the entire world of one's existence, which includes a very bodily mode of being in the world. In this connection it is interesting to notice that gnostic philosophies as well as many forms of schizophrenia

---

[29] Cf. Binswanger's discussion of the meaning of bodiliness in friendship. It is, however, puzzling that he did not apply his phenomenology also to the embrace of romantic love. *Grundformen*, pp. 447-450. Surprisingly enough, Jean-Paul Sartre, who has declared that "hell is other people," provided a keen phenomenological insight into the meaning of a caress in his *Being and Nothingness*, pp. 390-391.

are characterized by what an English psychiatrist has called the "unembodied self." [30] Especially within the reality of loving duality when one's bodiliness is affirmed by a quite distinct Other, one gains a deep sense of identity as a sexual, bodily being in the world. Historical and clinical evidence would suggest that when love does not provide an individual with an embodied sense of historical identity, the results may be expected to be unfortunate. Albert Camus has put a penetrating insight into the importance of bodily recognition within loving relationships and its significance for meaningful existence into one of his short stories about an explicitly sexual relationship. He observed of the principal female character: "Above all, she liked being loved, and he had showered her with attentions. By so often making her aware that she existed for him he made her exist in reality." [31] Precisely because this woman was loved as the feminine person she was, she was presented with a sense of identity which enabled her to become aware of herself as a sexual personal being.[32]

This brief phenomenology into bodiliness should not be misunderstood to suggest that the full sense of bodily historical identity will be actualized during adolescence any more than it should be interpreted as an open endorsement for uninhibited intersexual bodily encounter between teenagers. The purpose is to point out that one dimension of love's meaning pertains to the realization of genuine historical identity, which must include one's bodiliness. Real love, or intimacy, is a genuine possibility of adolescent being in the world. It is regrettable that taboos or misinterpretations which stress the sexual aspect of the relationship should conceal the grace which love bestows upon adolescent existence in its historical development toward mature personal meaning.

Failure to find a chum in preadolescence or a girl (or boy) friend during adolescence may seriously warp the person's development as far as intimate relations with other people are concerned. Our previous study of anxiety revealed the crucial role anxiety plays in the formation of the lived world. The self, being in the world, builds security operations, a self-system, to protect itself from anxiety. Thus the young person develops a

---

30 Cf. H.-C. Puech, *Le Manicheisme*, and D. Laing, *The Divided Self*, ch. 4.

31 A. Camus, "The Adulterous Woman," *The Fall and Exile and the Kingdom*, p. 154.

32 This was also the thesis which D. H. Lawrence notoriously and graphically spelled out in *Lady Chatterly's Lover*. By affirming each other's bodily sexuality in rather exaggerated fashion, the two lovers finally were led to discover that their existence was in fact structured by mutual presence or coinherent love.

defensive focal awareness of selective inattention, keeping out of sight those aspects of existence wherein might be discovered sources of anxiety. This dynamism of defensive focal awareness becomes particularly operative during the juvenile stage when one is naturally oriented toward the secular world, the realm of taking. Here one's perceptual and conceptual apparatus becomes highly developed, whereby one gains an orientation of life; [33] he makes his world, sizes it up, and takes it in stride. If anxiety is especially strong, an orientation, a philosophy of life, in fact a particular world, may evolve which allows for only a limited investment of interest in other people. A pattern of compulsive mediocrity designed to avoid danger may emerge; this pattern will include avoidance of the mystery and ecstasy of love as well as of ecstatic creative individuality. Life must be reduced to the avoidance of pain, the accumulation of pleasure, and the maintenance of a medium-gray color-tone in the world.

To many observers juvenile existence is becoming an all too frequent and widespread phenomenon in our culture: "The immature adult is the normal product of the process of acculturation in our civilization. . . . The individual is still struggling centrally with either preadolescent or adolescent problems, if he is not primarily stuck in the rut of antecedent ones." [34] Such adults may be considered well-adjusted, and moderate; they want things just enough, but never enough to take a risk or make a commitment. Their enjoyment comes not through creative encounter, but must be provided by the situation. They adjust to the secular situation in a businesslike fashion. They become organized within it and maintain loyally the "organization"; this includes upholding the juvenile virtues of competition, cooperation, and compromise and scorning individual or interpersonal ecstasy as dangerous and unhealthy. It is not surprising, however, that such existence vacillates between a feeling of weariness and an inner smoldering rage that life's possibilities are basically so few and its meanings so futile. [35]

Adults and children often share the same juvenile delight in successful competition. Yet when adults look longingly at the "great age of youth," adolescents become confused as to whether they are expected to grow older

[33] Cf. Pearce and Newton, p. 150.
[34] *Ibid.*, p. 137.
[35] Cf. *ibid.*, p. 168. See also Jules Henry, *Culture against Man*. One should not omit to mention the still important study by W. H. Whyte, Jr., *The Organization Man*. Erik Erikson's study of the problem of American identity is particularly penetrating and interesting, although it appears to be somewhat dated, or perhaps regional. See *Childhood and Society*, pp. 285-325.

toward personal maturity or younger in the direction of a juvenile world. Is it by coincidence or through selective inattention that while shouting loudly over fun and games our society is producing the most diabolical systems of destruction conceivable and engaging in warfare that has little if any rationally specified purpose? The trend to reduce existential problems to physical strivings, the debunking of love, and the glorification of a juvenile *Weltanschauung* might best be understood as clever but unfortunate dodges of anxiety. As our self-systems become institutionalized they present serious obstacles to personal relationships and maturation in our culture. The widespread refusal to confront honestly our general lack of intimacy and our fear of anxiety may well provide significant clues toward understanding our contemporary "juvenile" culture. Our culture in which adolescents are trying to grow up is faced with the horrendous problem not of repressed libido but of suppressed and smoldering hostility which emerges from a systematic frustration of basic personal possibilities.[36] The search for an adequate norm for personal maturity is not an idle pursuit either for adolescents or for those of us who can give thanks that the adolescent world crisis is behind us.

5. LOVE AND FRIENDSHIP

Much of our study has focused upon the phenomenon of romantic love, because it is particularly illuminative of certain distinguishing features of the new world of love and also because it is an extremely meaningful encounter within the development of persons which is too often overlooked, undervalued, or sentimentalized. I have not meant to suggest either that romantic love is the culmination of the existential history of love or that it is the most complete expression of the essence of love. It is unmistakably a brilliant phenomenon in which some of the glories, beauty, goodness, and truth of love become wonderfully manifest.[37] Another magnificent and highly significant moment of love is the phenomenon of true friendship, which is to be distinguished from social relationships or merely

---

[36] Frieda Fromm-Reichmann pointed out some time ago that the major problem of contemporary psychiatry is not sexual repression but hostility, which expresses itself in antagonisms, malevolence, and, we might add, the perpetuation of wars, the extension of gross injustices in class and racial conflict, and sadistic indifference to the suffering, bondage, and anxiety of others. See *Principles of Intensive Psychotherapy*, p. 84.

[37] Charles Williams makes this same point in his study of romantic love, *The Figure of Beatrice*. This should be read for itself, but also to offset the rather disparaging view presented by C. S. Lewis in *The Allegory of Love*.

friendly acquaintance. One rightly distinguishes between his beloved and his friends; nevertheless, romantic love, a loving marriage, and true friendship inhabit the same household of loving duality.

The mode of encounter in friendship has the essential structures of the phenomenon of loving interpersonal relationships already examined. Here one greets another in a direct, heart-to-heart way. There is a shared understanding of each other within a mutually formed world; it is a world of We-two which can interpenetrate the furthest boundaries of the world of singularity. Your good friend knows what is in your heart and on your mind. He knows who you are, and his knowledge can give you a sense of identity and integrity. The exchange of insight and affirmation is reciprocal; and it is sustained through mutual fidelity. In friendship you stand in a common world with a common destiny. There is a unity of purpose as each wills the best for his friend and the friendship. Similar to the dialectical unity of romantic love there is in friendship mutual exchange, give and take, making yourself present and receiving presence. Yet there are differences in the details; the slight alterations in the basic structures give friendship different specific meanings from those encountered in romance. The spatialization of friendship is slightly different, which is obvious merely in terms of respect for bodily distance.[38] Where lovers embrace for an extended duration, friends touch each other with a handshake or a brief hug. In romance there are often long moments of staring into each other's eyes, as though soul is merging into soul; friends are content with an exchange of looks. Yet in friendship as in romance, spatialization is a cooperative venture. To be with a good friend is to be at home in the world with another. The temporality of friendship is also constituted by an ecstasy of meaningful duration in which the whole history of each being is affirmed in mutual presence. The time when friends are together transcends the worry and attentiveness so apparent in the world of practical and social existence. The destiny of two friends as persons is encountered and affirmed as they stand with each other and for each other. Their mutual presence does not necessarily ring with the sounds of eternity as does the ecstasy of romance. The world of friendship is a world of We-two, yet there is a greater emphasis upon distance; there is more elbow-room for freedom to be a singular self. In the embrace of love the intentional structure is directed toward achieving a perfect union. The two become

[38] Binswanger also discusses friendship briefly in *Grundformen und Erkenntnis Menschlichen Daseins*, pp. 221 ff.

one flesh, not thereby losing freedom but uncovering *a freedom to be one* in a complementing, mutually enriching duality. In friendship's unity there is *a freedom to be two*. In both modes of communion there is transcendence over the distance established by social roles. In true love and friendship two persons confront each other openly without secrets, for they know that only as their freedom moves in concert will they forge a common world of personal freedom.

To mark off friendship more clearly from other forms of social relations, a suggestion from Binswanger is helpful; he pointed out that there are diverse forms of sharing. One can share a common cause, a common allegiance, a common activity, and even share an idea with another.[39] Though there is in some sense a common world, there is not necessarily a direct confrontation of an I with a Thou. The common historicity of sharing an idea or a social cause moves along the path of concern. Only when two persons engage one another so that their personal histories merge, as when they face a common fate together, does the reality of sharing partake of the personal world of We. The phenomenon of communication can and does occur within social existence as structured by concern; here one imparts content to my mind for me to analyze and think about. Yet communication can also be personal revelation and exchange in the mode of duality, as when an I communicates to a Thou not something about himself but communicates himself "in person," as we say. Impersonal conversation becomes genuinely personal communication when you realize that my language is me, and you receive not merely the words that I say but receive my world into yours.[40] Communication which focuses upon an impersonal content of words spoken or gestures made is within the modality of taking. Here individuals take hold of a meaning which they can agree upon. The meaning then has social validity.

Only as communication becomes an exchange not merely of things but more basically of persons with and to each other does it spatialize itself within the possibility of a loving We. If you tell me your problems I may feel sorry for you, and I may pity your plight; but not until I stand with

---

[39] *Ibid.*, pp. 227 ff.

[40] See again Beulah Parker, *My Language Is Me.* This psychiatrist reveals in detail the historical transaction between herself and a schizophrenic adolescent whose autistic and mechanical language, she discovered, was really his attempt to speak personally about himself and their relationship. By penetrating to the personal depths of his bizarre language, she was able to establish direct communication with his world; gradually he was able to identify with hers.

you in your place and face your historical destiny with you as We-two, so that this historical commitment is no longer yours but ours, is there the love rightly spoken of as friendship. In this context the French proverb proves right: "They only are true friends who think as one." The one who will help you lift your burdens from your chest may be a sympathetic acquaintance; he is not by that action alone the friend you rely upon for trust, from whom you derive the courage to face even the anxiety of death, and with whom you are free spontaneously to be yourself. Your friend becomes the voice of authentic conscience saying: "Become who you are!" A friend carries you in his heart and sees the world through your eyes; thus you see yourself through his love. Binswanger strongly emphasized the difference between the well-meaning stranger or acquaintance, perhaps a doctor, who is authentically concerned about your existence, your welfare, in Heidegger's phrase (*Fürsorge*), and the friend who gives you freedom by shaping with you the common world that transcends yours and mine in the new world that is ours.[41] We hope to encounter many benevolent acquaintances; but they will never take the place of one good friend. Perhaps the main trouble with Heidegger's characterization of authentic existence is that such an individual is not really lovable. He may stand out from the man sunk in frivolity and mediocrity, but he also is strikingly different from anyone I could call my "friend." The true friend is distinct from both the totally concerned being and the careless lover; although there is to be found more concern in friendship than in romance, nevertheless the underlying structure of friendship, the basis of its community, is the basic existential possibility of loving duality. As such, each friendship provides the possibility of enlarged freedom through the increased expansion of the interpersonal world. With each friend there is a new call of conscience toward one's personal destiny; for a friend also becomes the voice of conscience calling *us* to *ourselves*. Each friend provides a new criterion for decision and action as well as an impetus for greater existential meaning.

Yet each friend confronts us with another possibility of death, his death, which, within the world of We-two, will also be ours. Every time we lose a friend we die a little. Similarly there is also a greater possibility of loneliness, as well as a new possibility of the fall of love into concern, indifference, or alienation. The saying of the Son of Sirach remains wisdom for our day: "A faithful friend is a sturdy shelter: he that has found one

41 Binswanger, *Grundformen*, pp. 240 ff.

has found a treasure" (Ecclesiasticus 6:14). One highly unfortunate aspect of contemporary mobility is that people move so frequently that friends often do not find the geographic proximity to allow their friendship to grow. Even with regular correspondence it is difficult to mature together in a common world that is personally "ours" and not by and large the world of social existence. The effects of this problem reverberate through modern marriages, which in turn are made to carry most of the burden of intimacy; not surprisingly this leads some marriages to crack under the strain.

A brilliant portrayal of the phenomenon of friendship was made by Albert Camus in his deeply humanistic novel, *The Plague*. A self-sacrificing doctor, Rieux, has tirelessly given himself to minister to those suffering from a bubonic plague which has struck the Algerian city, Oran. During the course of the novel he is joined by a Frenchman, Tarrou, who has been trapped in the town by a quarantine act which has isolated the city. They freely share a common destiny, which is to bring relief to those who are afflicted with the plague. In their common battle against this evil and in pursuit of a commonly recognized good, they become more than coworkers; gradually they sense that they have become friends. One evening when they have a brief respite from tending to the sick, they are alone on a terrace overlooking the harbor. Tarrou asks: "Can I regard you as a friend?" Dr. Rieux answers, "Yes. Of course we're friends; only, so far we haven't had much time to show it." [42] With this vote of confidence, a mutual recognition of their friendship, Tarrou proceeds to tell Rieux the story of his life; that is, he shares his very private world with its experiences of value as well as horror, so that it also becomes part of Rieux's world.

Tarrou also confesses that he has a deep sense of corporate guilt over the deaths of thousands of people, because he has tacitly approved acts and principles that have been responsible for their deaths. He had come to realize that he was in the world *with* others, sharing with them a living humanity and also a responsibility for their well-being, a responsibility which he was aware that he had not fulfilled. The awareness of guilt caused him to be suspicious of himself and then of others, so that he had lost any sense of peace in the world.

We can't stir a finger in this world without the risk of bringing death to somebody. . . . We all have the plague, and I have lost my peace. . . . Each of us has the plague within him; no one on earth is free from it. And I know, too, that we must keep endless watch on ourselves lest in

[42] A. Camus, *The Plague*, pp. 227-228.

a careless moment we breathe in somebody's face and fasten the infection on him.[43]

Obviously he is speaking here of the plague equivocally and is also referring to an existential condition in which men are threats to each other, the cause of suspicion, *dis-ease*, and death. He sees three alternatives to existence: to be a victim; to avoid as far as possible by isolation the forces of the spiritual pestilence; and to be a true healer following the path of sympathy. To Tarrou that latter path means to become a saint; to Rieux it means to be a man. In friendship they maintain a common stance in a shared history which is directed toward the goal of fulfilled human existence and involves personal risk in warding off those forces which would prohibit it. Their relationship provides an unacknowledged fourth alternative of friendship, which makes the third both possible and richly meaningful.

Communication has been established, and the friendship has been sealed in mutual understanding. Then Tarrou suggests that they do something for friendship's sake. They agree to go for a swim. Walking together they move down onto the jetty, then onto the rocks against which the waves are breaking gently in the otherwise still, dark night.

> Before them the darkness stretched out into infinity. Rieux could feel under his hand the gnarled, weather-worn visage of the rocks, and a strange happiness possessed him. Turning to Tarrou, he caught a glimpse on his friend's face of the same happiness, a happiness that forgot nothing, not even murder.
>
> They undressed, and Rieux dived in first. After the first shock of cold had passed and he came back to the surface the water seemed tepid. When he had taken a few strokes he found that the sea was warm that night with the warmth of autumn seas that borrow from the shore the accumulated heat of the long days of summer. The movement of his feet left a foaming wake as he swam steadily ahead, and the water slipped along his arms to close in tightly on his legs. A loud splash told him that Tarrou had dived. Rieux lay on his back and stayed motionless, gazing up at the dome of sky lit by the stars and moon. He drew a deep breath. Then he heard a sound of beaten water, louder and louder, amazingly clear in the hollow silence of the night. Tarrou was coming up with him, he now could hear his breathing.
>
> Rieux turned and swam level with his friend, timing his stroke to his. But Tarrou was the stronger swimmer and Rieux had to put on speed to keep up with him. For some minutes they swam side by side, with the

[43] *Ibid.*, pp. 234-235.

same zest, in the same rhythm, isolated from the world, at last free of the town and of the plague. Rieux was the first to stop and they swam back slowly, except at one point, where unexpectedly they found themselves caught in an ice-cold current. Their energy whipped up by this trap the sea had sprung on them, both struck out more vigorously.

They dressed and started back. Neither had said a word, but they were conscious of being perfectly at one, and that the memory of this night would be cherished by them both. When they caught sight of the plague watchman, Rieux guessed that Tarrou, like himself, was thinking the disease had given them a respite, and this was good, but now they must set their shoulders to the wheel again.[44]

The two friends now clearly exist within a common world of We where they sense that they are united. Their experience is one of ecstasy in which they are no longer prisoners to the world of concern, suspicion, and fragmentation. The rest of the town lived as though it had no future, so burdened were the people by the past and the unbearable present. These friends were transported into the ecstatic unity of a meaningful personal history, into the time of presence, which recollected the past, affirmed the present, and which gave them the courage to face the future that included returning to their task in the social world with detached resignation and compassion. In a situation of universal alienation where each kept his distance from others as though each had been exiled from humanity, their friendship provided them with a home of trust, freedom, and joy. The townsfolk gradually had sunk down into the dreariness of an exiled life, losing "the power of imagining the intimacy that once was theirs, or understanding what it can be to live with someone whose life is wrapped up in yours." [45] As people had become separated from each other they ceased to be truly historical, losing their possible humanity by allowing the imagination and freedom of love to disappear, as though without a trace. What the rest were losing by submission to an oppressive present these two friends recovered through the transport of friendship, which opened to them a world that was authentically human because it was grounded in love.

As Camus's description would indicate, true friendship is a genuinely mature phenomenon; unlike adolescent chumship or romantic love it is fully aware of responsibilities within the secular world. It is love which is not only responsive to friendly coinherence and exchange but is also re-

44 *Ibid.*, pp. 238-239.
45 *Ibid.*, p. 169.

sponsible for the totality of being in the world which includes profound respect for another's individuality and for needs and rights of the society in which friendship occurs. Both true friendship and romantic love have a certain isolation from public life; friendship, however, can occur and express itself more easily in public view, within the framework provided by secular existence.

Binswanger suggested that psychotherapy is properly to be understood not as a curative technique, nor as an art, but as a form of friendship. The psychiatrist is secondarily treating a patient; primarily he is engaged with a person whose existence is extremely unfortunate. To understand and assist the patient the doctor must renounce somewhat his own particular perspective and enter the unfortunate world that confronts him. He is to see things through the patient's eyes, to become aware of his history and his destiny and to face with him his fate. *Mutatis mutandis* the same can be said for the teacher, the counselor, and the pastor. It is by sharing the weight of another's problems with him that the other finds the freedom to see beyond the hold his restricted world has upon him. As a sufferer is able to see that he no longer exists imprisoned in isolation, cut off from the warmth of intimacy; as he sees his world through friendship, he uncovers a history bright with meaningful freedom and hope that is grounded by love. St. Paul wrote, "Bear one another's burdens, and so fulfill the law of Christ" (Galatians 6:2). Phenomenological analysis would suggest that the realization of that exhortation and the fulfillment of that law within this fallen world will occur as we truly befriend each other and face our historical responsibilities not as resigned individuals but as persons who affirm the history which belongs to us both.

6. LOVE AND MARRIAGE

There is one possibility in interpersonal existence in which meanings of romance and friendship may interpenetrate to such an extent that a new world can evolve marked by deep personal happiness and fulfillment; this possibility is to be found in marriage. To celebrate love and marriage, however, is to acknowledge a possibility, not applaud a universal fact. That many people suffer marriage rather than enjoy it, and frustrate themselves jointly as well as individually, adding misery upon misery, is a fact too patent to be ignored or denied. Phenomenology is only interested in the truth of human existence; it has already exposed much sham and pretense in modern living and should continue to do. However it also serves to call attention to alternatives in which the truth may be found and lived. Some of the pain and misfortune encountered in many marriages arises from intense personality clashes, unrealistic or unfair demands and expectations placed upon the marriage partner, and from mutual selfishness, or what Erich Fromm in *The Art of Loving* aptly called "egoism *à deux*." Yet much of it is also due to faulty images of marriage, love, and personal existence; it is here that existential phenomenology can be of service by providing, as this book has attempted to do, an understanding of love and existence, as well as insight into some common roadblocks to authentic personal development. In this way the phenomenology of existence and love may alleviate some of our universal handicaps.

Though scores of witnesses have called attention to hazards of married life and its increasingly high mortality rate in our culture, nevertheless marriage and the family are recognized and established modern institutions. There is little question that these institutions will disappear; but there is little doubt that their meanings have altered considerably and will continue to do so. In the days of chivalry it would have been quite improper to attempt to integrate romance and marriage. Marriage was serious business designed to perpetuate the family and society and to socialize all the family members; romance served no such serious purpose. Our culture, however, has gone far in the attempt to idolize and institutionalize romance within marriage; this trend is responsible for a good part of the dilemma of modern marriage. As shown previously, the idolatry of romance is really one of the most serious enemies of love. Romance is a form of love, but it is not an enduring one; it is like a blossom that must die to the transformation which will produce the fruit. Another difficulty in contemporary culture comes from the fact that marriage is a mature institution, whereas many of our widespread values and behavior patterns are basically juvenile. In his disturbingly perceptive book, *Culture against Man*, Jules Henry noted the prevalence of juvenile attitudes in adult American society which are felt particularly in the family. Mature love involves suffering and requires a dying to an autonomous self; in a juvenile world this fact is unrecognized or misunderstood. Juvenile freedom is typically conceived individualistically; mature personal freedom is understood from within the world of loving duality. To juvenile adults the goal is thought of in terms of pleasure and individual satisfaction. Many marital relationships are unfortunately constituted by much wishful thinking and self-centered manipulation of another. If marriage is conceived as a juvenile relationship or within the framework of an individualistic social existence, then perhaps it makes sense to speak of a marriage relationship in terms of reciprocal gratification of needs and attempt to work out a mutually satisfactory system of rewards. But it has been a major aim of this book to resist reducing love to something else; to understand the truth of love it is essential to see it in terms of the basic intersubjective mode of duality.

Sensible and practical manuals of marriage do well to point out the dangers of identifying romance with marriage and are often useful guides to those who seek to make marriage into a positive working relationship. The trouble with those approaches which glorify romance is that they sentimentalize and thereby falsify both marriage and love; but those which disparage romance in favor of something more realistic and perhaps more honest neglect ecstasy. There seems to be a great "hunger" in modern culture for ecstasy; it is a legitimate hunger, for ecstasy is a "need" that human existence has to transcend the present facts into future possibilities and to move toward personal fulfillment. One aspect of ecstatic existence in love has been observed in romance. Certainly the newly married couple will continue for a while to taste romantic ecstasy; and it is entirely possible, perhaps desirable, that the couple will occasionally find the re-emergence of romance after the honeymoon. However, the greatest reward of marriage is not romance but intimacy. When two persons are married in love, their relationship is structured by duality. The two become one flesh; yet in this union their individual differences are affirmed. This is especially apparent in sexual intercourse. In sexual union grounded in love each partner discovers that he or she is at home with another who is very different and that their lives nevertheless have become one.[46] In the communion of love they sense that there is a bond uniting them; their individual histories interpenetrate to form a common history. They share in each

---

[46] For a Christian understanding of the theology of sex within marriage see D. S. Bailey, *The Mystery of Love and Marriage*. Bailey sees sex as a sacrament embodying and expressing the spiritual union of two persons, borrowing heavily from Buber's philosophy. For a perceptive discussion of the problems of contemporary married love as this is battered by rapidly changing cultural forces, see Gibson Winter's *Love and Conflict*. For a standard, positive study of the family see Robert F. Winch, *The Modern Family*; and also *Selected Studies in Marriage and the Family*. Winch unfortunately reinterprets love in terms of social existence in *Mate-Selection: A Study of Complementary Needs*. The mates he studied *took* an interest in each other; but if they only learned to gratify each other's needs, they have not yet found love.

other's world, they understand life in terms of a united destiny, and they rejoice in each other's presence. Love brings them into an ecstatic new world of peace and gladness. As they find themselves in common agreement and in mutual understanding they move toward the building of a new world founded upon We-two.

The transcendence of love does not, however, move in one direction. Existence in love is directed toward the fulfillment of the other, the fulfillment of self, and the fulfillment of this new world in which two are one. In marriages grounded on love it is a common experience that having pledged oneself to another, one discovers that he is also more free to be himself. Love interpenetrates singular existence, enabling an individual to cope more adequately with problems, to be more certain of insight and judgment, to be more courageous in developing a particular talent or pursuing a special interest. Love overcomes the terrors of anxiety and helps to break down the constriction of self-systems. While establishing communion, love also strengthens and enhances individuals: "Make thy love larger to enlarge my worth," Mrs. Browning wrote to her husband. The individuals whose marriage exists in the world of love find themselves increasingly glad to be alive and proud of their own unique contribution to existence. Yet there is a sense of gratitude that the new individual strength and freedom has been received as a gift from the other partner. In the special intimacy which emerges within married love the partners together develop skills particularly suited toward fuller personal existence, such as the ability to sympathize with another, communicate directly with feeling as well as with intelligence, and to relax in another's presence and be ready for surprises. The ecstasy of love in marriage is not a hot flash, but it carries a quiet awe that endures in peace.

Love in marriage also interpenetrates the concerns of social existence. There is a family to be cared for; and there is a society, a large common world, which must be served. Love strengthens persons toward freer and more fortunate involvement within society and in everyday practical concerns. The social direction of love in marriage will often become dominant with the appearance of children in the home. Erikson has suggested that at this point a new stage in personal evolution begins, which he referred to as *generativity*, in the sense that partners are engaged "primarily in establishing and guiding the next generation." [47] In this stage love definitely reaches into structures of concern, taking care for health, learning, the

[47] E. Erikson, *Childhood and Society*, pp. 266 ff.

development of character, social justice, and countless other important matters. Parents express love through concern, by caring about the whole being of each child. Parental love requires not merely the bestowal of trust and affection but also guidance according to intelligence, worldly knowledge, and self-restraint. In this stage it is particularly important for marriage partners to become collaborators, working in concert for the best interests of the entire family. As they share a common life and purpose, husband and wife develop the communion and mutual respect of good friends.

In this stage of human development the meaning of fidelity becomes more fully apparent. Like all personal histories, married love must endure tests of conflict and periods of loneliness. To endure in its own special truth, the new world of love requires fidelity. The faithfulness needed to make a true marriage exceeds the boundaries of sex. To be faithful to another means to affirm the truth of the other and at the same time to be faithful to the love in which the marriage is grounded. By being faithless to the other, one destroys intimacy; and one is thereby faithless to himself and the truth which the other has helped to create and make manifest. Faithfulness in marriage is also an affirmation of freedom; and for individuals to enlarge their freedom within love there must be reciprocal fidelity. Furthermore parents must not only be faithful to each other but to their children. Though couples may learn to respect the integrity of each other, their insight into the meaning of love seems to become myopic when it comes to their children. The truth of duality is that love demands a certain distance from the other with whom one shares communion. Personal union is not absorption; it involves affirmation of otherness. Yet parents frequently attempt to possess their children, to invade their privacy, to direct rather than guide their development, to curtail their freedom supposedly in their children's best interests. To become a good parent requires that one become a good and wise person; and in terms of love that means at least to encourage the other to develop his own distinctive singular existence. The phenomenology of love has indicated that apart from a deep sense of home and presence in the lived world an individual will evolve an unfortunate form of existence. But presence is not possession. To be present to another is to share in his freedom, not control it; to be present to another means to affirm his destiny, not define it. To be faithful in love is to affirm the freedom of others for a variety of encounters. To be faithful is to be open to the authentic possibilities of someone else as well as of oneself. As one learns to be true to his mate and to his children, the scope of his freedom is enlarged and the possibility of more meaningful personal involvement with increasingly more people is considerably improved.

In the home and presence of married love the ecstasies of duality and singularity are heightened. At least from this phenomenology of existence and love it would appear that the greatest possibility for the growth and fulfillment of personal existence is to be found in married love. In a justly celebrated sermon on the meaning of marriage Jeremy Taylor wrote:

> For there is nothing can please a man without love; . . . but when a man dwells in love, then the breasts of his wife are pleasant as the droppings upon the hill of Hermon, her eyes are fair as the light of heaven, she is a fountain sealed, and he can quench his thirst, and ease his cares, and lay his sorrows down upon her lap. . . . No man can tell but he that loves his children, how many delicious accents make a man's heart dance in the pretty conversation of those dear pledges; their childishness, their stammering, their little angers, their innocence, their imperfections, their necessities are so many little emanations of joy and comfort to him that delights in their persons and society. . . . She that is loved is safe, and he that loves is joyful. Love is a union of all things excellent; it contains in it proportion and satisfaction, and rest, and confidence. . . .[48]

In married love, persons encounter each other in ecstatic intimacy, believing in their common history but encouraging each other's singularity, rejoicing in each other's happiness and sorrowing in the other's disappointments and frustrations, bearing each other's burdens and yet at times forgetting the world of social existence to enjoy each other's presence. The family properly embraces a plurality of the modes of existence and love and in turn provides some of the richest meanings and the greatest joys that being in the world can attain.

7. LOVE AND PERSONAL MATURITY

Consideration of adult married love and the stage of generativity emerging in responsible family life points in the direction of that elusive phenomenon known as personal maturity. Unfortunately, in our effort to gain a trustworthy image of maturity social sciences, including psychoanalysis, have very little to say to us. The focus of psychoanalysis has been upon

---

[48] Jeremy Taylor, "The Marriage Ring," taken from *Master Sermons through the Ages*, W. A. Sadler, Jr., ed., pp. 115-116. I have attempted to state more fully the Christian meaning of marriage in a sermon; see "The Birth of a New Being," *The Pulpit*, Vol. XXXIX, No. 6 (June, 1968).

basic dynamic patterns in development up to or through adolescence; especially it has concentrated upon unfortunate processes and often it has given the impression that psychopathology is the guide for understanding normal life processes. It has also been highly unfortunate that some social scientists and psychoanalysts have suggested basic life goals which in reality pertain to very early developmental processes. Sullivan, for example, maintained that there were two general goals of living: satisfaction and security.[49] Yet Sullivan himself went far beyond these essentially infantile goals by his own repeated insistence that dynamisms are intentional structures; to understand and appreciate dynamisms we must attempt to discover their goals. He also stressed that human existence is oriented to meaning, that the person perceives significance.

We would logically expect life goals in Sullivan's system to have been formulated in terms of existential meanings rather than in terms of satisfaction of biopsychic tensions; certainly these minimal goals do not reveal the dynamisms motivating Sullivan as a courageous and compassionate therapist. His followers who have accepted his goals, have yet inevitably moved into discussions of the importance of insight for a changed attitude toward life and full self-realization; insight is a goal far beyond mere satisfaction and security.[50] Sullivan himself elsewhere admitted that human maturity does not really fall within the jurisdiction of psychiatry, largely because those persons who are mature do not present themselves for therapy or analytical scrutiny. Yet he suggested that from the process of therapy, understood from his perspective as a process of expanding interpersonal relationships, certain characteristics could be deduced. To him one of the most important accomplishments for a truly meaningful life was to establish intimacy successfully. Through intimacy one becomes sensitive to the needs, possibilities, limitations, interests, and anxieties of others. Certainly Sullivan moved beyond Freud's ambivalence toward love; his picture of maturity envisages an ever-expanding personality with widening and deepening interests and increasing involvement with more and more people.[51] The aim of psychiatry is to clear away those forces which restrict

[49] Sullivan, *Clinical Studies*, p. 10. Cf. the same view adopted by Frieda Fromm-Reichmann, *op. cit.*, pp. 8-9.

[50] See especially F. Fromm-Reichmann's approach to psychotherapy and life beyond it, *op. cit.* See also Clara Thompson, *Psychoanalysis: Evolution and Development*, ch. 11.

[51] Sullivan, *Interpersonal Theory*, pp. 309 ff. P. Rieff has demonstrated Freud's ambivalence to love. Though Freud proclaimed "love is the great educator," *op. cit.*, p. 169, yet he also portrayed love in dark shades reflecting greed, weakness, sadism, and irrationalism, etc., *Freud: The Mind of the Moralist*, pp. 234-241.

or prohibit truly collaborative, syntaxic experience, which is the foundation of maturity.

More recently, Doctors Pearce and Newton have suggested that the mature person is one whose life process is relatively unhampered by security operations and a dissociated past, who is thus free to move to the frontiers of experience and engage in ever-expanding consolidation of affectionate relationships.[52] These affectionate or loving relationships are clearly envisaged as involving both sharing with and commitment to another and at the same time freedom to develop one's own unique capacities. Furthermore, strong love between two persons is thought of not as an exclusive treasure to be hoarded but as the gaining of trust and understanding so as to give and accept mature love in an increasing circle of friends.[53]

These brief suggestions from American social science are nearly identical with those of Binswanger and European personalists. Within the perspective of existential phenomenology the deepest personal meanings of being in the world are to be found in historically open and creative individuality and in the give and take of personal exchange occurring within the coinherent reality of loving duality. The two basic modes of singularity and duality are not radically separate, nor do their histories follow parallel lines. The gift of true love provides the freedom for discovering the meanings of love and as well promotes the freedom for genuine self-expression. Love does not close the world to any basic possibilities except inauthentic ones. The dynamism of love actually opens up a plurality of worlds and holds them together in integral fashion so that an individual can embrace basic yet diverse meanings in his own history. The meaning of maturity seen through the eyes of love is existence becoming increasingly open to basic possibilities in the personal and secular worlds.

To reach the goal of mature personal existence requires that we become open. What I have in mind is not porousness like that of a sponge but what Marcel has called availability; this availability is more than an attitude, it is a way of being. The mature free man is one who is *available* in his situation. He is open to its movements, welcomes its presence, and responds to its calls. The man who has been freed from the threats of anxiety by love is free to be open to the totality of the strange and exciting

---

[52] Pearce and Newton, *op. cit.*, p. 118.

[53] *Ibid.*, pp. 193 ff. See also Fromm-Reichmann, *op. cit.*, pp. 34 ff. These writers would apparently have agreed with the humanistic convictions of L. Mumford who maintains that "no theory of human development is adequate that does not include this widening of the province of love" (*The Transformations of Man*, p. 173).

mystery of being in the world. As Marcel has suggested, this openness or availability is thoroughly historical. It is open to past, present, and future. Temporal openness directed toward existential truth involves penetrating reflection upon being in a particular historical situation. Existential reflection in the mode of availability is not confined to the present; its historicity involves being faithful to the past, being faithfully attentive to the present, and being creatively faithful to the future. Such reflection is the hallmark of wisdom, a virtue of maturity.

Personal maturity as availability is grounded in love; this love involves being honestly faithful to the past, trustful of the present, and hopeful of the future. Maturity is life which is both committed and free, loving and intelligent, receiving and giving, young in spirit and wise in understanding. To become mature is to become personal in an ever-expanding human world where one is rooted in the home of love and yet where one also moves to open up the frontiers of the world's horizon. Such a person is free, as we say, to be in love with life.

Erikson has suggested that the truly mature person has reached the last of eight stages of life, which he calls the stage of *ego integrity*. The word "integrity" refers to wholeness, which from our viewpoint may be understood as an ecstatic unity of historical being. To Erikson, integrity suggests an open acceptance of one's facticity; but beyond that it is an affirmation of man's "proclivity for order and meaning." We could say it involves becoming responsibly aware of the intentional structures of our existential historicity. Integrity is marked by existential integration within reasonable grounds; it is rewardingly meaningful existence which is at unity with itself. Integrity includes a deep appreciation of oneself that goes beyond narcissism, for it is essentially an affirmation of being in the world. This affirmation is in fact an expression of fidelity to the full possibilities of being in the world. Unlike narcissism, integrity includes the totality of being with others in genuine sympathy and understanding. Because integrity rests upon a deeply rooted trust not merely in one's own being but more so in the integrity of others, it is definitely grounded in love. Erikson's studies indicate that the integrity of an adult is actually born and nourished as he learned to trust in the integrity of his parents or some other significant adults.[54] The child is father of the man. If the man attains integrity, he is a man to be trusted, a person of compassion and good faith, and a reservoir of wisdom.

[54] E Erikson, *Childhood and Society*, pp. 268-269.

Clearly these insights will lead us beyond a conception of life's goal in terms of self-realization and toward an ethical understanding of maturity where goals are seen in terms of responsibilities and service to others. It is well and good to imagine ego identity in the heights, depths, lengths, and breadths of experience; but knowledge of the barriers to integrated and self-expressive historical existence should direct us toward responsible action to overcome them. In the words of another writer who represents a phenomenological approach, a mature personality will be "a totality which harmoniously integrates a multiplicity of modes of existence," in a dynamic process which is ever open to the realization of new and more profound meanings. The mature person is one who has come to himself, who has gained awareness of his historical being in the world; but his insight is that he has been called forth as a person by others. To fulfill the meaning of maturity involves openness to experience; but it also requires responsibility in experience: "the most fundamental characteristic of the true personality is constant readiness to respond fully to the demands of reality." [55]

Insight into the nature of human existence both leads into and provides a basis for genuinely humanistic ethics. To become deeply and intensively alive does not stop at self-realization; to Erikson, maturity requires the application of the Golden Rule in all phases of interpersonal life. Integrity means allowing that rule to be integrated into all stages of life. Being mature means to be open not merely to one's own possibilities but to those of others as well; it is to become actively engaged in supporting the other in his being in the world as you expect and need him to support you.[56] The application of the Golden Rule applies not merely to individuals but to families, societies, and even nations. In all aspects this involves an affirmation of the full historicity of the Other which will strengthen him in his development toward a goal which is recognized neither as exclusively his or mine but as ours. Our phenomenology has indicated that in the vision of love we can see the destiny of mankind in terms of what Erikson calls a "common future identity." [57] The common identity of man is a historical possibility that opens up in the world of duality. To develop insight into basic possibilities and to practice ethical responsibility

[55] A. van Kaam, *Religion and Personality*, pp. 80-81. A similar emphasis has been powerfully expressed by Teilhard de Chardin; see especially his books *Le Divin Milieu*, *The Hymn of the Universe*, and *The Future of Man*.
[56] E. Erikson, "The Golden Rule in the Light of New Insight," *Insight and Responsibility*, p. 233.
[57] *Ibid.*, p. 242.

based upon such insight is not a matter to be taken casually. In reminding us of our task and our promise as human beings, Erikson has written:

> The nature of history is about to change. . . . Joint survival demands that man visualize new ethical alternatives fit for newly developing as well as over-developed systems and identities. A more universal standard of perfection will mediate more realistically between man's inner and outer worlds than did the compromises resulting from the reign of moral absolutes; it will acknowledge the responsibility of each individual for the potentialities of all generations and of all generations for each individual, and this in a more informed manner than has been possible in past systems of ethics.[58]

Existential phenomenology would clarify and amplify Sullivan's and Erikson's schemes through the images of world and encounter. To discover that man is being in the world is to realize that all human living is historical encounter. To be in the world is to encounter it. To encounter people means two possibilities: to encounter them personally or impersonally, as members of society or as persons, though these possibilities obviously do not exclude each other. Both possibilities are legitimate and both are necessary to authentically personal life. To encounter another human being is not, however, to encounter an object in an external world; it means to meet another being in the world. To meet a person is to encounter another world. The security operations of our self-system lead us, however, to construct a world that is on the defensive. Our world sees another world as a possible threat. So in our encounter with others we often see them as strangers, as foreigners from a different world that puts our tidy world in jeopardy. The security forces in our defense system inevitably suggest that if we cannot eliminate this threat by violence or selective inattention which just "forgets" that the other world exists, then we must attempt to domesticate that unknown and potentially unruly world. The tactics we use are to convince the other that our world is better than his and so has a greater legitimacy of being. He may be persuaded to be robbed of his world and made a prisoner of our own. The loss unfortunately is twofold. Not only has his world been transformed out of all possible authenticity but our world has again successfully refused to profit from experience, so that our defense system is all the tighter. In this operation both of us have closed the doors to personal freedom.

Existential insight has suggested that to find the truth of being in the

[58] *Ibid.*, p. 157.

world one must recognize that his being in the world is with other world-designing beings. The voice of love does not repudiate another world but confirms its being and its authentic possibilities. To respond to the call of love means to encounter persons as personal worlds and to be open both to affirm their unique worlds and to expand our own by sharing in them. The way of love and maturity is for two worlds to interpenetrate. To respect and affirm a world is to support the other in his attempt to ward off anxiety by creating between us the trust that each of us needs to allow the human world to be open for healthy expansion toward personal possibilities. That is to make a home for personal existence to live in.

A second insight necessary for maturity is to recognize that to meet another person is to encounter a personal history. In the secular world we encounter people primarily in an instrumental fashion, which is to be aware of them as behavioral objects who perform particular functions within a given field. That is to be aware of them in terms of the present. But to meet a person is also to confront a past and a future; this involves becoming aware of another as a historical being. To see the Other historically is to recognize this being as a bearer of a plurality of historical meanings. To confront him in the present is to engage yourself with a person who has already experienced tensions and satisfactions, who has battled with anxiety, and has enjoyed victories and suffered defeats, who has known the freedom of love and the imprisonment of anxiety and loneliness, and whose past has been directed into this present which is leading into a future that may appear to him to be either desirable or horrible. To encounter another as a historical being is to be aware of the defenses and the hopes of the past that lead him to expect and need certain satisfactions in the present. To encounter another history in love is to affirm the basic possibilities of this particular history, which is to affirm the future of another in terms of its possible authenticity. To encounter a personal history is to look toward its destiny through the eyes of the other as well as your own so that he may gain a true vision of himself, a vision that comes through the eyes of one who sees him in love. In meeting a friend or a stranger, existence calls to us to act benevolently toward him, affirming both his world and his historical destiny. The classic parable of Jesus stated this truth dramatically. On the road to Jericho several priests passed by a man who had been violently interrupted on his journey. They looked upon him in terms of the present, as a stranger, a threat, a dying man. An unknown man from Samaria responded to the injured traveler not merely as a victim of the present but as a man with a history; he encountered him as a historical-personal being who had a possible future for the growth of freedom, love, and maturity. The Samaritan responded as one who affirmed the right of that other particular being in the world to exist, to continue to unfold in the mystery of the lived world. The wisdom of Jesus here was to indicate that whenever we go and do likewise the history of each of us will be infinitely richer.

The direction of this chapter has been toward the illumination of the centrality of love in the whole course of existence toward its authentic destiny. It has been my conviction that love is not only the power necessary for existence to develop positively through each stage of life toward genuine maturity but that love is also the key needed to open our understanding of distinctively personal existence. Lewis Mumford wrote:

> In the development of the person love is actually the central element of integration: love as erotic desire and procreativeness, love as passion and aesthetic delight, lingering over images of beauty and shaping them anew, love as fellow feeling and neighborly helpfulness, bestowing its gifts on those who need them, love as parental solicitude and sacrifice, finally, love with its miraculous capacity for overvaluing its own object, thereby glorifying it and transfiguring it, releasing for life something that only the lover at first can see. Without a positive concentration upon love in all its phases, we can hardly hope to rescue the earth and all the creatures that inhabit it from the insensate forces of hate, violence, and destruction that now threaten it. And without a philosophy of the person, who dares talk of love? [59]

One of the insights of existential phenomenology has been, of course, that it is precisely a concentration upon the phenomenon of love which provides us with a comprehensive and trustworthy philosophy of the person.

8. LOVE AND THE ULTIMATE MEANING OF EXISTENCE

Nevertheless, one cannot speak about a full understanding of the person without considering the phenomenon of religion. As Kierkegaard insisted, beyond the stage of ethical responsibility and philosophical reflection lies the final stage on life's way, religious existence. As he so characteristically put it, "It is really the God-relationship that makes a man a man." This disturbing voice of the past is still a provocative testimony to the final meaning of existence; and the religious modality he represented is owed an

[59] L. Mumford, *The Transformations of Man*, p. 176.

attentive hearing. Even without moving into the area of theology we must admit that the picture of man which has thus far emerged from within the new humanism of existential phenomenology is incomplete. We have not explored the particular historical encounter which has commonly been designated religious experience, or what from a theological perspective might be called graceful being in the world. Unless there is immediate and conclusive evidence to the contrary, it could be that religious existence constitutes a basic and decisive human possibility, in spite of a negative evaluation of religion from much contemporary theology.

According to William James, who was a pioneer in the scientific-humanistic approach to religious phenomena, the most profound kind of religious experience such as regeneration or redemption is "one fundamental form of human experience," regardless of what its source and ultimate significance might be.[60] The kind of religious experience which most interested James involved the individual's surrender of his total self to Reality; and yet after surrendering, the individual paradoxically found himself renewed in an extraordinary way. That is, the most profound religious experience is a type of the "dying and behold we live" variety. In his classic study of individual religious experiences James came to the conclusion that the quality of religious experience is unique, something that "we meet nowhere else." [61] Though he amply demonstrated numerous forms of psychopathology which have become attached to religion, he held that at its best religion is a personal experience which produces an expansiveness of the self that would seem even to transcend the ecstasy of existential openness already considered.[62] Unique effects of personal redemption, as James understood it, are to produce in the individual a sense of harmony (peace),

---

60 W. James, *The Varieties of Religious Experience*, p. 108.

61 *Ibid.*, p. 45. Similar to numerous theologians James distinguished religion from ethics. To him religion meant a kind of spontaneous and total response to a living presence considered to be divine. Ethics or morality, which requires volitional resignation toward a condition which is not yet present, is primarily concerned with an ought. James came close to the suggestion made by Erikson that religion deals with a basic trust in life; as such it is the foundation of man's radical openness to discovery, growth, and personal relationships. James would not have agreed with Rudolf Otto's insistence that religious experience is structured by a mental a priori; nor would he have moved in the direction of stereotyping religious experience in terms of a numinous *Mysterium Tremendum*. The point of his study was to demonstrate the varieties of religious experiences. Otto's study moves within an idealistic perspective in which there is a search for the essence of religious experience; James adapted a radically pluralistic perspective. The latter's position may also be contrasted with phenomenological studies by G. van der Leeuw and M. Eliade which have sought to construct formal essences of some supposedly ideal type of religious experience.

62 James, *Varieties*, p. 74.

a new awareness of the meaning of life through radical reorientation around a new center of interest (faith), and an insight into a bright new world wherein personal existence finds the dimensions in which fulfillment becomes a possibility (hope).[63] James was most concerned to find the pragmatic meaning of religion in terms of the psychological fruits produced by it. Those fruits which he discovered and prized highly were the acquisition of increased freedom and an expansive personality, a sense of historical continuity or identity, along with such virtues as courage, resignation, patience, trust, and love.[64]

Toward the conclusion of his study, in which he moved further away from analysis toward interpretation, he suggested that religious faith has a unique basic function in the economy of personal development, which is to awaken men to a divine Presence with whom human existence finds its highest perfection. Certainly our existential phenomenology has not explored this possibility of being in the world; and thus we must acknowledge that a complete vision of man in his wholeness, man as he is in truth, has not been attained through this new approach. Further studies of human transcendence, of man in ecstasy, are required; and these must include a focus upon religious phenomena, not merely in terms of individual experience but also in the form of interpersonal relationships and corporate existence. To further our understanding of man it is also highly desirable that a dialogue between existential phenomenology and theology occur. Here is not the place to pursue this matter; but a few suggestions can be made which will be relevant toward initiating conversation.

The first has to do with demanding some honest confessions from theology that some religious language is guilty of prevarication, particularly as a disguise for existential weaknesses. Self-criticism is a fact of life in the best philosophy and science; if the same does not exist in theology, then it just has not yet caught up to their level. Phenomenology in particular has attempted to get beyond mere words to experience itself. From Husserl onward the phenomenological movement has been discontented with traditional formulations, particularly those about the nature of man; we are well aware that human beings easily settle down with prejudices and abstractions which conceal more than they reveal about life. Existential phenomenology has sought to discover and verify meanings in the context of historical encounter. It would share contemporary suspicion about the existential meaning of much religious language. Like James we would want

---

[63] *Ibid.*, p. 242.
[64] *Ibid.*, pp. 266-273.

religion to be put to the pragmatic test; further, we want to discover how it actually works upon individuals and groups, apart from their own interpretations. For example, in theological language, a particular war may be a holy crusade; from every other point of view it is an act of violent self-assertion. Similar judgments could be made of a host of religious attestations. This is not to ask theology to engage in religious debunking so popular with numerous contemporary religious sociologists. What I am suggesting is that theology share in the question raised by numerous disciplines of a particular religious experience: What does this encounter really mean to our world?

As an example, phenomenology might challenge religious claims to salvation, or theological affirmations to the extent that some particular history is redemptive. Is the religious testimony at all commensurate with existential facts? Of course if a theologian asserts a complete dichotomy between the sacred and the profane, then any mutual communication is precluded. Supposing that division is not made, then there is evidence which has to be faced. Traditional language of salvation in numerous major religions of the world has claimed that religious experience provides the authentic way to achieve personal fulfillment and maturation; salvation means wholeness and refers to a process of discovering one's true identity and becoming fully integrated. Enormous amounts of evidence from a variety of social sciences indicate that much redemptive religion, such as Christianity, at least in contemporary society, is part and parcel with attempts to establish a kind of juvenile identity, to avoid mature responsibility for large problems by focusing selfishly upon trivial private ones, to perpetuate advantageous inequitable systems by appealing to an infallible divine law, and so forth. Religion has been used as a handy device to dodge facing oneself in depth, to gain cheap reassurance, to cover up numerous destructive dynamisms that retard the process of maturation in oneself and others.[65]

Since existential phenomenology has been particularly concerned to discover meanings of human existence in the light of basic historical possi-

---

[65] In addition to the classic work by James, many studies, particularly those in the Freudian psychoanalytic tradition, have more recently furnished us with evidence indicating the pathology of much individual religion. Other studies have indicated similar religious pathology on broader social dimensions, such as that done by G. Allport, *The Nature of Prejudice*. P. Berger's works in religious sociology make similar points dramatically; see, e.g., *The Precarious Vision*, and *The Noise of Solemn Assemblies*. For theologians who have shared this insight into pathological characteristics in religion without abandoning their convictions, see the essays dealing with moral and psychological objections to Christianity in A. Vidler, *Objections to Christian Belief*.

bilities and to set forth criteria for evaluating the process of personal maturation, we should question the meaning of theological language which speaks of salvation within a personal world that is more apparently the victim of terrifying anxiety. Numerous studies have indicated that for many, religion operates as a grandiose rationalization of primitive attempts to ward off anxiety; to use Sullivan's term, much religion could be understood as a universal self-system. Unfortunate forms of existence which are efforts to achieve security, even at the price of sacrificing personal maturation, have long been vested in sanctity. Now that we are aware of the massive threat anxiety plays in personal development it would be well to consider the possibility that much of what has traditionally been called sacred is little more than an elaborate self-system; and much traditionalism constitutes a massive self-system of corporate dimensions. The religious self-system has been made all the more secure because it has presented itself as above criticism or even above interpretation by worldly interests. Theology must be willing to recognize that much perverted and unfortunate existence has hidden itself in the skirts of religion, and that enemies to love and personal maturation have been tolerated through deferential attitudes to what is subsumed under the category of the sacred. What men in the past have called sacred we might today more wisely call sick. Much unfortunate high-flown existence has been revered as exceptionally pious; perverse eccentricity has been dubbed as quaint or has been tolerated, even revered, as loyal defense of sacred tradition; affected mannerisms have been evaluated as setting the style for truly religious existence; and thoroughly uncommitted, irresponsible existence has been lauded as otherworldly. What is needed is an investigation of the actual lived world from which religious testimony and interpretation have arisen and a willingness to assess the existential meaning of religious experience in a cooperative inter-disciplinary approach. The point here is not novel; but in spite of Freud, James, and a host of others, it has been all too easily ignored. Fortunately more and more theologians are becoming aware of the problem centering in the apparent discrepancy between religious language and existential truths. As one writer has tersely put it: "Now, as then, today as always, the Christian problem is to correlate the truth of Christianity with the empirical truths men live by, without confusing them." [66] The task to relate the

---

[66] G. Vahanian, *The Death of God*, p. 11. Strangely enough, after making this important point, Vahanian proceeds to criticize many truths men live by in a devastating fashion; and though his book terminates without a conclusion, he seems to imply a theological approach close to that of Barth, in which there is a sharp bifurcation between sacred and profane truths.

language of religious conviction to positive existential development does not, however, belong to Christianity alone. It is a responsibility which religion in general must assume and share with other disciplines in a common humanistic endeavor to understand man in terms of his highest possibilities.

A second step in the process of existential verification of the meanings of religious experience is more positive and even more challenging. The philosopher Ronald Hepburn stated a position which has importance beyond even his own concerns:

> If the theologian is to communicate at all, he must establish some sort of contact points between his special senses of the words he uses and the ordinary senses of these words. If he has modified their meanings in using them to speak of God, he must show clearly the direction in which the modification has taken place. He must convince us, too, that the change of meaning is not so drastic as to erode away the entire sense the word originally possessed.[67]

In its original context his argument was to direct theologians toward the philosophy of logical analysis so as to reach a common understanding of what religious words may mean. However his argument has even more merit if it directs theologians to other disciplines which study distinctively human phenomena, and encourages them to become informed of the refined senses of words which emerge through research. Like existential phenomenology, theology must also turn "back to the things themselves," to the actual historical experience and its effects upon those persons who give religious testimony to the most authentic meaning of life.

If, for example, theologians cannot speak perceptively about the mystery of human love, how can they hope to communicate the meaning of divine love as an existential power? Much theological analysis has centered upon meanings of ancient words, which hardly represents an open encounter with contemporary existential facts. An alternative approach has been grandly represented by Paul Tillich. Using an ontological approach to love, he affirmed: "Life is being in actuality and love is the moving power of life. . . . Love is the drive towards the unity of the separated . . . as the reunion of the estranged." [68] Few theologians have been more influential

---

[67] R. Hepburn, Christianity and Paradox, pp. 6-7.

[68] P. Tillich, Love, Power, and Justice, p. 25. I have elsewhere offered a systematic critique of Tillich's ontological approach; see my Ludwig Binswanger's Existential Phenomenology, pp. 311-351. My criticism here of Tillich's broad generalization about the

for our era in recovering the importance of love for theology as well as for life than Tillich; yet his extremely broad definitions have not done much to clarify the full scope of love's meanings. In fact much language about love as a drive for reunion reflects an individualistic perspective that existential phenomenology has sought to overcome; and it leaves out of account crucial existential-historical structures, wherein the meaning of love becomes manifest. Theology must learn to honor the invitation offered by other disciplines to share in the pursuit for concrete and reliable insight into and understanding of man's greatness and misery within the context of the lived world. The need for religion to test its convictional language through a disciplined attention to experience is as relevant to its mission as it is to the development of theology. A Christian laywoman, Jessica Furlong, has pleaded that what is needed "is a new understanding of love, the love that casts out fears and enables men to face the realities of their condition." What is distressing is that religion, in her case the Christian Church, has talked so little about love as it is needed for personal growth; the Church's failure to grow in its understanding of love as an existential power "means that we are seriously handicapped in offering the love which we claim to be the Christian contribution to society." [69]

The dialogue between existential phenomenology and theology will require an open collaboration in an effort to uncover basic existential meanings. This collaboration will establish points in common upon which communication can be initiated and fruitfully extended. It would appear that existential phenomenology is particularly relevant to that type of theology which is increasingly oriented toward the phenomenon of man rather than bound by authoritative religious texts or traditions. Some eminent theologians are insisting that in the modern world to speak with conviction theology must be rooted in personal experience. For example, Langdon Gilkey has portrayed the contemporary theological situation this way:

> Our theological analysis must begin with man. If we felt sure that the divine word in Scripture was the truth, then the Bible might be our starting point. Or if we felt some assurance that existence as a whole was coherent, a metaphysical beginning might be possible. But in our situation these two certainties are lacking. What remains for us, as remained for Augustine and Schleiermacher in not unsimilar straits, is man as we can

nature of love would apply also to Teilhard de Chardin, whose definition of love closely approximates that of Tillich.

[69] J. Furlong, *The Restless Church*, W. Kilbourn, ed., p. 45.

see him acting out his life around us, and as we feel the shape and depth of that human existence in ourselves. Such a "theological" study of man will of course be informed by our whole history, by the attitudes, feelings, and assumptions about life that our religious tradition has given us.[70]

Existential theology is a welcome addition to the search for man as he is in truth. Yet much of what has gone under the label of existential theology has merely incorporated various existential insights into an already established ontological system, such as with Tillich, or into a self-assured belief of the unquestionable validity of evangelical Christianity. Even as open a theologian as John Macquarrie has all too facilely stated that the question about the nature and destiny of man *inevitably* implies the need for divine grace.[71]

One serious difficulty with much existential theology is that it has reveled over the discovery of anxiety. This is particularly evident in the theology of Rudolf Bultmann, where the questionable interpretation of existential inauthenticity presented by Heidegger has been accepted as trustworthy. What is disturbing is that Macquarrie among other notable theologians sees Bultmann's approach as offering "the most promising way forward for Christian theology at the present time." [72] Granted the validity of demythologizing ancient views of man's nature in much modern theology—it is not at all evident, however, that in the grip of anxiety God alone can deliver man, as much evangelical and existential theology would indicate. A vast history of evidence suggests that what man needs most in his struggle with anxiety and search for personal maturity is trustworthy, intelligent, generous, reciprocal love. This is not meant to preclude divine grace as an answer to man's predicament. However, I suggest that for a dialogue to occur between existential phenomenology and theology, a common focus upon the mystery of human existence as illuminated in the phenomenon of love is in order. Insight into love will help to overcome a highly individualistic notion of freedom prevalent in much contemporary theology.

A truly existential theology will be strengthened if it can provide

70 L. Gilkey, "Dissolution and Reconstruction in Theology," *The Christian Century*, Feb. 3, 1965, pp. 135-139. See also his book, *How the Church Can Minister to the World without Losing Itself.*

71 J. Macquarrie, "How Is Theology Possible?" *New Theology No. I*, M. Marty and D. Peerman, eds., pp. 21-33.

72 J. Macquarrie, "Rudolf Bultmann," *A Handbook of Christian Theologians*, M. Marty and D. Peerman, eds., pp. 445-463. See also Macquarrie's earlier study, *An Existential Theology*. Perhaps the most substantial work of Bultmann's theology is his two-volume *Theology of the New Testament*.

faith's insights into the promises and joys of human existence as well as into its problems and responsibilities. The theologian Norman Pittenger has argued that the message of salvation refers not merely to the patching up of broken existence or to the recovery of humanity but to its attainment of the fullness of life. The ultimate meaning of salvation is not to be construed in terms of a rescue operation; salvation, the empowering of life by grace, is a crowning fulfillment of basic human values. Christ as the model of the truly religious man and as the incarnate expression of divine love is a revelation not merely of what we may become but to some extent of what in truth we already are.[73] To speak existentially in a way which is both honest to God and honest with men, theology must be appreciatively aware of the greatest human possibilities which various disciplines disclose, and then demonstrate with the help of faith how and in what way those meanings which give existence its distinctive characteristics and virtues are perfected by grace. A theology aware of man in his strength rather than obsessed with his weakness is very much in order.[74]

We cannot close, however, without clearly throwing the challenge in the other direction, and that is, as James indicated, to suggest that the full meaning and the final insight into human existence cannot be attained apart from the encounter of faith, or what might be called radical religious experience. The contemporary fashion in offbeat Christian theology to proclaim the death of God would supposedly preclude such a possibility. However, a phenomenological analysis of the world in which the death of God is dogmatically asserted would be illuminating and helpful; in a thoroughly secular world there seems to be no room for either the mystery of God or the mystery of personal being in the world.[75] Too often battles

[73] N. Pittenger, *The Christian Understanding of Human Nature*, ch. 7 especially. For a theological foundation underlying this approach, see Pittenger's exceptionally fine work, *The Word Incarnate*. Pittenger's efforts in theology have centered around the possibility of establishing genuine collaboration between theology and philosophy, particularly process philosophy and existentialism.

[74] This suggestion has also been made by D. Bonhoeffer, particularly in his *Ethics* and *Letters and Papers from Prison*. It is a position argued forcefully also by Teilhard de Chardin; cf., e.g., *Le Divin Milieu*.

[75] P. van Buren's *The Secular Meaning of the Gospel* is an example of the tendency of some modern theology to identify reality with the narrow conception of it formulated by an already outdated mode of logical analysis. The weakness of this approach to the reality of interrelations is easily in evidence in the above-mentioned study of Hepburn. Admittedly the language of thinkers such as Buber and Marcel is fantastically vague; but that does not legitimate the effort to reduce their meanings to a narrow secular world. The philosopher Leslie Dewart has recently made the provocative suggestion for both phenomenology and theology that the encounter of grace understood as divine love's "self-bestowal of the ultimate reality" places existence into a new

over existential meanings are fought within a restricted world of words where the actual phenomena from which words of conviction have emerged are forgotten, ignored, or only obliquely called into view. Existential phenomenology as a humanistic enterprise must admit that it has not focused upon or by any means accounted for the concrete existential possibility of encountering the grace which bestows ultimate meaning and eternal life as understood with any degree of theological precision and sophistication. The basic qualities of faith, gratitude, courage, and joy referred to by James, not to mention theologians, have scarcely been touched.

From a theological perspective an existential possibility in which man truly becomes a man is worship. We find intimations of worship in the plurality of worlds that constitute being in the world—in love, in ecstatic singularity, in art, and even in the secular world, especially in exciting discovery and notable achievement. Worship is not necessarily a possibility belonging to a world apart, nor does it necessarily fall entirely within one particular existential mode. Worship does not belong only to love or to the singular man alone before God in the act of faith. Rather, according to Evelyn Underhill, worship will best be understood as an existential response of the totality of man to Ultimate Reality, which not merely stands over against man but penetrates to the core of his being. Worship embodies, she wrote, a eucharistic principle by which is meant "the free offering and consecration of the natural life, that it may become the sensible vehicle of the Divine life." [76] As the human and divine mutually interpenetrate, human existence becomes open to its highest possibilities and at the same time discovers that its basic possibilities are authentically fulfilled. It may well be that in our fallen, anxiety-ridden world men must learn that worship, too, is a basic form of human life which opens up the

intentional structure. In his words, "grace transmutes mere spatio-temporal *facts* into ultimate religious *truths*." What this means for interpretation of an encounter which is believed to be "full of grace" is that it focus not upon some content but upon an existential-historical form of the event (cf. *The Future of Belief*, pp. 211 ff.). What we should hope to be able to accomplish with existential phenomenology would be to see into the world of religious encounter and to understand the particular meanings that grace brings to existence. To suggest that religious ecstasy is essentially no different from secular excitement is to capitulate to a barbarous lack of discrimination. It is possible to appreciate both Bach and the Beatles; but there is a discernible real difference between these two modes of music. If it is possible to make genuine artistic discriminations, then it surely should be possible to distinguish between the world opened up by the vision of true faith and that as seen through the eyes of strictly secular existence.

[76] E. Underhill, *Worship*, p. 341.

true ground of every existential mode. As Miss Underhill might put it, only as the creature learns to give himself totally to the Presence of Ultimate Reality will he wake up to what it means to be truly human and find within his own historical realization the destiny of living an abundant life in grace. Perhaps the challenge which religion presents to existence is true, and that to find ultimately meaningful life man must learn to bless the Lord of life.

In coming to the close of this attempt to lay the foundations for the phenomenology of personal existence I realize that the task opens up still greater possibilities and responsibilities for understanding and communication. Uncovering the truth of man requires dialogue. If, as much theology claims, man only becomes truly human as he becomes fully religious, existential phenomenology would suggest that religion as a human phenomenon which supposedly provides ultimate meaning to being in the world must enter into conversation with other disciplines which disclose essential human meanings; and in these conversations theology must seek to find a common world of discourse. Existential phenomenology proposes to any theology which concentrates upon existence some trustworthy criteria with which to examine and judge its evidence, and with which to expand insight and increase understanding of the meaning of being in the world. In addition to the possibility for an advance in existential truth which may result in a dialogue between existential phenomenology and theology there is another possible gain which religion may receive from the former. Kierkegaard once said that "the reward of the good man is to be allowed to worship in truth." [77] Certainly existential phenomenology cannot bestow goodness; but it can deepen our insight into the nature of human goodness and so anticipate a form of worship that is "in spirit and in truth." As existential phenomenology helps to uncover the centrality of love for authentic personal existence, it may help to enlarge and deepen our understanding of faith and hope. In the final analysis existential phenomenology and theology may be incommensurate. Yet with increased awareness of the meaning of love we may at least have caught a glimpse of the ultimate meaning of *existence in grace*. This new humanism is not far removed from the conviction expressed by a reputable theologian of another era: "He who does not love does not know God; for God is love. . . . No man has seen God; if we love one another, God abides in us and his love is perfected in us" (I John 4: 8, 12).

[77] *A Kierkegaard Anthology*, R. Bretall, ed., p. 271.

14

The Meaning and Mode
of Existential Phenomenology

1.

A common reaction to much reading of phenomenological literature is ambivalence. One is often impressed with the brilliance, perspicacity, and erudition of dedicated phenomenologists; but just as often one is frustrated by their results. Phenomenologists, particularly those in the tradition of Husserl, seem to become enmeshed in the discussion of method. The fundamental claim to allow basic phenomena to speak for themselves begins to grate when, after having perused volumes, one hears so little about concrete human situations. Surely one reason so many turned from pure phenomenology to existential philosophy was because the latter often did throw much needed light upon existence as it is felt, known, and lived in the everyday world. Unfortunately existential philosophy and phenomenology have often become confused, and in the process they have both been distorted.[1] An unfortunate and widespread reaction in our continent to

[1] A great service has been rendered to phenomenology by Herbert Spiegelberg, who has presented a careful, lucid, highly sympathetic study in two volumes, *The Phenomenological Movement*. In contrast we have been surfeited with a vast potpourri of skimpy summaries of existential philosophers. Some have been helpful, but often we discover in the most acute studies a negative reaction. See for example, M. Grene's *Dreadful Freedom*, H. Kuhn's *Encounter with Nothingness*, F. H. Heinemann, *Existentialism and the Modern Predicament*. See the Bibliography for further references. Of those studies which are both impressive and sympathetic, one of the best, which serves as an introduction, is John Wild's *The Challenge of Existentialism*; it should be noted, however, that Wild has considerably changed his viewpoint since writing that book.

both movements is to wave them aside as European eccentricities and therefore as basically irrelevant to American culture.

Undoubtedly some of the criticism which has been made of both movements is justified. Yet my contention is that by developing phenomenology in a thoroughly existential manner it is possible to achieve significant and trustworthy insight into the meaning of human existence. Furthermore, I am convinced that this new approach in existential phenomenology has affinities with American social sciences and even American pragmatism. All three approaches have a distrust of conceptual schemes which apparently are divorced from concrete historical existence and consequently make prejudiced judgments. I believe that many of the captious problems posed by traditional philosophical and theological anthropology can be solved only by following the advice of the late Professor J. L. Austin: "The right policy is to go back to a much earlier stage, and to dismantle the whole doctrine before it gets off the ground." [2] Thus in Part Two of this book I departed from a consideration of the philosophical background of phenomenology and a discussion of method and plunged into that source from which all doctrines flow, the lived world of experience. In a typically impatient American way, with a method imperfectly formulated, I started investigating, analyzing, and interpreting. There was a more solid reason than mere impatience; it has to do with a pragmatic reason associated with a slogan calling to mind John Dewey: Learn by doing. By actually applying a method not thoroughly formulated I trusted that a more reliable understanding of our method's means and contributions would emerge than if I had remained in the stage of critical reflection.

In this final chapter my task is to set forth as clearly as possible what I mean by existential phenomenology. The first step will be to review previous discussions so as to indicate how existential phenomenology stands in relation to other positions which are somewhat responsible for it. The second step will be to delineate the specific subject matter of this method, human transcendence as the personal world. A consideration of existential phenomenology as a synthesis of loving imagination and analysis, as a way of overcoming rational prejudices and intuitively getting to the heart of personal existence to reach genuine understanding will bring our study to a conclusion.

[2] J. L. Austin, *Sense and Sensibilia*, p. 142.

2.

To begin clarification, let us re-examine the term "phenomenology." As commonly used it is different from speculative methods that rely upon deductive logical processes. Generally speaking, phenomenology implies some kind of unprejudiced description which in turn depends upon an encounter with the things described. This vague way of speaking about phenomenology is far removed from the purpose and method of this book. Unfortunately even practicioners of phenomenology who have learned their lessons from Husserl occasionally suggest that phenomenology can be used to reveal any phenomena at all.[3] Surely this is not the case either. What is pertinent here is to determine what the word "phenomenon" is to be taken to mean. As previously noted, Heidegger argued at length that *phenomenon* does not mean appearance, as though implying something concealed behind it; rather, it means that which shows itself as it really is. Furthermore, it implied for him a direct manifestation of beings, and ultimately of Being itself. Let us get rid of the bogus Kantian dichotomy of thing and appearance; but Heidegger's clarification is not precise enough to take at face value.[4]

A continuing theme of phenomenology as studied thus far has been a relentless criticism of a naïve naturalistic attitude which is usually implicit in merely descriptive phenomenology as well as in narrow empiricism. We have constantly seen attacked what Werner Heisenberg referred to as the *illusion* of classical physics and of the "common-sense" ideas which lay behind it. It was once believed that we could describe the world without reference to ourselves and so arrive at a completely objective description of reality, one which contained no traces of man's measurements. The revolutionary changes in physics have drastically upset that belief. At this point modern physics and phenomenology join forces in pointing out that previ-

3 R. B. McLeod suggests this, though he also emphasizes that phenomenology applies to experience. Just what he means by experience does not become clear. See his "Phenomenology: A Challenge to Experimental Psychology," *Behaviorism and Phenomenology*, T. W. Wann, ed., pp. 47-74. John Wild explicitly states that phenomenology can reveal "anything which shows itself, in any mode, shape, or manner." Cf. his *Existence and the World of Freedom*, p. 34. This careless statement is implicitly corrected as he goes on to delineate the stages of phenomenology which involve opening up the lived world of human experience, which is really the phenomenon to which his method applies.

4 It should be remembered that Heidegger himself did not stop there, but went on to develop a peculiar doctrine of phenomena in terms of his own notion of Being.

ous attempts to force a sharp division between man as an investigator and objects being investigated in a supposedly determined universe were unwarranted and arbitrary. To understand any science we must be aware that our knowledge of objects is inseparable from the knowing subject. What we know of nature is not nature in itself but nature revealed through our particular way of questioning.[5] Before the discoveries of relativity and quantum mechanics had been made, Husserl had also decisively called attention to man's unique way of encountering the world; and he focused upon our experience of objects as they make sense to us. He advocated a thorough investigation not of objects as though divorced from us but precisely *as* they are experienced by us. Phenomenology, then, marks a radical return to experience and includes a strong critique of methods and assumptions of a former era which had attempted to leave experience out of account. At this stage we can make a preliminary conclusion that experience is the phenomenon which this new method attempts to study, though this rough conclusion will need refining and further clarification.[6]

Existential phenomenology focuses upon experience itself and attempts to understand it as a *human event*. It is adversely critical of narrow physicalist empiricism and of intellectualism, both of which level experience in an attempt to get beyond it; the former seeks to reduce experience to pure facts, making experience itself just one fact among others, while the latter endeavors to transcend experience to grasp universals. Merleau-Ponty once reminded us that "experience anticipates a philosophy, and philosophy is merely an elucidated experience."[7] However, this method is a return to experience, not to elucidate merely one particular form of it,

---

[5] Cf. W. Heisenberg, *Physics and Philosophy*, pp. 55-59.

[6] I may here point out affinities with American pragmatism, and particularly with William James's attempt to establish a radical empiricism, which would open up consciousness to the stream of pure experience. In advocating a radical empiricism James was attempting to develop a philosophy of pure experience by which he would overcome the dualism implicit in both philosophy and common sense, a dualism which separates subject from object, thought from things. Like my phenomenology, James was attempting to recover the unity of experience in which the various aspects of it, that are sorted out and analyzed by other methods, are grounded. See his *Essays in Radical Empiricism* and *A Pluralistic Universe*. An early and magnificent indication of how his radical empiricism works on experience is given in *The Varieties of Religious Experience*. Though he once said of the latter that it was all fact and no philosophy, it is definitely an exploration of pure experience. He plunged into realms wherein even angels fear to tread and was able to reveal to us something of the quality and existential meaning of intense and extraordinary religious experiences. See also the excellent recently published study by Hans Linschoten, *On the Way toward a Phenomenological Psychology: The Psychology of William James*.

[7] M. Merleau-Ponty, *Phenomenology of Perception*, p. 63.

but to illuminate experience as a whole. Existential phenomenology accepts the challenge to philosophy made by Merleau-Ponty when he said: "Either experience is nothing or it must be total." [8] In this sense of giving undivided attention to an elucidation of experience as a living phenomenon it may be said that existential phenomenology signifies a radical and new form of empiricism.

Husserl brought attention back to experience, back to the things themselves as we encounter them in their immediacy and in terms of their meaningfulness. Yet he had his own distinct notion of the "things" to which his method would be applied, a notion which has not been shared by many who have at first been attracted to his program. A quick review of what Husserl meant by phenomenology and the phenomena will help to distinguish his position from the one presented in the second part of this book. Husserl sought to recover and reveal the rational basis upon which all meaningful experience is founded. He advocated a transcendental phenomenology which was conceived as an investigation of human subjectivity by itself. This investigation, operating through the various stages of the phenomenological reduction, was believed capable of opening up the pure ego and its immediate relation to ideal essences.

Implicit in his conception of phenomenology, then, was a notion of human transcendence that finds expression in his theory of consciousness. This theory involved a peculiar doctrine of the intentionality of consciousness. For Husserl, consciousness is structured by a noetic intentionality of meaning-bearing acts in which ideal, noematic contents are immediately present to the pure ego. In his doctrine of consciousness he held that because of its intentional nature, consciousness itself is constitutive of meaningful experience. Phenomenology as he conceived it concentrates upon the acts and operations of consciousness as these make manifest the vast range of possible meanings; it thus reveals both the pure ego and the intended objects of consciousness, the *eidos* or ideal meanings. It is the latter, to which consciousness is directly related, which supposedly enable us to recognize any object of experience as meaningful and to determine the proper significance of any given experience. Because his phenomenology was designed to illuminate eidetic essences underlying all knowledge it was itself characterized as a rudimentary form of knowledge, as a science of the sciences. His phenomenology admittedly stood close to, if not in, the tradition of idealism, endorsing a unique privilege of consciousness as the

8 *Ibid.*, p. 258.

sole and universal medium of access to our knowledge of whatever exists.[9] This kind of phenomenology quite logically operates in a rarefied atmosphere of pure consciousness reflecting upon itself and upon ideal meanings which are unconditioned by historical development. The findings of this phenomenology present us with self-evident, apodictic truths which are consequently beyond question.

Husserl's phenomenological idealism demanded from the beginning a segregation of ideal essence from empirical fact. In contrast to the latter's phenomenology of pure subjectivity and ideal meanings there was Scheler's critique of idealism and his subsequent attempt to work out a phenomenology of the essential structures and values of personal existence. Scheler presented both a different notion of the phenomena and of phenomenology from that found in Husserl's writings; obviously Scheler had a different intuitive understanding of the nature of human transcendence. Further-

[9] My interpretation of Husserl here is, I believe, in line with that of Aron Gurwitsch, a leading disciple of Husserlian method. See, e.g., his *Studies in Phenomenology and Psychology*, pp. xvi–xix et passim. Gurwitsch argues that Husserl's transcendental, constitutive phenomenology is essentially a form of idealism and is thus to be distinguished from all existential phenomenology, including that of Merleau-Ponty. Consequently Gurwitsch and Husserl have a different understanding of the nature of phenomenological evidence and interpretation from that of others. The idealistic form of phenomenology maintains that truth is or becomes self-evident; thus its nature is apodictic. The search for essences is a pursuit of self-evident truths which are therefore unquestionable. This philosophical position is convinced that through the use of the mind it is possible to achieve, to use John Austin's neat phrase, incorrigible evidence. To many social scientists as well as to many philosophers this attempt to uncover apodictic truths and hence complete certainty in the sphere of human history and experience is an impossible one. For an existential approach the truth about man always has a tentative aspect; in view of Heidegger's disclosure of the historicity of being in the world, all descriptions of man in his wholeness are no less than conjectural interpretations, because the being of man stretches into an unknown future. Consequently it is surprising that Stephen Strasser, who has done so much to bring phenomenology and the social sciences together, has nevertheless retained an idealistic assumption about the nature of phenomenological truth. For he has maintained that phenomenology provides a foundation for social sciences because its intuitive grasp of phenomena presents evidence that does not stand in need of demonstration. Such evidence is the becoming evident of what is real; hence it is self-evident, the opposite of being covered up; cf. *Phenomenology and the Human Sciences*, pp. 249 ff. For existential phenomenology there is no evidence which does not stand in need of verification; as I have emphasized throughout this book, phenomenology needs the help of the sciences to purify, correct, amplify, and enrich its insights into the true nature of man. Perhaps the crucial dividing line between idealistic and existential phenomenologies is to be discovered most easily in the different notions they have about the nature of phenomenological evidence. The opposition between the two divisions in phenomenology parallels that in modern theology. Interestingly enough the division centers in both cases around the notion of revelation, be it of the truth of divine being or of human being. In both cases the existential approach lives with uncertainty.

more, Scheler began to elucidate a notion having to do with man's access to the truth about himself which was more rudimentary than that contained in a restricted emphasis upon consciousness; especially provocative were his suggestions about the revelatory power of both vital feelings and personal feelings of the heart, which above all make manifest the meaning of being a person within the phenomenon of love. His endeavors to expand awareness of the nature of experience suggested a possibility which was in part made explicit by Heidegger's phenomenology of existence; yet Scheler's insights into the intentional-historical reality of love as the foundation for genuine community were also extremely important in the process of expanding Heidegger's analysis.

In spite of reservations and criticisms which have been expressed toward it, Heidegger's existential analysis has been of crucial significance to the development of existential phenomenology. Under the impetus of Husserl the existential approach focuses upon experience first of all as a living event that contains and manifests significance; yet it refuses to acknowledge an exclusive privilege of consciousness to lay hold of meanings. The full truth of man can be achieved only by a return to human existence seen as a whole; this "turn" involves the entire man and not merely his consciousness. There is no direct path through consciousness to transcendentals. Heidegger subtly and deliberately set out to enlarge the notion of phenomena and thereby revolutionize the scope of phenomenology; he moved from eidos to Being, thereby setting phenomenological analysis within an ontological framework. Without any doubt he has broadened our understanding of the structure of experience. He has indicated that the constitutive process of our cognitive relation to meaningful reality is not to be envisaged as merely an intentional structure of consciousness but as being in the world. His main thrust has been to develop a radically new and fundamental ontology; yet in his early major work he drew attention to the transcendent character of experience in terms of man's radically historical mode of being in the world. As Scheler indicated the heart to have unique access to our knowledge of personal existence, Heidegger showed that feelings, moods, and particularly moral acts such as resolutely facing one's own death are indispensable for revealing the authentic meaning of existence. Consciousness was thus dethroned and set within the larger framework of temporal being in the world.[10] In terms of meth-

10 This development has been increasingly substantiated by social sciences, particularly as these have been influenced by phenomenological and existential insight. Cf. for example J. Lyons, *Psychology and the Measure of Man* and the pertinent essay by

odology Heidegger's existential approach greatly modified the phenomenological reduction. The truth of man, he maintained, will not be uncovered primarily in an act of reflection but will become manifest within man's authentic concern directed toward the historical actualization of his own most possibilities. Thus the acute phenomenological disclosures of human transcendence by both Scheler and Heidegger provide evidence of the possibility for a genuine phenomenology which is not forced to execute the phenomenological reduction in an idealistic fashion such as indicated by Husserl.

Nevertheless Heidegger's primary interest in ontology led him to neglect the full extent of human transcendence as he sought to uncover Being itself. In his scheme Being was affirmed as the fundamental phenomenon which becomes manifest, though this manifestation is primarily in terms of its not being there merely at hand or on hand. Phenomenology was conceived as the most appropriate method for the unveiling of Being. Just as existential phenomenology refused to settle with a naïve phenomenology of mere description or with an idealistic phenomenology, so it has resisted Heidegger's early attempt to push phenomenology into ontology. Heidegger's expansion of the noetic aspect of intentionality in terms of historical being in the world is heuristically valuable; his transmutation of noema into Being is not. With the assistance of Binswanger in particular it has been possible to keep phenomenology focused upon human transcendence as being in the world in terms of concrete historical encounters. Furthermore, by focusing upon existence in terms of the lived world it became evident that Heidegger's revelation of man had unfortunately omitted the extremely important world of intimate interpersonal relations; this in turn led to his omission of the basic structure of personal intersubjectivity as well as to his absolutization of existential concern.

A consistent failure in many existential approaches has been the inability to account for the reality of interpersonal participation in genuine community. The works of Marcel and Buber were particularly instructive in helping to rediscover the basic reality of intersubjectivity. Furthermore, it was suggested that one reason for the failure of a traditional Western approach to account for intersubjectivity is because it is riveted to visual imagery; not insignificantly, Buber was steeped in Jewish oral tradition and Marcel was a musician.

In the Greek heritage, the early aspects of which both Husserl and

Merleau-Ponty, "The Philosopher and Sociology," *Philosophy of the Social Sciences,* M. Natanson, ed., pp. 487-505.

Heidegger sought to revive, visual imagery has played a dominant role in the formation of concepts by which we understand reality.[11] Visual imagery frequently, however, does not symbolize at all adequately the realities of existential space, time, and interpersonal participation. By adopting an auditory image of reality so as to think of existence in the imagery of sound, we become better attuned to the phenomenon of interpersonal reality, which is characterized as much by interpenetration as by resistance, by harmony as much as by discord. Gabriel Marcel has said that phenomenology is a concrete approach which directs philosophy to return to one's neighbor. That one may discover one's neighbors as oppressive and greedy and so be led to articulate a distrustful individualism such as found in Sartre's writings, is an incontrovertible possibility. Yet by listening to the expressions of loving encounters a new possibility for being in the world becomes illuminated. In addition to the authentic possibility of being in the world toward one's true self there is also an authentic possibility of being with and for another being; this possibility has a particular structure which can be distinguished from that of singular concern. In other words, by focusing upon the phenomenon of the human world through "listening" as well as by "looking," we become aware of two distinct authentic possibilities, that of resolute singularity and of trustful, coinherent duality. Existential phenomenology has modified Heidegger's analysis of existence by focusing upon the existential world and by emphasizing interpersonal relations as the basic world structure in which personal existence originates. Thus it has modified and redirected Heidegger's expansion and alteration of Husserl's phenomenology.

3.

Existential phenomenology as I have come to understand and apply it is a method specifically and appropriately designed to illuminate the transcendental framework within which experience occurs and to uncover the basic meanings which constitute the significance of any given lived world. It enables man to interpret reliably his existence in terms of the fundamental structures of his historical existence in the distinctively human world. As a method existential phenomenology marks a radical return to experience;

11 C. M. Bowra, The Greek Experience, pp. 23 ff. He has provocatively remarked that the intense quality of light in Greece has a powerful influence on the Greek vision of the world, and hence had an extremely significant effect upon Greek habits of understanding, which in turn gave a definitive shape to their philosophy.

yet its distinctive focus is upon the broad framework of the lived world in terms of basic structural possibilities. Heidegger's rediscovery of the worldliness of human transcendence has led us to abandon traditional images of transcendence as beyond the world. Man's transcendence is not characterized by an ability to rise above the world but to encounter his total environment creatively and so make his world. Being in the world does not by any means suggest that existence is merely a plaything of determining forces. Human being is *in* the world, but his being is a historically creative process. In other words being in the world is not only constituted by meaning but at the same time by freedom. To be in the world is to be free in a field of meanings.

Freedom is frequently misinterpreted as a power which operates over against the world. However, the world and freedom are falsely opposed. The lived world provides the room in which freedom lives. Too often notions of freedom leave freedom up in the air. Notions found in much existential literature which consider freedom largely in terms of a separate act that intrudes itself into a predetermined world, which overemphasize man's free will and decision-making, have been misleading; they have not caught sight of the order within which freedom expresses itself. The phenomenon of human freedom cannot be understood apart from the structure within which it lives. Freedom constitutes the human world; but it is also constituted by that world. It could, then, be possible to consider existential phenomenology as an unveiling and an interpretation of the lived world of freedom.[12]

Again Heidegger's elucidation of the crucial character of temporality in the phenomenon of being in the world has helped to focus attention upon the history of the lived world. The world of human freedom is fundamentally historical. It cannot, therefore, be understood by concentrating upon a present, by observing and describing an individual in his immediate relationships with his environment. The world of freedom is alive with the past and also with future possibilities for the appropriation of existential meaning. Intentionality has thus been expanded not only in terms of worldliness but also in terms of historicity. Thus the essences which we have sought to uncover are basic existential possibilities within the history of the lived world which ground the existential meanings of any concrete encounter. To get at the meaning of existence it is necessary to hear the rhythm of a given history sounding not only in the present but

[12] Cf. J. Wild, *Existence and the World of Freedom*, especially pp. 129-135.

also from the past and the future. To use a musical analogy, one would not be expected to understand a symphony by examining the concert hall in which it is to be played or the instruments that will produce the sound, nor by listening to a few bars of the music. One must be caught up in the whole phenomenon of the sound from beginning to end to understand and appreciate its power and its meaning. So it is with an attempt to understand the phenomenon of man. Mere investigation of his environment or grasping hold of man for a few measures of his life will not reveal the quality and scope of his historical being in the world. Of course the obvious difference between man and a symphony is that we do not know how our history will end. Yet we can become aware that our existence is moving ahead and that there is the possibility that its conclusion will be such as to make the whole stretch of our history richly meaningful. In our relationship to our history we are like both the composer at work on an incomplete symphony who seeks to realize its fullest possibilities and members of the audience listening to a finished symphony for the first time, not knowing how it will end.

Using the analogy of music to understand the nature of existential historicity has also proved to be extremely helpful with respect to intersubjective existence. Historicity is not like a simple melodic line played out in an isolated chamber. An individual's historicity interpenetrates the histories of others. When we listen to the whole phenomenon of interpenetrating historicities it becomes apparent that an approach which concentrates upon one line at a time presents a distorted notion of what actually takes place in the world. Freedom strikes quite a different sound from the structure of personal coinherence than it does from a segregated structure of singularity. Personal existence is like polyphonic music which has a complicated chord structure. By attending to the world of being in love it became apparent that Heidegger's portrayal of the lived world was not merely ambiguous but too restricted. While the lived world does denote man's creative frame of reference whereby an individual expresses his freedom and finds it meaningful, Heidegger failed to consider the creativity of two people in love who form a new world of extremely significant possibilities. Two persons in love create an important new phenomenon, just as do two musicians who join to make music together. Being in love is a form of freedom which constitutes a new historical movement and a new frame of reference. This is the world of duality or personal coinherence. To be in the world of We-two does not mean that I am any less free than Heidegger's resolute individual; it does mean that human freedom includes various basic possibilities and that one of them moves within the direction of coinherent interpersonal relationships. The world of freedom as Heidegger revealed it simply must make room for the creative mutual presence of significant others. My being in the world is not primarily or authentically *mine*; in the deepest sense it is *ours*. Singularity emerges from duality, personal subjectivity from intersubjectivity. The first fact is not *I am* but *we are in the world*; as such, *we create the world*. Love is the foundation of personal existence and freedom.

From the perspective of love other possibilities within the personal world become more apparent, such as fallenness, the terror of anxiety, loneliness, and various forms of unfortunate existence. Leaders of existentialist thinking as well as social scientists have perhaps given too much attention to morbid aspects of existence in which human freedom is stunted and historicity perverted. This new approach in existential phenomenology has focused upon love, which clearly casts light upon the fallen condition of man but which also points toward a human world that resounds with maturity, integrity, wisdom, and personal happiness. Without insight into the greatest possibilities open to historical existence our understanding of the meaning of human life will be extremely inadequate. In addition to a reassessment of the meaning of individual and interpersonal existence, the existential phenomenology of love has been able to reinterpret everyday social existence, which has often been disparaged as the epitome of inauthenticity. By illuminating much of everyday life in terms of the structure of taking and being taken, it is possible to perceive the positive meaning as well as the dangers which this mode of existence has to an authentic life. Much existential and personalist literature has been horrified that men ordinarily relate to each other in ways similar to the way they relate to things, through the mode of taking. With the assistance of Binswanger, it became apparent that not only is it natural and necessary to take other people, but there are positive ways of doing so which in turn approximate love. I suggested that the basic existential mode of taking is particularly relevant to an understanding of the process of secularization. Secular existence has its own intentional structure, its own legitimate form of historicity, its own genuine possibilities which must be understood from within the context of its own historicity as well as in relationship to other basic possibilities. Finally the world of social intersubjectivity came into view, though much research is necessary before it is adequately understood.

Through its focus upon love, existential phenomenology has discovered that the lived world consists essentially in a plurality of worlds. Being in the world is a primordial structure, but it is constituted by a plurality of worlds which have their own specific space-time characteristics. To understand the whole world of freedom, it is necessary to examine the various basic intentional structures and consider the essential possibilities within which freedom lives and develops. Human transcendence is to be understood in terms of being in the world, but man's worldliness is like complex polyphonic music, not a single melodic line that either rises or falls; man transcends his present historically, by moving forward toward new and divergent possibilities of meaning. Authenticity or inauthenticity is not something which can be judged by one particular scale, or rhythm, or pattern. The inauthentic life is that which tries to compress the various directions into one or two; as in schizophrenia it seeks to reduce the number of basic possibilities, to stay alive by reducing risks. Authentic life is full of surprises; it is open to risks and allows various basic directions to interpenetrate. The shortcoming of many existential approaches is that in an effort to defend freedom they have tended to absolutize one particularly meaningful possibility and to see other possibilities as threats which might drown out the one which is particularly significant to them. The phenomenology of love sees the radical plurality of the lived world; it also suggests that a pluralistic approach to diverse human phenomena is requisite to account for and to do justice to them. With real openness to basic existential possibilities we are better prepared to appreciate the significance of human life in its misery as well as in its grandeur, in its growth as well as in its disintegration.

4.

One of the greatest obstacles to a fair and appreciative perception of the lived world is prejudice. Even though men of good will such as scientists and philosophers attempt to collaborate in deepening our understanding of human life they often engage not merely in a battle of words but in a "war of worlds." [13] The trouble seems to stem from a conflict in perspectives, as

---

13 Cf. J. Wild, *Existence*, pp. 80-97. Fortunately this conflict is less likely to occur if the scientist has come under the influence of the theory of relativity and quantum mechanics. According to Werner Heisenberg, one of the great contributions of modern physics is that it has brought about the dissolution of the rigid frame of concepts of the nineteenth century (cf. *Physics and Philosophy*, p. 198). Unfortunately some social scientists have not yet profited from the lessons of modern physics and

though each participant in the argument has absolutized his own frame of reference and cannot communicate with another if his perspective is radically different. Existential phenomenology has been particularly concerned about the breakdown in communication between intelligent and informed men and women who share a common purpose of understanding human existence. From the beginning phenomenology has sought to overcome what it believes to be the particular prejudice of contemporary Western culture which makes it especially blind to experience as it is lived. Phenomenology has thus sought to overcome not merely one particular form of prejudice but to get at the root of prejudice which obstructs men's insight and understanding into themselves. It has sought to get "back to the things themselves," that is, back to the lived world. Various kinds of phenomenological reductions have been suggested which supposedly relieve man of cultural or methodological blinders and bring him into immediate confrontation with his own reality. Rather than escalate the war of words about phenomenological reductions, it will be best to consider how methodological prejudice begins. Certainly the factor of cultural conditioning is extremely significant, not merely in terms of specific content, but also in terms of modes of perception. Yet psychoanalysis has achieved insights into the formation of perceptual prejudice which in turn are very relevant to existential phenomenology. With reflection upon these insights, it becomes easier to discover the nature of immediate experience and thus return to the lived world.

In a remarkably illuminating study of memory and childhood amnesia, Ernest Schachtel pointed out that there is a shift in the organization of perception as a human being develops into adulthood. This shift of perception involves gravitating from a sense of nearness to one's immediate situation, so characteristic of small children, to the individual's sense of distance to it.[14] This is especially the case in our culture, which emphasizes practicality and active, manipulative behavior to an extent quite foreign in other cultures, such as Africa. This shift in our mode of perception has in turn had a considerable effect upon the structure of our experience. Instead of being open and responsive to a presence which is immediately felt, the well-acculturated Westerner tends to step away from it, so as to perceive it

still argue as though the classical view of natural sciences is, or ought to be, applicable to their own pursuits. Thus, ironically, the philosopher may have more "trouble" with a friend who is a social scientist than one who is a mathematician, physicist, chemist, or even biologist.

[14] E. G. Schachtel, *A Study of Interpersonal Relations*, P. Mullahy, ed., pp. 26 ff.

as an object that can be taken in, examined, classified, and controlled. A new kind of relationship to our environment is thus formed; a different world is made. This distancing mode of experience constitutes a consistent perceptual pattern which in turn has a decided effect upon one's existential awareness. In this essay Schachtel was concerned to demonstrate the effect such a shift has upon memory, particularly the memory of childhood. In our culture the mentality of childhood is discouraged; this is in contrast to the African, who does not see the necessity of repressing insights into life's meaning which may come in childhood and are often expressed in the imagery of myth. Lacking encouragement and meeting constant repression, our childhood memory atrophies. In its place, a pseudo-memory emerges which recalls life through a screening process. Freud discovered this when he encountered massive resistance to childhood memories in some of his patients, although he interpreted this phenomenon quite differently from Schachtel. What the latter points out is that this resistance is often a result of one's vague consciousness that the traces of childhood memory are incompatible with adult life. A war of the worlds of childhood and adulthood occurs. The successful suppression of the childlike mode of experience is dubiously recognized as a sign of maturity.

During development a child's mode of experience is often forced into another mode which is more acceptable and functional in a particular culture. One dominant motive for giving in to what some have called the "rape of the mind" is the force of anxiety which drives the little person to seek security with the significant adults in his world. As the later mode of experience hardens it becomes nearly impossible to recover a fresh and close encounter such as is possible in childhood. Yet it does happen that people are able to get behind the pseudo-memory, especially during a time of crisis in which the self-system is so shaken that one becomes aware of an experience of presence which, as a poet put it, "is so freshly new." Schachtel refers to the recovery of the immediacy of childhood experience during the process of psychotherapy:

> In the course of growing up, the language label and the corresponding conventional memory schema replace the living perception of the object. Thus the significant individual perception is lost, the object loses its aura, and only its name remains; and its indifferent conventional cliché or picture may be recalled voluntarily by the conventional memory schemata. But sometimes it is possible, by insisting, to revive the former alive perception, the childhood aura of the object, and in this way to arrive also

at the significant emotional experiences of that time which endowed the object with its unique aura.[15]

In psychotherapy a patient is often able to recover the living present of the past through an interpretation of dreams and a probing analysis of his deepest feelings. The latter may be particularly revelatory, for what the mind has forgotten the body remembers. Feelings are a very important access to our past.

Though Schachtel was here attempting to understand a crucial phenomenon in the process of psychotherapy, his insight is extremely relevant to our own pursuit. The attempt to recover a fresh perception of existence, one unprejudiced by acculturation, is difficult; but it is neither impossible nor fantastic. Existential phenomenology does not so much seek to recover a lost childhood memory but childlike openness to our encounter with the world. To become open to the fullest possibilities of experience it is necessary to rediscover the world as presence. Only as we meet the world in terms of presence can we hope to reach the essential meaning of our existential encounters. Openness to the concrete as presence is remarkably vivid in certain artists, who through great skill are able to communicate their insight in art form. The presence of a face done by Rembrandt, or of still-life by Cezanne, or of a starry night by Van Gogh come to mind. The rudimentary sense of the world as presence is not the prerogative of a genius alone. It is frequently if not inevitably found in lovers, and it is apparently a universal quality of childhood. Scheler maintained that a true philosopher must overcome his egocentricity. In other words we must learn to lose our vanity and acquire an attitude much more akin to lovers and little children than one which is most respectable in the success-oriented adult society of the West.

The notion of recovering insight through a new kind of openness runs through phenomenological literature; and it implies a concept of intuition, which was of crucial importance to Husserl as well as to Scheler. In Husserl's usage intuition was thought of as a mental breakthrough, where the light shines, the finger snaps, and we say, "I've got it." This mental intuition supposedly provided consciousness with its special access to the universal meanings of reality. Heidegger radically altered the notion of intuition, replacing it with his own notion of the cognitive function of feelings, moods, states of mind, as as well as reflection and resolute acts. In

[15] *Ibid.*, p. 41.

Heidegger's scheme, however, this "existentialized" intuition relates to the understanding of the meaning of Being rather than to some ideal essences.

Existential phenomenology shares Heidegger's primary emphasis upon the role of feelings in developing intuition; they are fundamental to our understanding of being in the world. In this sense intuition refers to the immediate apprehension of the fact of being in the world as a living presence. It has been a great mistake in our culture to think of feelings as blind; part of the effort of existential phenomenology has been to correct our prejudice against feelings. Through feelings one is in touch with the lived world; through them one gets a notion of "how things are going" in a particular world. To trust one's feelings is part of what is meant by emphasizing the necessity of discovering that one *is* his body, as discussed by Marcel and Merleau-Ponty.[16] By affirming one's own bodiliness and trusting in the deep-lying feelings which reach out and envelope the world, one becomes aware of existentials such as time and space, one's life with others as well as in opposition to others, of love and the disjunctive force of anxiety. To understand existence one must first learn to listen to it before one looks intently at it so as to analyze it.[17] The intuitive listening to one's lived world through one's feelings is an essential step in the process of existential phenomenology; but it is also essential to take another step in the direction of interpersonal understanding, especially if we are to overcome the prejudice of individualism.

Particularly important to this phenomenological investigation of existence have been personal feelings. Scheler's epistemology at one point was an attempt to elaborate Pascal's saying: "Le coeur a ses raisons, que la raison ne connaît pas." The center of man's openness to life and especially to personal values, he maintained, was not in the head but in the heart. Binswanger's consequent affirmation and elaboration of the role of the heart in communicating existential knowledge has been particularly instructive. Avoiding the religious implications in the word "heart" found in

16 Extremely important at this point is the thorough discussion by Merleau-Ponty of the role of the body and feelings as the primary way of discovering existential meaning (cf. *Phenomenology of Perception*, pp. 90-199).

17 The importance of listening to existence before attempting a visual inspection was, of course, a deep insight embedded in Freud's development of psychoanalysis. While not looking at the therapist, the patient was encouraged to speak about his history; through a mutual listening to the whole sound of his life the patient and therapist reciprocally reached an understanding of the basic structures and their significance in this particular historical existence. Here again is another example of how phenomenology can and has learned from the social sciences, a point which perhaps cannot be emphasized too much.

the writings of Augustine and Pascal, he maintained that one's heart meta-phorically refers to a distinct and basic mode of moving (*Wandel*) through the world.[18] More specifically one's heart becomes most percep-tive in the structure of interpersonal duality, an insight touched but blurred by many theories of sympathy (*Einfühlung*). The heart is uniquely open to the other and can reveal what appearances so easily conceal. The heart shows us "how it goes" with the other and how our relationship is faring. In one's heart one senses if one is truly at home with another and whether or not one's meanings have been received, distorted, or rejected in communication. When openness between two persons has been achieved and they speak directly, we say that they talk "heart to heart." As my heart listens to what is in your heart a new form of communication becomes possible, which is characterized by unusual directness and mutual under-standing. When your heartfelt words go straight to my heart, what I receive is not merely your words but *you*. In heart-to-heart communication two persons become aware of each other as presence; and they sense the meaning of the new phenomenon of their mutually interpenetrating duality which both transcends and affirms the individuality of each.

Apart from coinherence, the voice of the heart becomes ambiguous and deceptive, and its blurred vision of meanings may be confusing rather than enlightening. In the words of Dylan Thomas, each of us may say:

> I have been told to reason by the heart,
> But heart, like head, leads helplessly.[19]

Yet by listening to the open encounter of heart to heart we become aware of the truth of genuinely personal existence and especially of love itself. Only as we open our hearts to receive what comes from the heart of another can we begin to perceive the depth of his dread and the heights of his aspirations, the degree of his passion and the warmth of his personality, the bitterness of his soul and the joy there which may overcome it. The heart does not dwell upon appearances but transcends them or penetrates through them. Our hearts can open up the horizon of inner life history, of man's struggle for freedom to attain his own most appropriate meanings. In this sense the truth that comes through the heart is incommensurable with secular knowledge, that mode of perception which emerges in the encounter of taking and being taken. The heart is aware of significance and

[18] Binswanger, *Grundformen und Erkenntnis Menschlichen Daseins*, pp. 106 ff
[19] D. Thomas, *Collected Poems*, p. 63.

of possibilities which do not become manifest by mere observation and reflection. It is in the heart that we become attuned to the wholeness of existence and to its personal dimension and meaning. When I perceive you with my heart I am not primarily aware of some part of you, such as a facial expression, a gesture, the sound of your voice; I become aware of you as a presence whose world interpenetrates with mine. Through the mode of heart-to-heart communication we become aware that the world is not exclusively yours or mine, nor its, nor his; we become aware that the world is *ours*. This insight of the heart opens up to us a new dimension of possibilities for the attainment of genuinely personal existence in a common world.

Illumination of the crucial significance of the heart indicates a new phenomenological reduction whereby it is possible to overcome prejudice so as to acquire personal insight into and knowledge of the intersubjective world. It is apparent that existential phenomenology stands far removed from either a method which stresses detachment for the purposes of reflective analysis or from one which calls for a bracketing-out of moods, feelings, and personal relationships. The phenomenology of personal existence demands involvement as well as analysis; it requires us to become fully engaged within the phenomenon of personal life and to be open to its meanings with the whole of our beings. Existential phenomenology means that we do not put man at the end of our method as though examining him under a microscope but, rather, we seek to put the whole man into the method itself. One cannot find the truth of man through cool calculation alone; on the contrary, one must put his heart into the task.

Nevertheless knowledge of the whole man cannot be attained merely through one mode of cognition. It should be clear from previous chapters that I am not advocating an irrational approach to life or in any way deprecating the rational reflection, patient analysis, and attention to evidence so often associated with scientific method at its best. On the contrary, rigorous discipline in method and conclusions is essential. Existential phenomenology attempts to be a radically empirical discipline which is particularly attuned to the unique phenomenon of human existence in its wholeness, with the hope of discovering a framework in which the partial knowledge purveyed by various sciences may be most reliably understood and interpreted. It is not my intention to debase reason, but to expand its boundaries and also the conditions of reasoning. One aim of existential phenomenology is to put the insights derived from detached observation and analysis back into the living context which afforded the possibility of such knowledge in the first place. The goal or reason with respect to human existence is not merely insight and knowledge; these mean little if they are not incorporated into personal understanding. The understanding which is most appropriate for personal existence comes from the heart; it is understanding which issues from participation in a common experience with another or, better, in a world that is shared.

5.

Lewis Mumford once wrote that "no one can understand another human being, unless he brings love as well as science to that task." [20] That insight has become a central conviction in the phenomenology of existence and love. The kind of understanding which emerges from genuine personal coexistence must be refined in collaboration with scientific method and data. Knowledge of the heart must be united with knowledge of the head; and this union requires a dialogue in which reasons from the heart and reasons from the head interpenetrate. Binswanger in particular sought to find a reconciliation between the knowledge of love and the knowledge that emerges through scientific concern.[21] Such reconciliation is certainly an ideal. But is it realistic? How is it possible really to bring together love and science within a radically empirical method?

To attempt an answer to this question we might first reconsider the special method used in many of the social sciences. Max Weber, to mention an important representative of a distinctive approach used in several of the social sciences, maintained that though the social scientist operates in a scientific and empirical manner, his approach differs from that of the natural scientist. Whereas the intention of the latter is to describe and analyze what he observes, predict its movements as nearly as possible and thus increase man's control over it, the former's intention includes a further aim, which Weber also referred to as understanding (*verstehen*).[22] To reach understanding of human action the scientist must cease being merely a spectator and become sympathetically identified with that action.

[20] L. Mumford, *Green Memories*, p. 108.
[21] Binswanger, *Grundformen*, p. 562.
[22] M. Weber, *The Methodology of the Social Sciences*, cf. pp. 40 ff., 53 ff., 77 ff., 83-93, 175-183. See also Talcott Parsons' study of Weber's method in *The Structure of Social Action*, chs. 16, 17. Parsons quite rightly points out that Weber made too much of a distinction between the natural and social sciences; we are now more aware that there is much less "objectivity" in the former than previously suspected. No science can divorce itself from values and subjective meanings, for every perception involves a selection of values.

His role is not merely to observe; as Harry Stack Sullivan was later to put it, he must be a *participant observer*. The obvious reason is that the energetic process which holds the attention of the social scientist is *human* action; and this involves meanings, or what Weber often referred to as motives. The social scientist wants to know of an action, be it individual or social: Why did he or they do it? and What did it mean to him or them? A peculiar task of a social scientist is to understand the human situation as a whole, as nearly as this is possible. He attempts to account for the subjectivity of concrete individuals and societies as "objectively" as possible, and this includes the attempt to see the human reasons involved in a certain action or event. In developing an empirical method which sought not merely knowledge but understanding, Weber directed social scientists to study existence as constituted by meanings. To grasp the meanings of a given human situation it is necessary to approach others not as laboratory specimens but as fellow participants in the drama of existence. To become a participant observer requires a suspension of one's own values and an identification with the meanings and values of others. This suspension is a kind of phenomenological reduction which is closely akin to what has also been referred to as love.

Insofar as any phenomenological reduction, intuition, or understanding entertains any claim to authentic knowledge of personal existence in terms of its wholeness, it must be founded upon love. This study has made it evident that love is crucial not only to the development of personal history but also to our ability to perceive and understand the meaning of the human world. We are all aware that truth, particularly that pertaining to human existence, does not come easily. Our senses may deceive, our minds fail, our attention may select out basic areas because anxiety is suspected to lurk there, and our perceptual patterns may be so culturally conditioned that we miss most of what is going on. In spite of such obstacles love is a cognitive power which can reveal the depth and breadth of existence in a privileged and unique way. Love has the power to break down prejudices and provincialisms and to open eyes and hearts to the immediate disclosure of personal existence in its wholeness, its diversified structures, and its basic meanings. At least in the sense that they are trustworthy and can be acted upon to bring about further insight, understanding, and direct communication, the disclosures of love are profoundly true.[23]

23 W. Luijpen attempts, without making much headway, to develop Heidegger's notion of truth as the disclosedness of Being. To American readers one of the most

This endeavor to unite love and intelligence in an active collaboration that achieves deep understanding will sound strange to scientific disciplines, though it has been encountered before in the history of philosophy and theology. However, what I am suggesting is not novel but a basic assumption within the world of artistic experience. Both existential phenomenology and the social scientists have something to learn from the arts, especially from the literary artist, when it comes to understanding human existence and articulating this understanding in an authentic way. The English critic, John Bayley, has pointed out that a great artist such as Chaucer, Shakespeare, or Tolstoy is able to portray human life authentically because he possesses the "neutrality of love." An artist who communicates a vision of life which we recognize to be true has relied upon love which penetrates into another's world yet maintains neutrality in the sense of affirming the uniqueness of the other. Love enables the artist to perceive his characters from within the boundaries of love as well as from outside them.[24] The artistic creation is convincing because the artist discloses a common world, one which he shares both with his major characters and with his readers; and yet at the same time he is able to affirm, appreciate, and illuminate his deep sense of human differentiation, a differentiation which applies to himself and his characters as well as to his readers. The world of Shakespeare's lovers, for example, is our world and yet also quite distinctly theirs. Their world and its meaning are "both inside us and outside. And this inside and outside effect is echoed by the characters that are drawn by the great neutral artist." [25] Such an artist draws us into another world and also helps us to see it as different from our own.

It is precisely the neutrality of love which is able to disclose not only another being but also our particular relationship to him; love is able to reveal the entire dynamic context, the whole situation of our encounter. Thus we can reflect almost simultaneously upon the significance of a character's action and our own response to it, regretting perhaps a boorish action on his part and laughing at our priggishness which prompted such a reaction. We do not, however, enjoy such freedom of reflection and objectivity in the encounter with romantic artists. As Bayley suggests, the ro-

interesting suggestions he makes pertinent to truth is that truthfulness should be considered in terms of the fruitfulness statements have. This sounds amazingly similar to our own pragmatic tradition. However a distinctive notion is presented by Luijpen, I believe, when he suggests that fruitfulness should be considered in terms of opening us up for dialogue with reality. Cf. his *Existential Phenomenology*, pp. 142-158, 166-167.

[24] J. Bayley, *The Characters of Love*, p. 33.
[25] *Ibid.*, pp. 33-34.

mantic approach to love, say in D. H. Lawrence, is "not an approach but a manifesto." [26] The romantic detaches himself from the common and ordinary aspects of reality so that the world of his characters is a one-dimensional abstraction. Similar to Bayley's distinction between the neutrality of love and romanticism, existential phenomenology is not akin to romanticism, even though it has focused upon romantic love. Through love existential phenomenology has tried to return to the common givenness of existence and to see it whole, as it really is.

In a way similar to literary artists, Binswanger maintained the objectivity of love and suggested an approach which blends love and reflection; what he advocated was a "loving thinking," as he called it. We can quite properly refer to this visionary power of love to see intimately as well as objectively into the structures and meanings of human-life *imagination*.[27] Imagination is the kind of reflection and vision which arises out of listening to our feelings and our hearts, indeed the whole human world as it encounters us with meanings and possibilities. It is not an alternative to reasoning; *imagination is reason operating within the boundaries of love.* As S. T. Coleridge pointed out long ago, the work of the imagination is unique; it alone is able to recover for us the living unity of experience after our reflective faculties have broken that unity through exact analysis.[28] Imagination should not reject or ignore the findings of scientific scrutiny but, rather, integrate them into a picture of the whole of existence, much the way a good writer or biographer does who wishes to bring his central character to life for the reader. As an example of how love and science combine in the understanding of existence, Binswanger suggested how he would go about reaching an understanding of his former teacher in psychiatry, Eugen Bleuler. He would acquire as much secular knowledge of him as possible, that is, knowledge of his personality and character, his traits and capabilities, his history and social context, etc. All such knowledge emerging from the discursive mode of concern is important if we are to assume that we know something about him. But to reach an understanding of Bleuler as a person demands a knowledge which arises from an encounter with him as a Thou. In order to reveal the being of Bleuler as a person

[26] *Ibid.*, p. 29.

[27] Binswanger, *Grundformen*, pp. 546, 642 ff. et passim.

[28] Cf. S. T. Coleridge, *Biographia Literaria*, chs. 13, 14. Roughly the same idea has been expressed by G. Marcel in his distinction of primary and secondary reflection; see *The Mystery of Being*, Vol. I, ch. 5. Marcel was influenced by Coleridge early in his development as an existential thinker.

requires a twofold knowledge emerging both from detached observation and from participation in the other within the bonds of friendship.[29] Binswanger's case studies and the many illustrations which are to be found in his other writings are indicative of the actual power of love and analysis as combined in imagination to break through fragmented and distorted images so as to enable us to see persons whole.

Loving imagination is the art by which we detect the deepest significance of another's particular acts and gestures. Though the capacity of such imagination has been discussed usually at highly sophisticated levels, its powers of discernment are commonly known, though perhaps often ignored. A popular song expresses the truth when it says:

There are smiles that have a tender meaning,
That the eyes of love alone can see.

Love can detect the true intention of a smile or word or gesture which can easily pass unnoticed to one not within the boundaries of love. It is really only through love that we can reach a personal understanding of "how it goes" with another person or group. For one to enter the world of another and to appreciate its otherness so as not to project one's own meanings into it, one needs imagination, sympathetic and creative vision which has become unclouded in love.

Imaginative personal thinking can represent a reconciliation of detached analysis or secular knowledge and the vision of love. To think imaginatively about another person is really to think from the heart. Through the work of loving imagination the existential phenomenologist gains an assured awareness of the meanings of another existence which may have been only dimly sensed in his feelings. The operation of the imagination is difficult at times, as any lover or artist or parent knows; but it can work and it does bring light and understanding amid confusion and uncertainty. Though it is often serious and sometimes involves suffering, imagination is also truly a form of play. To say this does not imply that existential phenomenology endorses sloppy or undisciplined methods. Existential phenomenology requires attentiveness to evidence, patience in careful analysis, and diligence in responsible reflection; yet unless these virtues are grounded in love and can merge with imaginative playfulness they will hardly disclose the ecstasies which make the freedom of existence authentically meaningful. Existential phenomenology must be grounded in loving

[29] Cf. Binswanger, *Grundformen*, pp. 597 ff.

imagination, and hopefully it will also be imbued with the spirit of wisdom and a touch of the poet. We must wait for circumstances to produce such combinations as were evident in Scheler or Heidegger or Binswanger, who have illuminated the great heights of human possibilities. However, most of us not so imbued can continue expanding our existential awareness with reason and imagination, so long as we do not completely lose touch with the freshness of childhood or grow indifferent or obdurate to the sympathy of love.

6.

Not only in this chapter but throughout this book have I attempted to formulate a workable conception of existential phenomenology and to indicate how, where, and why it is different from other phenomenological methods. This method in large part marks a new thrust in philosophy, involving total engagement in the endeavor to hear and see the whole man in terms of his being directed in and toward existential meanings. This approach in many ways is a product of our own particular era. In our rapidly changing historical situation where old human visions and patterns of life are being plowed up, the soil of human history strikes us with its promises as well as its barrenness. For growth to occur that will yield new visions and patterns for the development and well-being of distinctively human, personal life, it becomes incumbent upon us to ask anew the ageless questions about man and his significance in the world. What is the meaning of my neighbor's being in the world, of my enemy's, of my beloved's, of mine? And what is the meaning of our life together? To gain a perspective and an approach in which satisfactory answers to such fundamental existential questions may be achieved, we have prosecuted a radical return to the immediacy of concrete experience, trusting existence itself to reveal the meaningful structures of its encounters.

The results of this new approach are by no means the last word. Existential phenomenology does not signify a conclusion to an intense search; it stands emphatically as an opening, as an approach which is always beginning to discover, to understand, and to communicate. To employ this method, which is thoroughly and consciously grounded in existential historicity, we must stand open to illumination from the full extension of man's temporality as well as from the plurality of his worlds. The aim of existential phenomenology is not to defend a position; it offers a program of research. This element of research is characteristic of the operation of existential phenomenology and needs to be emphasized. Not only is its focus upon history which is always in the making, but its method itself is part of this same historical process as it moves toward the increase of insight, understanding, and wisdom. As a thoroughly historical discipline existential phenomenology does not represent a fixed view but one that is constantly developing. As a return to the rudimentary givenness of experience it is a kind of first philosophy or metaphysics. However, it does not represent a particular *Weltanschauung*, although it is particularly suited to illuminate and understand varieties of total perspectives held by individuals and groups. If described as metaphysics, then that label is only appropriate in the sense of a boldly inquisitive search for the meanings of human freedom.

This research is no less than a radical expression of human freedom. Yet it is also characterized by a firm commitment. We must understand that commitment is not necessarily an act of closure; it can also be an enduring affirmation of freedom. In existential phenomenology we are committed to stand open to the meanings constituted by human freedom. We are thus committed to truth. We are committed to the task of formulating as reliably as possible our insights and understanding of the full meaning of being in the world. Yet we should not claim that our truths have absolute validity. As Merleau-Ponty once expressed it, our formulations remain true until further notice. Since every interpretation is liable to reflect prejudice and distortion, we must search for the truth of man knowing that our testimony runs the risk of imparting half-truths or even untruth. The risk involved in the search for truth is a dare we must take; we are committed to it. Our research, then, is a new adventure, not merely for consciousness but for the whole of human existence in a historical quest for man as he is in truth. It is an endeavor to know and understand what personal existence really means. As an adventure in understanding, existential phenomenology is not merely an intellectual or academic endeavor. The late Swiss phenomenologist Pierre Thévanaz was certainly right when he said that it constitutes no less than a method "for changing our relation to the world, for becoming more aware of it." [30]

As existential phenomenology changes our relation to the lived world

[30] P. Thévanaz, *What is Phenomenology?*, pp. 90-91. This first essay which bears the same title as the book is one of the most solid introductions and discussions of mainline European phenomenology to be found in English.

through making us more aware of its meanings, it is correct to say that it marks a new form of humanism, for humanism, seeks not merely to know man but to serve him. The particular service existential phenomenology renders to the truth of being in the world involves communication. If truth is to set man free it cannot remain hidden or private; it must be shared. Existential truth is not a fixed set of propositions but itself is a historical possibility. This truth is an ever-developing emergent of the growth of insight and communication. As existential truth is communicated it alters and grows; if it were to become finalized it would become a lifeless abstract ideal, uninformed by the realities of newly emergent historical encounters. The truth of man is something each historical being must discover for himself; yet it is only through communication that insight gains clarity, finds validation, and becomes the wisdom by which a distinctively human world can be constructed. If communication breaks down, truth goes into hiding; and the freedom to become a man in the sense of the highest human possibilities is curbed. One insight to emerge from this research is that truth and love, though not synonymous, interpenetrate and serve each other. To keep men free for their ownmost possibilities and enlightened about the deepest and most enduring existential meanings, love is indispensable.

Existential phenomenology is then also an act of love in the service of the basic truths of distinctively human existence; it is, further, a true testimony to the meaning of love which grounds the most authentic possibilities for becoming a person. To practice existential phenomenology faithfully is to combine love and science, the heart and the mind, imagination and intelligence, so that men may come to know the truth of being human. The creativity of mutual exchange among various disciplines centering upon man is a richly rewarding possibility which our existential phenomenology has particularly sought to serve.

Two things finally should be said. I have emphasized that our aim is to see man in the truth, as he really is. We are all acutely aware that such truth is frequently ugly and painful; but we also know that the truth about man can be an epiphany of splendor. To discover that splendor and understand it as it becomes manifest in the myriad phenomena of love has been a principal task of this book. Partially, a motive for performing this task is to correct the notion that existential thinking only turns up dirt about man. Existential phenomenology reveals man's greatness and joy as well as his smallness and misery. There is a tremendous need for us to continue research so that we might have increasing insight into such basic human phenomena as personal well-being and ennobling suffering, cheerfulness and self-sacrifice, maturity and personal integrity, creative achievement and wisdom. Behind the realization of the need for much more healthy and humane research lies a conviction expressed well by Anton Chekhov in his notebooks: "Man will become better when you show him what he is like." Only if man becomes aware of the great possibilities of becoming a true person can he begin to understand and resist those possibilities which stand in his way of appropriating that truth.

To maintain that existential phenomenology stands open to truth about man as expressed in various media is to express the conviction that this method cannot remain isolated from others. As we seek to explicate experience, to grasp meanings, and to recover insight and gain understanding of existence as a whole, existential phenomenology operates as philosophy; but it is a philosophy which refuses to exist as a completely separate pursuit.[31] It exists for mutual exchange, for communication with other disciplines and in addition to enable them to communicate more readily with each other about human significance. This existential phenomenology has been reared in an interdisciplinary family, and it exists to serve various disciplines which study man. It is more than a philosophical means to bring together the various disciplines and to foster interdisciplinary discourse. Existential phenomenology is itself interdisciplinary by nature, sharing with science its careful scrutiny of evidence, with philosophy its struggle to see things whole, and with art its reverent attention to images and its creative ability to enter imaginatively into the heart of the world it seeks to understand and represent. Only as this philosophy is willing to step aside and lose itself in its openness to other witnesses can it hope to achieve a complete view of the phenomenon of man, of human existence as it is in truth.

[31] Cf. the portrayal of true philosophy by M. Merleau-Ponty, *Phenomenology of Perception*, pp. xx, 456. He wrote: "Philosophy is not the reflection of a pre-existing truth, but, like art, the act of bringing truth into being. . . . True philosophy consists in relearning to look at the world, and in this sense an historical account can give meaning to the world quite as 'deeply' as a philosophical treatise. . . . Whether it is a question of things or of historical situations, philosophy has no function other than to teach us once more to see them clearly, and it is true to say that it comes into being by destroying itself as a separate philosophy."

BIBLIOGRAPHY

Bibliography

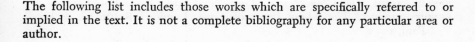

The following list includes those works which are specifically referred to or implied in the text. It is not a complete bibliography for any particular area or author.

BOOKS

ABRAHAMSON, MARK. *Interpersonal Accommodation*. Princeton: Van Nostrand, 1966.

ADLER, ALFRED. *The Practice and Theory of Individual Psychology*. Paterson: Littlefield, Adams, and Co., 1959.

ALLEN, E. L. *Existentialism from Within*. London: Routledge & Kegan Paul, 1953.

ALLPORT, GORDON W. *Becoming: Basic Considerations for a Psychology of Personality*. New Haven: Yale University Press, 1955.

———. *The Individual and His Religion*. New York: Macmillan, 1957.

———. *The Nature of Prejudice*. Garden City: Doubleday & Co., 1958.

———. *Pattern and Growth in Personality*. New York: Holt, Rinehart and Winston, 1964.

ARGYLE, MICHAEL. *Religious Behavior*. Glencoe: The Free Press, 1959.

ARIETI, SILVANO, ed. *American Handbook of Psychiatry*. New York: Basic Books, 1959.

AUDEN, W. H. *Collected Shorter Poems 1930–1957*. London: Faber & Faber, Ltd., and New York: Random House, 1966.

AUGUSTINE. *Basic Writings of Saint Augustine*. New York: Random House, 1948.

AUSTIN, J. L. *How to Do Things with Words*. London: Oxford University Press, 1962.

———. *Sense and Sensibilia*. London: Oxford University Press, 1962.

AYER, A. J. *The Concept of a Person*. London: Macmillan, 1963.

BAILEY, DERRICK S. *The Mystery of Love and Marriage.* New York: Harper & Row, 1952.

BAINTON, ROLAND H. *What Christianity Says about Sex, Love, and Marriage.* New York: Association Press, 1957.

BAKAN, DAVID. *The Duality of Human Existence.* Chicago: Rand McNally & Co., 1966.

BALLY, GUSTAV. *Der Normale Mensch.* Zurich: Polygraphischer, 1952.

————. *Vom Ursprung und von den Grenzen der Freiheit: Eine Deutung des Spiels bei Tier und Mensch.* Basel: Benno Schwabe, 1945.

BARRETT, WILLIAM. *Irrational Man.* Garden City: Doubleday & Co., 1958.

BARTH, KARL. *Dogmatics in Outline.* London: SCM Press, 1957.

————. *Evangelical Theology.* Garden City: Doubleday & Co., 1964.

————. *The Humanity of God.* Richmond, Va.: John Knox Press, 1960.

————. *The Word of God and the Word of Man.* New York: Harper & Row, 1957.

BAYLEY, JOHN. *The Characters of Love.* New York: Basic Books, 1960.

BENOIT, HUBERT. *The Many Faces of Love.* London: Routledge & Kegan Paul, 1955.

BERDYAEV, NICOLAS. *Dream and Reality.* New York: Macmillan, 1951.

BERGER, PETER L. *Invitation to Sociology.* Garden City: Doubleday & Co., 1963.

————. *The Noise of Solemn Assemblies.* Garden City: Doubleday & Co., 1961.

————. *The Precarious Vision.* Garden City: Doubleday & Co., 1961.

BERNE, ERIC. *Games People Play.* New York: Grove Press, 1964.

BINSWANGER, LUDWIG. *Ausgewählte Vorträge und Aufsätze.* Vol. I. Bern: Francke Verlag, 1947.

————. *Ausgewählte Vorträge und Aufsätze.* Vol. II. Bern: Francke Verlag, 1955.

————. *Being-in-the-World.* Trans. with introduction by Jacob Needleman. New York: Basic Books, 1963.

————. *Drei Formen Missglückten Daseins.* Tübingen: Max Niemeyer, 1956.

————. *Grundformen und Erkenntnis Menschlichen Daseins,* 2nd ed. Zurich: Niehans Verlag, 1953.

————. *Der Mensch in der Psychiatrie.* Pfüllingen: Neske, 1957.

————. *Schizophrenie.* Pfüllingen: Neske, 1957.

————. *Sigmund Freud: Reminiscences of a Friendship.* New York: Grune & Stratton, 1957.

BLOY, MYRON. *The Crisis of Cultural Change.* New York: Seabury Press, 1965.

BOHANNAN, PAUL. *Africa and Africans.* Garden City: Doubleday & Co. (Natural History Press), 1964.

BOSS, MEDARD. *The Analysis of Dreams.* London: Rider, 1957.

————. *Einführung in die Psychosomatische Medizin.* Bern: Hans Huber, 1954.

————. *Indienfahrt Eines Psychiaters.* Pfüllingen: Neske, 1959.

————. *Körperliches Kranksein als Folge Seelisher Gleichgewichtsstörungen*, 5th ed. Bern: Hans Huber, 1956.

————. *Psychoanalyse und Daseinsanalytiker*. Bern: Hans Huber, 1957.

————. *Psychoanalysis and Daseinsanalysis*. New York: Basic Books, 1963.

————. *Sinn und Gehalt der Sexuellen Perversionen*. Bern: Hans Huber, 1947.

————. *Der Traum und Seine Auslegung*. Bern: Hans Huber, 1953.

BOWERS, MARGARETTA K. *Conflicts of the Clergy*. New York: Thomas Nelson & Sons, 1963.

BOWRA, C. M. *The Greek Experience*. New York: New American Library, 1959.

BRILL, A. A. *Lectures on Psychoanalytic Psychiatry*. New York: Vintage Books, 1955.

BRONOWSKI, J. *The Common Sense of Science*. London: Penguin, 1960.

BROWNING, ELIZABETH BARRETT. *Sonnets from the Portuguese and other Poems*. Garden City: Doubleday & Co., n. d.

BRUNNER, EMIL. *The Divine Imperative*. Philadelphia: Westminster Press, 1947.

BUBER, MARTIN. *Between Man and Man*. Boston: Beacon Press, 1955.

————. *Eclipse of God*. New York: Harper & Row, 1952.

————. *I and Thou*, 2nd ed. New York: Charles Scribner's Sons, 1958.

————. *Two Types of Faith*. New York: Harper & Row, 1961.

BULTMANN, RUDOLF. *History and Eschatology*. New York: Harper & Row, 1962.

————. *Jesus Christ and Mythology*. New York: Charles Scribner's Sons, 1958.

————. *Theology of the New Testament*. 2 vols. New York: Charles Scribner's Sons, 1951, 1955.

BUYTENDIJK, F. J. J. *Das Menschliche*. Stuttgart: Koehler Verlag, 1960.

CAMUS, ALBERT. *The Fall and Exile and the Kingdom*. New York: Random House, 1957.

————. *The Plague*. Trans. by Stuart Gilbert. New York: Alfred A. Knopf, 1948.

CASSIRER, ERNST. *An Essay on Man*. Garden City: Doubleday & Co., 1953.

CHISHOLM, RODERICK M. *Theory of Knowledge*. Englewood Cliffs: Prentice-Hall, 1966.

COLERIDGE, S. T. *Selected Poetry and Prose*. New York: Rinehart & Co., 1951.

COLLINGWOOD, R. G. *The Idea of History*. New York: Oxford University Press, 1956.

COLLINS, JAMES. *The Mind of Kierkegaard*. Chicago: Henry Regnery Co., 1953.

COPLESTON, FREDERICK. *Contemporary Philosophy*. London: Burns & Oates, 1956.

COULSON, C. A. *Science and Christian Belief*. Chapel Hill: University of North Carolina Press, 1955.

COX, HARVEY. *The Secular City*. New York: Macmillan, 1965.

DALBIEZ, ROLAND. *Psychoanalytic Method and the Doctrine of Freud*. 2 vols. London: Longmans, Green, & Co., 1941.

D'ARCY, MARTIN C. *The Mind and Heart of Love*. New York: Meridian Books, 1956.

DAVID, H. P. and BRACKEN, H., eds. *Perspectives in Personality Theory*. New York: Basic Books, 1957.

DESCARTES, RENÉ. *Descartes Selections*, R. Eaton, ed. New York: Charles Scribner's Sons, 1927.

DEWART, LESLIE. *The Future of Belief*. New York: Herder & Herder, 1966.

DEWEY, JOHN. *Art as Experience*. New York: G. P. Putnam's Sons, 1958.

―――. *Reconstruction in Philosophy*. New York: New American Library, 1952.

DILTHEY, WILHELM. *Dilthey's Philosophy of Existence*, W. Kluback & M. Weinbaum, eds. New York: Bookman Associates, 1957.

DONDEYNE, ALBERT. *Contemporary European Thought and Christian Faith*. Louvain: E. Nauwelaerts, 1958.

DONIGER, SIMON, ed. *Sex and Religion Today*. New York: Association Press, 1953.

DURKHEIM, ÉMILE. *The Elementary Forms of the Religious Life*. London: George Allen and Unwin Ltd., 1915.

―――. *Essays on Sociology and Philosophy*, K. Wolff, ed. New York: Harper & Row, 1964.

EDDINGTON, ARTHUR. *The Nature of the Physical World*. Ann Arbor: University of Michigan Press, 1958.

ELIADE, MIRCEA. *Myth and Reality*. New York: Harper & Row, 1963.

―――. *The Myth of the Eternal Return*. New York: Pantheon Books, 1954.

―――. *Patterns in Comparative Religion*. Cleveland: World Publishing Co., 1963.

―――. *The Sacred and the Profane*. New York: Harper & Row, 1961.

ERIKSON, ERIK H. *Childhood and Society*, 2nd ed. New York: W. W. Norton, 1963.

―――. *Insight and Responsibility*. New York: W. W. Norton, 1964.

―――. *Young Man Luther*. New York: W. W. Norton, 1962.

FIRTH, RAYMOND, ed. *Man and Culture: An Evaluation of the Work of Bronislaw Malinowski*. New York: Harper & Row, 1964.

FRANK, ERICH. *Philosophical Understanding and Religious Truth*. New York: Oxford University Press, 1956.

FRANKFORT, H. & H. A.; WILSON, J.; JACOBSEN, T. *Before Philosophy*. Baltimore: Penguin, 1949.

FRANKL, VIKTOR. *From Death Camp to Existentialism*. Boston: Beacon Press, 1959.

―――. *The Doctor and the Soul*. New York: Alfred A. Knopf, 1955.

―――. *Homo Patiens*. Vienna: Franz Deuticke, 1949.

―――. *Logos und Existenz*. Vienna: Amandus, 1951.

―――. *Der Unbedingte Mensch*. Vienna: Franz Deuticke, 1949.

————. *Der Unbewusste Gott*. Vienna: Amandus, 1949.

FREUD, ANNA. *The Ego and the Mechanism of Defense*. New York: International Universities Press, 1946.

FREUD, SIGMUND. *Collected Papers*. 5 vols. New York: Basic Books, 1959.

————. *Civilization and Its Discontents*. London: Hogarth Press, 1957.

————. *The Future of an Illusion*. New York: Liveright Publishing Co., 1953.

————. *A General Introduction to Psychoanalysis*. New York: Garden City Publishing, 1943.

————. *New Introductory Lectures on Psychoanalysis*. London: Hogarth Press, 1957.

————. *An Outline of Psychoanalysis*. London: Hogarth Press, 1955.

FRIEDMAN, MAURICE S. *Martin Buber: The Life of Dialogue*. New York: Harper & Row, 1960.

FROMM, ERICH. *The Art of Loving*. New York: Harper & Row, 1956.

————. *The Heart of Man*. New York: Harper & Row, 1964.

————. *Man for Himself*. New York: Rinehart & Co., 1947.

————. *Psychoanalysis and Religion*. New Haven: Yale University Press, 1959.

FROMM-REICHMANN, FRIEDA. *Principles of Intensive Psychotherapy*. Chicago: University of Chicago Press, 1961.

FURLONG, MONICA. Chapter in *The Restless Church*, W. Kilbourn, ed. Toronto: McClelland and Stewart, 1966.

VON GEBSATTEL, V. E. *Prolegomena Einer Medizinischen Anthropologie*. Göttingen-Heidelberg: Springer, 1954.

————. *Christentum und Humanismus*. Stuttgart: Klett, 1947.

GILSON, ETIENNE, ed. *Existentialisme Chrétien: Gabriel Marcel*. Paris: Plon, 1947.

GOLDBRUNNER, JOSEF. *Cure of Mind and Cure of Soul*. London: Burns & Oates, 1958.

————. *Holiness Is Wholeness*. New York: Pantheon Books, 1955.

————. *Individuation*. New York: Pantheon Books, 1956.

GREEN, HANNAH. *I Never Promised You a Rose Garden*. New York: New American Library, 1965.

GRENE, MARJORIE. *Dreadful Freedom*. Chicago: University of Chicago Press, 1948.

————. *Martin Heidegger*. New York: Hillary House, 1957.

GURWITSCH, ARON. *Studies in Phenomenology and Psychology*. Evanston: Northwestern University Press, 1966.

HABER, R. N., ed. *Current Research in Motivation*. New York: Holt, Rinehart & Winston, 1966.

HALL, C. S. and LINDZEY, G. *Theories of Personality*. New York: John Wiley, 1957.

HARPER, RALPH. *The Sleeping Beauty*. New York: Harper & Row, 1955.

HEGEL, G. W. F. *The Phenomenology of Mind*. Trans. by J. B. Baillie. London: Swan Sonnenschein and Co., 1910.

HEIDEGGER, MARTIN. *Being and Time*. New York: Harper & Row, 1964.

_____. *Einführung in die Metaphysik.* Tübingen: Max Niemeyer Verlag, 1953.

_____. *Holzwege.* Frankfurt am Main: Klostermann, 1957.

_____. *An Introduction to Metaphysics.* New Haven: Yale University Press, 1959.

_____. *Platons Lehre von der Wahrheit mit Einem Brief Über den Humanismus.* Bern: Francke Verlag, 1954.

_____. *Sein und Zeit.* Tübingen: Max Niemeyer Verlag, 1957.

_____. *Vom Wesen des Grundes.* Frankfurt am Main: Klostermann, 1955.

_____. *What Is Philosophy?* & *The Question of Being.* New York: Twayne Publishers, 1958.

HEINEMANN, F. H. *Existentialism and the Modern Predicament.* New York: Harper & Row, 1958.

HEISENBERG, WERNER. *Philosophic Problems of Nuclear Science.* London: Faber and Faber, 1952.

_____. *Physics and Philosophy.* New York: Harper & Row, 1962.

HENDIN, HERBERT. *Suicide and Scandinavia.* Garden City: Doubleday & Co., 1965.

HENDIN, HERBERT; GAYLIN, W.; CARR, A. *Psychoanalysis and Social Research.* Garden City: Doubleday & Co., 1965.

HENRY, JULES. *Culture against Man.* New York: Random House, 1963.

HEPBURN, RONALD W. *Christianity and Paradox.* London: Watts, 1958.

HETTLINGER, RICHARD F. *Living with Sex.* New York: Seabury Press, 1966.

HODGES, H. A. *The Philosophy of Wilhelm Dilthey.* London: Routledge & Kegan Paul, 1952.

HOFMANN, HANS. *The Ministry and Mental Health.* New York: Association Press, 1960.

HOOK, SIDNEY, ed. *Philosophy and History.* New York: New York University Press, 1963.

VON HÜGEL, F. *Essays and Addresses on the Philosophy of Religion.* 2 vols. London: J. M. Dent & Sons, 1921, 1926.

_____. *Eternal Life.* Edinburgh: T. & T. Clark, 1948.

HUIZINGA, JOHAN. *Homo Ludens: A Study of the Play Element in Culture.* Boston: Beacon Press, 1955.

HUSSERL, EDMUND. *Cartesianische Meditationen und Pariser Vorträge.* The Hague: M. Nijhoff, 1950.

_____. *Cartesian Meditations.* The Hague: M. Nijhoff, 1960.

_____. *Ideas.* Trans. by B. Gibson. New York: Macmillan, 1931.

_____. *The Idea of Phenomenology.* The Hague: M. Nijhoff, 1964.

_____. *Die Idee der Phänomenologie,* 2nd ed. The Hague: M. Nijhoff, 1958.

_____. *Ideen zu einer reinen Phänomenologie.* Halle: Niemeyer, 1922.

_____. *The Paris Lectures.* The Hague: M. Nijhoff, 1964.

_____. "Phenomenology," article in *Encyclopaedia Britannica.* Vol. 17. Chicago: University of Chicago Press, 1947.

_____. "Phenomenology and Anthropology," article in *Realism and the*

Background of Phenomenology, R. M. Chisholm, ed. Glencoe: The Free Press, 1960.

———. *Phenomenology and the Crisis of Philosophy*. Trans. with introduction by Q. Lauer. New York: Harper & Row, 1965.

HUXLEY, JULIAN. *Man in the Modern World*. New York: New American Library, 1953.

JACOBI, JOLANDE. *The Psychology of C. G. Jung*. London: Routledge & Kegan Paul, 1951.

JAHODA, MARIE. *Current Concepts of Positive Mental Health*. New York: Basic Books, 1959.

JAMES, WILLIAM. *Essays in Pragmatism*. New York: Hafner Publishing Co., 1949.

———. *Essays in Radical Empiricism & A Pluralistic Universe*. New York: Longmans, Green, & Co., 1947.

———. *The Principles of Psychology*. 2 vols. New York: Dover, 1950.

———. *The Varieties of Religious Experience*. New York: Random House (Modern Library), n. d.

JASPERS, KARL. *Man in the Modern Age*. Garden City: Doubleday & Co., 1957.

———. *The Perennial Scope of Philosophy*. New York: Philosophical Library, 1949.

JONES, ERNEST. *The Life and Work of Sigmund Freud*. 3 vols. New York: Basic Books, 1953, 1955, 1957.

JUNG, CARL G. *Modern Man in Search of a Soul*. London: Routledge & Kegan Paul, 1953.

———. *Symbols of Transformation*. New York: Pantheon Books, 1956.

KAUFMANN, WALTER, ed. *Existentialism from Dostoevsky to Sartre*. New York: Meridian Books, 1960.

KAZANTZAKIS, NIKOS. *Zorba the Greek*. New York: Simon and Schuster, 1959.

KEGLEY, C. and BRETALL, R. *Reinhold Niebuhr: His Religious, Social, and Political Thought*. New York: Macmillan, 1961.

———. *The Theology of Paul Tillich*. New York: Macmillan, 1956.

KIERKEGAARD, SØREN. *Concluding Unscientific Postscript*. Princeton: Princeton University Press, 1941.

———. *A Kierkegaard Anthology*, R. Bretall, ed. Princeton: Princeton University Press, 1951.

———. *Purity of Heart Is to Will One Thing*. New York: Harper & Row, 1956.

KITAGAWA, DAISUKE. *Africa in Transition*. Geneva: 1962.

KLUCKHOHN, C.; MURRAY, H. A.; SCHNEIDER, D. M. *Personality in Nature, Society, and Culture*, 2nd ed. New York: Alfred A. Knopf, 1959.

KÖHLER, LUDWIG. *Hebrew Man*. Nashville: Abingdon Press, 1958.

KÖHLER, WOLFGANG. *Gestalt Psychology*. New York: New American Library, 1959.

KOYRÉ, ALEXANDER. *From the Closed World to the Infinite Universe.* New York: Harper & Row, 1958.

KUHN, H. *Encounter with Nothingness.* Hinsdale: H. Regnery Co., 1947.

KWANT, REMY C. *Phenomenology of Social Existence.* Pittsburgh: Duquesne University Press, 1965.

LAING, R. D. *The Divided Self.* London: Tavistock Publications, 1960.

LAMPERT, E. *The Divine Realm.* London: Faber & Faber, 1944.

LANGAN, THOMAS. *The Meaning of Heidegger.* London: Routledge & Kegan Paul, 1959.

LANGER, SUSANNE. *Philosophy in a New Key.* New York: New American Library, 1948.

LAUER, QUENTIN. *Phenomenology: Its Genesis and Prospect.* New York: Harper & Row, 1965.

LEE, E. N. and MANDELBAUM, M., eds. *Phenomenology and Existentialism.* Baltimore: Johns Hopkins Press, 1967.

LESSA, W. A. and VOGT, E. Z. *Reader in Comparative Religion.* New York: Harper & Row, 1962.

LEWIS, C. S. *The Allegory of Love.* London: Oxford University Press, 1946.

LINSCHOTEN, HANS. *On the Way toward a Phenomenological Psychology: The Psychology of William James.* Pittsburgh: Duquesne University Press, 1968.

LORSCHEID, BERNHARD. *Max Schelers Phänomenologie des Psychischen.* Bonn: Bouvier, 1957.

LÖWITH, KARL. *Denker in Dürftiger Zeit.* Frankfurt am Main: Fischer, 1953.

LUIJPEN, WILLIAM. *Existential Phenomenology.* Pittsburgh: Duquesne University Press, 1960.

LYONS, JOSEPH. *Psychology and the Measure of Man.* New York: Macmillan, 1963.

MACQUARRIE, JOHN. *An Existential Theology.* London: SCM Press, 1955.

————. "How is Theology Possible?" in *New Theology No. 1*, M. E. Marty and D. G. Peerman, eds. New York: Macmillan, 1964.

————. "Rudolf Bultmann," chapter in *A Handbook of Christian Theologians*, M. E. Marty and D. G. Peerman, eds. Cleveland: World Publishing Co., 1965.

MALINOWSKI, BRONISLAW. *Magic, Science and Religion.* Garden City: Doubleday & Co., 1955.

————. *Sex and Repression in Savage Society.* New York: Meridian Books, 1955.

MANNHEIM, KARL. *Ideology and Utopia.* New York: Harcourt, Brace, and Co., 1936.

MARCEL, GABRIEL. *Being and Having.* New York: Harper & Row, 1965.

————. *Creative Fidelity.* New York: Farrar, Straus, & Co., 1964.

————. *The Existential Background of Human Dignity.* Cambridge: Harvard University Press, 1963.

————. *Homo Viator.* Chicago: Henry Regnery Co., 1951.

————. *L'Homme Problematique*. Paris: Aubier, 1955.

————. *Metaphysical Journal*. London: Rockliff Publishing Corp., 1952.

————. *The Mystery of Being*. 2 vols. London: Harvill Press, 1950–51.

MARCUSE, HERBERT. *Eros and Civilization*. Boston: Beacon Press, 1955.

MASLOW, ABRAHAM H. Chapter in *Religion, Science, and Mental Health*, New York: New York University Press, 1959.

————. *Motivation and Personality*. New York: Harper & Row, 1954.

MAY, ROLLO; ANGEL, ERNEST; ELLENBERGER, HENRI F. *Existence: A New Dimension in Psychiatry and Psychology*. New York: Basic Books, 1959.

MCADOO, H. R. *The Structure of Caroline Moral Theology*. London: Longmans, Green, and Co., 1949.

MCLEOD, R. B. "Phenomenology: A Challenge to Experimental Psychology," in *Behaviorism and Phenomenology*, T. W. Wann, ed. Chicago: University of Chicago Press, 1964.

MCLUHAN, MARSHALL. *Understanding Media*. New York: New American Library, 1966.

MEAD, G. H. *The Social Psychology of George Herbert Mead*, A. Strauss, ed. Chicago: University of Chicago Press, 1956.

MERLEAU-PONTY, MAURICE. *Phenomenology of Perception*. London: Routledge & Kegan Paul, 1962.

————. *Sense and Non-Sense*. Evanston: Northwestern University Press, 1964.

MICHALSON, CARL, ed. *Christianity and the Existentialists*. New York: Charles Scribner's Sons, 1956.

MIEGGE, GIOVANNI. *Gospel and Myth in the Thought of Rudolf Bultmann*. London: Lutterworth Press, 1960.

MOONEY, CHRISTOPHER. *Teilhard de Chardin and the Mystery of Christ*. New York: Harper & Row, 1964.

MOUSTAKAS, CLARK E. *Loneliness*. Englewood Cliffs: Prentice-Hall, 1961.

MULLAHY, PATRICK, ed. *A Study of Interpersonal Relations*. New York: Grove Press, 1949.

MUMFORD, LEWIS. *The City in History*. New York: Harcourt, Brace, & World, 1961.

————. *Green Memories*. New York: Harcourt, Brace, & World, 1947.

————. *The Transformations of Man*. New York: Collier Books, 1962.

MUNROE, RUTH L. *Schools of Psychoanalytic Thought*. New York: Dryden Press, 1955.

MUNZ, PETER. *Relationship and Solitude*. London: Eyre & Spottiswoode, 1964.

NATANSON, MAURICE. *Literature, Philosophy and the Social Sciences*. The Hague: M. Nijhoff, 1962.

————, ed. *Philosophy of the Social Sciences*. New York: Random House, 1963.

NIEBUHR, REINHOLD. *Faith and History*. New York: Charles Scribner's Sons, 1949.

————. *Man's Nature and His Communities*. New York: Charles Scribner's Sons, 1965.

————. *The Nature and Destiny of Man*. New York: Charles Scribner's Sons, 1949.

NIETZSCHE, FRIEDRICH. *The Philosophy of Nietzsche*. New York: Random House, 1937.

NOCK, A. D. *Conversion*. Oxford: Clarendon Press, 1952.

NUTTIN, JOSEPH. *Psychoanalysis and Personality*. London: Sheed & Ward, 1954.

OATES, WAYNE E. *The Religious Dimensions of Personality*. New York: Association Press, 1957.

OPPENHEIMER, ROBERT J. *Science and the Common Understanding*. London: Oxford University Press, 1954.

OTTO, RUDOLF. *The Idea of the Holy*. London: Oxford University Press, 1952.

PARKER, BEULAH. *My Language Is Me*. New York: Basic Books, 1962.

PARSONS, TALCOTT. *Essays in Social Theory*, rev. ed. Glencoe: The Free Press, 1954.

————. *The Structure of Social Action*. Glencoe: The Free Press, 1937.

PASCAL, BLAISE. *Pensées and the Provincial Letters*. New York: Random House, 1941.

PEARCE, JANE and NEWTON, SAUL. *The Conditions of Human Growth*. New York: The Citadel Press, 1963.

PFUETZE, PAUL E. *Self, Society, Existence*. New York: Harper & Row, 1961.

PIAGET, JEAN. *Play, Dreams, and Imitation in Childhood*. London: Routledge & Kegan Paul, 1951.

PITTENGER, W. NORMAN. *The Christian Understanding of Human Nature*. Philadelphia: Westminster Press, 1964.

POLANYI, MICHAEL. *Personal Knowledge*. Chicago: University of Chicago Press, 1958.

————. *Science, Faith, and Society*. London: Oxford University Press, 1946.

————. *The Study of Man*. London: Routledge & Kegan Paul, 1959.

PROGOFF, IRA. *The Death and Rebirth of Psychology*. New York: Julian Press, 1956.

PUECH, H-C. *Le Manichéisme*. Paris: Civilisations du Sud (S. A. E. P.), 1949.

RANK, OTTO. *Beyond Psychology*. Camden, N.J.: Haddon Craftsmen, 1941.

RIEFF, PHILIP. *Freud: The Mind of the Moralist*. New York: Viking Press, 1959.

ROBERTS, DAVID E. *Psychotherapy and a Christian View of Man*. New York: Charles Scribner's Sons, 1950.

ROBINSON, JAMES M. and COBB, J. B., eds. *The Later Heidegger and Theology*. New York: Harper & Row, 1963.

ROSTAND, JEAN. *Can Man Be Modified?* New York: Basic Books, 1959.

ROUBICZEK, PAUL. *Existentialism For and Against*. Cambridge: Cambridge University Press, 1964.

RUITENBEEK, HENDRIK, ed. *Psychoanalysis and Existential Philosophy*. New York: E. P. Dutton & Co., 1962.

SADLER, WILLIAM A., JR., ed. *Master Sermons through the Ages*. New York: Harper & Row, 1963.

SARTRE, JEAN-PAUL. *Being and Nothingness*. New York: Philosophical Library, 1956.

―――. *Existentialism*. New York: Philosophical Library, 1947.

―――. *No Exit and Three Other Plays*. New York: Vintage Books, 1955.

SCHELER, MAX. *On the Eternal in Man*. London: SCM Press, 1960.

―――. *Vom Ewigen im Menschen*. Bern: Francke Verlag, 1954.

―――. *Der Formalismus in der Ethik und die Materiale Wertethik*. Bern: Francke Verlag, 1954.

―――. *Man's Place in Nature*. New York: Farrar, Straus, and Cudahy, 1962.

―――. *The Nature of Sympathy*. New Haven: Yale University Press, 1954.

―――. *Philosophical Perspectives*. Boston: Beacon Press, 1958.

―――. *Schriften aus dem Nachlass*. Vol. I. Bern: Francke Verlag, 1957.

―――. *Die Stellung des Menschen im Kosmos*. Munich: Nymphenburger, 1949.

SHAKESPEARE, WILLIAM. *The Complete Plays and Poems of William Shakespeare*. Boston: Houghton Mifflin Co., 1942.

SHIDELER, MARY MCDERMOTT. *The Theology of Romantic Love: A Study in the Writings of Charles Williams*. New York: Harper & Row, 1962.

SOLOVYEV, VLADIMIR. *The Meaning of Love*. London: Centenary Press, 1945.

SONNEMANN, ULRICH. *Existence and Therapy*. New York: Grune & Stratton, 1954.

SPIEGELBERG, HERBERT. *The Phenomenological Movement*. 2 vols. The Hague: M. Nijhoff, 1960.

STERN, KARL. *The Flight from Woman*. New York: Farrar, Straus & Giroux, 1965.

STEVENS, WALLACE. *Poems*. New York: Vintage Books, 1959.

STRASSER, STEPHAN. *Phenomenology and the Human Sciences*. Pittsburgh: Duquesne University Press, 1963.

SULLIVAN, HARRY STACK. *Clinical Studies in Psychiatry*. New York: W. W. Norton, 1956.

―――. *The Interpersonal Theory of Psychiatry*. New York: W. W. Norton, 1953.

SULLIVAN, J. W. N. *Beethoven: His Spiritual Development*. New York: New American Library, 1954.

SUTTIE, IAN D. *The Origins of Love and Hate*. Harmondsworth: Penguin, 1960.

TABOR, EITHNE. *The Cliff's Edge: Songs of a Psychotic*. New York: Sheed and Ward, 1950.

TAYLOR, JOHN V. *The Primal Vision*. London: SCM Press, 1963.

TEILHARD DE CHARDIN, PIERRE. *Le Divin Milieu*. London: Collins, 1961.

―――. *The Future of Man*. New York: Harper & Row, 1964.

―――. *Hymn of the Universe*. New York: Harper & Row, 1965.

―――. *The Phenomenon of Man*. London: Collins, 1959.

THÉVENAZ, PIERRE. *What Is Phenomenology? and Other Essays*. London: Merlin Press, 1963.

THOMAS, DYLAN. *Collected Poems 1934–1952*. London: J. M. Dent & Sons, 1952.

THOMPSON, CLARA. *Psychoanalysis: Evolution and Development*. New York: Grove Press, 1957.

TILLICH, PAUL. *The Courage To Be*. New Haven: Yale University Press, 1953.

———. *Dynamics of Faith*. New York: Harper & Row, 1957.

———. *Love, Power and Justice*. New York: Oxford University Press, 1954.

———. *The Protestant Era*. Chicago: University of Chicago Press, 1951.

———. *The Religious Situation*. New York: Meridian Books, 1956.

———. *Systematic Theology*. 3 vols. Chicago: University of Chicago Press, 1953, 1957, 1964.

———. *Theology of Culture*, R. Kimball, ed. New York: Oxford University Press, 1959.

TIRYAKIAN, EDWARD A. *Sociologism and Existentialism*. Englewood Cliffs: Prentice-Hall, 1962.

TOURNIER, PAUL. *Guilt and Grace*. London: Hodder & Stoughton, 1962.

———. *The Meaning of Persons*. New York: Harper & Row, 1957.

TROBISCH, WALTER. *I Loved a Girl*. New York: Harper & Row, 1965.

TYMIENIECKA, ANNA-TERESA, ed. *For Roman Ingarden*. The Hague: M. Nijhoff. 1959.

UNDERHILL, EVELYN. *Mysticism*. New York: Noonday Press, 1955.

———. *Worship*. London: Nisbet & Co., 1936.

VAHANIAN, GABRIEL. *The Death of God: The Culture of Our Post-Christian Era*. New York: George Braziller, 1961.

VAN BUREN, PAUL M. *The Secular Meaning of the Gospel*. London: SCM Press, 1963.

VAN KAAM, ADRIAN. *Religion and Personality*. Englewood Cliffs: Prentice-Hall, 1964.

VIDLER, A. R., ed. *Objections to Christian Belief*. New York: J. B. Lippincott, 1964.

WACH, JOACHIM. *Sociology of Religion*. Chicago: University of Chicago Press, 1958.

———. *Types of Religious Experience*. Chicago: University of Chicago Press, 1951.

WALKER, NIGEL. *A Short History of Psychotherapy in Theory and Practice*. New York: Noonday Press, 1959.

WATKIN, DOM AELRED. *The Enemies of Love*. London: Burns & Oates, 1958.

WEBER, MAX. *Ancient Judaism*. Glencoe: The Free Press, 1952.

———. *From Max Weber*, H. H. Gerth and C. Wright Mills, eds. New York: Oxford University Press, 1958.

———. *General Economic History*. Glencoe: The Free Press, 1950.

———. *The Methodology of the Social Sciences*. Glencoe: The Free Press, 1949.

————. *The Protestant Ethic and the Spirit of Capitalism*. New York: Charles Scribner's Sons, 1930.

————. *The Sociology of Religion*. Boston: Beacon Press, 1964.

WEINBERG, HARRY L. *Levels of Knowing and Existence*. New York: Harper & Row, 1959.

WELCH, E. PARL. *The Philosophy of Edmund Husserl*. New York: Columbia University Press, 1941.

WILD, JOHN. *The Challenge of Existentialism*. Bloomington: Indiana University Press, 1955.

————. *Existence and the World of Freedom*. Englewood Cliffs: Prentice-Hall, 1963.

————. *Human Freedom and Social Order*. Durham: Duke University Press, 1959.

WILLIAMS, CHARLES. *All Hallows' Eve*. New York: Pellegrini & Cudahy, 1948.

————. *Descent into Hell*. New York: Pellegrini & Cudahy, 1949.

————. *The Descent of the Dove*. London: Faber & Faber, 1950.

————. *The Figure of Beatrice*. London: Faber & Faber, 1957.

WILLIAMS, DANIEL DAY. *The Spirit and the Forms of Love*. New York: Harper & Row, 1968.

WINCH, ROBERT F. *Mate-Selection: A Study of Complementary Needs*. New York: Harper & Row, 1958.

————. *The Modern Family*, rev. ed. New York: Holt, Rinehart and Winston, 1963.

————. *Selected Studies in Marriage and the Family*, R. McGinnis, and H. Barringer, eds. New York: Holt, Rinehart and Winston, 1962.

WINTER, GIBSON. *Love and Conflict*. Garden City: Doubleday & Co., 1958.

————. *The New Creation as Metropolis*. New York: Macmillan, 1963.

————. "Theology and Social Science," in *The Scope of Theology*, D. Jenkins, ed. Cleveland: World Publishing Co., 1965.

YINGER, MILTON J. *Religion, Society and the Individual*. New York: Macmillan, 1957.

————. *Toward a Field Theory of Behavior: Personality and Social Structure*. New York: McGraw-Hill Book Co., 1965.

ZUCKERKANDL, VICTOR. *Sound and Symbol: Music and the External World*. New York: Pantheon Books, 1956.

ZUURDEEG, WILLEM F. *An Analytical Philosophy of Religion*. Nashville: Abingdon Press, 1958.

ARTICLES

ALEXANDER, FRANZ. "Impressions from the Fourth International Congress of Psychotherapy," *Psychiatry*, Vol. 22 (1959).

ARONSON, JASON. "The Positive Role of Mental Crisis," *Saturday Review* (Dec. 5, 1964), pp. 82–84.

BIEMEL, WALTER. "Husserls Encyclopaedia-Britannica Artikel und Heideggers

Anmerkung Dazu," *Tijdschrift Voor Philosophie*, Vol. 12 (Feb., 1950).

BLOY, MYRON B. JR. "The Christian Function in a Technological Culture," *The Christian Century*, Vol. LXXXIII, No. 8 (Feb. 23, 1966), pp. 231–234.

BOOTH, GOTTHARD. "Values in Nature and in Psychotherapy," *Archives of General Psychiatry*, Vol. 8 (Jan., 1963), pp. 38–48.

ERIKSON, ERIK H. "Youth: Fidelity and Diversity," *Daedalus*, Vol. 91, No. 1 (Winter, 1962), pp. 5–27.

FINK, EUGEN. "Die Phänomenologische Philosophie Edmund Husserls in der Gegenwärtigen Kritik," *Kant Studien*, Vol. 38 (1938), pp. 331–383.

FRANKL, VIKTOR. "The Spiritual Dimension in Existential Analysis and Logotherapy," trans. W. A. Sadler, Jr., *Journal of Individual Psychology*, Vol. 15 (Nov., 1959).

FROMM-REICHMANN, FRIEDA. "Loneliness," *Psychiatry*, Vol. 22 (Feb., 1959).

GILKEY, LANGDON. "Dissolution and Reconstruction in Theology," *The Christian Century*, Vol. LXXXII, No. 5 (Feb. 3, 1965), pp. 135–139.

———. "Secularism's Impact on Contemporary Theology," *Christianity and Crisis*, Vol. XXV, No. 5 (April 5, 1965), pp. 64–67.

PRUYSER, PAUL W. and MENNINGER, KARL. "Review of *Existence*, by R. May, et al." *The Christian Scholar*, Vol. XLIII (Dec., 1959), pp. 305–306.

RYCROFT, CHARLES. "The Analysis of a Paranoid Personality," *The International Journal of Psycho-Analysis*, Vol. 41, part 1 (Feb., 1960).

SADLER, WILLIAM A., JR. "The Birth of a New Being: The Christian Meaning of Marriage," *The Pulpit*, Vol. XXXIX, No. 6 (June, 1968), pp. 18–20.

SCHRADER, GEORGE A. "Existential Psychoanalysis and Metaphysics," *The Review of Metaphysics*, Vol. 13, No. 1 (Sept., 1959).

STRUPP, HANS H. "Toward an Analysis of the Therapist's Contribution to the Treatment Process," *Psychiatry*, Vol. 22, No. 4 (Nov., 1959).

WILD, JOHN. "Contemporary Phenomenology and the Problem of Existence," *Philosophy and Phenomenological Research*, Vol. XX, No. 2 (Dec., 1959), pp. 166–180.

INDEX

Index